THE POLITICAL
ECONOMY OF THE
CANADIAN NORTH

THE POLITICAL ECONOMY OF THE CANADIAN NORTH

An Interpretation of the Course of Development in the Northern Territories of Canada to the Early 1960s

K. J. REA

Published in Association with the University of Saskatchewan by University of Toronto Press

SBN 8020 1527 1

FOR NAT

Preface

A STATEMENT concerning the background of this long essay on the development of Canada's northern territories may be useful to the reader who may well wonder why the matter was thought to merit any attention at all—especially from an outsider with no direct personal experience in the north. Certainly some of my professional colleagues have found it difficult to understand why anyone should devote some years to worrying about the economy of a part of Canada which contributes a statistically negligible part of the national produce and which supports a population of barely forty thousand persons. The project began at the University of Saskatchewan in 1954 when the late George Britnell suggested that northern development could become a political issue in this country and that the studies of development in the underdeveloped countries might throw some light on the economic questions which would be involved. The latter possibility was subsequently explored in "The Canadian Northwest: A Study in Sub-Arctic Economic Development 1898–1958," an unpublished Ph.D. thesis for the London School of Economics and Political Science. While I was so engaged, the question of northern development did indeed become an issue in Canadian federal politics. The ensuing confusion of economic arguments and political controversy demonstrated vividly the disorderly state of our national thinking about the north. It also impressed upon me the inadequacy of any narrowly "economic" approach to the supposedly new "problem of northern development." I was consequently encouraged to try to develop a broader approach to the matter—an approach in which the political influences involved in the development of the federal lands of the north were explicitly introduced. Although some of the "economics" used here are taken from the original thesis, along with some of the descriptive material, the following constitutes a completely re-thought and much more extensive approach to the matter of this development. Because of the explicit treatment of the interrelationship between the political and the economic elements in the process it seemed appropriate to revert to the old term "political economy" to characterize the approach. And because so much of the argument developed is speculative I should prefer to represent what follows as an "essay" rather than as a piece of "research" devoted to the discovery of new facts and "truths." Although a good deal of factual material has been included here, little of it is new. It is, however, difficult to find most of it collected elsewhere.

How extensively I am indebted to the work of others is indicated, I hope adequately, in the usual footnotes. The responsibility for the interpretation of this and the rest of the material is, of course, my own. In so far as I have made some use of the original thesis in the present work I should like to record here my debt to the late Professors Britnell and Fowke at the University of Saskatchewan; to A. D. Knox and Dr. Anne Bohm at the London School of Economics; to Dean Vincent Bladen at the University of Toronto; and to Mrs. Graham Spry—all of whom provided me with badly needed help, advice, criticism and encouragement. So far as the present work is concerned I have benefitted from a summer spent at the Institute for Economic Research at Queen's University and from the facilities made available to me by the University of Saskatchewan.

KENNETH REA

University of Saskatchewan
Saskatoon

Contents

I. AN INTRODUCTION TO THE AREA

1 The Land and Its Native Population

The Yukon, with its mountains, valleys, and broad plateaux; its mixture of white and Indian population, bears almost no relation to the Mackenzie Valley next door with its low, flat land covered with endless forest and muskeg. Neither one is remotely like the endless rock of the Canadian Shield and the Arctic Islands which make up the true Arctic—an area vast beyond the comprehension of anyone who has not seen it. [R. G. Robertson, Commissioner of the Northwest Territories, December 1957][1]

THE LAND AREA chosen for this study is contained within the political boundaries of the Yukon Territory and the Northwest Territories. The area so delimited is in no sense a "region" as either the geographer or the economist might use the term.[2] Nevertheless, all parts of the area referred to here share a remote location, a cold sub-arctic or arctic climate, a sparse population, and a territorial form of government. The practical advantage of this choice of boundaries is that it facilitates the use of available statistical material and it minimizes the number of political jurisdictions involved. The choice does, however, exclude territory which has strong geological, geographical and even economic relationships with the area selected. It will be seen below, for example, that the topography, climate, and resources of the economically important southern part of the Yukon are much more like those of northern British Columbia than they are like those of Mackenzie District in the Northwest Territories. It will also be seen by glancing at a map that the latter area

[1] R. G. Robertson, "The New North," a series of four lectures delivered at Carleton University, Ottawa, December, 1957 (Ottawa: Department of Northern Affairs and National Resources press release), p. 5.

[2] See, for example, W. C. Wonders, "Assessment by a Geographer," in F. H. Underhill, ed., The Canadian Northwest: Its Potentialities (Toronto: University of Toronto Press, for the Royal Society of Canada, 1959), p. 23.

is geographically and economically linked to northern Alberta and its commercial centre of Edmonton.

The main concern of this study, however, is with the development of a frontier area and, as at least every western Canadian must know, the development of such an area can be as intimately associated with political as with geographical factors. If the natural affinities are between Yellow-knife and Edmonton, or between Whitehorse and Vancouver, they are also between Regina and Minneapolis. It is true, of course, that the 60th parallel of north latitude, which defines the southern boundary of the area considered in this study, is not an international boundary. But it does separate land under federal jurisdiction from land under provincial jurisdiction, a separation of great traditional significance in the history of Canadian development.[3]

By seeming to ignore certain obvious physical factors in delimiting the area of the north for this study, attention is directed to cultural factors—notably to political organization—and also to technology as major influences shaping the development of an area which in many physical respects is surprisingly similar to the developed parts of this country.

THE LAND[4]

The most immediately perceptible characteristic of the territorial north is its sheer size. The Yukon Territory alone comprises 207,076 square miles. As presently constituted the Northwest Territories adds another 1,304,903 square miles, making a territorial total of 1,511,979 square miles—almost forty per cent of the total area of Canada.[5] Combine this with a population of 37,626 in 1961 and it is apparent that we are here concerned with one of the most sparsely populated parts of the world.[6] It is an area not only of vast internal distances, but of remoteness from major centres of population. It is over 500 air miles from the southern boundary of the territorial north to most points on the arctic coast-line. It is over 600 direct air miles from Fort Smith, the administrative centre of Mackenzie District, to Whitehorse, the capital of the Yukon. Actual travel distances are much greater, of course. The nearest large centre of population in

[3]See, for example, the discussion in V. C. Fowke, *The National Policy and the Wheat Economy* (Toronto: University of Toronto Press, 1957), Part One, pp. 3–84.

[4]One reference which the reader requiring a more detailed description of the geography of the territorial north and its relation to the geography of Canada as a whole may find useful is P. Camu, E. P. Weeks, and W. Sametz, *Economic Geography of Canada* (Toronto: Macmillan, 1964).

[5]Dominion Bureau of Statistics (hereafter cited D.B.S.), *Canada Year Book 1961* (Ottawa: Queen's Printer, 1962), p. 50.

[6]D.B.S., *1961 Census of Canada.*

Canada is Edmonton, 800 miles south of the mining centre of Yellow-knife on Great Slave Lake. And it is relevant to note that Edmonton itself is 2,000 miles distant from the chief industrial centres of eastern Canada.

Second only to its size the north is characterized physically by the great variety in its physiographic features. The area with which this study is concerned contains three of the five main physiographic regions of Canada—the Canadian Shield, the Interior Plains, and the Cordillera. These three regions in the north are merely northern parts of regions which extend throughout all of western Canada.

The Yukon Territory falls almost entirely within the Cordillera. This region is itself composed of three main systems of mountain ranges, the Eastern, Central, and Western. The Eastern system is present in the Yukon as an extension of the Rocky Mountains and comprises the Mackenzie, Franklin, and Richardson ranges.

The crest of the Richardson system divides the Yukon from the North-west Territories. These mountains are economically significant in Canada because the foothill structures on their eastern side are apparently geologically suitable for the accumulation of natural gas and oil. Major oil and gas fields have been developed in this region far to the south in Alberta and also at Norman Wells on the Mackenzie River in the North-west Territories.[7] During the 1950s extensive exploratory work was done in the territorial north by oil and gas companies interested in further exploitation of this resource.

The Central Cordillera is very complex, consisting of eleven ranges surrounding a large central plateau. The western system shuts off most of the Yukon from the Pacific Ocean with three great ranges of moun-tains—the Cascade, Coast, and St. Elias ranges.[8] The best known and economically most developed part of the Yukon consists of a large bowl-like area known as the Yukon plateau. This is predominantly an area of rolling uplands with large hills and a few isolated mountain peaks. The plateau is cut by many deep valleys through which flow the main rivers of the territory. The great central valley system, which runs northwest through the plateau, contains the Yukon River and its large tributaries, the Pelly, Stewart, Klondike, and Fortymile Rivers. Due perhaps to the arid climate, there are few lakes in the Yukon interior.

[7]W. K. Buck and J. F. Henderson, "The Rôle of Mineral Resources in the Development and Colonization of Northern Canada," in V. W. Bladen, ed., *Canadian Population and Northern Colonization* (Toronto: University of Toronto Press, for the Royal Society of Canada, 1958), p. 78.

[8]See G. H. T. Kimble and D. Good, *Geography of the Northlands* (New York: American Geographical Society, 1955), pp. 316–17.

In addition to the petroleum deposits found on the east of the Cordillera, the entire region contains important deposits of metals and asbestos. The consensus is that the mineral resources in the northern parts of the region are probably just as prevalent as in the south, with the greater concentration of mines in the southern areas being attributable to "the greater attention the more accessible areas have received."[9] It will be seen in a later chapter that mineral development in the Yukon has depended upon the mining of gold, silver, lead and zinc from deposits accessible by water transport.

Moving east from the Cordillera the next principal region is the Mackenzie lowland, a region which has been described by the geological survey of Canada as a "continuation northward of the Great Central Plain of North America which holds on its forested surface a great many lakes and muskegs drained by small streams meandering through shallow valleys."[10] The few commercially valuable stands of timber in the Northwest Territories are located in some of these river valleys in the more southerly parts of Mackenzie District.

The northern portion of the interior plains possesses essentially the same geological characteristics as western Canada. Underlying the entire region are sedimentary formations consisting of flat-lying limestones, sandstones and shale. It has been noted that, "the rocks underlying the plains of the Northwest differ little from those of the more southerly parts of the western Canada sedimentary basin, where most of the oil and gas and much of the coal is produced at present."[11] Unlike the southern plains region, however, the northern extension has little in the way of large-scale agricultural potential. Given existing agricultural techniques the soil and climatic conditions are relatively unfavourable. As will be shown later, however, small-scale agriculture has been practised both in Mackenzie District and in the Yukon. It will be seen that the limits to such development to date have been imposed more by market than by physical conditions. While little is known of the extent of lands suitable for agriculture in the territorial north, some estimates have placed it in the neighbourhood of 1,500,000 acres.[12] Lloyd has

[9]Buck and Henderson, "The Rôle of Mineral Resources," p. 79.

[10]Canada, Department of the Interior, *The Northwest Territories 1930,* by F. H. Kitto (Ottawa: King's Printer, 1930), p. 13.

[11]A. H. Lang and R. J. W. Douglas, "Minerals and Fuels," in Underhill, ed., *The Canadian Northwest: Its Potentialities,* p. 42; see also C. S. Lord, *Mineral Industry of District of Mackenzie, Northwest Territories,* Geological Survey of Canada Memoir 261 (Ottawa: King's Printer, 1951), pp. 4–5.

[12]B. G. Sivertz, "The North as a Region" (Ottawa: Resources for Tomorrow Conference, 1961), Vol. I, p. 569.

suggested that at least some of this is "every bit as good as that now being broken for new settlers in northern Finland and Norway."[13] Nevertheless, only a fraction of one per cent of this area has been brought under cultivation to date.

The eastern part of the territorial north comprises the northwestern section of the Canadian Shield, a great system of worn-down Pre-Cambrian rocks which dominates all of central and north-eastern Canada. The western limit of the Shield is clearly defined by the series of large lakes which straddle the contact zone between the Shield and the interior plains lying to the west of it. These lakes run the length of Canada and two of them, Great Bear Lake and Great Slave Lake, lie within the area of this study.

The region east of this demarcation line displays the characteristic topography of the Canadian Shield. It is a rather level plateau with an extremely rough surface characterized by an apparently endless pattern of slight elevations and depressions. The latter are often filled with water. Indeed, water frequently covers as much as 25 per cent of the visible landscape. The dry areas interspersed among the wet are either bare, exposed rock or they are covered with glacial deposits supporting varying amounts of vegetation depending upon the prevailing climate. In many places climatic conditions permit the formation of a peat-like soil called "muskeg."[14]

It is important to note that although surface vegetation on the Shield varies considerably from the parts of it lying just north of the United States boundary to the parts lying far north of the arctic circle, the geology is essentially the same throughout. It is in the geological structures of the Shield that the great bulk of the metallic minerals such as copper, gold, iron, nickel, uranium and cobalt produced in Canada are found. It is now generally established, despite the lack of detailed studies, that the northern parts of this region are probably as rich in these minerals as are the parts lying further south.[15] It has been pointed out by Buck that:

The concentration of producing mines along the southern fringe of the Shield is surely due to accessibility and consequently more thorough geological

---

[13]Trevor Lloyd, "The Future Colonization of Northern Canada," in Bladen, ed., *Canadian Population and Northern Colonization*, p. 153.

[14]Canada, Department of Mines and Technical Surveys, *An Introduction to the Geography of the Canadian Arctic* (Ottawa: Queen's Printer, 1951), p. 36.

[15]R. G. Robertson, *The Northwest Territories—Its Economic Prospects, A Brief Presented to the Royal Commission on Canada's Economic Prospects* (Ottawa: Queen's Printer, 1955), p. 7.

mapping and prospecting. Equally important, largely because the deposits are accessible, costs of exploration, development, and mining are lower in the south. Because the geological environment does not change, we have reason to expect that the distribution and abundance of ore deposits in the northern, less accessible parts of the Shield are comparable to those in the southern fringe.[16]

The north, then, contains three major physiographic regions—the mountainous Cordillera, the flat plains, and the rocky Shield, all of which possess much the same physical characteristics found in the same regions further south. It is unlikely that many Canadians find it difficult to conceive of the nature of the north so far as these physical characteristics of the land are concerned. The same cannot be said for its climatic features.

It is essential to an understanding of the economic situation of the north to appreciate that because this area is northerly in terms of latitude, it is not generally an arctic region as that term is used in relation to climate. If an arctic climate is defined as one in which the average mean temperature for the warmest month is less than 50 degrees Fahrenheit, the arctic and sub-arctic parts of the north may be separated by drawing a line on the map south-eastward from the Mackenzie delta to the port of Churchill on Hudson Bay. North of this line the average temperature is less than 50 degrees in the warmest month and average winter temperatures are all below 32 degrees. In the sub-arctic regions southwest of this line similar average winter temperatures prevail, but average summer temperatures there are above 50 degrees.[17] The demarcation between the arctic and sub-arctic areas so defined happens to correspond to the tree-line as well.

The isotherms lying across the north of Canada run southeasterly and not from west to east. Hence, the sub-arctic climate extends far into the north for more than 600 miles in the Mackenzie valley—well above the arctic circle—in the western part of the continent.[18] On the east, however, the arctic climate pushes south far below the arctic circle.[19]

It will be seen from Table 1.1 that all parts of the north have cold winters, although differences in average daily mean temperatures for January between north and south are perhaps less than most Canadians

---

[16]Buck and Henderson, "The Rôle of Mineral Resources," p. 76.

[17]J. L. Robinson, "Weather and Climate of the Northwest Territories," *Canadian Geographical Journal*, XXXII (March, 1946), 126.

[18]The arctic circle itself (66°32' North) is merely the circle of latitude north of which there is one day in the year during which the sun does not set.

[19]Canada, Department of Mines and Technical Surveys, *An Introduction to the Geography of the Eastern Arctic* (Ottawa: Queen's Printer, 1951), p. 20.

would expect. On the other hand, the winters do tend to be longer than those in the south. The low temperatures set in earlier and last longer. Furthermore, lows reached during the "cold snaps" also tend to be more severe than in the more settled areas of the Canadian West. As is also true further south on the prairies, however, the duration of the cold periods is so variable that the over-all character of the winter may be very different from one year to the next.

It is equally difficult to generalize about the summers of the north. It is not generally recognized that summer temperatures in the north are quite similar to those experienced in the south of Canada—as will be seen from the table. Because of these relatively favourable summer temperatures, and because of the unusually long hours of daylight in northerly latitudes in the summer months, various forms of heavy vegetation abound in the north during this season. The tree-line, for example, extends north all the way to the arctic coast in the Mackenzie valley. Trees and smaller plants in the area show, of course, the effects of the relatively short growing season. The average frost-free period in both the Mackenzie valley and in the Yukon is around 70 days, although the effect of local topography often exerts a marked influence on these conditions. Even more important, perhaps, is the effect of precipitation levels on plant life in the area and also the effect of permanently frozen soils in many areas. Both Mackenzie District and the Yukon Territory have dry climates. Mean precipitation at the major settlements in the Yukon during the year varies from about 10 to 13 inches and similar values are characteristic of the Mackenzie area as well.[20] The effects of cold or permanently frozen soils on plant life are not yet well understood but, while it appears to restrict growth by keeping the soil cool, it also appears to serve a useful purpose in keeping moisture near the surface.[21] In fact, it has sometimes been suggested that the low precipitation of the north is in general counteracted by the tendency for moisture to be retained longer than in southerly regions, "for the low temperatures reduce the amount of evaporation and the permanently frozen sub-soil prevents underground drainage."[22] More recent studies (based on the Thornthwaite classification) have suggested, however, that the need for moisture by growing plants in the north is high and that consequently

[20]W. Dickson, "Northern Agriculture," in C. A. Dawson, eds., *The New North-West* (Toronto: University of Toronto Press, 1947), Table I, p. 161 and Table III, p. 175.

[21]R. G. Robertson, *The Northwest Territories—Its Economic Prospects*, p. 18.

[22]Canada, Department of Mines and Resources, *The Northwest Territories* (Ottawa: King's Printer, 1943), p. 12.

the climate is, in general, sub-humid.[23] This would seem to be supported by the fact that, except in limited areas where soils and precipitation are unusually favourable, the forests of the north contain trees of small diameter and sharp tapers, characteristics which greatly reduce their commercial value. Nevertheless, these forests do provide cover for important numbers of fur-bearing animals. The smaller vegetation of the area also provides adequate food to maintain herds of caribou, both in a wild and in a semi-domesticated state.

The relative shortness and dryness of the summer season in the north are conditions which impose significant limits not only on the growth of living resources in the area, but also on the use which can be made of the rivers and lakes for transportation purposes.[24] The north has two large river systems, the Mackenzie and the Yukon, both flowing northwest to the sea. The navigable part of the Mackenzie system begins at the northern Alberta settlement of Waterways as the Athabaska River which flows north into Lake Athabaska. The Slave River connects Lake Athabaska with Great Slave Lake, a body of water having a total area of 10,980 square miles. It is only in the Slave River part of the waterway that a complete interruption of navigation occurs. Between Fort Fitzgerald, Alberta, and Fort Smith, Northwest Territories, the Slave falls 109 feet in sixteen miles and necessitates a portage for that distance. At the far western end of Great Slave Lake the Mackenzie River proper begins and it falls without interruption to the Arctic Ocean. The total length of the system is 1,700 miles.

The duration of the navigation season on the Mackenzie varies with spring ice conditions on Lake Athabaska and Great Slave Lake, and also with the water levels prevailing at certain critical points in the rivers themselves, especially late in the season when summer precipitation has been low. On an average the system is open only for about four months each year.

The Yukon River system drains the central part of the Yukon Territory in much the same way that the Mackenzie drains the western part of the Northwest Territories. The system is navigable from Whitehorse, in the southern Yukon, all the way through Alaska to Bering Strait. The distance from Whitehorse to the sea by river is 1,777 miles, of which 637 miles lie within Canadian territory. The river has a number of tributaries,

[23]M. Sanderson, "Is Canada's Northwest Subhumid?", *Canadian Geographical Journal*, XLI (September, 1950), 143.

[24]H. A. Innis, *Problems of Staple Production in Canada* (Toronto: Ryerson Press, 1933), p. 14.

of which the most important in Canadian territory are the Lewes, Pelly, White, Stewart, Klondike, and Fortymile rivers. Although there are a number of critical low water points on the main system, there are no portages on it. Again, however, the river is open only about four months of the year.

The effect of climate on river transport in the north is illustrative of the general significance of the region's climatic conditions. Although careful studies of the effects of cold, of temperature extremes in general, and of perma-frost on economic life in the north are only beginning, it is already clear that such conditions raise the costs of living and in various ways handicap the exploitation of northern resources. An attempt will be made later in this study to assess the relative impact of climatic factors on development in the territorial north, for it is important that these should be neither ignored nor overstated. The historical record of development in the north will show that while climatic factors have had a significant effect upon costs of production there, they have not constituted a barrier to production in any absolute sense. As one experienced northern administrator has put it, "If resources are found which are rich enough to compete with those closer to present markets, climate will not be a principal obstacle impeding development of the Canadian Northwest."[25]

THE NATIVE POPULATION

The native population of the territorial north consists of North American Indians living principally in the interior and of Eskimos situated in the northern and eastern Arctic coastal regions. The Indian population of the Yukon and Northwest Territories appears to have a common origin, for all groups in the area speak either the Athapaskan language or the very similar Kutchin tongue. Little is known of the origin of these people for they had no written language and their oral traditions are said to be of little use as a source of factual information about the distant past.[26]

When Europeans first came into contact with these native people in the early eighteenth century, they were found to be occupying the entire area of what is now the Northwest Territories and the Yukon as far

[25]J. L. Robinson, "Weather and Climate of the Northwest Territories," *Canadian Geographical Journal*, XXXII (March 1946), p. 139.

[26]For a description of these people see D. Jenness, *The Indians of Canada* (Ottawa, Queen's Printer, 1955), chap. 23.

north as the tree-line. The truly arctic regions north of the tree-line were occupied only by the Eskimos who had developed a highly specialized technology which enabled them to live in the barren lands of Keewatin and on the arctic coasts. Thus, the Indians of the territories were traditionally dependent upon the woodlands for their living. They had no agriculture but depended upon hunting and fishing for subsistence— occupations which prevented them from establishing permanent settlements. The Eskimos were also nomadic, being dependent upon the migratory caribou for much of their food supply and upon the fish and mammals of the coastal seas.

The environment of even the Indian population was harsh and its technology was hardly adequate to meet the difficulties it imposed upon them. They were probably worse off than most of the other native groups in North America and their numbers were small even before the coming of the Europeans. Certainly their difficulties were increased by this event. It has been estimated that the Athapaskans may have numbered about 13,000 early in the nineteenth century.[27] Within a century this number had been reduced by at least 50 per cent. Although inter-tribal conflict among the Athapaskan people came to an end early in the nineteenth century the new ways of life introduced by the fur-traders and missionaries proved disastrous. More and more the Indians (and later, the Eskimos) tended to congregate about the fur-trading posts, to adopt European clothing and dwellings, and to become economically dependent upon the trapping of furs for a living. The proceeds were used to buy the flour, beans, bacon, and other imported foods of the white man, thereby permitting further specialization of native labour in trapping fur-bearing animals for their pelts. Simultaneously, the native of the far north, like his fellows elsewhere in Canada, was subjected to the ravages of previously unknown diseases, especially tuberculosis, and to the effects of alcohol. His primitive religion was overwhelmed and Christianity was introduced in its place. Virtually all the Indians of the territories today are classed as adherents to either the Anglican or Roman Catholic faith. Unlike the other Indians of Canada, however, most of the Indians of the north escaped being confined to reservations by virtue of the fact that only negligible amounts of land were required by the white settlers in the north. The fur-trading relationships between Europeans and natives have never disappeared in the

[27]D. Jenness, "The Indians of the Northwest Territories and the Yukon," in Canada, Department of Mines and Resources, *Canada's Western Northland* (Ottawa: King's Printer, 1937), p. 60.

north as they have in those parts of Canada which proved suitable for agricultural settlement. Consequently, in a way, the natives of the territorial north were not subjected to the same pressures of adaptation to the white man's society as were the Indians located further south.

It should be noted, however, that there has been extensive intermarriage between Indians and Europeans in the north, so that for many years now it has been possible to say that "in the whole area there are probably few Indians of pure stock."[28] This makes it difficult to classify the population of the area for statistical purposes and, in practice, the definition of "Indian" is usually based upon the legal status of the individual in terms of the Dominion Indian Act of 1880. Although this act was modified in 1951, its effect has been to force Indians to choose between becoming wards of the state entitled to special assistance, but lacking citizenship, or to becoming citizens without such special assistance.

Because of this problem of classification and the remote location of the native population of the north, it has always been difficult to estimate its size. The data collected in the quinquennial census of Indians conducted by the federal government suggests that the total number of Indians in the Yukon and the Northwest Territories was more or less stationary, with the figure ranging from five to six thousand from early in this century until after World War II, and that since then it has been growing at a rapid rate. In 1962 the total reported by the Indian Affairs Branch (Department of Citizenship and Immigration) was 7,204.

Despite the great romantic appeal the Eskimo and his way of life have had since the early explorers first encountered these people, remarkably little factual information was obtained concerning them until quite recently. One reason for this was that it was not until this century that they were closely bound into the fur trade and, even then, because of their nomadic habits and confusing names, it proved difficult to estimate their numbers. The first rough count was made in 1927, at which time the total Eskimo population of Canada was estimated at 7,103, of which about 5,000 were probably located in the territorial north as that term is being used here. By 1961 this number had increased to 8,017. The data, and the causes of this population growth, will be examined further in subsequent chapters.

[28]Canada, Department of Mines and Resources, *The Northwest Territories— Administration, Resources, Development* (Ottawa: King's Printer, 1948), p. 22.

2 The Administration of the Territorial North

THE PART OF CANADA referred to as the territorial north for purposes of this study is administered jointly by various departments of the federal government and by two territorial governments, the Government of the Yukon Territory and the Government of the Northwest Territories. The evolution of this dual form of administration has been long and complicated.

The concept of territorial government in Canada, as distinguished from that of provincial government, originated in 1869 when the newly formed Government of Canada passed "An Act for the Temporary Government of Rupert's Land and the North-Western Territory when United with Canada."[1] Rupert's Land consisted of all those lands drained by rivers flowing into Hudson Bay and Hudson Strait which had been ceded to the Hudson's Bay Company by the charter of 1670. The North-Western Territory consisted of all the remaining land, in what is now Canada, lying between Rupert's Land on the east and the Crown Colony of British Columbia on the west. In 1870 title to Rupert's Land, the North-Western Territory and the arctic islands claimed by Britain was given by the British government to the Dominion of Canada. While a general administrative jurisdiction was maintained over these lands by the federal Department of the Interior, a form of territorial administration was provided for by the act of 1869. This was entrusted to a North-West Council, sitting in what is now Winnipeg, and to the Lieutenant-Governor of Manitoba. Manitoba itself was a small area carved out of the North-West Territories and given a provincial form of government in 1870.

The remaining part of the Territories was ruled under these arrange-

[1]*Statutes of Canada*, 32–3 Vic., c. 3 (1869).

ments for another five years, but in 1875 the federal government passed the "North-West Territories Act" which established a separate territorial administration under a resident Lieutenant-Governor. The Lieutenant-Governor was to be assisted by a North-West Council of not more than five persons appointed by the Governor-General in Council. This Council was given both executive and legislative responsibilities, the latter including powers to raise revenues by taxation for local and municipal purposes; to administer justice, property, and civil rights; to provide for public health, police, roads, highways and bridges; and, in general, to legislate in all matters of a purely local and private nature.[2]

As Lingard has pointed out, an ingenious provision was included in this Act, which would make possible a gradual evolution of this Council into an elected legislative assembly. It provided that when the Lieutenant-Governor was satisfied that any part of the Territories not exceeding 1,000 square miles in area had a population of at least 1,000 persons, other than un-enfranchised Indians and aliens, it was to be made an electoral district sending a member to the Council. When the elected members numbered 21, the Council was to be designated a Legislative Assembly.[3] This came about over a period of 10 years and in 1888 the first Legislative Assembly of the Northwest Territories was constituted with 22 elected members and three legal experts appointed by the Governor-General-in-Council.[4] Although the North-West Territories Act of 1888 provided that the Lieutenant-Governor was to select four members of the Assembly to advise him on financial matters, there was still no provision to enable the Assembly to control the spending of money by the government in the Territories.[5]

In 1891 a new act was passed by the federal government to amend these arrangements for territorial government. The North-West Territories Amendment Act of 1891 gave the territorial Assembly authority to legislate in virtually all matters assigned to the provinces by the British North America Act, except for the raising of funds on the public credit of the Territories and the administration of natural resources in the Territories. This included authority over the spending of territorial funds whether raised by taxation or granted by the federal government.[6] The committee elected by the Assembly to "advise" the Lieutenant-Governor

[2]*Ibid.*, 38 Vic., c. 49 (1875).

[3]C. C. Lingard, *Territorial Government in Canada* (Toronto: University of Toronto Press, 1946), p. 4.

[4]*Ibid.*, p. 5.

[5]*Statutes of Canada*, 51 Vic., c. 19 (1888).

[6]*Ibid.*, 54–5 Vic., c. 22 (1891).

on such spending evolved over the next six years into a fully responsible executive committee of the legislature. In 1897 the North-West Territories was formally granted responsible government similar to that existing in the provinces but, unlike them, lacking authority to borrow money or to administer the natural resources of the area.[7] By this time the population of the Territories was still small but it was growing rapidly. Between 1891 and 1901, according to census data, the population of the Territories grew from 98,967 to 165,555.[8]

The area under the jurisdiction of this territorial government when it became fully responsible in 1897 still included all the land between Manitoba and British Columbia and extending north to the Arctic Ocean, except for an area lying north of Manitoba and Ontario as those provinces were then constituted. This area, designated the District of Keewatin, was removed from the North-West Territories in 1876 and was apparently to be reserved as a separate district until such time as it might be added to the provinces of Manitoba and Ontario.[9] In 1882, some of the more settled parts of the Territories were designated as the Provisional Districts of Assiniboia, Saskatchewan, Alberta, and Athabaska. Three years later, in 1885, the additional Provisional Districts of Yukon, Mackenzie, Franklin and Ungava were established.[10] Residents of the first four Provisional Districts mentioned, or parts of them at least, were represented in the Legislative Assembly. Those living in the latter Provisional Districts were not.

The rapid influx of agricultural settlers to the southern plains of the Territories in the last years of the century led to a great population increase and a growing demand for those government services assigned to territorial government by the Act of 1891. Education and the establishment of suitable roads were major, and very costly, requirements. At the same time territorial revenues were limited to the rather small amounts available from property and other local taxes, and from grants made by the federal government. Being denied the power to borrow funds to finance investment in social overhead capital made the financial situation of the territorial government precarious.

The fact that the territorial government was also denied any power to

[7]Ibid., 60–1 Vic., c. 28 (1896–7).

[8]Canada, Department of Agriculture, Census Office, Census of Canada, 1891 and Ibid., 1901.

[9]C. C. Lingard, "Administration of the Canadian Northland," Canadian Journal of Economics and Political Science, XII (February 1946), 47.

[10]L. H. Thomas, The Struggle for Responsible Government in the North-West Territories 1870–97 (Toronto: University of Toronto Press, 1956), pp. 97–8.

regulate the development of natural resources in the Territories was another, and in some ways related, source of irritation and frustration for the residents of the area. The use of the agricultural lands of the Territories for the purpose of national development by the federal government was often felt to impose unreasonable burdens upon the residents of the Territories.[11] Out of this situation emerged the struggle for provincial status which was to lead to the establishment of the provinces of Saskatchewan and Alberta in 1905.

Even before this major alteration in the administration of the North-West Territories occurred, however, one of the remote Districts was given a special status and removed from the jurisdiction of the North-West Territories. This took place in 1898 when the Yukon District was established as a separate Territory. The exact boundaries of this new Territory lying north of British Columbia were not immediately defined, but its creation greatly reduced the area of the North-West Territories. In 1905 this area was further reduced by the creation of the provinces of Saskatchewan and Alberta. As Lingard has shown, the precise selection of the area to be given provincial status and indeed the decision to divide this territory once selected into two provinces instead of making it one, was made on rather dubious grounds.[12] The selection of the 60th degree of north latitude as the northern boundary of the area was apparently based upon the assumption that this was the northerly limit of agricultural settlement. The eastern boundary was taken as that established for the province of Manitoba in 1881 and the western one that already established for British Columbia. The decision to further divide this area into two parts apparently rested upon some belief that a province of such a vast area would be disproportionately large in comparison with the other provinces already in Confederation.

The administration of the remaining part of the old North-West Territories was revised by the Northwest Territories Amendment Act of 1905.[13] In the same year the District of Keewatin was enlarged by the addition of those parts of the old Provisional Districts of Athabaska and Saskatchewan not included in the new province of Saskatchewan, and the whole area assigned to the newly delimited Northwest Territories. The latter remained intact, however, for only seven years. In 1912 the northern boundaries of the provinces of Quebec, Ontario, and Manitoba were extended northward to their present limits. Since

[11]See Lingard, *Territorial Government in Canada*, p. 14.
[12]*Ibid.*, pp. 199–206.
[13]*Statutes of Canada*, 4–5 Edw. VII, c. 27 (1905).

then, boundaries of the Northwest Territories have remained unchanged. The present subdivision of the Territories into the districts of Mackenzie, Keewatin and Franklin was established by order-in-council in 1918 and made effective in 1920. The present boundaries of the Yukon Territory date from the settlement of the Alaska Boundary dispute in 1903.

The foregoing outline of the establishment of territorial government in Canada and of the eventual creation of the Yukon and Northwest Territories as we know them today, has necessarily focused attention on those parts of the great public domain which developed, economically and politically, to the point where provincial status became inevitable. The actual jurisdiction of the old North-West Territories' government and of the federal Department of the Interior over those parts which today comprise the Territories existed more in principle than in practice. While it is true that these areas were formally administered by the federal departments in Ottawa and by the territorial government (sitting first in Winnipeg and later in Livingston on Swan River [1876–7], still later in Battleford [1878–1882], and from 1882 until 1905 in Regina), they were in practice virtually ungoverned frontier areas possessing neither population nor economic significance until the 1880s in the case of the Yukon and until the early 1920s in the case of the Northwest Territories as presently constituted. Until these dates in each jurisdiction, the actual administration was carried out chiefly by the Royal Northwest Mounted Police. In both cases this *de facto* police administration was superseded only when there was an awakening of interest in the economic potentialities of each area.

In the Yukon the only important resource before the 1880s was fur. This was exploited by the Hudson's Bay Company until it withdrew from the area in the middle of the nineteenth century. Thereafter, the country drained by the Yukon River was worked by American traders operating upstream from Alaska. A desultory trade in furs was carried on by the Alaska Commercial Company which also provided supplies to a few miners prospecting for gold in Canadian territory. In 1887 one of these prospectors made an important gold strike on Fortymile Creek not far from the Alaska Boundary. Although the Treaty of St. Petersburg had defined the greater part of this boundary as the 141st meridian, it had never been actually located. Consequently, in 1887, the Canadian government financed an expedition to explore the country drained by the Yukon River and to survey the boundary with Alaska. This expedition was conducted under the direction of Dr. G. M. Dawson.

Following the gold discovery on Fortymile, there was increased activity in the area made accessible by the Yukon River and its tributaries. The fact that this river provided access to the area and made it contiguous with Alaska undoubtedly encouraged those using it to think of the Yukon as a continuation of American territory. Certainly the early commercial life of the Yukon ignored the international boundary. The Alaska Commercial Company was joined after the strike on Fortymile by the North American Transportation and Trading Company. The latter had its head office in Chicago, but its main distributing point was at Cudahy in Canadian territory.[14]

This situation eventually attracted the attention of the Canadian government which in 1894 sent an officer of the Royal Northwest Mounted Police into the Yukon "to ascertain officially and authoritatively the condition of affairs."[15] As a consequence of this investigation, the Department of the Interior reported as follows:

The facts clearly established—first, that the time had arrived when it became the duty of the Government of Canada to make more efficient provision for the maintenance of order, the enforcement of the laws and the administration of justice in the Yukon country, especially in that section of it in which placer mining for gold is being prosecuted upon such an extensive scale, situated near to the boundary separating Northwest Territories from the possessions of the United States in Alaska; and, second, that while such measures as were necessary to that end were called for in the interests of humanity, and particularly for the security and safety of the lives and property of the Canadian subjects of Her Majesty resident in that country who are engaged in legitimate business pursuits it was evident that the revenue due to the Government of Canada, under its customs, excise and land laws, and which would go a long way to pay the expenses of Government, was being lost for want of adequate machinery for its collection.[16]

To meet this situation the federal government established a detachment of 20 Royal Northwest Mounted Police officers in the Yukon. The detachment commander was authorized "to represent where necessary and until other arrangements can be made, all the departments of Government having interests in that region."[17] The making of these "other arrangements" became urgent after the great gold strike of August 16, 1896, set off the Klondike Gold Rush. The magnitude of this

[14]Canada, Department of the Interior, *Report of the Deputy Minister of the Interior for the Year 1895* (Ottawa: King's Printer, 1896), p. 9.
[15]Canada, Department of the Interior, *Information Respecting the Yukon District* (Ottawa: King's Printer, 1897), p. 7.
[16]*Report of the Deputy Minister of the Interior for the Year 1895*, p. 4.
[17]*Ibid.*, p. 6. The Royal Northwest Mounted Police administration was under the command of Major T. M. Walsh, who had previously established Fort Walsh in the Cyprus Hills and brought law and order to the southern prairies in the 1870s.

development is suggested by the fact that within two years Dawson, a small camp at the confluence of the Yukon and Klondike rivers, was to become a city of 25,000 inhabitants.

This influx of population, combined with the distance of the Yukon from Ottawa, encouraged the federal government to separate the Yukon district from the rest of the Northwest Territories. In establishing this separate Territory, the Yukon Act of 1898 followed for the most part the principles of the Northwest Territories Act of 1875.[18] It provided for a chief executive officer called a commissioner who was to administer the territorial government under instructions given him from time to time by the Governor-General-in-Council or by the Minister of the Interior. The commissioner was to be assisted in this task by an appointed council of not more than six persons, including the judges of the territorial court. The act conferred upon this territorial government authority over the same matters in the Yukon as those for which the Government of the Northwest Territories had authority in its area of jurisdiction. The existing ordinances of the Northwest Territories were to have force in the Yukon until amended or repealed by the competent authority.[19] New legislation of the Yukon government was to be subject to disallowance by the Governor-General-in-Council for a period of two years after being passed.

The commissioner appointed in 1898 was assisted by a Council consisting of six persons appointed by the Governor-in-Council. The persons appointed were in fact the chief federal administrative officers in the Territory including the commissioner of the police, the judge of the territorial court, and the registrar of land titles. In 1899 the gold commissioner, another federal official in the Territory, was added to the Council.

The wholly appointed Yukon Council existed for only one year. In 1899 the Yukon Act was amended to permit British subjects in the Territory to elect two members of the Council for a term of two years.[20] The same amendment empowered the Commissioner-in-Council to pass ordinances regulating and licensing various kinds of businesses, such as shops and taverns, and to devise public health regulations for the Territory.

It was soon found that these new arrangements were not acceptable to many of the residents of the Yukon. One acute, but perhaps not

---

[18]Lingard, "Administration of the Canadian Northland," p. 48.
[19]*Statutes of Canada*, 61 Vic., c. 6 (1898).
[20]*Ibid.*, 62–3 Vic., c. 11 (1899).

unbiased observer, has written that the "administration of criminal law continued to be by the North-West Mounted Police—sound, swift, relentless, and effective, but that of civil affairs, under the Government of the day, reeked with graft and crookedness, and will ever be a blot on Yukon history."[21] Much local discontent apparently derived from the conviction that the Council, as constituted, represented federal interests rather than those of the Territory. As in the old North-West Territories the attack on this non-responsible form of territorial government was concentrated on the matter of government expenditures, although the question of granting large areas of placer mining lands to certain private interests was also a matter of great local concern.[22] In 1904 the Yukon Council defeated by a vote of six to two a motion to send a memorial to the federal government requesting "that the laws governing the Yukon Territory and particularly those acts governing and defining the duties of the Yukon Council and the Commissioner, be so amended as to provide . . . the elected members of the Council [with] more control over the spending of public monies than they at present possess."[23] A related proposal to establish a board of three council members to advise the Commissioner between sessions of Council was also defeated. Similar motions were proposed and defeated in 1906 and in 1907.

Despite the obvious reluctance of the federal government's agents in the Yukon to permit the establishment of responsible, or even truly representative government at the territorial level, the residents of the Yukon eventually succeeded in obtaining the latter. They also obtained representation in the House of Commons. Indeed, federal representation was won more easily than representation on the Territorial Council.

The agitation for federal representation began in earnest in 1900 when a mass meeting in the Yukon sent a petition to Ottawa requesting the right to send two representatives to the House of Commons so that "important and pressing questions relating to the Yukon Territory may be properly brought before the House of Commons by members . . . acquainted with the conditions" of the Yukon.[24] No action was taken on this request by the federal government until 1902 when the Yukon Territory Representation Act was passed.[25] This act gave male British

[21]Mrs. George Black, *My Seventy Years* (London: Nelson, 1938), p. 186.

[22]*Ibid.*, pp. 188–9.

[23]Yukon Territory, *Journals of the Yukon Council* (1904), IV, 26.

[24]Canada, Parliament, House of Commons, *Official Report of Debates* (hereafter cited as *House of Commons Debates*), 1900, cols. 7773 and 7780, cited in Lingard, "Administration of the Canadian Northland," p. 49.

[25]*Statutes of Canada,* 2 Edw. VII, c. 37 (1902).

subjects, excluding Indians, the right to return one member to the House of Commons. It also sought to specify in some detail election procedures thought suitable to a remote and sparsely settled frontier region. In view of the subsequent difficulties associated with federal elections in the Yukon there is reason to believe that these provisions were either badly conceived or badly administered, or both. The campaign of 1904, for example, was enlivened by a narrowly avoided lynching of the returning officer in Dawson.[26]

The same year that the Yukon Territory Representation Act was passed, the Yukon Act itself was amended to meet some of the other requests of the residents of the Yukon.[27] The amended act increased the size of the Council from seven to ten members by providing for three additional members to be elected for two-year terms. This still did not give the elected members a majority when the Commissioner voted. Three other provisions of the act also represented at least partial acquiescence to the demands of the Yukon residents. First, the Commissioner-in-Council was given the same powers to make ordinances for the Yukon as were possessed by the Lieutenant-Governor of the Northwest Territories acting with the advice of the Territorial Legislative Assembly. Secondly, it provided that the ordinances passed by the Governor-in-Council for the Yukon should not remain in force longer than the next ensuing session of Parliament unless approved by resolution of both Houses.[28] The importance of this was that it restricted the power of the Governor-in-Council to make mining lands concessions in the Yukon by order-in-council without approval from Parliament, a matter frequently raised in the Yukon Council by the elected members. Thirdly, the amended Yukon Act gave the territorial government authority to control liquor in the Territory. As noted below, the latter concession was to be of great financial importance to the territorial government.

Despite these concessions, agitation for more representation on the Council continued. In the Council itself, motions were introduced during the sessions of 1904, 1905, and 1906 to request the federal government to make the Council wholly elected. Each time such motions were introduced they were either defeated or side-tracked.[29] The matter was also carried to the House of Commons as a result of petitions and the efforts of the Member for the Yukon. In the course of the Commons debate in

[26]Mrs. George Black, My Seventy Years, p. 191.
[27]Statutes of Canada, 2 Edw. VII, c. 34 (1902).
[28]Lingard, "Administration of the Canadian Northland," p. 50.
[29]See, for example, Journals of the Yukon Council (1905), V, 17.

1906, it was established that what was wanted was not provincial status, but merely a form of government similar to that provided for the old North-West Territories prior to 1905. It was two years, however, before any progress was made in this direction.

In 1908, an "Act to Amend the Yukon Act" was passed providing for a wholly elected Council of ten, sitting apart from the Commissioner and having annual sessions during a three-year term.[30] This Council, which met for the first time on July 15, 1909, was given some measure of control over the public purse, in so far as the Act provided that all money bills calling for the appropriation of any part of the public revenue of the Territory or for the imposition of any tax were to originate in the Council. But at the same time it provided that no such bill could be adopted unless it had first been recommended to the Council by the Commissioner.[31] As Lingard has pointed out:

It is evident that the Yukon did not receive responsible government. While the elected representatives of the people possessed legislative power within well-defined limits, the Commissioner was responsible to the federal government alone in respect to his wide executive and administrative functions. The people's representatives might initiate and pass legislation for the Commissioner's approval, disapproval or reservation for the assent of the Governor-in-Council, but they possessed no control over its execution. Clearly, the success of the system would largely depend upon the wisdom, good sense, and executive ability of the Commissioner on whom the Federal authorities depended for efficient and intelligent administration of the Territory.[32]

The Council itself was obviously dissatisfied with its status, for one of its first acts in 1909 was to set up a committee "to prepare and forward memorials to the Government and Parliament of Canada praying that the Yukon Act be amended so as to confer greater powers on the Yukon Council than at present possessed. . . ."[33]

Such prayers were not heard in Ottawa, however, and the form of territorial government established in the Yukon in 1908 remained virtually unchanged for the next ten years. The only attempt made to increase the power of the Council occurred in 1912 when George Black, after seven years as an elected member of Council, became Commissioner. In his first message to Council in that year he announced that a Superintendent of Public Works was to be appointed from among the members of Council in order to give Council "more direct control of

[30]*Statutes of Canada*, 7–8 Edw. VII, c. 76 (1908).
[31]*Ibid.*
[32]Lingard, "Administration of the Canadian Northland," p. 52.
[33]*Journals of the Yukon Council* (1909), IX, 83.

the expenditures, and securing for the Territory in effect a measure of responsible government."[34] The weakness of this entire system of territorial government was to be fully revealed six years later.

So far, to the writer's knowledge, no serious attempt has been made to assess the effect individual personalities had upon the development of territorial government in the Yukon. When such a study of the Yukon administration is done, however, the figures of George Black and his wife will loom large. When George Black resigned as Commissioner in 1916 in order to organize and lead the Yukon Infantry Company, the affairs of the Territory, already in sharp decline, deteriorated still further and the established government organization began to disintegrate. When the fourth wholly elective Council met in April, 1917, the chief executive officer was G. N. Williams who was styled "administrator" of the Territory. When Council met for the 1918 session it found that the Administrator had been replaced by another, and apparently even less prestigious officer, the Territorial Gold Commissioner. That the Council was never in any way consulted concerning these changes in the territorial government is clear from a rather plaintive telegram it immediately sent to Ottawa. It requested that "before drastic changes are made in the Government and administration of the Territory the Council be given an opportunity to express an opinion regarding same." It added that "the Council is uninformed as to changes already made or those proposed to be made."[35]

In fact the federal government had decided that the great reduction in population in the Yukon after 1910 made a drastic reduction in the administrative structure of the territory necessary on purely economic grounds.[36] It was also under some pressure to reduce all costs of government in the territory. In 1917, for example, a critic remarked in the House of Commons as follows:

I went through the Estimates last year and found that very little short of $1,000,000 was being paid by Canada for the 9,000 people, or thereabouts, in the Yukon. That is a huge figure. In going through the various items last year, I did not find that the slightest regard was paid to the changed conditions. . . . It simply amounted to this, that it cost about $100 per head to keep those 9,000 people in the Yukon. When the proposition is put that way it does not look very economical.[37]

That administrative economy was the federal government's primary concern was clearly indicated by the reply received by the Council to

[34]*Ibid.* (1909), XII, 9.   [35]*Ibid.* (1918), XVII, 8.   [36]See Table 11.2.
[37]*House of Commons Debates*, 1917, p. 1736.

its telegram quoted above. The Minister of the Interior bluntly informed the Council that "it is the intention of the Government to abolish the Yukon Council and to substitute therefore a simpler form of local administration."[38] This intention was carried out by Order-in-Council P.C. 745 on March 28, 1918, which abolished the positions of "Commissioner" and of "Administrator" and transferred the duties of these officials to the Gold Commissioner of the Yukon Territory. At about the same time, the government introduced a bill in the House to ratify its reduction of the number of administrative officials in the Yukon and to authorize the Governor-in-Council to abolish the existing Yukon Council. Provision was made for the appointment of a Council of two or more members by warrant of the Governor-General under his Privy Seal.[39]

This new federal policy with respect to the Yukon had two important implications, one obviously relating to the concept and status of a territorial government in Canada and the other having to do with the related question of economic development in regions so governed.

So far as the structure of territorial government is concerned, the new arrangements were clearly designed to eliminate local influence in governing the Territory altogether, apparently in order to eliminate the costs of electing and maintaining a representative body. The Council itself suggested that its membership be reduced from ten to five so as to lower these costs. But at the same time it insisted that "any other form than that of representative government would be unsatisfacory and repugnant to the people of this Territory, the large majority of whom are British subjects."[40] In the face of such opposition the federal government relented and in 1919 another amendment was made to the Yukon Act providing for an elected council of three members (with a sessional indemnity reduced from $600 to $400).[41] Commenting on this in the House, the Minister of the Interior expressed the hope that this would reduce total federal government expenditures in the Yukon to "something commensurate with the size of the population."[42]

Some of the economic implications and effects of this federal economy campaign in the Yukon will be considered below, where it is shown that these measures coincided with a critical phase in the economic development of the Yukon territory. During the early 1920s an effort was being

---

[38]*Journals of the Yukon Council* (1918), XVII, 33.
[39]*House of Commons Debates*, 1918, pp. 464, 682, and 2221.
[40]*Journals of the Yukon Council* (1918), XVIII, 43.
[41]*Statutes of Canada*, 9–10 Geo. V, c. 9 (1919).
[42]*House of Commons Debates*, 1919, p. 593.

made to develop lode mining in the Yukon to offset the continuing deterioration of the placer gold mining industry there. In particular, promising silver developments in the Mayo area at this time gave new hope for the recovery of the territorial economy and they were used by the Territorial Council in 1923 to support a request to the federal government for an increase in the size of the Council and in the amount of the sessional indemnity. The federal government's policy with respect to the Yukon remained unchanged, however, and so did the structure of the territorial government.[43]

The statutory basis for this structure was embodied in the *Revised Statutes of Canada 1927*, c. 215. No major legislative changes were made until after World War II. Indeed, the only alterations made in the structure of the territorial government during this period occurred in 1932 when all the powers of the Gold Commissioner were transferred to a "Comptroller" by Order-in-Council.[44] The following year the office of Gold Commissioner was abolished and for the next sixteen years the Comptroller functioned as the chief executive in the Yukon government.[45]

After World War II, for the first time since 1919, the federal government apparently became convinced that some elaboration of the territorial administration could be justified in terms of population increase and, perhaps, economic considerations. Legislation was passed in 1948 to permit the Governor-in-Council to "appoint for the territory a chief executive officer to be styled and known as the Commissioner of the Yukon Territory."[46] It also provided for the restoration of the Administrator to execute the functions of the Commissioner in the absence of the latter. The same act provided an increased sessional indemnity of up to $1,000 for members of the Council. The latter was felt to be justified because "during recent years the length of the session and the amount of legislation which they must consider have been greatly increased."[47] Provision was also made for living and travelling expenses connected with Council duties. During this same year (1948) several other territorial officers were installed, including a public Administrator, a Deputy Registrar of Land Titles, and a Legal Advisor to the territorial government.[48]

This strengthening of the Yukon territorial government was carried a

---

[43]*Ibid.*, 1923, pp. 3943–4.
[44]Canada, P.C. 1481, June 30, 1932.
[45]See *House of Commons Debates*, 1948, p. 5181.
[46]*Statutes of Canada*, 11–12 Geo. VI, c. 75 (1947–8).
[47]*House of Commons Debates*, 1948, p. 5180.
[48]Canada, Department of Mines and Resources, *Annual Report 1949*, p. 148.

step further in 1951 when the Council was expanded from three members to five.[49] This was done by creating new electoral districts so as to give more adequate representation to the growing population of the southern parts of the Territory. The first three-man council elected after the upheaval of 1919 represented the districts of Dawson, Klondike, and Whitehorse. With the development of the Mayo area in the early 1920s the Klondike district had been replaced by a new Mayo electoral district and this arrangement lasted until 1952. The first new five-man council was elected in that year to represent the districts of Dawson, Mayo, Carmacks, Whitehorse East, and Whitehorse West. The shift in the centre of population to the south was also responsible for the decision to move the territorial seat of government from Dawson City to Whitehorse. This move was made early in 1953.[50]

Throughout this post-World War II restoration of the framework of territorial government in the Yukon, there was no significant formal alteration in the nature of the Council's relationship with the appointed chief executive officer. The Council continued to sit apart from the territorial Governor and to initiate and pass ordinances for his consideration. He, in turn, continued to approve, disapprove, or reserve such bills for the assent of the Governor-in-Council. But although the volume of such legislative business increased greatly, the elected Council could exercise no direct control over the execution of government business in the Territory. This continued to be the formal responsibility of the appointed Governor of the Territory and the practical task of federal government departments and their employees in the Yukon, aided by a small territorial "civil service." The latter functioned primarily in the fields of education, road maintenance, and liquor control. And it should be noted that this territorial civil service remained under the sole management of the Commissioner.

It was not until 1960 that any progress was made in establishing some measure of responsible government in the Yukon. In that year legislation was passed which provided that there was to be an "Advisory Committee on Finance consisting of three members of the Council to be appointed by the Commissioner upon the recommendation of the Council." It further provided that "the Commissioner shall consult with the Committee in the preparation of the estimates of expenditures and appropriations required to defray charges and expenses of the Public Services of the Territory for each fiscal year." At the same time the

[49]*Statutes of Canada*, 15 Geo. VI, c. 23 (1951).
[50]Canada, Department of Resources and Development, *Annual Report 1953*.

Council was again increased in size from five to seven members.[51] Both measures were implemented, according to the Minister of Northern Affairs and National Resources, in response to a formal resolution passed by the Territorial Council and after consultation with the Yukon's Member of Parliament.[52]

TERRITORIAL GOVERNMENT IN THE YUKON

As the preceding outline of the historical development of the formal apparatus of territorial government in the Yukon indicates, there was no significant alteration in the constitutional status of that government between 1908, when representative government was established, and 1960, when a tentative step was taken toward providing a small measure of responsible government at the territorial level. During a good part of the fifty-two years intervening the actual conduct of government in the Territory was more an administrative function than a legislative one, for even in the area of territorial jurisdiction it would seem that what initiative there was came largely from the federal authorities. There were good reasons why this was so. Paramount, of course, was the inability of the elected council to exercise any initiative in the spending of public monies, even those raised by taxation in the Territory. Throughout its long history, the Yukon Act provided that, "It shall not be lawful for the Council to adopt or pass any vote, resolution, address, or bill for the appropriation of any part of the public revenue of the Territory, or of any tax or impost, to any purpose that has not been first recommended to Council by message of the Commissioner, in the session by which such vote, resolution, address, or bill is proposed."[53] Under these conditions it would be misleading to suggest that those powers assigned by the Yukon Act to the territorial government were in fact under the control of the local citizens acting through their elected representatives on Council. When reference is made to the territorial government, it must be remembered that this means the Commissioner operating in his dual role as chief federal civil servant in the Territory and as the non-responsible chief executive of the territorial government.

That there is in fact a danger of thinking of the Yukon Council as the

---

[51]*Statutes of Canada*, 8–9 Eliz. II, c. 24 (1960). The sessional indemnity and related payments to members of Council had been revised in 1955.

[52]*House of Commons Debates*, 1960, p. 7050.

[53]*Statutes of Canada*, 1–2 Eliz. II, c. 53 (1952–3).

effective part of the Territorial Government is suggested by the following statement by the Minister of Northern Affairs and National
Resources:

The set-up in the Northwest Territories and the Yukon is that we have given
jurisdiction to elected councils to look after matters concerning the territories,
with the exception of natural resources, education and social welfare for the
Indians and Eskimos.[54]

In fact, these matters were customarily "looked after" by the territorial
government, which in practice meant the Commissioner. The effective
power of this official was perhaps so great *vis à vis* the Council simply
because he had to act not only as the person responsible to the federal
government for carrying out the duties assigned to the territorial
government, but because he was even more directly responsible for
administering the duties performed on behalf of the federal government
itself in the territory.

The formal division of powers between the federal government and the
territorial government in the Yukon was made, with a few significant
exceptions, along the same lines as established in the British North
America Act between the federal government and the provincial governments. The legislative powers of the Commissioner-in-Council enabled
him to make ordinances for the government of the Territory in relation
to direct taxation within the Territory, the establishment of territorial
offices, municipal institutions, election of members to Council, intoxicants, game, prisons, business licences, incorporation of certain kinds of
companies, marriage, hospitals, roads, agriculture, property and civil
rights, and "generally all matters of a merely local or private nature in
the Territory." The territorial government was also given jurisdiction
over the administration of justice in the Territory, including the right to
establish courts of civil, but not of criminal, jurisdiction. Education was
also made a territorial responsibility subject to the provision that a
majority of ratepayers in local areas might establish such public schools
as they thought fit and that Roman Catholic or Protestant minorities in
such areas could establish separate schools and be exempt from public
school rates.[55] The Yukon Act provided that all ordinances made by the
territorial government were to be subject to disallowance by the
Governor-in-Council within a period of two years.

It will be noted that the chief omission from the corresponding list of
provincial powers was the power to administer natural resources in the

[54]*House of Commons Debates*, 1960, p. 7055.
[55]*Statutes of Canada*, 1–2 Eliz. II, c. 53 (1952–3).

Territory. In addition to this, throughout most of its history the Yukon government was unable to incur debt. In the revised Yukon Act of 1952–3 provision was made to enable the Commissioner-in-Council to borrow money, subject to the approval of the Governor-in-Council, on behalf of the Territory for meeting its annual expenditures pending receipt of annual revenues and for the purpose of lending money to municipalities for the construction of roads, waterworks, sewers or other municipal works. These borrowing and lending powers were broadened somewhat by an amendment in 1958 which made it possible for the Commissioner-in-Council to borrow money for territorial purposes, municipal purposes, or local purposes.[56] The same amendment authorized the Commissioner to lend money to municipalities and to school districts in the Territories and to invest surplus money standing to the credit of the Yukon Consolidated Revenue Fund.[57]

These changes in the financial powers of the territorial government reflected the population increase in the Territory after the beginning of World War II which, combined with the emergence of new standards of community services in the area, had brought about a large demand for such local services as streets, waterworks, sewerage systems and, of course, education, public health, and welfare facilities. Because even today municipal organization in the Yukon is rudimentary, the provision of such local services and works has remained largely in the hands of the territorial administration itself. Although there is, for example, provision under the municipalities and taxation ordinance to create incorporated cities in the three areas of Whitehorse, Dawson and Mayo, only the first two at time of writing have actually become municipalities as the term is applied in the provinces.

The Yukon Act, as noted above, also provided for the creation of local school administrations in the Territory. Again, however, providing education remained a function of the territorial administration itself. In fact, the actual arrangements for education in the Yukon never did have much relation to the legislative provisions made for it and as a result of the acceptance of these *ad hoc* arrangements, at time of writing there were still no locally administered public schools.

Throughout the history of the Yukon, three main functions absorbed most of the time and money of the territorial government. These were

[56]These "local purposes" included the financing of schools and hospitals in the Territory. See *House of Commons Debates*, 1958, p. 2290.

[57]*Statutes of Canada*, 7 Eliz. II, c. 9 (1958).

the providing of transportation facilities, education, and public health and welfare. The exercise of the first function had an unusual importance in view of the undeveloped nature of the Territory and its economic dependence upon the discovery and opening up of mineral deposits. The desperate efforts made by the territorial council in the first decades of this century to promote the development of lode mining drew attention to the problems of transportation within the area. In the early phases of development in the Mayo district, for example, the cost of transporting ore from Mayo to San Francisco was approximately twenty-two dollars per ton, of which almost twenty dollars per ton was attributable to the first twenty miles it had to be moved from the mines to the river![58] Some of the difficulties experienced by the territorial government in providing what local interests considered adequate roads and other transportation facilities will be noted when the whole question of transportation is considered in a later chapter.

The emphasis on transportation, education, and public health and welfare in the territorial administration's work is shown by breakdowns of territorial expenditures. The general pattern in the early 1960s is suggested by Table 2.1 which shows that in the fiscal year ending March 31, 1960, 33 per cent of the total territorial expenditures went to transportation and communications, about 28 per cent to education, and about 18 per cent to health and welfare. It is interesting to note that this distribution of outlays was not unlike that of the provincial governments in the same year. A more detailed breakdown of these expenditures (in 1959) is given in Table 2.2.

Unlike its pattern of expenditures, the revenues of the Yukon government have differed greatly from the pattern in the provinces. Throughout most of its history the Yukon territorial government derived more of its revenue from the sale of liquor than from any other single source. The only other important sources of revenue have been federal grants, sales taxes, licences and permits. Table 2.3 shows that in 1960, for example, the provinces derived an average of about 8 per cent of their total revenues from profits on liquor sales, whereas the Yukon drew almost 39 per cent of its revenue from this source. The sale of "privileges, licences and permits" in the Yukon yielded 10.6 per cent of total revenues compared to an average of over 20 per cent in the provinces and total taxes accounted for only about a quarter of total revenues

[58]Canada, Department of Mines, Mines Branch, *Annual Report on the Mineral Production of Canada 1916*, p. 148.

instead of the almost 50 per cent they brought to the provinces. Federal subsidies, it will be noted, were about the same in the Yukon as in the provinces other than the Maritimes.

Prior to the end of World War II, the Yukon government was heavily dependent upon federal grants for revenue to be used for territorial purposes. The size of this grant fluctuated considerably over the years. The contraction of federal support for the Territory at the end of World War I brought a sharp drop in the size of the federal grant from over $200,000 annually to less than $100,000 in the early 1920s. There was some increase in the grant in the late 1920s and early 1930s, but the depression of that decade brought another sharp drop in revenues from this source. The grant fell even further during World War II to a low of less than $50,000 in 1941. During this period the federal grant was apparently thought of as a device for raising total territorial revenues to the minimum level required to maintain the functions assigned to the territorial government. In 1943, for example, a $60,000 federal grant was made to the Yukon and the Minister of Mines and Resources explained to the House of Commons sitting in Supply that, although there had been some increase in the expenditures of the Yukon government, "fortunately the revenue obtained by the Yukon territorial council has also increased, so that it has not been necessary to increase this vote."[59] Throughout the remaining years of the war and during the early years of post-war reconstruction, the federal grant remained at about this same level. The structure of federal support for territorial government in the Yukon was altered, however, in 1948. In that year the federal government entered into a five-year financial agreement with the territorial government similar to those it made with the provinces.

The agreement of 1948 provided for an annual grant of $60,000 in lieu of the previous federal grant in support of government in the territory. Added to this was a *per capita* subsidy of 80 cents (based on a population of 8,000) yielding $6,400 the first year. Finally, a tax-rental arrangement provided that the territorial government would rent its personal and corporate income tax and succession duties powers to the federal government in return for a guaranteed annual minimum return of $89,365.[60] In 1948 this agreement brought to the territorial government a total of almost $200,000. An interesting provision of this agreement was that whenever net profits from the sale of alcoholic beverages exceeded $185,000, the excess was to be "set aside and applied to pro-

[59]*House of Commons Debates*, 1943, p. 5304.
[60]Canada, *Public Accounts 1949*, p. M-30.

mote the development of the natural resources of the Territory by the providing of roads, bridges, and other public works." In 1948–9 this amounted to $217,687.[61]

Similar agreements were entered into in 1952 and again in 1957 and under each of them the amount of money made available to the territorial government was increased. It amounted to between $250,000 and $300,000 from 1952 to 1956 and thereafter to over $400,000.[62] A detailed breakdown of total territorial revenue for 1959 is given in Table 2.4.

THE ROLE OF THE FEDERAL GOVERNMENT IN THE ADMINISTRATION OF THE YUKON

The preceding summary of the development, constitution, and functions of the Yukon territorial government has indicated the relative weakness of that government. Constitutionally the functions of the territorial government have been more limited than those of the provincial governments, the chief restriction being in the area of natural resource administration. Given the dependence of the territorial economy on mining, it is not surprising to discover that a relatively large amount of the day-to-day administration of the Territory has always been entrusted to federal officials and employees. But the weakness of the territorial government constitutionally and financially has also meant that it has had to depend heavily upon federal employees to carry out functions nominally under the control of the territorial government. Thus, while road building and maintenance, for example, is a territorial responsibility, much of the actual work has been under the direction of the federal authorities, partly because of the absence of territorial organization and equipment and partly because of federal involvement in road construction arising out of resource development. This is true of most functions of government in the area even today when a real territorial civil service is beginning to develop. The chief exception is in the field of education where direct federal involvement is relatively slight.[63] Perhaps

[61]*Ibid.*
[62]D.B.S., *Financial Statistics of Provincial Governments, Revenue and Expenditure,* published annually 1956–60. Because of the post-war inflation the increase in revenues from these agreements is considerably exaggerated. In terms of constant (1949) dollars the real increase was from about $150,000 before 1952 to approximately $223,000 by 1955 and to just over $250,000 by 1960.
[63]The Yukon school system is described in Chapter IX.

the nature of this reliance upon federal facilities is suggested by the fact that even the ordinances of the Yukon Council have had to be sent to Ottawa for drafting because no staff was available in the Territory for such work.

Although at time of writing there was a move afoot to reduce the dependence of the Yukon upon federal administrative facilities, throughout the period with which this study is concerned, this dependence was generally very great and, in most fields, total. Because this federal administration in the Yukon was provided by the same departments that administered the Northwest Territories, it will be convenient to defer a description of it until the development of territorial government in the Northwest Territories has been sketched.

TERRITORIAL GOVERNMENT IN THE NORTHWEST TERRITORIES

The general nature of territorial government as formally constituted in the Northwest Territories is similar to that of the Yukon. The chief formal difference lies in the much slower development of representative provisions and in the greater centralization of all branches of territorial government in Ottawa. Associated with the latter has been an even greater territorial dependence upon federal departments for the actual administration of territorial affairs than has been the case in the Yukon.

The structure and powers of the Northwest Territories government were defined by the "Northwest Territories Amendment Act" of 1905 which provided for the appointment of a chief executive officer, to be known as the Commissioner of the North West Territories, and a Council of not more than four members to assist in the administration. The Commissioner and his Council were all to be appointed by the Governor-in-Council.[64] This territorial government was given authority to pass ordinances for the governing of the Territories under instructions from the Governor-in-Council or from the responsible federal minister in the same fields as were assigned to the Yukon government and to the provinces—except for roads, wills, married women's property, coroners and inquests, controverted elections, intoxicants, hospitals, and agriculture. As in the Yukon the existing ordinances of the old Northwest Territories passed before 1905 were continued in force until repealed or amended.

[64]*Statutes of Canada*, 4–5 Edw. VII, c. 27 (1905).

These arrangements for territorial government in the Northwest Territories had little importance from an administrative standpoint between 1905 and 1921. During this period the Northwest Territories remained the preserve of the fur trade and were actually administered almost entirely by the Royal Northwest Mounted Police under the direction of Lieutenant-Colonel F. White, Comptroller and Deputy Head of the police force and also Commissioner of the Northwest Territories. Although the Canadian government sought to extend the area of its northern territories to, or even beyond, the north pole during these years, it found it unnecessary either to establish a council or to make new ordinances for the government of these areas before 1921.[65] Federal expenditures in the Northwest Territories amounted to about six thousand dollars annually during these years, this amount being appropriated for purposes of "general government."

It was not until a private company discovered commercial quantities of petroleum near Fort Norman on the Mackenzie River that any official enthusiasm, or even interest, developed in connection with the Northwest Territories. This discovery at what was to become Norman Wells led Mr. Meighen to make in Parliament the then original observation that, "It is a great mistake to assume that the area of the Northwest Territories is wholly—or, indeed, in any substantial degree—barren." He went on to prophesy that, "The time will come when it will be a prized part of the Dominion."[66]

As a consequence of this new interest in the area, the federal government appointed the four-member council for the first time early in 1921 to assist the Commissioner, W. W. Corry, Deputy Minister of the Department of the Interior, who had succeeded Lieutenant-Colonel White a year earlier. At the same time a branch of the Department of the Interior was organized to carry out the active work of administration, and some local offices were established in Mackenzie District.[67] Later in 1921, the Council was increased from four to six members, and provision was made for one member to be appointed Deputy Commissioner

---

[65]M. Zaslow, "A Prelude to Self-Government: The Northwest Territories, 1905–1939," in F. H. Underhill, ed., *The Canadian Northwest: Its Potentialities*, p. 91. The government's pursuit of sovereignty in the high arctic during this period is described in G. W. Smith, *Territorial Sovereignty in the Canadian North: A Historical Outline of the Problem*, Northern Co-ordination and Research Centre (Ottawa: 1963), pp. 7–10.

[66]*House of Commons Debates*, 1920, p. 3281.

[67]*Minutes of the Council of the Northwest Territories*, June 14, 1922, I, 28. The administration building at Fort Smith was opened on August 15, 1921.

and empowered to exercise the powers of the Commissioner in his absence.[68]

This structure of territorial administrative facilities remained unaltered from 1921 to 1951. During this thirty-year period the government of the Territories was entrusted in effect to a group of senior civil servants. The Council itself during this period has been described as "an inter-departmental advisory committee, co-ordinating the activities of several federal departments within the Territories. . . ."[69] In the early 1930s, for example, the Council consisted of the Assistant Deputy Minister of the Department of the Interior; the Deputy Minister of the Department of Mines; an official of the Dominion Lands Board, Department of the Interior; the Commissioner of the Royal Canadian Mounted Police; the Deputy Superintendent General, Department of Indian Affairs; and the Director of the Northwest Territories and Yukon Branch of the Department of the Interior.[70] The functions performed by the Council after 1921 had to do chiefly with modifying the old North-West Territories ordinances to bring them into conformity with the different and changing social and economic environment of the new Territories. During the 1920s and most of the 1930s this involved the Council in relatively little legislative activity for, despite the high hopes entertained for rapid economic development in Mackenzie District in the early 1920s, the fur trade continued to dominate the entire area until the Yellowknife gold quartz-mining boom of the 1930s. An impression of the activities of Council during most of these two decades might be gained from the following account of a fairly representative year's proceedings:

During the year seven meetings were held. At these a number of important matters were dealt with, including the re-drafting of the game regulations, the consideration of grants for the protection of native orphan children and for assisting the carrying on of hospitals and schools, the establishment of permanent radio stations, and the organizing of a system of fire-ranging and game protection by wardens. New ordinances concerning the fur export tax, legal time zones in the Territories, and Eskimo ruins were passed and careful consideration given to the draft of the revised ordinances of the Northwest Territories.[71]

The legislative powers of the Commissioner-in-Council were essentially the same as those assigned to the Yukon territorial government.

---

[68]_Statutes of Canada_, 11–12 Geo. V, c. 40 (1921).

[69]Zaslow, "A Prelude to Self-Government: The Northwest Territories, 1905–1939," p. 92.

[70]_Minutes of the Council of the Northwest Territories_, I and II.

[71]Canada, Department of the Interior, _Report of the Director of the Northwest Territories and Yukon Branch 1929–30_ (Ottawa: King's Printer, 1931), p. 10.

The North-West Territory Act provided the Commissioner-in-Council with power to make ordinances for the Government of the Territories under instructions from the Governor-General-in-Council, or the responsible minister, respecting direct taxation within the Territories in order to raise revenue for territorial or local purposes, establishment and tenure of territorial offices and the appointment and payment of officers, maintenance of prisons, municipal institutions, licences, solemnization of marriages, property and civil rights, administration of justice and generally all matters of a local or private nature in the Territories.[72] All ordinances made under this authority were subject to a federal veto. It was not until the later years of the 1930s, however, that the territorial government began to use most of these powers.

The sudden development of mining at Yellowknife and at Port Radium in the late 1930s brought about a substantial increase in population and in the level of economic activity in the Mackenzie District. Furthermore, these changes quite altered the character of the area which had previously been dominated by the fur trade. The territorial administration found itself increasingly confronted by the demands of a new white population for modern facilities and amenities. These included schools, hospitals, water and sewerage systems, streets and roads, electric power, and a wide range of administrative services such as regulation of retail trade, urban planning, enforcement of sanitary standards, and social welfare provisions.

It is interesting to note that throughout the history of the territorial north, the provision of such services tended to lag considerably behind the demand for them. That this should be so is not surprising, perhaps, in view of the uncertainties facing development based upon mining operations in such a remote part of a large country. It may be that such a lag is only prudent under such circumstances. If that be so, the system of governmental organization which existed in the Territories (and only to a slightly lesser degree that which existed in the Yukon) throughout the 1930s and 1940s was well designed to ensure that no rash decisions should be made in allocating resources to provide such facilities in that area. In the areas of jurisdiction specifically assigned to the territorial government the reluctance to use public funds to provide even rudimentary forms of social overhead capital was evidenced by the administration's continued reliance upon religious institutions to provide schools, hospitals, and a measure of social welfare work.

The demand for community services in the Territories was, of course,

[72]*Statutes of Canada*, 4–5 Edw. VII, c. 27 (1905); *R.S.C.* 1906, c. 62; *R.S.C.* 1927, c. 142; 15 Geo. VI, c. 21 (1951).

greatest in the larger settlements growing up in connection with mining and the related new economic activities. The chief settlements emerging in the late 1930s were Fort Smith, the administrative centre for Mackenzie District, Yellowknife on the Great Slave Lake, and Port Radium on Great Bear Lake. The latter was completely a company town and the company provided what facilities it needed. Of the other two, only Yellowknife was large enough to develop a form of local government before the development of the District was halted by World War II.

Under the authority of the Local Administrative District ordinance for the Northwest Territories, an area of about 39 square miles was constituted the Yellowknife Administrative District in October, 1939. The affairs of this district were placed under the management of a Local Trustee Board made up of an appointed chairman, two elected, and three appointed, members.[73] The size of the Board was increased from five to seven by the addition of two more elected members effective January, 1946. The specific powers allotted to the Board by the territorial ordinance gave it authority to impose taxes on real and personal property, to levy a poll tax, and to pass by-laws for the relief of the poor; for public health; road, street and sewer construction; for regulating traffic; and for the support of schools.[74] In 1940, a public school district was also established and a school board of three members elected.

The issues involved in the creation and subsequent operation of such institutions of local government in the Northwest Territories were complex and difficult ones. Nevertheless, the fundamental problem underlying these difficulties was, from the outset, simple and obvious enough. With the growth of population in the area, the residents, and especially the new residents, wanted a say in the administration of local affairs—but they lacked a local tax base large enough (and well-enough established) to finance the operations of local governments. The nature of the problem was certainly well appreciated by the Northwest Territories Council, which, as is apparent from its Minutes, was generally hostile to pleas for "administrative reform" from the residents of the area during this period.

The development of such institutions of local government and, indeed, the agitation for reform of the territorial administration itself,[75] ended with the outbreak of World War II. The effects of the war on the

[73]Canada, Department of Mines and Resources, *Annual Report 1940* (Ottawa: King's Printer, 1941), p. 69.

[74]Lingard, "Administration of the Canadian Northland," p. 68.

[75]For a brief description of this agitation see Zaslow, "A Prelude to Self-Government: The Northwest Territories, 1905–1939," pp. 92–9.

Territories are discussed elsewhere in this study, but in the most general terms, they transformed not only the economic life of the area but also the attitude of the federal government toward its responsibilities for development there. The subsequent growth of government activities in the Northwest Territories was marked by renewed efforts on the part of the residents to obtain a greater say in the conduct of public affairs. While such efforts led to no sudden or dramatic alteration in the system of territorial government in force since 1921, by the early 1950s the federal government was able to concede that "with the increase in population and the development of the territories, it is considered that there should be some elected representatives in the council."[76] In the spring of 1951 the government introduced into the House of Commons a Bill to amend the Northwest Territories Act having a "regard to the growth of the Northwest Territories." A cabinet minister explained that "It is the opinion of the government that the time has come to recognize that growth and to give to the people of the Northwest Territories some elected representation in the Northwest Territories Council."[77] This was done by providing for a council consisting of eight members, one of whom was to be Deputy Commissioner. Of these eight, three were to be elected by the people of Mackenzie District to represent three constituencies in Mackenzie District, and five were to be senior federal officials appointed by the Governor-in-Council as before.[78] The first elected members were J. Brodie, a trader, resident in Fort Smith representing Mackenzie South; F. Carmichael, a trapper from Aklavik representing Mackenzie West; and M. Hardie, a clerk in Yellowknife, representing Mackenzie North. The revised statute provided that these elected members would sit for three-year terms. It also called for at least two sessions of Council per year, one of which was to be held in the Territories and one at Ottawa. The elected members were granted a stipend of $50.00 per day but not exceeding $1,000 per year, and certain travelling and living expenses connected with their council duties.[79]

In reply to criticisms directed at the rather slight progress this new arrangement represented in terms of granting representative government to the people of the Territories, the responsible minister pointed out that only a small part of the cost of government in the Territories was borne by local residents and he concluded that "I should think the people of

[76]*House of Commons Debates*, 1951, p. 1536.
[77]*Ibid.*, p. 1540.
[78]*Statutes of Canada*, 15 Geo. VI, c. 21 (1951).
[79]*Ibid.*, 2–3 Eliz. II, c. 8 (1954).

Canada generally would expect the people of the territories to be capable of bearing a larger share of total government expenses in the territories before they can reasonably expect to have a fully elective council."[80]

One year after the provision of the partly elected council in 1951, the federal government introduced a bill to "transfer additional revenues to the territorial government and to place upon it additional responsibilities more in keeping with its new status."[81] Specifically, a territorial revenue account was established and the council was made responsible for roads, wills, the property of married women, coroners, inquests, controverted elections, intoxicants, hospitals, and agriculture.[82]

Further steps taken in the 1950s to meet local demands for control over territorial affairs included the establishment of a form of municipal government in the settlements of Hay River, Fort Smith, and Fort Simpson. The latter two were established as Local Improvement Districts in 1954.[83] In the same year one more elective seat was added to the Territorial Council, making four elected to five appointed members (not including the Commissioner).[84] When this provision was debated in the House of Commons the government indicated its willingness to add a fifth elected member, thereby giving the elected members a majority of the seats in the Council, but it was felt that this provision should be held in reserve pending further development in the Territories.[85]

Throughout the 1950s, then, a Council dominated by appointed members continued to govern the Northwest Territories. The elected members provided a measure of representation for the residents of the Territories, at least for those who lived in the more economically developed District of Mackenzie. The eastern or arctic part of the Territories did not share directly in the small degree of representative government built into the territorial system during the post-World War II period. The electoral districts established by the Commissioner were all in Mackenzie District. Consequently, although the federal departments of government continued to execute not only federal but also the territorial policy throughout the entire area of the Territories, the residents of the western regions had some voice, however small, in the determination of this policy, while those of the eastern regions did not.

[80]*House of Commons Debates*, 1951, p. 1606.
[81]*Ibid.*, 1952, p. 3407.
[82]*R.S.C.*, 1952, c. 195 and c. 331. The Northwest Territories Act was revised in 1952, but the new act did not come into force until after the amendment of the Criminal Code in 1955.
[83]*Minutes of the Council of the Northwest Territories.*
[84]*Statutes of Canada*, 2–3, Eliz. II, c. 8 (1954).
[85]*House of Commons Debates*, 1953–4, p. 1237.

The development of representative institutions at the territorial level of government during the post-war years was accompanied by an equally modest transfer of government responsibilities from the federal department in charge of territorial administration to the Council. This policy was initiated, as noted above, in 1952 when certain additional powers were placed under territorial jurisdiction and the federal government undertook to provide the territorial government with additional revenues. The latter provision indicated that this was essentially a matter of transferring administrative duties from a federal department to a territorial government controlled by that department and dependent upon federal finance for most of its undertakings. Aside from federal grants, territorial revenue sources were limited to liquor profits, licences and fees, and certain local taxes. During the post-World War II period these proved entirely inadequate to meet the growing demands for community services in the Territories. While most of these demands were in fact met through direct federal investments in schools, hospitals, hostels and even in complete "model communities" such as Inuvik,[86] measures were introduced during the 1950s to increase the degree of financial competence and independence enjoyed by the territorial administration. These consisted of amendments to the Northwest Territories Act to enable the territorial government to borrow money and for the institution of a financial agreement between the federal and territorial governments similar to that which had been made earlier with certain provinces and with the Yukon Territory.

The financial relationship between the territorial and the federal government was reorganized in 1953 when the old system of federal grants in support of the territorial government was replaced by a so-called "Tax Rental Agreement." The federal payments to the Territories under this and subsequent agreements became, next to liquor profits, the chief source of revenues for the territorial government.[87]

The original agreement was superseded by a new one in 1957 which provided for annual payments to the territorial government based on the population of the Territories and on the Gross National Product of Canada. Although the revenue yielded by the agreement rose to $520,000 during the 1957–58 fiscal year,[88] close to double the 1952–53 figure, the demands upon the territorial government for capital outlays

---

[86]Most of the capital cost of school construction in the Northwest Territories, for example, was met by the federal government during the 1950s. See the remarks made by the Minister of Northern Affairs and National Resources on this subject in *House of Commons Debates*, 1958, pp. 4028–9.

[87]See Tables 2.3 and 2.4.

[88]D.B.S., *Financial Statistics of the Government of Canada*.

on education, water and sewerage systems and similar local undertakings grew even faster. During the decade of the 1950s the population of the Territories grew by approximately 40 per cent and territorial outlays rose from $430,000 in 1952–53 to $2 million in 1959–60.[89] It was understood in the 1957 agreement that if territorial expenditures were increased beyond the level contemplated in the agreement, the territorial government would have to find the additional revenues required on its own initiative.[90] The problem here, of course, was that the Northwest Territories Act made no provision whereby the territorial government could borrow money. And the federal government recognized, in 1957, that the time had come when some borrowing powers had to be conferred upon the territorial government if it was in fact to perform the duties nominally assigned to it.[91] Consequently, the Northwest Territories Act was amended during the 1957–58 session of Parliament to enable the Commissioner-in-Council to make ordinances (*a*) for the borrowing of money by the Commissioner for territorial, municipal or local purposes on behalf of the Territories and (*b*) for the lending of money by the Commissioner to municipalities and school districts in the Territories.[92]

While this amendment represented a formal improvement in the constitutional position of the territorial government, it must be noted that in practice there was little actual alteration in its financial dependence upon the federal government. As in the Yukon, where the territorial government had for some time enjoyed similar borrowing powers, there was little possibility that the borrowing could in fact be done through the bond market. It was recognized that so long as the federal government retained jurisdiction over the natural resources of both territories, any borrowing they did would have to be from the federal government rather than from private or commercial sources.[93]

The main functions of the territorial government in the Northwest Territories have been even more limited than has been the case in the Yukon. Table 2.1 shows that as late as 1960 the government of the Northwest Territories was spending approximately two-thirds of its total budget on two functions, education and health. In the Territories these and all other territorial functions in practice have been carried out

[89]Council of the Northwest Territories, *Votes and Proceedings 1961*, mimeographed, p. 2.
[90]*Ibid.*, p. 46.
[91]See *House of Commons Debates*, 1958, p. 4028.
[92]*Statutes of Canada*, 6 Eliz. II, c. 30 (1957).
[93]See *House of Commons Debates*, 1958, p. 4028.

by federal employees. At time of writing there was still no territorial civil service. To an even greater extent than has been the case in the Yukon, then, throughout the period of this study, the territorial government of the Northwest Territories has had little constitutional power, and even less *de facto* power to influence significantly the course of development in the area nominally under its jurisdiction. Throughout the entire area of the territorial north, the real responsibility for development has been almost completely centred in the federal capital. The small population of the area has had relatively little opportunity to initiate public undertakings or to supervise their execution. Even the great expansion of public activities in the Northwest after World War II had little effect on this situation. By the end of the 1950s, in the fiscal year 1959–60, for example, the combined expenditures of the territorial governments were about 3 million dollars. Direct expenditures by federal departments in the area during the same year amounted to over 76 million dollars.[94]

The extent to which there has been local influence exerted on this kind of federal activity in the north is difficult to assess. Some influence, especially in the Yukon, has undoubtedly been channelled through the territorial councils and, in very recent years, there may be some evidence to suggest that the Council of the Northwest Territories has begun to provide a channel of communication between local residents and the federal administration. Another connection has been by way of federal officials and employees stationed in the north, especially the members of the R.C.M.P. The most direct avenue of access to the federal authorities, however, has been through the measure of representation in Parliament which has been provided for residents of the Yukon since as early as 1902 and for residents of the Northwest Territories since 1947.

The Yukon won its parliamentary representation in 1902 after several years of petitioning the federal government for this right. In that year the Yukon Territory Representation Act established the Yukon as an electoral district and provided for it to send one member to the House of Commons.[95] Over the years this Yukon constituency has been ably represented in the House. During much of the history of the Yukon its chief spokesman "outside" was George Black who won the Yukon seat for the Conservative Party in four successive federal elections—those of

---

[94]Territorial expenditures from D.B.S., *Financial Statistics of Provincial Governments, Revenue and Expenditure (Actual), 1959*, p. 8. Outlays of federal departments based on data attributed to Department of Northern Affairs and National Resources and cited in *House of Commons Debates*, 1961, p. 4384.
[95]*Statutes of Canada*, 2 Edw. VII, c. 37 (1902).

1921, 1925, 1926 and 1930. During his first term George Black was responsible for carrying through several amendments to the Yukon Act concerning judicial procedures in the Territory and for securing the passage of the Yukon Quartz Mining Act. The latter legislation was, and continues to be, highly esteemed in the Yukon because, like the Placer Mining Act which preceded it, it put the control of mining in the Territory under statute instead of administration by order-in-council. This local preference for statutory regulation of the industry was justified by the Yukon's representative on the grounds that "the government was far removed from the scene of operations" and very often the regulations were found to be very undesirable in their effect.[96]

In 1930 Black was elected Speaker of the House. When he withdrew from public life in 1935 his wife, running as an independent Conservative, won the Yukon seat (thereby confirming, as she reports in her autobiography, the saying that there were two parties in the Yukon— the Liberals and the Blacks).[97] Black took over again in 1940 and continued to represent the Yukon in the House until 1948. Before leaving the House, he was able to remark that the Conservative Party had held the seat for 42 of the 46 years it had been represented in Parliament. This was not, he felt, because the great majority of the Yukon voters were supporters of the Conservative party, but because of their dissatisfaction with the federal government's policies in regard to the Yukon.[98]

The question of providing Parliamentary representation for the Northwest Territories was not raised until the 1920s. According to Zaslow, local demands for such representation increased when the beginning of mining in Mackenzie District in the 1930s "added a new element of discontent in the form of prospectors, mining company employees and businessmen of many sorts who were attracted to the District of Mackenzie."[99] In 1938 the Minister of Mines and Resources remarked in the Commons that although no request for representation of the Territories had been received, he "should not be surprised if it did arrive within a few years."[100] The outbreak of war in 1939, however, disrupted the development of the mining industry in Mackenzie District and the question of Parliamentary representation for the area disappeared for several years. But with the great increase in the rate of development

---

[96]*House of Commons Debates,* 1924, p. 636.
[97]Mrs. George Black, *My Seventy Years* (London: Nelson, 1938), p. 309.
[98]*House of Commons Debates,* 1948, p. 1761.
[99]Zaslow, "A Prelude to Self-Government: The Northwest Territories, 1905–1939," p. 99.
[100]*House of Commons Debates,* 1938, p. 725.

in Mackenzie District at the end of the war it became obvious that the population growth of the District made some measure of representation necessary. The federal government's solution was to annex, in 1947, part of Mackenzie District to the Yukon electoral district, thereby creating a giant constituency known as Yukon–Mackenzie River. According to the member returned by this constituency, this was done "notwithstanding the many many protests by the peoples of the Mackenzie River district and the Yukon Territory." The people of the two areas, he argued, had no community of interest and, because of the high cost of campaigning by air, they could not be adequately represented by one member.[101] His predecessor, George Black, described the arrangement as being "so impossible and impractical that one wonders if those sponsoring the bill are really in earnest. If they are, it shows them to be totally lacking in knowledge of conditions in those areas or willing to discard all proprieties."[102] This highly unpopular measure was finally remedied by the Representation Act of 1952 which provided for a member for Yukon Territory and a separate member for Mackenzie District.

Through these representatives the residents of the Yukon and of the more developed western part of the Northwest Territories have had some voice in the formation of federal policy as it relates to the administration of the regions north of 60 degrees. And they have had access through their representatives in Parliament to information concerning the federal government's activities in the north. The latter function of these representatives has been unusually important in the case of these northern constituencies because, as we have seen, the territorial governments have had little real responsibility for the day-to-day conduct of government activities in the north, partly because of their very limited constitutional powers, and even more limited financial resources, but chiefly because even the carrying out of territorial affairs has normally been entrusted to the various federal officials and departments established in the area.

THE FEDERAL ADMINISTRATION IN THE TERRITORIAL NORTH

Over the years a rather complex system of government administrative facilities has been built up in the territorial north. From the outset, however, one federal department has always borne the main responsibility

---

[101]*Ibid.*, 1949, p. 1361.
[102]*Ibid.*, 1947, p. 1208.

for the conduct of government business throughout the area. This federal department has been charged with the duty of administering the provisions of the Yukon and Northwest Territories acts and any ordinances passed by the Yukon and Northwest Territories councils. The same department has also been responsible for the administration of the federally controlled resources of the two territories. Initially, this overall administration of the Territories was entrusted to the Department of the Interior which exercised these duties until 1936. In that year, as an economy measure, four government departments, including the Department of the Interior, were combined to form the Department of Mines and Resources. Northern affairs became just one of a great many matters which included mining, immigration, mapping and surveys, Indian affairs, national parks and forest resources, assigned to the new department. The "Lands, Parks and Forests Branch" of the Department was entrusted with the administration of the north.[103] In 1947 this branch was abolished and the administration of the Territories was put under the "Lands and Development Services Branch" of the same department.[104]

The expansion of federal resource development activities after World War II was the reason given for the abolition in 1950 of the Department of Mines and Resources (along with the Department of Reconstruction and Supply) and the creation of three new departments, "Resources and Development," "Mines and Technical Surveys," and "Citizenship and Immigration." The Department of Resources and Development was made responsible for a great range of matters including forests, irrigation projects, national parks, archaeology, ethnology, fauna and flora, tourist information and services, housing, and the Trans-Canada Highway. The new department's first annual report mentions that "The control and management of the affairs of the Northwest and Yukon Territories and other federally-owned lands are also responsibilities of the new department,"[105] and the implication that this was regarded as a rather minor responsibility is heightened by the internal organization of the new department which initially split the management of territorial affairs among several sub-divisions of the "Development Services Branch." Later in the year the department was reorganized and a new branch, the "Northern Administration and Lands Branch," was created. It was

[103]Canada, Department of Mines and Resources, *Annual Report 1936–7* (Ottawa: King's Printer, 1938), p. 61.

[104]Canada, P.C. 37–4433, November 1, 1947.

[105]Canada, Department of Resources and Development, *Annual Report 1949–50* (Ottawa: King's Printer, 1951), p. 7.

in turn divided into two divisions, the "Northern Administration Division" and the "Lands Division." The former was made responsible for administering the affairs of the Yukon and Northwest Territories and the latter for administering all federal lands not administered by any other agency of government.[106]

While this change did much, on paper at least, to simplify the locating of the responsibility for general administration of the Territories, the fact remained that this function was still regarded as a minor one. A reader of the annual reports of this new department would get the impression that the administration of the Territories was hardly as important a function of the department as the administration of the National Museum. The federal government itself was clearly aware that this impression was being created. In an important speech in the House on December 8, 1953, the Prime Minister (Mr. St. Laurent) conceded this and admitted further that, "Apparently we have administered these vast territories of the north in an almost continuing state of absence of mind."[107]

As part of a proposed renewal of federal activity in the north, the Department of Resources and Development was re-named the "Department of Northern Affairs and National Resources" in 1954. It was explained that the purpose of this change was not to establish a new department, nor "to add to the scope of government in any way, nor even to add new functions to those discharged by the department affected" but "to give new emphasis and scope to work already being done, and to indicate that the government and parliament wish to see such greater emphasis made a continuing feature of the operation of government."[108] It was suggested also that the new name itself was significant for it was held to be "indicative of the fact that the centre of gravity of the department is being moved north."[109]

In its first annual report, the Department of Northern Affairs and National Resources stated that its functions were essentially the same as those of the old department, but that its responsibilities in relation to the north were more fully and clearly defined. Furthermore, the Minister was now specifically responsible for co-ordinating the activities of all government departments in the Northwest Territories and the Yukon and for promoting development there.[110]

[106]*Ibid.*
[107]*House of Commons Debates*, 1953, p. 698.
[108]*Ibid.*, p. 696.   [109]*Ibid.*, p. 697.
[110]Canada, Department of Northern Affairs and National Resources, *Annual Report 1953–4* (Ottawa: Queen's Printer, 1954), p. 9.

After the re-naming of the department in 1954 there was an almost continuous re-organization going on within the department. The chief purpose of this was apparently to de-centralize its operations, especially in the Northwest Territories. In 1959 the Northern Administration Branch reported that "the rapid pace of northern development as reflected in the growth of the Branch made desirable a complete re-organization of the Branch. . . ." This re-organization was designed "to meet changing conditions in the north and through its emphasis on decentralization gave much more administrative responsibility to the field."[111] In the Northwest Territories the field duties of the Branch were entrusted to the Administrator of the Mackenzie and to the Administrator of the Arctic, the latter being responsible for administration in the less developed eastern part of the Territories. By 1961 it was becoming apparent that the Northern Administration Branch was in the process of establishing an administrative system in the Northwest Territories which would serve as the basis for separating Mackenzie District from the rest of the Territories and constituting a separate "Territory of Mackenzie," having its own partly independent administration similar to that of the Yukon, while the remaining part of the Territories remained under the more direct jurisdiction of the federal department in Ottawa.

A brief sketch of the activities of the more important federal departments operating in the north in the early 1960s will perhaps make clearer the nature of the role played by the federal government there and the nature of the division of responsibilities between the federal and the territorial administrations at that time.[112]

In the early 1960s the Department of Agriculture carried on continuing studies of agricultural possibilities in the north. It operated experimental farms at Whitehorse in the Yukon and at Fort Simpson and Inuvik in the Northwest Territories.

The Indian Affairs Branch of the Department of Citizenship and Immigration administered the Indian Act throughout the territorial north. This involves it in attempting to develop employment opportunities for Indians, in providing education and training facilities, in providing housing, regulating trapping and fishing practices and in carrying out the various Indian Treaty obligations of the federal government.

[111]Canada, Department of Northern Affairs and National Reseources, *Annual Report 1958–9* (Ottawa: Queen's Printer, 1959), p. 24.
[112]Most of the information in this section is derived from a memorandum periodically prepared in the Department of Northern Affairs and National Resources for the Advisory Committee on Northern Development.

The provision of educational facilities for Indians in the north brought the Indian Affairs Branch into close contact with the territorial governments. Although special Indian schools have been provided in the north from time to time, historically the federal authorities provided for Indian education by subsidizing mission schools operated by the Roman Catholic and Anglican churches. In more recent years, as the territorial governments came to provide schools primarily in response to demands made by local white residents, the Indian Affairs Branch steered Indian students into these "territorial schools" under cost-sharing agreements with the territorial governments.

The Department of Fisheries was responsible for enforcing the Fisheries Act, the Fish Inspection Act, and the various regulations made under these acts throughout the territorial north. It also co-operated with the Fisheries Research Board in surveying lakes in the area with the object of developing limited commercial fishing. The chief development of this kind was the commercial fishery based on Great Slave Lake which is described elsewhere in this study. The Fisheries Research Board has also undertaken investigation of sport fishing possibilities in the arctic and along the coastline of Mackenzie District.

The Department of Forestry was responsible for surveying and for formulating forest management plans for the forests of the Northwest, all of which were reserved to the Crown.

The Department of Justice was directly responsible for the administration of justice in the territories. This included the organization of the courts, both of civil and of criminal jurisdiction. The Royal Canadian Mounted Police was responsible for all law enforcement in the northern territories. This federal police force had sole responsibility for enforcing federal statutes, territorial ordinances, and the criminal code both in the Yukon and in the Northwest Territories. It also policed the municipalities of Yellowknife, Hay River, Whitehorse and Dawson. Historically the R.C.M.P. officers throughout the north also performed a great variety of tasks on behalf of the various federal departments. Police officers were frequently, and in some areas still are, registrars of vital statistics, collectors of various kinds of government revenue, inspectors of fisheries, Indian agents, postmasters, and administrators of pensions, family allowances and other welfare provisions. The amount of this kind of civil administration was reduced after World War II by the stationing of increased numbers of departmental employees in the north.

In the absence of territorial departments of labour, the federal department provided conciliation services, certified trade unions as bargaining agents for employees in both territories and administered policies respecting fair wages and employment practices.

A number of functions particularly important to the development of resources in the north were performed by various branches of the Department of Mines and Technical Surveys. The Geological Survey of Canada, for example, was responsible for most of the surveying and geological mapping of the north and its mineral resources. The Mines Branch, and its predecessors, played an important role in providing technical assistance for the development of mining and metallurgy in the north. The Surveys and Mapping Branch carried out all the geodetic, topographic, oceangraphic, and legal surveys in the north.

The federal Department of National Health and Welfare was responsible, in effect, for the operation of all health facilities in the north. Its Northern Health Service was directly responsible for carrying out all the responsibilities of the federal government for health in the area. It operated, for example, a system of nursing stations and hospitals throughout the north including those once operated by the Indian Health Service. But it also carried out all the responsibilities of the territorial governments in the field of health as well—except for the hospital insurance programme. It directed the operation of the Yukon Health Plan and was directly involved in the provision of hospital and public health facilities in the Yukon under cost-sharing agreements made between the territorial and the federal governments. In the Northwest Territories virtually all health facilities and programs were administered by Northern Health Services.

A similar integration of territorial and federal responsibilities was being developed in the field of public welfare during the late 1950s. The Department of National Health and Welfare not only administered the federal Family Allowances and Old Age Security programmes in the north, but it also participated in the provision of Old Age Assistance, Disabled Persons Allowances, Blind Persons Allowances and, under the Unemployment Assistance Agreements, social assistance measures in the Territories. All these services were provided on the basis of federal-territorial cost-sharing agreements. Some of the actual administration of these programmes in the Yukon Territory in more recent years was done by a territorial Department of Welfare, while in the Northwest Territories it continued to be done by federal employees of the Northern Welfare Service, an agency of the federal Department of Northern Affairs and National Resources.

The responsibilities of the federal Department of Public Works in the early 1960s provides a further illustration of the federal-territorial division of administrative responsibilities and of the somewhat greater independence of the Yukon territorial government. The federal department was responsible for federal building projects throughout the north and for a great deal of road and bridge construction both in the Yukon and in the Northwest Territories. In the Yukon, however, a territorial Department of Public Works had begun to undertake some construction, including road building and maintenance, whereas in the Northwest Territories the "territorial" projects continued to be entrusted, along with federal ones, to the federal department.

Reference has already been made to the general role of the Department of Northern Affairs and National Resources, the federal department which was specifically charged with co-ordinating government activities in the north and with exercising general administrative authority over the affairs of the Territories according to the provisions of the Yukon Act, the Northwest Territories Act, and other federal statutes. This department also carried out a number of specific functions in the north, most of them related to resources. Its Canadian Wildlife Services, for example, made surveys and other studies of wildlife resources throughout the north; the Education Division operated a school system for all children in the unorganized areas of the Territories; the Engineering Division planned and designed roads, buildings and public utilities for the north and provided engineering services to the territorial governments; the Industrial Division studied and organized programmes to promote industrial development in the Northwest Territories; and the Resources Division administered the Crown-owned mineral rights, forests and lands in the Yukon and Northwest Territories.

From this sketch of territorial and federal government in the north it will be apparent that up to the early 1960s there had been little fundamental change in the concept of territorial government in Canada since the establishment of the Yukon in 1898. Indeed, at time of writing the present status of the two territorial governments was little different from that of the old North-West Territories in the 1880s. The Yukon and part of the Northwest Territories were represented in Parliament. The Yukon had an elected council and the Northwest Territories a partly elected one. Neither had responsible government. Instead, even in the Yukon, the appointed Commissioner remained, in effect, the territorial government, for the elected council continued to function in a purely advisory capacity. Both territorial governments continued to rely heavily on federal grants for finance. And, although the Yukon government had the beginnings of a territorial civil service, the bulk of the actual execution of government responsibility in both the Yukon and the Northwest Territories was still being carried out by federal departments. It should be noted also that in the Yukon the territorial civil service was under the direction of the appointed Commissioner.

It is also important to appreciate that the amount of government activity of all kinds in the north was very much greater in the early 1960s than could even have been imagined ten years earlier. Throughout most of the history of the north, government was not a conspicuous factor. This was true even in the economic life of the area, a feature which served to distinguish it from the experience of most other parts of this country.

The extent to which government ignored the north was suggested in a remarkable speech delivered by the Deputy Minister of Northern Affairs and National Resources in 1957 when he stated that:

So completely did we forget the north that as recently as ten years ago—with the sole exception of the mining town of Yellowknife—there was not in the Northwest Territories one single school . . . that had been built by any government—national, territorial or local. The north was left to the missionaries, the fur traders, the Eskimos and the Indians.[113]

Speaking in the Commons in 1957 the Minister of Northern Affairs and National Resources gave as reasons for this "obliteration of the north from the national mind" the nation's preoccupation with western settlement, World War I, the Great Depression, and World War II.[114]

If a slightly defensive note is discernible in these remarks it may be explained by the new attitude which developed in Canada toward the question of northern development after World War II. The most extraordinary manifestation of this "new view" of the north was its incorporation into the Diefenbaker phenomenon of 1957–58. While a consideration of the development and practical effects of this new enthusiasm for the north will be possible only much further on in this study, it may be useful here to consider briefly the question of why, aside from the question of party politics, the historical absence of vigorous government activity in the north should have been a reason for recriminations in the 1950s.

The fact of the matter is that throughout the history of the north

---

[113]R. G. Robertson, "The New North," a series of four lectures delivered at Carlton University, Ottawa, December, 1957 (Ottawa: Department of Northern Affairs and National Resources press release, mimeographed), p. 6.
[114]*House of Commons Debates*, 1957, p. 1197.

it has on several occasions attracted the attention of Canadians and their political representatives. The reasons have been varied, but they may be divided into three main categories, those relating to defence, economic benefits, and the problems of the native people.

Considerations of defence have on four specific occasions attracted public attention to the Canadian north and, on each occasion, have stimulated an increase in government activity in the area. The threat on two occasions has come from the United States, on the other two from Japan and the Soviet Union respectively. The defence problem was, of course, different in each case. The threat from the United States was on both occasions non-military and stemmed from the possibility that the United States would establish *de facto* jurisdiction over territory claimed but not effectively occupied by Canada. The first instance was in the 1870s and 1880s when it became apparent that the most active traders and prospectors in the Yukon were United States citizens. In 1896 William Ogilvie reported to the Canadian government on the situation in the Yukon and suggested that some currency be sent to the Yukon partly in order to provide a medium of exchange more satisfactory than gold dust, but also because it "would emphasize the existence of Canada." He added that "what coin and bills are here are largely American."[115]

The second instance of Canadian concern over possible establishment of *de facto* United States control over territory claimed by Canada occurred in the 1950s when Canada and the United States initiated the elaborate system of continental defence which involved establishing radar stations and other defence installations in largely unoccupied Canadian territory. Although these measures were themselves initiated out of fear of a Russian attack on North America, they led to some concern in Canada when, on a number of occasions, it appeared that jurisdiction had passed to United States authorities over personnel and facilities located on Canadian territory.[116] The same kind of alarm created by the tendency of some Americans around the turn of the century to refer to the Yukon as though it were not part of Canada was again generated in the 1950s by such things as a reference in an American periodical to Ellesmere Island lying "north of Canada." The latter item was brought before the House of Commons and the Minister of

[115]Canada, Department of the Interior, *Information Respecting the Yukon District* (Ottawa: King's Printer, 1897), p. 53.
[116]See, for example, the article in *McLean's Magazine*, May 26, 1956; also *House of Commons Debates*, 1956, p. 6889.

Northern Affairs and National Resources reassured the House that he agreed "we should do everything to assert our sovereignty in those Arctic Islands. . . ."[117]

The two remaining occasions on which national interest in the north was stimulated by considerations of defence were in the 1950s when, as already noted, the north was regarded as a strategic territory over which a Soviet air attack on North American population centres might be launched and in the early years of World War II when it was feared that Japan might invade North America by way of Alaska or the Pacific Northwest coast. The elaborate military undertakings in both periods attracted a great deal of public attention to the "forgotten lands" of the north—and a great deal of public investment and government activity as well. They also contributed to the development of a new national awareness of the problems of the native Indian and Eskimo population of the north.

In view of the over-all weakness of local influence on government in the Territories historically, and also because of the federal government's inclination to leave matters of health and welfare in the area to non-governmental agencies, it is not surprising that there had previously been little specific concern for the conditions of life for the native population of the north. The attitude of government throughout most of the history of the north toward the problems of the native people in general is implicit in a comment made by the Minister of the Interior in the House in 1925. In referring specifically to the Eskimos he stated that they had "not received very much attention at the hands of this government, but we are becoming more alive to our responsibilities in that regard."[118] It was not until after World War II, however, that Canadians became at all conscious of the social and economic problems faced by the Indians and Eskimos of the north. As Professor C. A. Dawson wrote in 1947, " recent visitors to the North from the United States and Canada have been appalled by their ill-health and meagre health facilities."[119] He went on to suggest that an independent outside survey of the Indian and his problems, as preparation for a new Indian programme, be undertaken at once.

As a consequence of increasing knowledge of what was going on in the north during the post-World War II years, the nature of these

---

[117]*House of Commons Debates*, 1954, p. 4680.
[118]*Ibid.*, 1925, p. 4083.
[119]C. A. Dawson, "The New North-West," Part 11 of C. A. Dawson, ed., *The New Northwest* (Toronto: University of Toronto Press, 1947), pp. 310–11.

natives' problems came to be better understood. It had long been recognized that the social problems of native people coming into closer contact with European civilization were serious. Indeed, much of the Canadian government's inactivity in the north prior to World War II may have been the result of a more or less conscious policy of not disturbing the pattern of native life which had been created by the fur traders and missionaries.[120] The post-World War II period, however, brought increasing awareness of the inadequacy of the fur trade as a source of income for the native population and of the mission system as a source of education, medical care, and welfare services. Above all, it became obvious that the long-run prospects for improving conditions of life for the native people of the north could not be separated from the question of general economic development of the northern Territories. During the 1950s one of the strongest arguments in favour of measures designed to accelerate the rate of economic development in the north has been that such a programme is essential to saving the native population from poverty on the one hand and from the debilitating effects of living on unearned income on the other. In his submission to the Royal Commission on Canada's Economic Prospects in 1955, the Commissioner of the Northwest Territories made this point in the following terms:

The people of the north—the Indians and the Eskimos—are used to the country and its climate. With proper training and adjustment they can contribute greatly to the development of northern Canada in the years to come. But many will not be there to aid in that development if it does not occur sufficiently soon or at a sufficiently rapid pace to provide the economic means of life for them. And those who are there may be less able to participate if, over a period of years, they have become accustomed to reliance on relief.[121]

Whether or not the logic of this argument is defensible, it does appear to have had something to do with the re-awakening of public interest in the north in recent years. And it brings us to the third question which, during the 1950s, as in the 1890s, the early 1920s and the 1930s, prompted at least temporary national interest in the north—the question of the potential economic benefits to be derived by Canada from the

[120]The Minutes of the Northwest Territories Council during this period contain frequent references to the undesirability of white immigration into the Territories because of its deleterious effects upon the native Indians and Eskimos. The main concerns appear to have been to protect the native trappers from competition with "white" trappers and to minimize the possibility of indigent whites becoming a charge upon territorial revenues.

[121]R. G. Robertson, *The Northwest Territories—Its Economic Prospects, A Brief Presented to the Royal Commission on Canada's Economic Prospects* (Ottawa: Queen's Printer, 1955), p. 17.

exploitation of northern mineral resources. Although the attempts to exploit such resources will be examined in some detail later in this study, it should be noted here that on at least four occasions the interest of the Canadian public and the interest of the federal government in the north has been stimulated by such developments. What is particularly interesting is the way the federal government responded to such interruptions in the routine of administering its vast but politically unimportant hinterland.

Canadian economic and political historians have long accepted the view that the origins and purposes of the federal government are to be understood in terms of the problems confronting an economic area dependent upon the export of certain "staple" commodities, the commercially feasible production of which presupposed heavy public expenditures on capital facilities such as canals and railways. This aspect of the "national policy" had been brought to completion, presumably, by 1930 when the lands of the western plains were turned over to the provinces of Saskatchewan and Alberta, having served their national purposes of providing a major staple export, a commercial frontier for the Canadian industrial and business sector located in the St. Lawrence area, a means of attracting immigrants, and a means of financing part of a national transcontinental railway.

The federal lands of the west, then, were used as a major component in the programme aimed at national economic development. Earlier in this chapter the process of political evolution in these areas was described. The lands left over from the creation of Saskatchewan and Alberta and the extension of the other provinces to their present boundaries were "remnants" in every sense of the word. They were lands of patently inferior quality from the standpoint of economic potential. While Canadians had no intention, as we have seen, of discarding them or of letting some other country use them, they were set aside, presumably in the hope that they would be useful in the future if not in the present. That they were not completely without value even in "the present" was shown by the placer gold development in the Klondike as early as the 1880s, although national awareness was not developed until the rush into the Klondike. The next flurry of national interest in the economic potential of the north occurred in the early 1920s, when commercial quantities of petroleum were discovered near Fort Norman on the Mackenzie River. And in the middle of the 1930s further interest in the resources of the north was generated by the pitchblende discovery on Great Bear Lake and by the gold quartz discovery at what is now

Yellowknife on Great Slave Lake. These were the major developments to attract national attention to the economic potential of the "left over" national lands. There were many smaller discoveries, of course. The ones mentioned, however, had some discernible political significance. The Klondike placer gold development led to the establishment of territorial government in the Yukon and federal representation for the Territory. The petroleum development at Norman led to the activation of the Northwest Territories Council, and the developments of the 1930s brought about the introduction of a measure of representation to this Council. Not even these relatively "major" resource developments, however, led to any important change in the role of the northern territories in the national economy. They served to remind Canadians of their economic potential. But they also necessitated some increase in the expense of administering the national lands. And they also forced the federal government to go beyond maintaining peace and order in the north and obliged it to provide, either directly or through the territorial governments, *some* funds for transportation, communications and other essential services in the north.

The impression one gains from reading debates in *Hansard* on the provision of funds for administration and the provision of other services in the north is that for the first half of this century most speakers were less than convinced of the economic justification for such expenditures. Certainly there were no suggestions during this period that government expenditures should *precede* the demand for them.

It has already been noted, for example, that when gold mining in the Yukon passed out of the boom stage early in the century, the reaction of the federal government was to reduce its expenditures and to restrict its operations in the Yukon rather than to expand its activities in the hope of stimulating the flagging economy of the Territory. The local council, on the other hand, representing people with some stake in the future of the Territory, sought to encourage the development of new mineral industries by building roads and granting subsidies. These efforts were not entirely unsuccessful but, given the financial and constitutional restraints Ottawa imposed on the territorial government, they could hardly be undertaken on a scale adequate to do more than slow down the rate at which the Yukon economy was deteriorating. The federal government's attitude is illustrated by the following exchange in June, 1920, during Committee of Supply:

MR. DENIS This appears to be a large appropriation for a population of 4,300. Has a like appropriation been made each year for several years past?

MR. MEIGHEN Oh, no, the appropriation that has been made yearly for several years past has been far more. In the last two or three years the appropriation has been very much reduced, somewhat to the indignation, I fear, of the population of the Yukon. I did not feel that the number there warranted the expenditure that was being made. It is only a short time since the expenditure was twice the amount we are asking now.[122]

Much of the reduction in federal spending in the Yukon was made during this period by reducing the grant in support of road construction, which may have accounted for some of the "indignation" felt by the residents of the Yukon who saw in road construction the chief device for opening up the lode mining properties they hoped to see come into production to supplement the output of the dwindling placer gold reserves. In 1922 the new Minister of the Interior, still under attack for spending too much money on the Yukon, defended his request for funds on the grounds that he had "discovered a persistent demand for road construction to enable the people engaged in mining to get out the products of the mine." At the same time, however, he assured the House that he hoped to present a "much reduced estimate on this head next year."[123] Again there is a suggestion in such a remark that attempts to develop new mining properties in the Yukon were something of a nuisance to the federal government in so far as they obliged it to spend money on supporting administration and services. Certainly it was not felt that the federal government should initiate measures aimed at developing resources in the Territory *directly*. This was, of course, quite consistent with the *laissez-faire* principles of the government of the day. However much the government might have violated these principles in order to promote and accelerate economic development in the other parts of Canada during the first half of this century, it adhered quite scrupulously to them when the question of developing the resources under its own direct control in the Yukon and Northwest Territories arose.

By 1920 a distinct policy with respect to these resources began to emerge. Simply stated, this northern development policy was aimed at leaving the northern lands alone except for providing the natives with some protection against glaring abuses by white men (through protecting their hunting and trapping opportunities, for example) and except for giving some indirect and usually technical assistance to private companies prospecting for and developing mineral resources in the Territories. This policy of leaving territorial development to the initiative of

[122]*House of Commons Debates*, 1920, p. 3281.
[123]*Ibid.*, 1922, p. 1034.

private enterprise in almost all fields accounts for the relative absence of effective government institutions charged with the administration of the Territories. Although this policy was never precisely formulated it appears to have reigned unchallenged in Ottawa until well into the 1950s. Certainly examples of vigorous government activity in the north can be found before then, but they were motivated by considerations of defence or concern for native welfare as such and did not reflect a change in the attitude toward the economic potential of the area. This potential, while often recognized, was seen as a very "chancy" one. It was frequently referred to in glowing terms by Canadian politicians, but it was not seen as something upon which federal funds could be gambled. Alternative uses for such funds were assigned a much higher priority. If private enterprise was willing to risk investments in the Territories, the policy of the government was to not discourage such ventures. But it did little to encourage them and it was reluctant to enter into any closer financial involvement with such ventures until they had become proven commercial successes. Public funds invested at that stage could be invested with little risk either of economic loss or of political criticism.

When oil was discovered in the Northwest Territories at the beginning of the 1920s the government's policy was explained as follows: "The Government are merely laying the scientific basis and in that way enabling these investigations to proceed along sound and sensible lines."[124] When asked if the government provided any assistance to those looking for oil, the Prime Minister replied that such undertakings were supported by "private capital, not the capital of the government," and that those who discovered oil would reap their own reward.[125] How little the federal government's policy changed over the next several decades is suggested by the reply given to similar queries by the responsible Minister in the House in 1955 and 1957. In 1955 Mr. Lesage explained, again in Committee of Supply, that "what we try to do in my department is to create an economic climate under reasonable terms of expenditures. I am sure the hon. member . . . will agree that we should not go to the extent of creating an artificial development which would be more costly than sound economics would warrant."[126] Just what the Minister understood by "sound economics" in this context was made clear in a speech he made in the House two years later:

In a broad sense there is an underlying agreement on the fundamentals of resource management, that it should make the best possible use of resources

---

[124]*Ibid.*, 1920, p. 3281.   [125]*Ibid.*   [126]*Ibid.*, 1955, p. 3729.

in the public interest, that renewable resources should be managed in a way to renew them in perpetuity, that their development should be economic and that the best means to ensure that it will be economic is, in general, private enterprise.[127]

Of course, government expenditures in the north increased tremendously over the period which separates the remarks of Mr. Meighen and those of Mr. Lesage. But the initiative in northern investment normally came from "private enterprise." This policy was described in rather blunt terms by Mr. N. Byrne, a mining consultant resident in the north for many years, as follows:

People on the outside look on the north as a romantic country developed by the government. But what has the government done to develop the country? All the development here has been done by private enterprise and not the government. Their policy seems to be, "You spend the money opening up the country, and then we'll think about helping you or paying you back"—just the opposite to the point of view the government should have.[128]

Mr. Byrne supported the latter point on the grounds that mining companies need help to get into production, not after they have got into production. Providing the help before hand is very risky; providing it afterwards is less risky, but less rewarding.

Because this issue must remain with us throughout the present study, it will be useful to adopt the terms "Social Overhead Capital" and "Directly Productive Activity" (abbreviated SOC and DPA respectively) to distinguish between the two kinds of investments or expenditures to which we have been referring. The nature of this distinction has been formulated most usefully for our purposes by Albert Hirschman:[129]

The distinction between Social Overhead Capital (SOC) and Directly Productive Activities (DPA) is a recent one. Like all such classifications it must be judged not by its logic, which is far from compelling, but by its theoretical and practical usefulness, which has been considerable. SOC is usually defined as comprising those basic services without which primary, secondary, and tertiary productive activities cannot function. In its wider sense, it includes all public services from law and order through education and public health to transportation, communications, power and water supply, as well as such agricultural overhead capital as irrigation and drainage systems. The hard core of the concept can probably be restricted to transportation and power.

---

[127]*Ibid.*, 1957, pp. 1200–1.

[128]Quoted in D. Oancia, "Why Capital Avoids the North," *Saturday Night*, January 19, 1957, p. 22.

[129]A. O. Hirschman, *The Strategy of Economic Development* (New Haven: Yale University Press, 1958), pp. 83 and 86.

And further:

Some SOC investment is required as a prerequisite of DPA investment. Access to an area by sea, road, rail, or air is indispensable before other economic activities can unfold there. But within rather wide limits, the relationship between SOC and DPA is not technologically determined. Within these limits, the cost of producing any given output of DPA will be the higher, the more inadequate the SOC of the economy.

It will be shown in Part II of this study that the level of development in the Canadian north has been so low the provision of SOC has in fact been restricted almost entirely to the area of the lower limit referred to in the last passage quoted—that is, the question has been one of providing SOC to "open up" for development a previously *undeveloped* part of the country.

Whether or not public expenditures upon such original SOC required to permit subsequent development of an undeveloped area will or will not be made must depend upon a great many factors, both economic and political. Some of these are considered in the context of territorial development in Canada in the concluding chapter of this study where an attempt is made to assess the possibilities of using objective investment criteria, such as may be provided by the now quite orthodox techniques of benefit-cost analysis, to arrive at explicit and consequently politically justifiable decisions concerning such uses for public funds. But whatever promise such techniques may hold for future policy-making, they have not been used in the past. What can be said with certainty now is that in the past, as in the present, policy decisions relating to public spending on SOC for development purposes have been more influenced by highly subjective considerations—pre-eminent among which has been simply the nature of the expectations held by the policy-makers concerning the future economic (and perhaps political) potential of the area in question. If there is any enthusiasm concerning the future of the area, estimates of future returns to public investments there will tend to run high and there will be a corresponding tendency to discount high risk factors. Under these circumstances, it is naturally more likely that policies aimed at "leading" private investments in DPA by making the necessary public investments in SOC ahead of time will be adopted than if there is pessimism respecting the possibilities of bringing about economically worthwhile and self-sustaining growth in the area.

It is at this point that the connection between the form of political organization and the nature of economic policy becomes apparent. If the less developed area is dependent upon a larger economic and political unit, its economic potential is bound to be assessed in terms of the national benefit by the central government. In the Canadian prairie west late in the nineteenth century, for example, the relevant question was, "What can the west do for Canada" in return for outlays (or other commitments) of public funds for the development of its resources? Similarly, in the case of the north, the same question must be asked in Ottawa. Historically the tendency has been for the central government, rightly or wrongly, to place a low estimate on the north's economic potential in these terms. And, consequently, public investment in SOC in the north has lagged DPA investment by private concerns.

A very different approach to the question is likely to be taken by residents of the undeveloped region themselves and this would explain at least part of the confused public discussion of the question of northern development in this country over the years. Residents of the area concerned naturally associate their economic prospects with those of the area in which they live. They must be optimistic about its potential.[130] So must the "outsiders" who have invested in resource development or commercial undertakings in the area. If there is a local government, its policies will naturally reflect this confidence, and so it is likely to pursue measures whereby public investment in SOC will lead private investment in DPA. But, for reasons which will already be apparent, this possibility has been negated in the case of the Canadian north. By denying citizens of the Territories responsible government and by removing jurisdiction over natural resources from the competence of the territorial governments that were established, the federal authorities obviated any possibility of a direct regional influence on development policy. This is not to say, of course, that had the territorial governments been given the authority to legislate on such matters they could have found adequate public funds to finance major territorial SOC investments or that they would have used such funds wisely. Had they possessed such power, however, even relatively small amounts of public funds might have effectively been used in the strategically right place at the right time by a government which was both more immediately aware of what the obstacles to specific development projects actually were, and at the same time more confident of the long-run economic prospects for the area.

In any event, the close inter-connection between political institutions

---

[130]This was a conspicuous common characteristic of briefs presented by northern residents and communities to the Royal Commission on Canada's Economic Prospects.

and economic development in the Territories has been clearly demonstrated in the past seventy years. And its implications must be appreciated by those presently charged with planning the future evolution of the north both politically and economically. In the following chapters an attempt is made to set out the broad lines of economic development in the north to date. The organization of these chapters is dictated by the nature of the development problem as it exists in the Canadian north.

THE DEVELOPMENT PROBLEM

The Canadian north is remote from the markets and industrial centres of the world. Economically, it is characterized by the presence of large stocks of land resources and the absence of any significant local supplies of skilled labour and capital, both of which must be imported from distant centres. As noted above, although the land resources of the north are owned and administered by the state in Canada, with few exceptions private enterprise has been entrusted with initiating their development. Under these circumstances the expectation has been that skilled labour and capital would be diverted from alternative employments elsewhere in Canada and applied to the northern land resources whenever private *entrepreneurs* became aware of profitable opportunities to do so.

It is apparent from the map that profitable opportunities to exploit northern land resources are certain to be limited by their remoteness both from markets and from sources of supply. Commodities exported from the northwest to compete with similar commodities produced elsewhere in Canada would be at a disadvantage if for no other reason than because of the distance which they must be transported to market. Under given conditions of market demand, labour and capital must be more efficiently combined with northern land than with less remote land if the products yielded in the north are to compete in world markets. Because the technology used in these operations has usually been imported from outside the area, the only "efficiency" to be realized in the north is that obtained from operating on unusually high-grade land. The size of this grade differential necessary to attract labour and capital to the north depends upon the size of the transport costs and any other locational disadvantages to be overcome.

Measures designed to overcome these disadvantages of location, especially the "distance" factor, impose high overhead costs upon these northern operations. Most of the developments undertaken will be seen to have been of small scale with the result that, given existing technology, individual producers found it difficult to make use of facilities such as railways and hydro-electric power plants which require relatively large markets if they are to yield the low unit cost benefits of which they are capable. The development of such markets was frequently thwarted by the geography of the north and by the scattered character of individual projects in such a vast area. The traditional Canadian technique of using public funds to finance the provision of such facilities until local markets made them self-sustaining was rejected, until at least the post-World War II period, because of the policies of the federal government described above. The only alternatives remaining for sufficiently determined private producers were to use inefficient small-scale devices such as roads or trails, instead of railways, and power generated by small internal combustion units instead of by "hydro." And, as would be expected under the circumstances, a persistent tendency toward concentration of ownership and integration of individual operations manifested itself in the north in response to the underlying economic forces which were allowed to operate there.

The various kinds of directly productive activities which have been established in the territorial north may be divided into two categories—the industries which produce for markets outside the north and those which sell in the local territorial markets. This is a fundamental distinction characteristic of the traditional Canadian approach to the study of economic development and it has seemed appropriate to use it in this study of what is still an economically very primitive part of Canada. For ease of reference, however, the terminology used here will be that of the more recent American practitioners of this type of analysis. Hence, the term "export-base industry" will be applied to those industries which sell in outside markets and the term "residentiary" to those which produce mainly for local markets. In terms of development theory the implication of this distinction is that the export-base industries provide the impetus for economic growth in the area concerned, while the residentiary industries subsequently become established on this initial base.[131] Thus the development of principal export-base industries in the Yukon and Northwest Territories is considered in the next two chapters and the residentiary industries are taken up in Chapter 5.

[131]For a further description of these terms, and a discussion of the approach they represent in the context of regional and urban growth theory, see H. S. Perloff, E. S. Dunn, E. E. Lampard, and R. F. Muth, *Regions, Resources, and Economic Growth* (Baltimore: Johns Hopkins Press, 1961), pp. 57–62 and 104–6. See also D. C. North, "Location Theory and Regional Economic Growth," *Journal of Political Economy*, Vol. 63 (June, 1955).

II. PRIVATELY SPONSORED ACTIVITY IN THE TERRITORIES

3 The Export-Base Industries: Trapping, Fishing, Tourism

The barren land running inland from the Arctic Sea will in certain districts remain forever useless. Mackenzie River district is still the famous scene of the fur trade, and may long continue so, though there is always the possibility of any portion of the vast waste of the Far North developing, as the Yukon territory has done, mineral wealth rivalling the famous sands of Pactolus or the riches of King Solomon's Mines. [George Bryce, *The Remarkable History of the Hudson's Bay Company* (Toronto: Briggs, 1900), p. 475.]

THE MOST IMPORTANT industries in the economy of the north have been those based upon the simple staple products, fur and minerals, familiar to all students of Canadian economic history. Although the fur trade has been for many years now an industry of declining relative importance in terms of the gross output of goods and services in the north, it has continued to be the most important source of earned income for the native population of the area. Neither the Indians of the north nor the Eskimos had an opportunity to develop an agricultural economy. Consequently, they have remained throughout their history dependent upon the fish, mammals and birds of the north for their food, clothing, shelter and, especially in the case of the Eskimo, even for light and heat and transportation. Thus, the traditional native economy of the north has always been based upon the animal resources of the area.

Before the appearance of the Europeans this dependence was direct. The population lived on the fish and game available. A great variety of edible fish was found in the many inland lakes and rivers and also in the coastal waters, especially the river deltas. The kind of mammal life available varied greatly from one part of the north to another. In the Yukon area, where there is a great deal of forest cover in the southern and more mountainous regions, moose, caribou, sheep and goats, and grizzly bear were, and still are, available. In the southern parts of the Mackenzie area, moose, woodland caribou, and bison were found. Further east, in the large areas of lightly forested and non-forested "barren lands," immense herds of caribou and musk-ox lived by feeding directly on the lichens and other small plants growing on the tundra. These herds have apparently been greatly reduced in modern times. The barren land caribou, for example, have been estimated to have numbered between 1.5 and 3 million around 1900. In 1948 the number was estimated at 670,000 and ten years later it was less than half that.[1] These barren land caribou, and the once almost-exterminated musk-ox, range far north, even into the Arctic islands where, in fact, the largest part of the present musk-ox population is located. In these far northern and coastal regions where the Eskimo groups are located, seals, walrus and whales have also been utilized to support human life.

In addition to these major species of "game animals" almost every part of the north has some species of animals prized more for their pelts than their meat. Some of these, such as the polar bear and the white or arctic fox, are found chiefly in the arctic regions of the north. Others, such as the beaver, black bear, lynx, marten, mink, muskrat and squirrel are confined to the more temperate and forested regions. These also yield the red, cross, and silver foxes. Hares, mice, and lemmings, upon which many of the larger fur-bearing animals feed, are distributed widely throughout the entire area of the north.

THE TRAPPING INDUSTRY OF THE YUKON AND NORTHWEST TERRITORIES

The traditional native economy of the north continues to exist in a fairly pure form in some particularly remote regions. And throughout the north much of the population continues to draw at least some part of its needs directly from the land through fishing and hunting. But for almost two centuries the native economy of the north has been subjected to varying degrees of commercialization by Europeans and their descendants in North America. Since the middle of the eighteenth century the native economy of the north has been basically a "fur trading economy" —an economy in which the natives provided the labour and skills

---

[1]D. S. Rawson, "Biological Potentialities," in Underhill, *The Canadian Northwest: Its Potentialities*, p. 66.

required to produce furs for export from the north in return for a wide range of imported wage goods (and a certain amount of capital in the form of steel traps, rifles, and other instruments of the trade). The history of the fur trade in Canada has been thoroughly detailed elsewhere.[2] In brief summary here, the northern fur industry was first established in the arctic regions by the Hudson's Bay Company formed in 1670. This company established its first trading posts in the eastern arctic at the mouths of the rivers emptying into Hudson Bay and James Bay. The French fur traders operating from the St. Lawrence region to the south pursued a more aggressive policy of establishing posts far inland, at first only in the south but, as competition in the trade developed, more and more toward the northwest. To prevent the occupation of its inland "fur shed" by these far-ranging traders operating inland from the St. Lawrence, the Hudson's Bay Company was forced to move inland from the west coast of Hudson Bay. In this way, a series of trading posts was established in the eastern arctic and northern coastal regions of what was to become the Northwest Territories. Although many private traders operated in these regions, and although larger organizations such as Revillon Frères Trading Company sometimes competed with the Hudson's Bay Company for the trade there, the latter company has dominated that trade for almost three hundred years.[3]

The development of the trade in the western arctic and sub-arctic regions of the north originated with the establishment of the North-West Company by a group of Montreal merchants in 1784. This company pushed rapidly north-westward through the interior of British North America in the late eighteenth century. Following Alexander Mackenzie's exploration in 1789 of the river which bears his name, the North-West Company occupied the northern plains area. Mackenzie, himself a partner in the North-West Company, was responsible for establishing the fur-trading posts which to this day constitute many of the "settlements" in Mackenzie District. This system of posts stretches from Fort Smith on the Slave River all the way down the Mackenzie River system to Aklavik near the arctic coast, the intervals between posts varying from about 150 to 200 miles.

This western part of what is now the Northwest Territories eventually became the point of confrontation between the Hudson's Bay Company,

---

[2]See H. A. Innis, *The Fur Trade in Canada* (Toronto: University of Toronto Press, 1962, Canadian University Paperbooks edition).
[3]Revillon Frères Trading Company was absorbed by the Hudson's Bay Company in 1935.

working westward from the coasts of Hudson Bay, and its traditional rivals working inland from the St. Lawrence to the Pacific northwest. The first two decades of the nineteenth century were marked by vigorous competition between the North-West Company and the Hudson's Bay Company in the Mackenzie Country as rival posts were established at strategic points by the Hudson's Bay Company. In 1821 the struggle ended with the amalgamation of the two competitors under the name of the Hudson's Bay Company.

After 1821 the Hudson's Bay Company pushed the fur-trading frontier still further into the northwest corner of North America. The exploration of what was to become the Yukon Territory was first done by officers of the Company seeking to develop this last new source of furs under the direction of Sir John Simpson who had been appointed Governor-in-Chief of Rupert's Land in 1820. The exploration of the Yukon Territory was undertaken from both the north and the south during the early 1840s. By virtue of a special licence of 1838 the Company was authorized to trade in "British Territories to the west and north-west of Rupert's Land."[4] That this included what is now the Yukon Territory had been established by a treaty made between the governments of Russia and Great Britain in 1825 whereby Russia relinquished to Britain her claims not only to the western coastal regions south of 54°40', but also to the interior lands up to the frozen ocean.[5]

In 1840, following the abandonment of a post at Dease Lake in northern British Columbia, Robert Campbell was instructed by Simpson to explore the north branch of the Liard River to its source and to cross the divide in search of a river flowing westward.[6] Campbell ascended the Liard to a lake which he named Finlayson's Lake and then struck out overland until he reached a large river flowing north-westward which he named the Pelly in honour of Governor Pelly of the Hudson's Bay Company. Two important trading posts were established as a result of this exploration, one at Pelly Banks in 1842 and another, Fort Selkirk, at the confluence of the Pelly and the Lewes in 1848.[7]

At about the same time that Campbell was penetrating the Yukon

---

[4]See E. E. Rich, *The History of the Hudson's Bay Company 1670–1870* (London: Hudson's Bay Record Society, 1958), Vol. II, p. 779.

[5]Canada, Department of the Interior, *The Yukon Territory: Its History and Resources* (Ottawa: King's Printer, 1916), pp. 2–3.

[6]*Ibid.*, p. 4.

[7]L. J. Burpee, in A. H. Murray, *Journals of the Yukon 1847–8*, Publications of the Canadian Archives, No. 4 (Ottawa: Government Printing Bureau, 1910), pp. 8–9.

Territory from the south and establishing trading posts on the southern tributaries of the Yukon River, other Hudson's Bay Company men were pushing into the northern Yukon from the Mackenzie Delta region. This northern exploration was initially prompted by Franklin's reports of abundant fur-bearing animals along the Peel River which flows into the Mackenzie and, in fact, forms one of its channels in the delta area. The eastern parts of the Peel were explored by John Bell in the summer of 1839 and the following year a post, Fort McPherson, was established. Although this development was part of the Mackenzie River operations of the Company, Bell's further explorations in the far northern areas eventually led to a major discovery of great importance to the development of the fur trade in the Yukon. This was the realization in 1846 that the Porcupine River was actually a tributary of the Yukon and that it could be used as a convenient link between the Mackenzie Valley and the central Yukon country by taking advantage of the Rat River connection between the Yukon and Mackenzie watersheds.[8]

The following year, Alexander Murray was sent to establish a trading post near the confluence of the Porcupine and Yukon rivers. This post, named Fort Yukon, was intended to give the Hudson's Bay Company access to the furs collected by the Indian tribes of the central interior despite the fact that Russian traders had already established contact with these Indians from the west. In fact, Fort Yukon was established a good 4° of longitude inside Russian territory in Alaska. Although the Alaska boundary had not been located at that time, it is clear from Murray's own journal that he was well aware that he was building his post in Russian territory.

The operations of the Yukon fur trade after 1850 were focussed on Fort Yukon and the northern link with the Mackenzie operations. In the late 1840s Campbell journeyed from the posts on the southern tributaries of the Yukon down the river to Fort Yukon, then up the Porcupine, over the mountains to Fort McPherson and up the Mackenzie to Fort Simpson. Because the route from the Yukon to the Mackenzie via the northern rivers was much easier than by way of the Liard to the south, the Porcupine became the regular trade route between the Mackenzie and the Hudson's Bay Company posts in the Yukon after the middle of the century.

[8]Canada, Department of the Interior, *The Yukon Territory: Its History and Resources*, p. 8. For a detailed discussion of this interesting development see V. Stefansson, *Northwest to Fortune* (London: Allen and Unwin, 1960), chap. 14.

The Hudson's Bay Company continued to trade at Fort Yukon until 1869. In that year, with Alaska now in United States hands, the Company was unceremoniously ejected from Fort Yukon. The Company appeared determined to continue its operations in the area, however, and it promptly relocated further up the Porcupine at Rampart House. This post was later moved another twelve miles east because of doubt concerning the boundary location. In 1889 a United States survey showed that it was still twenty miles inside United States territory and in 1890 the post was again moved.[9]

This concern of the United States authorities over the incursions by the Hudson's Bay Company into its new territory is rather surprising in view of the activities of United States traders in British territory during the 1870s and later decades. In 1869, the same year that the Hudson's Bay Company was turned out of Fort Yukon, the Alaska Commercial Company was formed. This American-owned company established posts along the Yukon and during the 1870s it became the dominant commercial organization in the Yukon country. In 1874 it established a post at Fort Reliance near Dawson and its agents operated posts at the site of Fort Selkirk,[10] and at Ogilvie located on the Yukon River near its junction with the Sixty-mile River. The Alaska Commercial Company, and after 1892, a competing firm known as the North American Transportation and Trading Company, played an important part in developing the western parts of the Yukon Territory late in the nineteenth century. Partly because of their influence and also because of the water and rail transportation systems developed in conjunction with the great placer mining boom in the Yukon during the 1890s, the Yukon fur trade and the Yukon economy in general broke their connection with the Mackenzie River fur trade. The subsequent economic and political development of the Yukon and of the Mackenzie area remained quite distinct—with the Yukon coming to be established more as a hinterland of Alaska, the ports of the Pacific coast and the Mackenzie area remaining as a hinterland of central and western Canada.[11]

[9]Burpee, p. 6.

[10]Fort Selkirk was destroyed by Indians in 1852 and abandoned by the Hudson's Bay Company.

[11]It should be noted that the northern part of Mackenzie District as well as the northern coast of the Yukon had some connection with Pacific Coast ports such as Vancouver by way of the western arctic sea route. This route was used extensively by whalers and also by fur traders who sailed through Bering Strait to such centres as Herschel Island and other settlements along the western arctic coast.

It is interesting to note that the far eastern arctic regions of the north were not developed as established fur trading regions until long after the most distant parts of the northwest had been opened up to the trade. Posts were not established there until after 1910. During the second and third decades of this century a series of posts were opened along the coasts of Hudson Strait and Baffin Island. Because these arctic posts had to be serviced by ocean vessels sailing out of eastern Canadian ports, the far eastern arctic became yet another quite distinct economic region in the north.

The Fur Trade and Northern Development

The fundamental significance of the fur trade in the development of the north lies in the fact that it gave an economic value to the region in the minds of "outsiders." Because of this, non-residents were induced to invest in the north. This investment was primarily, as we have seen, in exploration and in the scattered fur trading posts which to this day represent the majority of the "settlements" in the area. Developed in conjunction with these trading posts were the transportation systems which linked them together and which connected them to the markets and sources of supply outside. Given the nature of the fur trade's production techniques, no elaborate capital facilities were required, nor was it necessary to import significant quantities of labour. The trading posts were essentially retailing establishments dealing in imported trade goods and credit. The transportation systems were river or ocean routes to which a variety of specialized vessels were adapted.

These fur-trading routes, vessels, and cargo-handling systems proved to be difficult to adapt to the requirements of other kinds of business activity, a factor of some importance in the subsequent economic development of the north. At the same time, the fur trade's method of satisfying its transportation requirements virtually eliminated any question of public involvement in providing transportation facilities in the area. By adapting vessels to the physical characteristics of natural waterways the fur traders evaded the question of heavy investment in more or less permanent capital facilities such as canals, dredged channels, roads, or railways. They consequently did not have to concern themselves with the possibility that competitors would benefit from their investments without recompense. It is difficult (although not impossible) to prevent someone using a river channel you have dredged or a road that you have built through the wilderness, but it is easy to prevent someone from shipping goods in your boat without bearing some share of the capital costs involved in providing the boat. Because of its particular needs and its way of providing for them, then, the fur-trading industry did not have to, or did not choose to, solicit public assistance in the form of public investments in such things as transportation facilities.

Similarly, in meeting its labour requirements, the fur-trading industry was again able to take advantage of natural conditions. Just as natural waterways were utilized to avoid heavy capital imports to the area, so was the native population used to provide the great bulk of the labour inputs required. This native labour force had the great advantage that it could, in part at least, "live off the country," when necessary. It did not have to be provided with even the amenities required in a mining or lumbering camp. Thus, again, investment in fixed capital was minimized. This is not to suggest that the labour was necessarily "cheap." While the opportunity cost of native labour (its value in the best alternative employment) has nearly always been low in the north, competition among traders and the exigencies of northern living made necessary significant outlays not only in the form of wage goods exchanged for furs but also upon credit relief during "seasons of distress," and traditional "gifts." What investment was made in schools, hospitals, and other social capital facilities for the benefit of this labour force was, until very recent years, made chiefly by religious or charitable organizations whose agents established themselves in many of the settlements which grew up around the fur-trading posts. Thus, neither the industry nor any other governing body had to accept the burden of this responsibility.

We see, then, that because of its fundamental technical requirements, the fur-trading industry was able to adapt itself very well to the conditions of the country in which it had to operate. Nature provided a good part of the labour force required and waterways for transportation which, despite the deficiencies of both, enabled the industry to operate without significant public assistance or support. Partly because of this, perhaps, but also because of the general lack of outside interest in any other aspect of the northern territories until late in the nineteenth century, the fur trade also remained relatively free of public regulation and control. Even when such interest did develop in the case of the Yukon in the 1880s, the circumstances there were such that when institutions of government did appear and did concern themselves with the affairs of the Territory, the fur trade escaped serious attention.

Although the Yukon Council passed a "Game Ordinance" and amended it from time to time, so great was the preoccupation of government with mining in the Yukon that, as late as 1947, the North Pacific Planning Project could report that "Yukon Territory has no program of active management of fur resources."[12]

This lack of interest in the trapping industry on the part of government created a serious situation for a native population dependent upon trapping for its income. As we have seen, during the last half of the nineteenth century the fur trade was established throughout all but the most remote arctic regions of the north. Consequently, by the turn of the century, the life of most of the native population of the north had been "commercialized" and the bulk of the population had become dependent upon trapping furs for its living. With the advent of mining in the north, beginning with the Yukon placer gold mining in the 1870s and 1880s, however, there was a greatly increased movement of white population into certain parts of the north. Some of this population became involved in trapping either on a part- or full-time basis. The result was a proliferation of small trading companies and competition between white and native trappers for furs. Furthermore, as the competition for these furs increased, "over-trapping" caused the supply of certain species to decline. The initial large influx of white trappers associated with the Klondike gold rush was augmented by those attracted by the high fur prices following World War I and by those who went into the Northwest Territories during the Norman Wells oil boom of the early 1920s.

The subsequent concern for the welfare of the native population and for the preservation of fur-bearing species of animals led, in the Northwest Territories, to the implementation of control measures by the federal government. When the Northwest Territories Council was named in 1921 and local offices of government established in the Territories, steps were taken under authority of the Northwest Game Act of 1917 to bring hunting and trapping under control by requiring white trappers to obtain licenses and by imposing restrictions upon the trapping of certain species in various areas from time to time. In 1923 three native game preserves were established in which only Indians, Eskimos, Métis leading the native life, and a few white trappers already in the areas concerned, were permitted to hunt and trap. The area of these preserves (the Yellowknife, Slave River, and Peel River preserves)

[12]North Pacific Planning Project, *Canada's New Northwest* (Ottawa: King's Printer, 1947), p. 132.

totalled 75,452 square miles. Similar preserves were established in 1926 (the Arctic Islands Preserve) and in 1938 (the Mackenzie Mountain Preserve). Of these the largest is the Arctic Islands Preserve which has a land area of 772,302 square miles and comprises all the arctic islands of Canada as well as large portions of the mainland in the District of Keewatin.[13] Other control measures taken by the government in the Northwest Territories included creation of the 15,000-square-mile Thelon Game Sanctuary located partly in the eastern part of Mackenzie District and stretching into Keewatin District, and Wood Buffalo Park straddling the border between Alberta and Mackenzie District. Trapping in the Park was limited in a way similar to that in the native game preserves.

Further measures designed to discourage white trappers from competing with natives for fur in the Northwest Territories included the implementation of a licencing system for whites which limited hunting and trapping privileges to British subjects who had completed four years residence in the Territories or who had carried on the business of trading and trafficking in game for a period of four years.[14]

Thus, beginning in the 1920s, the federal government did undertake to regulate fur trapping in the Northwest Territories. The enforcement of its regulations required, of course, the expenditure of some public funds on the previously unregulated (and virtually ungoverned) federal lands of the north. The federal government almost immediately sought to recover these outlays by imposing a tax on furs exported from the Northwest Territories. In 1924 it introduced a bill to implement such a tax on the grounds that despite the "rather heavy" licence fee already imposed on white trappers in the Territories their numbers were "steadily increasing" and that the tax was justified by the greater costs of administration being incurred as a consequence.[15] This bill was successfully opposed on the grounds that it constituted an undesirable tax on a primary industry and that it also violated the principle of "no taxation without representation." Nevertheless, three years later the government introduced the measure again and, despite similar objections, succeeded

[13]Canada, Department of Mines and Resources, *The Northwest Territories— Administration, Resources and Development* (Ottawa: King's Printer, 1948), p. 53.

[14]Despite the increasingly severe restrictions placed upon white trappers in the Territories during the 1920s, it was reported that during the 1930–1 season 21 per cent of the fur taken there was taken by non-resident British subjects and 4.5 per cent by aliens; see *Minutes of the Council of the Northwest Territories*, February 4, 1931, 1, 160.

[15]*House of Commons Debates*, 1924, p. 3238.

in amending the Northwest Territories Act to permit the imposition of such a tax.[16] In debate on the bill the Minister of the Interior pointed out that because the various provinces had taxes on furs and since the Yukon Territory had imposed such a tax some years earlier, the Northwest Territories remained the "only happy hunting ground in which there was no tax on furs." The reason for imposing such a tax was that since "the residents of that country are having a very considerable amount of money spent in improvements and facilities for carrying on their work and earning their livelihood," surely "there is no good reason why a small tax should not be placed upon these furs." The Minister indicated that he had a tax of about 5 per cent in mind.[17] The implementation of the tax was effected in 1929 by way of a "Fur Export Tax Ordinance" of the Northwest Territories administration.[18] The yield from this tax fluctuates with the value of output, but during the 1930s it provided between $50,000 and $100,000 annually. Since then it has seldom exceeded $100,000 (although in 1948 the yield was an exceptional $141,423) and has often fallen to near $50,000. The tax levied in the Yukon Territory was at a lower rate and has usually yielded about $10,000 annually.[19]

The regulations designed to reduce competition in the Territories between white and native trappers were further strengthened in 1938 when hunting and trapping licences were limited to those residents of the Northwest Territories who on May 3, 1938, held hunting and trapping licences and who continued to reside in the Territories, and to "the children of those domiciled in the Northwest Territories for the past four years provided that such children continue to reside in the Northwest Territories."[20] As a consequence of this policy, by the middle of the 1950s only about 200 of the 1,500 persons licensed to hunt and trap in Mackenzie District were not natives.

Following World War II, and as part of a general development of public interest in the north and its problems, a much more positive

[16]*Statutes of Canada*, 17 Geo. V, c. 64 (1927).

[17]*House of Commons Debates*, 1927, p. 1312. Manitoba, Saskatchewan, Alberta, and British Columbia had agreed to impose such a tax in 1922.

[18]Canada, Department of the Interior, *Report of the Director of the North West Territories and Yukon Branch 1929–30* (Ottawa: King's Printer, 1931), p. 21.

[19]Data from annual reports of Department of Mines and Resources 1937–1949; Department of Resources and Development 1950–53; Department of Northern Affairs and National Resources 1953–58.

[20]Canada, P.C. 977, May 3, 1938. The Northwest Territories Game Regulations were consolidated by *Order in Council* P.C. 1925, July 22, 1939.

policy with respect to fur conservation and the development of trapping as a predominantly native occupation was adopted. In the years immediately following the end of the war, intensified research programmes were undertaken relating to fur-bearing and game animals in the north, and special studies of the management and sociological aspects of the fur industry were also initiated. In 1947, for example, resident mammologists were stationed in such areas as the Mackenzie Delta where native population was relatively dense.

This new government involvement in the fur trade was reflected in the repeal of the Northwest Game Act in 1949 and its replacement by a Northwest Territories Game Ordinance in the same year. The Ordinance was intended to continue "the policy of conservation of the wildlife resources for the use and benefit of the resident aborigines," but it also provided a new feature in the form of regulations establishing registered trapping areas in Mackenzie District.[21] The purpose of the registered traplines provisions instituted in 1949 in the Northwest Territories and in 1950 in the Yukon was primarily to encourage trappers to manage fur resources carefully by giving them exclusive trapping privileges in limited areas. It also made possible, of course, much more thorough supervision and administration of trapping by public authorities.

By 1952, 425 registered trapping areas had been established in the Northwest Territories, 104 of them operated by groups and 321 by individuals. The number of trappers involved as of March 31, 1951, was 1,106 of which 136 were white, 786 Indian, and 184 Eskimo.[22] By 1955, over 50 per cent of the reasonably accessible trapping country (estimated at about 387,000 square miles) in Mackenzie District had been brought under registration. Because of the nomadic life of the Eskimos, no attempt was made to establish registration in the Keewatin and Franklin Districts.[23]

In the Yukon Territory the registration of traplines begun in 1950 was completed by 1955. By that time 376 individual traplines had been registered in the area lying south of 65°, while further north 51 family registrations had been made by nomadic bands of Indians.[24] By 1961 the administration of many of these registered trapping areas was being

---

[21]*Minutes of the Council of the Northwest Territories*, 1948, XVII, pp. 3639–40.
[22]Canada, Department of Resources and Development, *Annual Report 1952*, p. 70.
[23]D.B.S., *Canada Year Book, 1955*, p. 616.
[24]Canada, Department of Northern Affairs and National Resources,' *Annual Report 1956*, p. 111.

done by government officials acting in consultation with trappers' councils organized in some of the larger communities.[25]

We see, then, that during the twentieth century there has been a major change in the amount of public intervention in the affairs of the northern fur trade. This has come about largely as a result of concern over the welfare of the native population of the north which had, by the turn of the century, become heavily dependent upon trapping and the imported consumer goods to be had in exchange for furs. Although, like the northern parts of the provinces, the Yukon and Northwest Territories retained their character as wilderness areas, the influx of outsiders and a growing awareness of the dangers of over-trapping valuable species prompted the government to introduce numerous regulations and controls designed to preserve the trade for the benefit of the native population of the area. Unfortunately this only served to guarantee for the native population the dubious privilege of participating in an industry declining in terms both of its relative and absolute importance in the economy of the Canadian north.

Fur Production in the Yukon and Northwest Territories, 1900–61

The statistical record of fur production in the areas with which we are concerned begins in 1910. Records of raw fur production in Canada between 1900 and 1920 are confined to the decennial censuses in which attempts were made to take account of the number and value of pelts obtained by trappers. According to the 1901 and 1911 censuses the value of furs trapped in the Yukon and Northwest Territories was $899,645 in 1900 and $1,927,550 in 1910. Because of the uncertainty of the boundary of the Territories before 1905, however, these figures cannot be compared with those subsequently recorded. It was not until 1920 that annual figures became available. These were collected by the Dominion Bureau of Statistics through an annual survey of raw fur production based upon returns from licenced fur traders. After 1945 the Bureau's figures are based upon the probably much more complete returns obtained from government agencies responsible for administering trapping.

The production of raw fur in the Yukon and Northwest Territories annually since 1920 is given in Table 3.1. It will be seen that the level of output fluctuates greatly from year to year and that there is also a suggestion of an erratic cyclical fluctuation over roughly a ten-year

[25]Canada, Department of Northern Affairs and National Resources, *Annual Report 1962*, p. 21.

period. The occurrence of major peaks will be noted in 1921–22, 1930–31, 1939–40, 1948–49. It is tempting to attribute whatever periodicity is suggested by these figures to natural phenomena in the case of this particular industry. The apparent cycle in the prevalence of certain important fur-bearing species of mammals has attracted a great deal of study. There appears to be no question but that biological factors must account, at least in part, for the fluctuations shown in fur production. But it is equally certain that a number of other factors are also involved.

One important influence on physical output in this industry is the price of the product itself. In the late 1940s, for example, the decreased production of fox furs in the Northwest Territories was reported by the federal Department of Resources and Development to be "partly due to prevailing low prices for fox furs, and partly to the numerical decline of white foxes reported in most areas."[26] Since trapline registration was introduced, this influence of price on productive effort has been made even more clear. In the Yukon, for example, there were 376 registered traplines in 1954–55, but this number declined to 224 in 1956–57 and to 190 in 1957–58. It was reported that "a large number of traplines are not being used because of the poor fur market during recent years."[27]

In some parts of the north the interest of natives in trapping furs has undoubtedly fluctuated with the prevalence of alternative employment opportunities, such as those created by construction projects, some kinds of which offered much higher incomes than could be obtained from trapping. But even in the more remote areas there has been an observed tendency for some groups of natives during periods of low fur prices "to rely on relief or to turn their attention more toward hunting and living off the country."[28]

The high degree of instability in the physical output of raw furs in the north is reflected in the violent fluctuations in the gross value of this output measured in money terms. But the price instability already alluded to adds to these fluctuations. Because of this, trapping has been a highly uncertain source of money income for those engaged in it. And in the longer term it has been a diminishing source of such income, for after World War II, the total current dollar income generated by raw

[26]Canada, Department of Resources and Development, *Annual Report for the Fiscal Year Ending March 31, 1950*, p. 32.
[27]Canada, Department of Northern Affairs and National Resources, *Annual Report for the Fiscal Year Ending March 31, 1958*, p. 120.
[28]Canada, Department of Northern Affairs and National Resources, *Annual Report for the Fiscal Year Ending March 31, 1954*, p. 116.

fur production in the north has been lower in most years than was the case during the depression of the 1930s. But even worse, when we consider two additional factors not shown in these statistics—the decline in the value of the dollar and the growth of the native population during the 1940s and 1950s, it will be apparent that these people have been denied any possibility of earning a reasonable income from such employment. How much more drastic the decline in the value of northern fur output was when allowance is made for price changes may be suggested by noting that in terms of constant dollars the 1953–54 output was worth less than one-third of even the relatively low value produced in the 1937–38 season.

The slight growth in the total value of territorial fur production during the decades of the 1940s and 1950s also helped to reduce the importance of this industry to the northern economy generally. Whereas trapping yielded as much as 66 per cent of total northern production (excluding construction and agriculture) in 1924 and 1927, for example, and never fell below 21 per cent before 1949, after 1949 it consistently ran at from 13 per cent to 3 per cent annually.[29] While trapping thus became a less and less significant source of income and employment in the north, it nevertheless remained the chief source of earned income for the native population of the area.

Territorial Fur Production in Relation to National Fur Production

The relative importance of Yukon and Northwest Territories fur production in relation to total fur production in Canada declined greatly after the turn of the century. In 1910 the Yukon and Northwest Territories produced about 34 per cent of the gross value of Canadian fur output. As will be seen from Table 3.2, however, from the early 1920s to the end of World War II the Yukon and Northwest Territories contributed only from about 9 to 18 per cent of this total. After the war, this share of national output declined even further, and in the early 1960s ran as low as approximately 3 per cent.

It might, at first, seem surprising that the far northern hinterland of a rapidly growing agricultural and industrial country should suffer a relative decline in importance as a source of a commodity such as furs. After all, the Northwest Territories, and the Yukon especially, were developed for the fur trade in the nineteenth century largely because of the encroachment of settlement on the trade in less remote parts of

[29]See Table 11.13.

the continent. Rich has pointed this out in the following passage from his *History of the Hudson's Bay Company 1670–1870*:

One of the remarkable features of the fur trade during the great era of European emigration, the middle years of the nineteenth century, was that the fur frontier moved steadily north. Edward Ellice told the 1857 Committee of the British House of Commons that the fur trade in the United States was virtually extinct save for a small trade from the Missouri, and that in general terms the supply of peltry had fallen off by a half, perhaps by two-thirds, since the early years of the century. "All the countries easily reached have been entirely destroyed." The profitable fur trade of the Company, he said, came from very far north, and he put the southern frontier of the fur trade at about 60° north.[30]

Yet, as we have seen, the area north of 60° has accounted for a decreasing percentage of Canadian fur production during the present century. The explanation for this must be found in the revolution in techniques for producing raw furs which occurred late in the nineteenth century in this country.

Fur farming was begun in Canada on Prince Edward Island about 1887 and in Quebec in 1898. The number of farms in this country grew gradually until 1920 (when 587 were recorded) and much more rapidly between then and the beginning of World War II.[31] By 1938, 10,454 fur farms were reported. Since then, largely because of a deterioration in the relationship between operating costs and product prices, the number of fur farms in Canada has decreased to about 2,100. Because the output of furs from fur farms has continued to increase, however, it appears that the decline in numbers has been caused by the elimination of smaller, less efficient operators. The proportion of total Canadian fur production coming from the fur farms has risen steadily from around 4 per cent in the early 1920s to 64 per cent by 1962.[32]

Although many attempts have been made to establish fur farming in the Yukon and Northwest Territories, it has not been successful there. Consequently, northern fur producers continued to rely upon the trapping of wild fur-bearing animals and to suffer the attendant instability of output and income which characterizes such operations. And, like other wild fur producers, they found it difficult to adapt to changing demands for particular types of fur in the long run.

While a detailed study of the reasons for the failure of fur farming

[30]E. E. Rich, *The History of the Hudson's Bay Company 1670–1870* (London: Hudson's Bay Record Society, 1958), Vol. II, p. 779.
[31]Data on fur farming from D.B.S., *Canada Year Book 1963–4*, p. 632.
[32]D.B.S., *Canada Year Book*, "Fur Farms," annually 1922–63.

in the Yukon and Northwest Territories remains to be done, it is possible to deduce some of these reasons from the limited information available. Studies of fur production in northern Saskatchewan have shown that fur farming is not initially compatible with the native way of life which has developed in the northern regions.[33] Fur farming requires continuous supervision, a great deal of routine labour, and a fairly large scale of operation. Even if natives in the north were willing to make the major social adjustments required for such an undertaking, a serious economic obstacle would remain—the need for a relatively large amount of financial backing to undertake the capital investment required. The possibility exists, however, that white immigrants to the north might undertake fur farming there because of suspected locational advantages. These advantages could include a climate conducive to early "priming" of furs (a marketing advantage), low-cost native labour and, perhaps, even low-cost feed obtained by utilizing the fish resources of northern lakes. It is significant in the light of this speculation that commercial fur farming was initiated in the Yukon Territory with its proportionately large white population much earlier and practised much more continuously there than in the Northwest Territories where the white population has been relatively small. Fur farming was undertaken in the Yukon as early as 1914, in which year the Yukon Council passed an ordinance regulating the export of live foxes from the Territory.[34] As will be seen from Table 3.3, by 1923 there were 21 fur farms in the Yukon. This number declined steadily until, in 1944, the Dominion Bureau of Statistics reported no fur farms operating in the Yukon. Thereafter, some ranch-raised mink and fox production was occasionally reported from the Territory, but no significant regular production of such furs had been re-established at time of writing.

In the Northwest Territories, the Northwest Territories Game Act and Regulations made provision for the establishment and licensing of fur farms in the 1920s.[35] By 1940 there were only eight fur farms licensed in the Northwest Territories and of these only four were both fur farms in the usual sense and actually stocked with any number of animals.

---

[33]See, for example, H. Buckley, J. E. M. Kew, and J. B. Hawley, *The Indians and Métis of Northern Saskatchewan* (Saskatoon: Centre for Community Studies, 1963).

[34]See *Journals of the Yukon Council* (1914), XIV, 81. During the early years of fur farming in Canada new farms were established in such numbers that the chief product of established farms was breeding stock rather than pelts.

[35]Canada, Department of the Interior, *Regulations Respecting Game in the Northwest Territories*, authorized by P.C. 807, 15 May, 1929 (Ottawa: King's Printer, 1930).

The number of these farms fluctuated but showed no tendency to increase during the 1950s.

The statistics of fur production referred to above, then, reflect almost entirely the product of wild fur trapping in the case of the Yukon and Northwest Territories but, in the case of national figures, ranch-raised fur accounts for more than half the total output. To date, at least, there is no evidence to suggest that this pattern will develop in the Territories and thereby enable the area to maintain fur exports despite the declining wild fur trapping industry. It is notable that the difficulties experienced by this industry have in recent years caused considerable concern in government circles, largely, of course, because of the implications for the welfare of the native peoples. This has led, as we have seen, to increased government expenditures on conservation measures such as trapline registration, restrictions on trapping privileges, biological investigations, forest fire prevention and warden services. Efforts have also been made more recently to promote sales of important furs such as white fox. Nevertheless, the official outlook has been pessimistic, uncharacteristically so even in the case of the federal department of Northern Affairs and National Resources. The Deputy Minister of that Department and Commissioner of the Northwest Territories submitted to the Royal Commission on Canada's Economic Prospects in 1955 that:

For the long term, the outlook for fur trapping in the Northwest Territories seems limited. It is a static industry capable of little or no expansion. It is not inconceivable that the future may see some further decline brought about by developments in the fields of low-priced synthetic fur fabrics. These may serve to reduce the demand for some types of natural furs.[36]

It is worth mentioning here that apparently no serious attention has been given to encouraging fur farming as a source of employment and income for natives. A necessary first step toward this end would be a study of the attempts already made to establish such operations in the Yukon and Northwest Territories and the reasons for their lack of success. Some of the considerations for such a study were suggested in the Report of the North Pacific Planning Project in 1947:

Fur-farming may well be suitable for the North Pacific Region, but there is no reason for expecting ranch fur from this region to be any better than any other ranch fur. Costs of handling may well be higher than in older settlements. Food is one of the most important factors. There is no game available

---

[36]R. G. Robertson, *The Northwest Territories—Its Economic Prospects, A Brief Presented to the Royal Commission on Canada's Economic Prospects* (Ottawa: Queen's Printer, 1955), pp. 11–12.

for food, but in some areas there may be a surplus of freshwater fish, especially coarse fish, which could be used in a ration formula in sufficient quantity to make fur-farming economical. Along the Arctic Ocean, there are other possibilities. It might be possible to make good use of the meat of marine mammals in fur-farming and there is a large supply of fish that may be too far from market to be utilized for many years as an export for human consumption. In addition, the abundant plankton of Arctic waters might be adaptable for processing into animal food. It must always be remembered that the preparation of balanced rations for fur animals is a complicated business, and that regular, dependable supplies are important.[37]

In short, the commercial feasibility of fur farming in the territorial north has yet to be demonstrated. What past experience does suggest is that even if the basic economic problems of supplying the necessary raw materials and capital facilities can be overcome, additional problems of a social and cultural nature would have to be solved before fur farming could become an important source of native employment and income in the area. This conclusion is supported by the experience in at least two other enterprises based upon living resources in the northwest—the commercial fishery described in the next section of this chapter and the reindeer experiment described in Chapter 9 below.

THE COMMERCIAL FISHERIES OF THE TERRITORIAL NORTH

Although the lakes, streams, and coastal waters of northern Canada are the habitat of a large variety of fish and marine mammals, it is only in quite recent years that the extent and nature of these resources has been scientifically assessed—and even today this work is only in its early stages. A great deal remains to be done before it will be possible to assess the adequacy of these resources for their traditional domestic uses and for potential commercial development either as the base for an export food industry or as a tourist attraction. The rapidly changing technology available in the north greatly complicates such assessments in the case of these resources. For example, one of the chief uses for fish there has been to feed sled dogs. But as dogs are replaced by other forms of motive power in the north, the need for dog feed is declining. Similarly, changing tastes have an important influence upon the demand for locally produced food supplies in domestic markets. Experience has shown that as alternative sources of human food are made available in the north the domestic utilization of local fish declines. It has been

[37]North Pacific Planning Project, *Canada's New Northwest*, pp. 132–3.

reported, for example, that in the Great Slave Lake area, "When they can, local Indians buy canned fish from 'outside' instead of using the excellent quality fish which abounds within sight of their homes."[38] Nevertheless, Great Slave Lake, the Slave River, the Mackenzie and Yukon Rivers, Great Bear Lake, the major rivers of the arctic coast, and many of the smaller lakes throughout the Territories have sustained important domestic fishing operations for many years.[39] The most important species have been the whitefish, found in nearly all the northern lakes and streams, the lake trout found especially in the deeper lakes of Mackenzie and Franklin Districts, the inconnu found in most of the larger streams west of the Anderson River, and the pike found in many inland lakes and streams and also in some coastal areas. Of the latter, the Mackenzie Delta has been particularly important.

The possibility of establishing commercial fisheries based upon these resources was first scientifically examined at the end of World War II, although commercial fish production in the Yukon Territory was recorded during the 1930s. The best year for these operations in the Yukon appears to have been 1935 when output was valued at $20,735. Production appears subsequently to have declined, however, and when a biological survey of the waters of the Yukon was made in 1945 it was reported that the prospects for commercial fisheries were relatively poor, although the sport fishery appeared capable of considerable expansion.[40] Similar surveys were conducted by the federal Department of Fisheries in Mackenzie District in 1944. Studies of the Mackenzie River, Great Bear Lake and Great Slave Lake indicated that the latter at least was capable of sustaining a major commercial fishery.[41]

The Great Slave Lake Fishery

The waters of Great Slave Lake have long been known to contain large fish populations, chiefly whitefish and trout, which, along with some other species, supported a considerable domestic fishery for local Indians.

[38]W. A. Kennedy, *The First Ten Years of Commercial Fishing on Great Slave Lake*, Bulletin Number 107 of the Fisheries Research Board of Canada (Ottawa, 1956), p. 4.

[39]See D. S. Rawson, "Biological Potentialities," in Underhill, ed., *The Canadian Northwest: Its Potentialities*, pp. 68–9.

[40]See V. C. Wyne-Edwards, "The Yukon Territory," in *North West Canadian Fish Surveys 1944–5*, Bulletin Number 72 of the Fisheries Research Board of Canada (Ottawa, 1947), pp. 5–20.

[41]The basic investigations of the lake were conducted by Dr. D. S. Rawson of the University of Saskatchewan and the subsequent development of the fishery was supervised by Dr. W. A. Kennedy of the Fisheries Research Board of Canada.

The surveys of the lake made in 1944 led to a preliminary estimate that the lake could support an additional commercial fishery taking about 3.5 million pounds (dressed weight) of all species annually. This was the equivalent of about 4 million pounds of whitefish and trout before dressing and it was assumed that the domestic fishery would remove another million pounds to make a total annual permitted output of 5 million pounds.

The fact that Great Slave Lake and the marine resources sustained by it were under the direct control of the federal government made possible an exercise in regional resource development by a government newly awakened to the potential importance of the north by the experiences of World War II. Here was an opportunity to develop a new industry in Mackenzie District—an industry, moreover, which at first sight would appear capable of providing employment opportunities of a kind well suited to the employment of local low-opportunity-cost labour. The land resources were there, a potential labour force was present and there was reason to believe that markets existed for the product. And, as already noted, the exploitation of the resource was directly controllable from the outset to ensure a long life for the industry. All that remained to be provided was the necessary capital, a suitable organizational structure, and a technology capable of ensuring delivery of a high-quality food product to the distant markets.

The latter requirement appears to have dictated the nature of the subsequent development of the Great Slave Lake fishery—given the government's apparent assumption that the actual operation of the fishery should be left in the hands of private operators who would be regulated and advised by such government agencies as the Fisheries Research Board. In any event, it was apparent that only a relatively large organization, private or public, could hope to overcome the problems connected with transporting a perishable product from Great Slave Lake to the large markets in eastern North America. A partial solution was seen to lie in maximizing the value of the product per unit weight by filleting the fish and by maintaining a very high standard in selecting it. A further possibility lay in applying the technology of quick-freezing and shipping the fish to market in the frozen state. Both approaches required large inputs of capital in the form of freezing plants and specialized transportation facilities. The latter was a particularly difficult requirement given the conditions prevailing in Mackenzie District in 1945. The only transportation facility linking Great Slave Lake to the outside rail and road systems was the southern portion of the Mackenzie waterway system. Under these circumstances it was necessary to provide vessels capable of carrying a refrigerated cargo.

All these requirements, as it turned out, could be met by a commercial fishing company, MacInnes Products Corporation Limited, already engaged in fishing on Lake Athabaska and transporting frozen fish to the southern terminus of the Mackenzie waterway at Waterways, Alberta. Not only was this company experienced in the kind of fishery operation required on Great Slave Lake, but most of its "plant" was constructed on barges which could be quite easily transported over the waterway to Great Slave Lake.[42]

This relatively large, already established firm began operations on Great Slave Lake in the summer of 1945, working from a base established on the north shore of the lake at what is now known as Gros Cap. Fish caught in the nearby deep-water areas of the lake were brought to this base where most of the catch was processed as fillets, quick-frozen by mechanical freezing apparatus and then transported in refrigerator barges across the lake, up the Slave River to the rapids at Fort Smith, portaged in special trucks, reloaded in refrigerated barges and taken up the remaining part of the system to Waterways, Alberta. At Waterways the fish were transferred to refrigerated railway cars for shipment to southern markets. In 1947 the company experimented with air transport from the lake to railhead, but the costs of this mode of transportation were found to be too high at the time. In any case, the following year brought completion of the Mackenzie all-weather highway from Grimshaw, Alberta, to Hay River, a small settlement on the south shore of Great Slave Lake. The establishing of this new transportation facility brought about major changes in the organization and operation of the Great Slave Lake fishery after 1948.

As early as the winter of 1946–47 the rough winter road which preceded the Mackenzie Highway was used to transport fish to market. The winter fishery thus inaugurated attracted several fishing companies to the lake and during the second winter fishery, that of 1947–48, they produced almost 1,300,000 pounds roundweight of trout and whitefish. This compared with the 1947 summer fishery's catch of 2,138,000 pounds of these species.[43] The operations involved in these winter and summer fisheries were, of course, quite different.[44] In the summer fishery,

---

[42]Kennedy, *The First Ten Years of Commercial Fishing on Great Slave Lake*, p. 4 and p. 5 note 2.

[43]Canada, Department of Mines and Resources, *Annual Report 1948*, p. 156.

[44]The Great Slave Lake fisheries are described in detail in Kennedy, pp. 6–14.

licensed fishermen operated from two bases, Gros Cap and Hay River, using a variety of rather small vessels usually rented from the fish company to which the catch was sold. In the winter fishery, based at Hay River, pairs of fishermen operated from "cabooses" out on the ice sending their catch back to Hay River by means of a "snowmobile" or even by dogsled. Like the summer fishermen they were normally financed by fish companies.

Both the summer and the winter fishing operations were greatly encouraged by the completion of the highway from Hay River to Grimshaw, Alberta, for this made it possible to ship fish much more efficiently on a year-round basis. Using the new road it became possible to ship fresh fish to railhead both winter and summer, for trucks could cover the 389 miles of highway in from 12 to 18 hours. The general quality of the product was also improved by this relatively fast means of transport for only five days were required to move fish from the nets in Great Slave Lake to market in Chicago.[45]

Removal of the main transportation bottleneck in the fisheries operation in 1948, combined with an upward revision of the catch limits to 9 million pounds the following year, permitted a great expansion in the industry. With highway transport available, small companies could now enter the industry and they did so in considerable numbers. The summer fishery of 1949 attracted six companies operating 57 boats and 212 licences were issued. The winter fishery of 1949–50 was conducted by over ten companies and 611 licences were in effect.[46] The actual catch in the 1949–50 seasons was the largest ever recorded with almost the entire limit of 9 million pounds taken, the only time this has occurred. Largely because of the development of this industry, the population of Hay River grew from about 200 late in 1948 to around 1,000 in a year's time. It would be easy, however, to overestimate the significance of the rapid development of the commercial fisheries on the economy of the Great Slave Lake area. Although some employment opportunities for local native labour were created in this industry and in the various related operations such as transportation and other local service enterprises, mostly transient labour was employed in the actual fishing operations. Kennedy reports that although a few local residents participated in the commercial fishery, most of the summer fishermen came in from the northern lakes of the prairie provinces for the season and returned

[45]Canada, Department of Fisheries, *Annual Report 1948–9*, p. 34.
[46]Canada, Department of Resources and Development, *Annual Report 1950*, pp. 85–6.

home when it closed in September. The winter fishermen generally comprised an entirely different group and were chiefly farmers from northern Alberta and Saskatchewan who engaged in the fishery from December 1 to March 31—at which time they, too, returned home.[47]

The earnings of these fishermen fluctuated considerably as a result of variations not only in prices but also in the size of the catch. The latter was greatly affected by weather conditions both winter and summer. Although the winter operations were often hindered by bad weather, they were seldom completely halted by it. In the 1951–52 season, for example, operations were carried on in temperatures as low as 65° below zero. In that year the total earnings of fishermen were $654,450. This amounted to an average of about $1,300 per fisherman in the summer fishery and about $1,280 per fisherman in the winter fishery.[48] Often the difference between earnings in the two fisheries were more marked, however. In 1952–53 the average gross income in the summer fishery was $1,840 compared with $770 in the winter.

During the 1950s the industry improved considerably in efficiency, but it did not grow significantly. Some development was apparent in the extension of commercial fishing to other smaller lakes in the area, but most of these ventures remained "marginal" despite increasing government encouragement. Similarly, the industry gave little sign of becoming a more important source of employment for local natives—again despite increasing governmental efforts to encourage this.

The increasing efficiency of the Great Slave Lake operations during the 1950s is suggested by the fact that although the level of production declined, as shown in Table 3.4, from the peak reached in 1949, labour inputs decreased more rapidly. Estimating labour inputs on the basis of commercial fishing licences issued indicates an output of about 11,000 pounds of fish landed per fisherman in 1949, 12,000 pounds per fisherman in 1956, and 17,000 pounds per fisherman in 1961. By 1961 the number of persons employed in all primary fishing operations in the Northwest Territories was down to 336 from the 500 or more employed during the early 1950s.[49] Although this reduction in employment coincided with improved earnings for the fishermen involved, it reduced the possibility of making this new industry an important source of jobs for natives in the Great Slave Lake area. In 1957 the federal Indian

[47]Kennedy, pp. 7 and 10.
[48]Canada, Department of Fisheries, *Annual Report 1951–2*, p. 69.
[49]Based on data published in D.B.S., *Fishery Statistics of Canada*. The basis for reporting employment in the territorial fisheries varies considerably from one official publication to another.

Affairs Branch assisted a group of Treaty Indians to participate in the commercial fishery. It was subsequently reported, however, that "the turnover of fishermen was large and not more than 14 Indians were employed at any one time in seven camps."[50] Throughout the 1950s, by far the largest part of the labour employed directly in the fisheries continued to be provided by non-residents. Although the reasons for this have not yet been determined, it has been suggested that the local Indians were not considered to have "the skills necessary to ensure volume production, nor were they able to navigate large boats out of sight of land as required on Great Slave Lake."[51]

The future value of this industry as a source of native employment will depend upon the success of government efforts to train local residents in the skills required. But it will also depend, of course, upon the possibility of expanding the commercial fishery operations rapidly enough to offset its apparent tendency to devise labour-saving methods and to use increasing capital inputs.[52] It is evident that to time of writing the level of output in the industry has not been limited by the supply of natural resource involved. It is one of the distinguishing characteristics of the fisheries in the Territories that they have been developed under strict government control and in accordance with "scientific" resource management procedures. Indeed the Great Slave Lake fishery has been described as "the first, if not the only, fishery which has been opened commercially following scientific investigations" and which has subsequently been managed on the basis of "research and scientifically applied conservation measures."[53] The same procedure was followed in opening up to commercial fishing a number of smaller lakes in the vicinity. But, with only one exception (in 1949), the limits imposed to conserve the resource remained above the actual catch of the commercial fishing companies. We may conclude, therefore, that the level of development in this industry was limited more by economic factors than by the availability of fish as "scientifically" determined by the Fisheries Research Board.

[50]Canada, Department of Fisheries, *Annual Report 1957–8*, p. 26.

[51]Council of the Northwest Territories, *Votes and Proceedings, 1962*, p. 10 (mimeographed).

[52]Operators on Great Slave Lake have used increasing amounts of capital equipment, especially in the winter fishery where it shows up largely in the form of mechanized vehicles to transport fish to the processing plants and men and equipment to the fishing sites.

[53]Canada, Department of Resources and Development, Northern Administration and Lands Branch, *Industries of the Northwest Territories* (Ottawa, 1953), p. 23.

It is true that because of the system whereby Great Slave Lake was divided into areas with catch-limits assigned to each, the operators frequently reached the limit in one or two of the most accessible areas (especially that nearest Hay River). But this experience (and the apparent lack of enthusiasm shown by commercial firms to operate in the smaller lakes) suggests that it was production costs which imposed the effective limit on production and not any inadequacy of the resource base itself. In view of the fact that the most intensive fishing effort was restricted to the most accessible parts of Great Slave Lake despite the availability of fish elsewhere, it is apparent that, as one would expect, operating costs were found to increase significantly as fishing operations moved further away from the main processing, shipping, and supply centres. Transportation problems were even greater, of course, when crews were sent to other lakes, especially when the operations there were so small as not to warrant investments in plant at the site of the fishing operations. The development of a commercial summer fishery on Kakisa Lake, for example, was reported to have been discouraged by the fact that ice for storage purposes had to be flown in from Hay River—making this, in the rather restrained words of the Department of Fisheries, a "costly operation."[54] By 1960, although six other lakes were fished, only 25,000 pounds were taken from them in total.

Because of these economic obstacles confronting the fisheries in the Northwest Territories, at time of writing the possibility of future major development of this industry seems unlikely. The one important development during the period being considered here came about when the major improvement in transportation facilities was made in 1948 and it is possible that future transportation improvements might further stimulate its development. But during the 1950s, as the production figures shown in Table 3.4 indicate, the industry actually contracted both in terms of absolute levels of annual production and in terms of its share of the total Canadian inland fishery output. The latter fell from about 10 per cent in 1949 to less than 5 per cent in the early 1960s. The relative importance of the commercial fishing industry in the territorial economy is suggested by the fact that, even with the development of the Great Slave Lake operations, this industry came to account for little more than two per cent of the net value of commodity production in the Yukon and Northwest Territories combined.[55]

[54]Canada, Department of Fisheries, *Annual Report 1955–6*, p. 65.
[55]See Table 11.13.

TOURISM

The preceding sections of this chapter have outlined the development of two industries—trapping, and fishing—through which the territorial economy earned its living from the "outside." In regional, as in international trade, however, not all exports have to be "visible" in the form of commodities—they can include "invisible" items as well. Of these, one of the most important in many countries is made up of those highly subjective benefits bestowed upon the tourist: "one who makes a tour or tours; especially one who does this for recreation, one who travels for pleasure or culture, visiting a number of places for their objects of interest, scenery, or the like."[56]

It would be difficult to find a better example than "tourism" of an industry which depends upon the availability of transportation. While there are always a few tourists who thrive on hardship encountered in travel, perhaps partly because this increases the scarcity value possessed by a remote place of interest, it is difficult to think of an "industry" developing under such circumstances. Few travellers can afford "custom" travel when it involves long flights by chartered aircraft or long weeks of canoeing. If numbers of tourists are to be attracted to an area it must possess not only "objects of interest, scenery, or the like," it must be accessible to other than the very wealthy or the professional traveller and it must have at least some minimum of accommodation for the tourist when he gets there.

Like most other parts of Canada the territorial north possesses scenery, often distinctive, and some objects of considerable interest. During the period with which this study has been concerned, however, the only identifiable "tourist centre" was Dawson, the centre of the Klondike. For many years a small tourist business was done in the Yukon catering to travellers who traditionally voyaged up the inland passage on the West Coast to Skagway, boarded the White Pass and Yukon Route railway and travelled through the spectacular White Pass to Whitehorse. From there, river steamers carried the tourists to Dawson City and back again. (After the abandonment of the river operations in 1955, this part of the journey was made, less glamorously, either by highway or by air on a scheduled flight.) And once the Alaska Highway was opened to civilian traffic after World War II, hardy automobilists were able to travel the more than 1,000 miles from Dawson Creek,

[56]*Oxford Universal Dictionary*, 3rd Edition.

British Columbia, to Whitehorse and from there to Dawson or on to Alaska.

In the early 1960s a great effort was made to turn Dawson City into a major tourist centre. Prompted in part by a growing concern for the preservation of the rapidly disintegrating buildings of Dawson, and partly, too, by the dwindling reserves of placer gold which threatened the area's only industry, territorial and federal authorities organized the Dawson Festival complete with a new Broadway musical play to be performed in the restored Dawson opera house. Extensive additions to the accommodation facilities in Dawson were made and a massive publicity campaign was launched to induce large numbers of tourists to visit Dawson during the summer. This venture, despite heavy government subsidization, was far from being a success. As one member of the Yukon Council said subsequently, while this effort "did not work out as planned," it did indicate that another approach to the problem had to be made. There is perhaps a touch of the spirit of the Klondike, but also some evidence of desperation, in his proposal that gambling should be legalized in Dawson City, thereby making possible its preservation "at absolutely no expense to the Canadian taxpayer."[57] At time of writing the proposal had not been implemented and Dawson City appears to have reverted to its pre-Festival status as a minor tourist attraction in a very remote part of North America.

The tourist industry in the Northwest Territories is even less developed than that of the Yukon. Lacking a major centre of attraction, the Northwest Territories until recently has had to rely upon the small-volume, high-cost business of catering to sportsmen with sufficient means to fly in to fishing and hunting camps. Until 1960 there was no highway route into any part of the Northwest Territories beyond Hay River. In that year the completion of the Mackenzie Highway made the town of Yellowknife accessible to tourists travelling by automobile and since then some tourist business of a less specialized variety has developed in that centre. In 1961 about 35 per cent of the approximately 1300 tourists visiting the Northwest Territories spent some time in Yellowknife.[58] The volume of such business is expected to increase considerably in future, partly because of further transportation improvements and also because of measures being taken by governments, both

[57]Yukon Territorial Council, *Votes and Proceedings, 1963*, Vol. II, Sessional Paper No. 55.

[58]See L. S. Bourne, *Yellowknife N.W.T.—A Study of Its Urban and Regional Economy* (Ottawa, Northern Co-ordination and Research Centre: Department of Northern Affairs and National Resources, 1963).

federal and territorial, to promote such a development. For example, the Northwest Territories Council has helped organize a Northwest Territories Tourist Office and a Northwest Territories Tourist Association to encourage the development of tourist camps, camp-grounds along the Mackenzie Highway, improved hotel accommodation, etc. A particularly interesting attempt to develop further a "luxury trade" buffalo hunt in the southern Mackenzie District was initiated in 1959. A limited number of buffalo hunting licences was authorized (100 initially), outfitters were licenced, guides trained, and various regulations were devised to ensure that the private outfitters would provide adequate facilities for their clients. The average expenditures by alien non-resident buffalo hunters in 1960 amounted to $1,691 which indicates that this type of tourism could be of some importance to the local economy.[59] Attempts were also made to encourage the development of camps for other kinds of hunting and for sport fishing at various points in the Northwest Territories. It must be emphasized, however, that even in the 1960s the tourist trade was still in so rudimentary a form that it had no measurable role to play in the territorial economy.

The employment possibilities of the tourist trade have not been overlooked by those concerned with the problems of the native population of the north. It would appear obvious that this industry could be relatively satisfactory in this regard in so far as native guides and camp workers would be able to make use of traditional skills to obtain wage employment. It would be easy to exaggerate the possibilities of this, however, for not only has the absolute amount of this type of work been very small, but experience has shown that considerable training is necessary for the development of suitable guides and a considerable amount of supervision of their work is required. This has been the experience in northern Saskatchewan and it has been confirmed by the buffalo hunting experiment in Mackenzie District already referred to. In view of this it seemed unlikely that tourism could create job opportunities very much more accessible to natives than had other industries such as mining.

[59]Council of the Northwest Territories, *Votes and Proceedings, 1961,* Sessional Paper No. 10, Appendix "A".

4 The Export-Base Industries: Mining

THE DISCOVERY OF mineral deposits in the Yukon and Northwest Territories occurred during the eighteenth century. As early as 1771 Samuel Hearne was exploring the rumoured copper "mine" in what is now known as the Coppermine River area northeast of Great Bear Lake. In 1789 Alexander Mackenzie located coal deposits on the Great Bear River and noted also the presence of petroleum seepages on the Mackenzie River.[1] Unlike the fur resources discovered at the same time, however, and despite later discoveries, the mineral resources of what is now the Northwest Territories were not developed at all until the decades of the 1920s and 1930s. In the Yukon Territory, where significant exploration did not take place until well into the nineteenth century, the first mineral deposits were not noted until 1869 when gold was discovered on the Yukon River. Subsequent discoveries of placer gold on the tributaries of the Yukon led to the first mineral production in the northwest in the early 1880s.

Whether or not the known mineral resources of the north could be made competitive in national or international markets depended upon the supply conditions underlying their production—and the most significant of these were the transport problem, which presented the chief locational disadvantage, and the grade of the available land resources, which offered the greatest possibility for offsetting this disadvantage. Other factors, however, introduced an element of flexibility within the limits imposed by these conditions. These were never of sufficient strength before 1939 to permit the development of deposits which did

[1]D.B.S., *Mining Events 1604–1956*, Reference Paper No. 68. A brief description of these early mineral discoveries will be found in A. H. Lang and R. J. W. Douglas, "Minerals and Fuels," in Underhill, ed., *The Canadian Northwest: Its Potentialities*, pp. 45–50.

not contain some precious metals, but they did affect the extent to which such deposits could be utilized with respect to grade. The most significant of these were techniques to improve the efficiency of the northern mining operations themselves and the related, but more inclusive, factor of industrial organization. The earliest, and crudest, attack upon the mineral resources of the northwest depended upon sheer richness of grade to overcome the disadvantages of the area, but later development depended more and more upon technical and organizational devices to achieve this end.

MINERAL DEVELOPMENT IN THE YUKON TO 1914

Although some placer gold deposits were being worked on tributaries to the Yukon River as early as 1881, the first important discovery was made in 1887 when coarse gold was found on Fortymile Creek near the Alaska border. This development was eclipsed by the remarkable Klondike strike of 1896, but it marked the beginning of the first stage in the development of the Yukon alluvial gold mining industry, a stage characterized by the virtual absence of public regulation and control and by the organization of private enterprise in small, producing units of one or more men using simple capital equipment of a rather primitive kind.

These early miners were obliged to adapt the placer-mining techniques developed in California and British Columbia to the sub-arctic conditions of the Yukon area. In so far as the physical mining operation itself was affected by these conditions, the most difficult problem was presented by the prevalence of permanently frozen ground. During the great "rush" of 1896 it was found that much of the land in the Klondike district was permanently frozen to bedrock, which lay from 15 to 40 feet below the surface. Because the "pay dirt" lay near, or even *in*, the surface of the bedrock, the frozen overburden had to be removed. The initial richness of the deposits encouraged the application of crude techniques which depended more upon local wood supplies than upon imported capital equipment for reaching the gold-bearing gravels. Shafts were sunk in stages by burning large pyres of wood on the site to thaw the ground, which was then shovelled out, successive burning and digging being continued until bedrock was reached. About twelve inches of this rock, along with the rich gravels lying upon it, were then mined, hoisted to the surface, and sluiced to separate the gold. The disadvantage of this method was that it was slow and, as the timber was cut back from the creeks, it required increasing inputs of labour to maintain the fuel supplies. Fortunately, little timber was required for the workings themselves, for the frozen ground permitted construction of horizontal drifts at the bottom of the shaft without the labour and expense of timbering.

This technique of placer mining was used in the Klondike for the first two years following the strike on Bonanza Creek in 1896. During these years gold-seekers continued to arrive in large numbers. The main part of this rush did not reach the Klondike until the spring of 1897 and many migrants did not arrive until the spring of 1898, but by the summer of that year most of the richest creeks had been staked and, although there were periodic "stampedes" to new areas for the next eight years, there were no new strikes of great importance made.

Although the level of Yukon gold production fluctuated widely from year to year it remained relatively low until the discovery of Bonanza in 1896. If the years 1886 to 1900 are taken as marking the first stage in the development of the Yukon gold placers, the value of production may be said to have fluctuated between $40,000 and $300,000 over the first ten years of the period, rising sharply and rapidly after 1897 to a peak value of $22,275,000 in 1900.[2] This rapid increase in production was chiefly due to the development of new techniques for working established creeks such as "Bonanza" and "Eldorado." The steam-thawing process introduced in the winter of 1898 used a system of perforated probes driven into the ground and connected to a boiler. With these "steam points" operators were able to excavate from eight to ten feet per day instead of the two to three feet possible with the wood fires.[3] The other techniques which were developed to meet the peculiar difficulties encountered in northern placer mining were the cold-water and open-cut methods. Both of these used water for thawing the frozen ground overlying the gold-bearing gravels.

The equipment required by all these methods was relatively light, being limited in the main to small boilers, pumps, retorts, and hand tools. Supplying even these "hardware" items, however, along with food and building supplies, did provide the basis for a considerable wholesale and retail trade in Dawson. With reference to this trade Ogilvie, the government surveyor, noted the difficulties presented by the inadequate

[2]Canada, Geological Survey, Section of Mines, *Annual Report on the Mineral Industry of Canada 1904*, published as Sessional Paper 26a (Ottawa, 1906), p. 38.
[3]Canada, Department of the Interior, *The Yukon Territory: Its History and Resources* (Ottawa, 1909), p. 38.

transport facilities and observed in this "the great obstacle to the development of the district."[4]

The influx of labour and capital to the Klondike placers in the late 1890s took place under conditions which closely approximated those presupposed by the orthodox market theory. Labour and capital resources were transferred almost overnight from the old placer areas further south for there was a minimum of "official" interference with their free access to the Klondike. This was, indeed, limited to the regulations established by the police for the safety of those making the perilous passage over the passes into the Yukon before the railway was built.

The year 1900 marked the end of the first phase in the Yukon placer developments because, until that time, the main properties in the Klondike were sufficiently rich to permit profitable exploitation by small operators using relatively simple equipment. After 1900 most of the high-grade deposits had been worked to the point where that kind of operation was no longer profitable. The small operator was subsequently replaced by large organizations using quite different techniques. This revolution was effected during the first decade of the century through the introduction of power dredges and large hydraulic plants.

The first dredge was brought into the Yukon in 1900 and, although its initial trial on the Yukon River was a failure, it was relocated on Bonanza Creek where it was reported to have "demonstrated the possibility of low-grade ground being worked at a profit that could not otherwise be worked."[5] During the next ten years a number of dredges were constructed by mining companies in the Yukon and, because they usually operated on electric power, large investments in generating plant were necessary. In the absence of public power supplies, these were made by the larger private companies operating in the Klondike. In 1909, for example, the Yukon Gold Company built three new dredges on Bonanza Creek and invested $200,000 in a 1,650 horsepower hydro-electric plant on the Twelvemile River.[6]

The technique of dredging placer deposits and the technology embodied in the dredges themselves was borrowed from the placer-mining fields of California despite the quite different operating conditions which

[4]Canada, Department of the Interior, *Information Respecting the Yukon District* (Ottawa, 1897), p. 12.

[5]Canada, Department of the Interior, *The Yukon Territory: Its History and Resources*, p. 52.

[6]Canada, Department of Mines, *Annual Report of the Division of Mineral Resources and Statistics on the Mineral Production of Canada in 1909* (Ottawa, 1911), pp. 20–1.

prevailed in the Yukon. Because the earlier dredging operations in the Yukon were confined to mining naturally thawed gravels, the chief difference in conditions was the short Yukon operating season. But, although the dredges in California operated all year, the long hours of summer daylight in the Yukon permitted virtually 24-hour operation during the season so that the rate at which these heavy, capital-intensive plants could be utilized was not as much lower as might have been expected. The Yukon climate proved to be a more serious obstacle to the application of the other large-scale mining technique, hydraulic mining.

Because of the relatively dry Yukon climate, expensive investments in water-supply systems were necessary prerequisites for establishing hydraulic mining operations there. Small operators were consistently thwarted in their attempts to utilize this technique by a chronic shortage of water. The obvious source of the large volume of water required was the creek itself, but this presupposed the installation of pumps to create a "head" of sufficient force to wash down the banks of gravel. It was found that the operating costs of such pumping operations were prohibitive. After 1900, several large operators conceived the idea of using the spring "run-off" water by capturing it before it flowed into the creeks, but because this water was available only when the snow was melting, it was necessary to construct large reservoirs to store an amount adequate for a season's operation. Because this water was a resource falling under federal jurisdiction, the government sent an engineer into the Yukon in 1905 to investigate the possibility of constructing a system of public reservoirs to provide water to operators throughout the Klondike district.[7] Such direct public investment in the Yukon placer operations was subsequently rejected, however, in favour of a policy of granting large blocks of placer claims and water rights to a few very large mining organizations. The largest of these was the Yukon Gold Corporation, which built an impounding dam (collecting water from an area of 35 square miles) and a seventy-mile-long distributing system to supply water to its operations on Bonanza and Eldorado Creeks. By 1909 this company had invested approximately four million dollars in such facilities. In that year the Department of the Interior reported that such private developments had "obviated the necessity of subsidizing or undertaking as a public utility the construction of a large water scheme for the Klondike District."[8]

[7]Canada, Department of the Interior, *The Yukon Territory: Its History and Resources*, p. 57.
[8]*Ibid.*, p. 57.

The large mineral and water concessions which underlay this private investment in overhead capital facilities were granted by the federal government under a system whereby the land resources of the Yukon were regulated by orders-in-council on an *ad hoc* basis.[9] These grants, and the system of regulations which made them possible, were widely opposed in the Yukon, particularly by the remaining small operators in the area. The government eventually yielded to pressure from within the Yukon and in 1906 passed the Yukon Placer Mining Act which, with its amendments, governs placer mining in the Yukon to this day. Many years later a spokesman for the Yukon asserted that this act "did more to establish confidence in mining and to do away with the unrest and dissatisfaction in that Territory than anything else that had been done up to that time."[10]

The conversion of the Yukon placer mining industry from small to large-scale production was a gradual process. While it was taking place, as shown in Table 4.1, actual gold production from the Yukon declined steadily from the peak reached in 1900. During the first seven years of the century physical production of gold fell by over 100,000 fine ounces per year to reach a low of 152,381 fine ounces in 1907. In 1906 British Columbia replaced the Yukon as Canada's most important gold-producing region.[11] By 1907, however, the conversion to large-scale techniques had been completed and most of the large plants were functioning at capacity.[12] But, although annual output increased every year after 1907 until 1913, even the output of that year was still only about 25 per cent of the production achieved in 1900. As a result of this decline in the largest mining industry of the Yukon and partly because of the industry's conversion to capital-intensive techniques, the level of economic activity in the Territory dropped sharply. By 1914 the population had fallen to 8,512.

Despite these adverse developments, some optimism with respect to the future of the Yukon Territory was kept alive by modest success achieved in the search for new primary industries. Between 1900 and 1914 attempts were made to exploit copper, silver, and lead deposits in the Yukon and, although great difficulties were encountered, some of

[9]See page 44 above.

[10]*House of Commons Debates*, 1928, p. 2243.

[11]In 1906 British Columbia produced 48.5 per cent and the Yukon 40.6 per cent of Canada's total output of gold.

[12]Canada, Department of Mines, Mines Branch, *Annual Report on the Mineral Production of Canada 1907 and 1908* (Ottawa, 1910), p. 44. This series of reports is hereafter cited as Canada, *Mineral Production*.

these demonstrated the possibility of exporting metals other than gold from the Territory.

The Whitehorse copper belt is located in the extreme south of the Yukon Territory, lying in places only forty miles north of the British Columbia border. Several outcroppings of copper were reported there in 1897 by miners on their way to the Klondike and the first claim was staked in the summer of 1898. By the turn of the century the district had been thoroughly prospected and five major claims had been located. During the next several years exploratory work was done on these claims and occasional shipments of ore made. A group of mining engineers who visited the area in 1905 reported as follows on the development there:

The copper belt presents a considerable number of promising "prospects" of high grade ore, some of which will doubtless be successfully developed in the near future. . . . The reported offer of a rate of $5.00 per ton for ore in sacks, or $6.00 in bulk from Whitehorse to the . . . smelter at Ladysmith on Vancouver Island (a distance of 112 miles by rail and 900 miles by water) leaves some margin of profit on the mining and shipping of rich copper ores; and this operation may be expected to promote the development of mining on a much larger scale, and the realization of economies in all the departments (including transportation) which will make ores of lower grade profitable.[13]

The optimism of this report proved to be ill-founded, however, for actual shipments of copper ore from these properties remained small and although a production of 3,530 tons was achieved by all six mines taken together in 1907, output dropped sharply in 1908 and ceased altogether in 1909.[14]

The initial failure of these mines was attributable to the high freight rates charged by the White Pass and Yukon Route railway and the inadequacy of transport facilities between the mines and Whitehorse. Although all the mines were less than ten miles from Whitehorse, the cost of moving ore over the roads built by the territorial government averaged between three and four dollars per ton. How costly this was may be judged from the fact that the next 1,000 miles to the smelter cost six dollars per ton.[15] Even this remarkable disadvantage could have been overcome if shipments of very high-grade ore could have been maintained, but only small amounts of such ore were available in these deposits. Occasional shipments of high-grade ore were made after 1909 by hand-sorting the ores mined, and this served to keep the mines in existence, if nothing else.

[13]American Institute of Mining Engineers, cited in Canada, Department of the Interior, *The Yukon Territory 1909*, p. 61.
[14]Canada, *Mineral Production 1909*, p. 39.
[15]Canada, *Mineral Production 1907–8*, p. 44.

In 1910 the federal government was induced to give some encouragement to the development of these deposits by exempting them from the general tax levied on mineral production in the Yukon, but this concession had no apparent effect upon the supply conditions impeding their development.[16] It was not until the White Pass and Yukon Route railway reduced its freight rates in 1912 that the Whitehorse copper mines came back into serious production. As a result of this alleviation of the underlying transport problem, shipments of copper ore rose within a year to three times the previous record reached in 1907 and a relatively high level of production was maintained to 1914.[17] A similar pattern of development is to be observed in the attempts to develop lode-silver properties in the Yukon during the same period.

Some silver has always been produced in the Yukon as a by-product of the alluvial gold-mining operations. In the period before World War I, about one ounce of silver was produced along with every five ounces of crude gold bullion. Because this ratio remained roughly constant, the production of silver from the Yukon varied with the quantity of gold produced, rising to a peak of 290,000 fine ounces in 1900 and falling off with gold production to a low of 35,000 fine ounces in 1907.

In 1905 "promising deposits" of high-grade silver ores were discovered near Lake Tagish in the southern part of the Territory. The initial problems of development at these properties resembled those described in connection with the Whitehorse copper deposits. Some of the claims contained pockets of very rich ore which could be shipped to outside smelters despite the high transport cost incurred but, as is suggested by the erratic production recorded in Table 4.2, it was impossible to establish adequate reserves of such high-grade ore. In 1912 interest in this type of mining was diverted to the Mayo area and the Tagish Lake silver mines were eventually abandoned.

Although an important deposit of silver-lead ore was staked in the Mayo district as early as 1906, no development work was done there until 1912 when two separate attempts were made to prove this and several neighbouring deposits in the district. Despite the large development costs incurred and the absence of any means of transporting the ore for forty miles over uneven terrain to the Stewart River, some trial shipments of hand-sorted ore were made in 1912 and 1913. In 1914 a shipment of commercial size was achieved.[18] In view of the transport costs involved in this shipment, the fact that it yielded a profit suggests

---

[16]See *House of Commons Debates*, 1928, p. 2242.
[17]Canada, *Mineral Production 1914*, p. 71.
[18]*Ibid.*, p. 31.

that the ore must have been of very high-grade and silver content indeed. Data recorded by the federal Department of Mines in 1914 indicates that the shipment made in 1914 from the Mayo district yielded a smelter return net of transport and treatment costs amounting to approximately $128 per ton. Under the circumstances this was a remarkable development for the ore had to be hauled forty miles overland to the Stewart River at Mayo Landing where it was loaded onto small river-boats and taken to the junction with the Yukon River where it was transferred to larger river-boats and taken up-river to Whitehorse. From Whitehorse it was carried by rail 110 miles to Skagway and then by sea to smelters in San Francisco. In the early years of the development the cost of hauling the ore to the river was about twenty dollars per ton using sleds and horses on a frozen winter road. The cost of shipping the ore from Mayo to San Francisco was approximately twenty-two dollars per ton.[19]

Summarizing these developments in the Yukon, we have seen that, during the last two decades of the nineteenth century, labour and capital were attracted to the Canadian northwest by extraordinarily rich land resources in the form of placer gold. The significance of placer gold in this context is that the development of this resource minimized the main obstacle to industrial production of any kind in this area: the absence of transport facilities. Placer gold could be worked with very little capital, on a small scale; hence, the problem of moving heavy equipment and process supplies into the area did not exist to any critical degree. The very high value of the product minimized the problem of transporting it from the area. The chief transportation requirements were for the movement of labour into the area, communications within the Territory itself and the importation of foodstuffs, building materials, and other supplies needed for the maintenance of the population. These requirements were satisfied from the standpoint of the placer-mining operations by the construction of the White Pass and Yukon railway, the connecting river transportation system, and a system of crude winter roads.[20]

Following the turn of the century the richest land resources in the Klondike had been worked out and the placer-mining industry was converted to large-scale organization. Small, labour-intensive operations were replaced by capital-intensive dredging and hydraulic operations, a conversion which was facilitated by the federal government's policy of granting large land concessions to the private organizations willing to undertake these operations and the large overhead capital investments in

[19]Canada, *Mineral Production 1916*, p. 148.
[20]The development of these transportation facilities is described in Chapter VII.

power and water utilities associated with them. The large population loss associated with the decline of the placers and their conversion to large-scale operation brought about a general decline in the level of economic activity in the Yukon after 1900.

Largely as a result of discoveries associated with the development of the Klondike, however, several minerals other than gold were discovered in the Yukon, and with the decline of the placers, some attempts were made to develop them. All of these minerals were present as lode deposits, however, so their development presupposed the existence of much better transport facilities than did the placer gold deposits. The attempts to develop copper, silver, and lead properties in the Yukon during this period demonstrated the critical importance of the transport factor to this type of mining in the north. Although some development was achieved during this period on the basis of very high-grade ore shipments, little progress was made toward the solution of the under-lying transportation problem itself.

STAGNATION AND RETRENCHMENT IN THE YUKON MINERAL INDUSTRIES 1914–1929

The promise which the prospect of developing new primary production in the Yukon held for those most intimately connected with affairs in the Territory after 1900 was not appreciated by most other Canadians. By 1914 the public conception of the Yukon as a land of quick wealth had been transformed into a growing conviction that the Territory was not worth the expense associated with maintaining it—an attitude fostered by the continuing decline in gold production from 247,940 fine ounces in 1914 to 25,601 ounces by 1926. Because this decline in the alluvial gold-mining industry was not offset by sufficiently large production of the "new" minerals during this period, total mineral production fell by 47 per cent between 1914 and 1929 and, in the absence of alternative employment opportunities, an immediate loss of population resulted. By 1921 even the small population recorded in 1914 had been halved to stand at 4,157, a level at which it was to remain for the next twenty years.[21]

The years of the First World War were unusually favourable for metal producers everywhere and the struggling copper- and silver-lead–mining firms in the Yukon were given a new lease on life, at least temporarily.

[21]The population of the Yukon is shown in Table 11.12.

As a result of the war, world copper prices rose sharply, with the annual New York average price climbing from 17.275 cents per pound in 1915 to 27.202 cents in the following year. This permitted a substantial increase in copper production from the Yukon and total shipments rose from 533,216 pounds in 1915 to 2,807,096 pounds in 1916, the highest annual production figure ever attained by the industry.[22] Once the war ended, copper prices fell to more normal levels and Yukon copper production once again declined. By 1919 output had fallen back to 165,184 pounds and two years later shipments ceased altogether. Except for intermittent trial shipments in 1925, 1926, and 1927, no copper production has since been recorded for the Yukon Territory.

It is clear that in the case of this copper-mining industry, failure to solve critical transport problems made production commercially possible only under the influence of prices inflated by an unusual demand or in the presence of extraordinary grades of ore. The physical nature of the deposits meant that reserves of such ore could not be maintained.

In some respects the same seemed to be true of the silver-lead–mining operations in the Yukon. The rise in lead prices following the outbreak of war encouraged a rapid expansion of output, which reached a peak in 1916. When market conditions returned to normal, output was sharply curtailed, falling quite rapidly toward the end of the war and ceasing altogether in 1919. Unlike the experience in the copper-mining industry, however, the post-war period saw the discovery of new reserves of very rich silver-lead ore and their development by an organization sufficiently large and vigorous to attack the transport problems which plagued the industry.

The largest part of the Yukon's production of silver-lead ore during the war came from the established Silver King mine on Galena Creek. Production there reached 955,222 pounds in 1916, but fell off with the decline in wartime demand to cease entirely in 1919. Prospecting carried out during these years, however, resulted in the discovery of important silver-lead deposits on six separate hills in the Mayo district. L. Beauvet, the original discoverer of these deposits, struck a very rich silver-lead outcropping on top of Galena Hill in 1919. The Yukon Gold Company, one of the chief placer operators in the Klondike at this time, sponsored further exploration of this deposit and thereby stimulated a significant staking rush in the area. The original claim and a group of others were secured by the Yukon Gold Company which then created a subsidiary,

[22]Yukon copper production is given in Table 4.3.

the "Keno Hill Limited," to develop them. Mining was begun by this company late in 1920.[23]

The early 1920s were years of optimism in the Mayo district. Despite its formidable transportation problems, the Keno Hill Company succeeded in mining and shipping 4,300 tons of high-grade silver-lead ore in 1922. At the same time, a large group of claims in the area was taken over by the Treadwell Yukon Company of San Francisco. This company's operations in 1922 were very encouraging, as the following report suggests:

Development work on these properties has been vigorously prosecuted throughout the year, the results exceeding all expectations. . . . Such large high-grade ore bodies were developed during the winter . . . that the planned production was more than doubled.[24]

Even with the discovery and development of these new sources of very high-grade ore, however, production in the Mayo district continued to be handicapped by the lack of local transportation facilities. As supplies of very rich ores were depleted, it was apparent that further exploitation of these deposits would depend upon improvements being made in transportation facilities or upon the use of procedures to concentrate the ore mined, thereby improving the product's ability to withstand the high transportation charges.

After the failure of a private company organized and chartered for the purpose of building a fifty-mile railroad line along the Stewart and Mayo Rivers, the Mayo district mining operators undertook the improvement of transportation facilities on their own initiative. In 1922 the Treadwell Yukon Company revolutionized winter transport in the north by introducing tractors to haul ore over the forty-mile route to Mayo Landing. The Yukon Gold Commissioner reported in that year that the tractors had reduced hauling costs by over 75 per cent and that the company had decided to use them exclusively in the future.[25]

With this important improvement in the transportation situation combined with continuing high prices for both lead and silver, production from the Mayo region rose to record heights in 1923. That year 6,771,113 pounds of lead were produced along with 1,914,438 ounces of silver. Most of this production was attributable to the two large

---

[23]A. D. Pike, *Brochure on the Yukon Territory,* prepared for the Commonwealth Mining and Metallurgical Congress, September, 1957, and published by United Keno Hill Mines, Limited, p. 16.

[24]D.B.S., *Mineral Statistics 1922,* p. 67.

[25]*Ibid.,* p. 167.

producers already named. Several small companies also produced significant amounts of ore at this time, but due to their small capital they were unable to finance heavy investments in power and transport facilities. Because of this, they were obliged to sell their output to the two large producers who then shipped it to the smelters. In 1923 it was reported that this practice had "greatly encouraged these individual efforts and has materially assisted in the development of the camp."[26]

More intensive utilization of the Mayo district silver-lead deposits was made possible in 1924 when the Treadwell Yukon company invested in a concentrating mill. The problems of operating such a mill under sub-arctic conditions were quickly overcome and by 1924 the mill was processing ores being mined in the district not only by Treadwell Yukon but by many smaller operators as well. In the same year, the position of Treadwell Yukon was further strengthened when it acquired the assets of the United Keno Hill Company. These included the important "Sadie" claim, a waterfront lease on the Stewart River and a small, wood-burning thermal electric power plant. By 1924 the expanding operations of Treadwell Yukon were providing employment for about 100 men in the district.[27]

Under the influence of record prices for silver and lead, production of concentrates and ores from the Mayo district continued to grow and extensive exploratory work maintained ore reserves at a satisfactory level. Because of the successful alleviation of the transport problem through the development of new transport techniques and the construction of the concentrating mill, the district was able to withstand the sharp drop in the prices of these metals which occurred in 1927. Although there was a reduction in total output that year, the chief effect of the price change was to hasten the concentration of production in the Treadwell Yukon Company through the elimination of a number of smaller operators. By 1929 total lead production was up to a record level of 8,395,603 pounds and silver production reached the highest level attained in the Territory to that date. Almost all of this production came from the operations of the Treadwell Yukon Company.

The successful establishment of the Mayo silver-lead mining industry during the period between 1914 and 1929 owed something to unusually favourable metal prices. The fact that it was able to withstand sudden drops in these prices suggests, however, that the industry had progressed beyond a position of marginal existence, depending upon high grades

[26]D.B.S., *Mineral Statistics 1923*, p. 170.
[27]D.B.S., *Mineral Statistics 1924*, p. 158.

alone to maintain its competitive position in outside markets. This had been largely achieved through investment which reduced transport costs. But this investment had been in expensive hauling equipment and in a concentrating plant, so it presupposed, in the absence of public investment in transport, the organization of private enterprise on a rather large scale. So great were the advantages of scale in this situation that one company soon absorbed most of the smaller operators in the district. The same tendency was discernible in the evolution of the Yukon placer gold-mining industry during this same period.

The period from 1914 to 1929 was once again one of steadily decreasing production from the Yukon gold placers. Some signs of recovery were appearing toward the end of the period but, even so, by 1929 total output was down to 35,982 ounces from the 282,838 produced in 1913. The lowest point during the period was reached in 1926 when production fell to 25,601 ounces.

The organization of this industry had become quite stable by the end of the war. Although the actual numbers varied from time to time, three large firms dominated the industry while as many as eighty very small operators continued to exist. The large firms were consistently responsible for about 75 per cent of the total output.

The largest of these was the Yukon Gold Company which had made the extensive investments in water and power facilities described earlier in this chapter. In 1912 this company employed about 143 men in its various operations. The next largest company was the New Northwest Corporation, operating two dredges and employing about 115 men. This company, too, operated a hydro-electric plant, located on the north fork of the Klondike River, which provided power to the company's own dredges and also to the dredges of the Burrall and Baird company, the third of the large operators of the 1920s.[28]

The concentration of power in the Yukon alluvial gold-mining industry which took place throughout the 1920s was essentially a continuation of the process by which company organization had replaced individual entrepreneur-ship during the preceding period. At that time most individual operators were forced out of existence by what were essentially technical problems—as the very rich, easily accessible deposits were exhausted, more and more material had to be handled to obtain a given amount of gold. This could be done only by large-scale processing methods which involved increasing capital inputs to offset the declining value per unit of land used in the production process. As the placer

[28]D.B.S., *Mineral Statistics 1922*, p. 154.

deposits were worked it became necessary to carry this substitution farther and farther, and only large organizations had the financial support to do this. It is doubtful, however, if this process could have been carried much farther than it had been by the middle of the 1920s. By that time it was apparent that the placer operations in the Klondike could be expanded only by developing new land resources. Already, some dredges were operating on land which had been processed once before with the large-scale techniques. But, just as the application of the large-scale techniques had presupposed the existence of large organizations with extensive financial reserves, so did the technical problems associated with prospecting for new low-grade placer sites. These sites could be proved only by exploration, using power drills, carried on over very large areas of ground. In 1920 the federal government incurred the displeasure of the advocates of small-scale mineral development by amending the Yukon Placer Act in order to make even larger land concessions in the Klondike area to the large operators there.[29] This was probably one factor underlying the consolidation of the 1920s. But another was the greater advantage of larger organizations in applying a new technique developed in 1923 for bringing into production previously unworkable placer sites. Until that time, the dredges had been able to work only on gravels that were thawed during the hot Yukon summers. Some of the gravels, however, were permanently frozen and these had not been workable with the dredges. During the 1923 season the Burrall and Baird company demonstrated the feasibility of thawing these frozen gravels in advance of the dredge by using an elaborate system of hydraulic "probes." Drills were used to cut holes, set about 75 feet apart all over the dredging site, into which were fitted pipes connected to a hydraulic pressure system which forced water into the holes to thaw the gravels. By 1926 a large part of the placer gold produced in the Yukon was from artificially thawed gravels.

The advantages of large-scale, integrated operations in this type of operation were obvious. Roads, reservoirs, pumping stations, pipe-lines, power plants and electrical distribution systems were indispensable and could not be efficiently constructed or operated by a number of small independent organizations. Consequently, in 1929, a number of existing interests in the Klondike formed a new company, the Yukon Consolidated Gold Corporation to integrate these various operations. It acquired the dredges operated by the three large companies previously described and undertook the further development of the North Forks power plant

[29]See *House of Commons Debates*, 1920, p. 3107.

which was made the central power source for the whole Klondike district.

The actual production of gold in the Yukon, as shown in Table 4.1, declined steadily from 1914 until 1926 when a slight recovery began. Even so, by 1929 physical production was still only 14 per cent of the 1914 level. Because the price of gold remained constant at $20.67 per ounce throughout this period, the main cause of this deterioration of the industry was the increasing difficulty experienced in locating gravels which could be profitably worked with the existing facilities and organization of the industry. The Dominion Bureau of Statistics report on the industry in 1929 characterized the preceding 20 years as a period of "clean-up extractions and declining recoveries."[30]

As a result of the great decline in gold production in the Yukon between 1914 and 1929 this industry lost its position as the principal primary economic operation in the Territory. Not only did its decline reduce total mineral production by 47 per cent in this period, but by 1929 it contributed only 29 per cent of the total value of mineral production in the Yukon. As a result, the Mayo silver-lead mines surpassed the gold placers as a source of personal income in the Yukon. In 1929 wages and salaries paid in the Mayo operations amounted to $557,260 compared to $372,153 in the Klondike placers.[31]

Although the effect of an 86 per cent reduction in the value of gold output in the Yukon between 1914 and 1929 was partly offset by other mineral production this was not sufficient to prevent a substantial reduction in the general level of economic activity there. This, it will be recalled, was used to justify a considerable reduction in public spending just at a time when such spending could have materially assisted in the development work being attempted by private capital. Evidence was presented in Chapter II which suggested that the federal authorities were not unaware at this time of the underlying obstacles to the development of unusally rich mineral deposits in the Yukon. But, except for some assistance in road building, no direct action was taken to provide the basic capital facilities needed for this kind of development. Instead, the effect of public policy in the Yukon was to encourage the development of local producing monopolies sufficiently large to undertake the provision of these facilities themselves. Although the policy of the government with respect to the disposal of placer lands in the Klondike would suggest that this was a deliberate objective of the

---

[30]D.B.S., *Mineral Statistics 1929*, p. 68.
[31]*Ibid.*, p. 69.

government at this time, it seems more likely to have been a natural consequence of the absence of public investment in certain kinds of capital facilities. In the Klondike placer industry the most important forms of overhead capital were electric power plants and water systems. In the Mayo district silver-lead–mining industry, the provision of transportation facilities was the critical investment of this type. Because of the "lumpiness" of such investments and the substantial economies of scale involved in the operation of the capital facilities created by them, only relatively large private organizations could develop the miniature industrial "complexes" necessary in the absence of public provision of these facilities.

In the Yukon, these larger organizations were created locally out of smaller organizations already located there. To a large extent this appears to have been virtually spontaneous for, in both industries, the smaller operators tended to associate themselves with the larger operators so as to make use of the latter's overhead capital facilities. In the Klondike this took the form of larger operators selling power to those too small to finance their own power supplies. In the Mayo district, the largest operator overcame the transportation problem by acquiring tractors to reduce the cost of the intial transportation stage and by investing heavily in a concentrating mill to make the product better able to withstand the transport costs involved. Smaller producers, unable to undertake such investments themselves, used these facilities on a custom basis and were eventually absorbed into the larger organization. In this way private enterprise was able to establish the beginnings of an efficient mining industry in the Yukon despite the reluctance of the public authority to attack the underlying economic problems involved.

MINERAL DEVELOPMENT IN THE YUKON AND MACKENZIE DISTRICT, 1929–39

The world economic collapse of 1929 created conditions highly favourable to the production of gold, so it is not surprising that there was renewed interest in the mineral resources of the Canadian northwest at that time. Even before the price of gold was officially increased to $35.00 an ounce the declining general price levels and the resulting increase in the purchasing power of an ounce of gold caused producers to subject existing gold deposits to more intensive working: and prospecting, aided by the aeroplane, swept into the undeveloped District of Mackenzie.

The gross value of mineral production in the Yukon during this period fell by almost 50 per cent during the first five years, from a total of $2,521,588 in 1930 to $1,302,308 in 1935. During the next five years this downward trend was reversed and by 1939 the total was up to $4,961,321, the highest value recorded since 1916. This recovery in value terms was chiefly attributable, however, to the increased price of gold.

The principal gold producer in the Yukon, the new Yukon Consolidated Gold Corporation, was well established by 1931 with five dredges and several large hydraulic plants in full-scale operation.[32] The Yukon Gold Commissioner reported in 1932 that: "Throughout the whole Yukon an increased interest has been shown in placer mining. Creeks which were abandoned are now claiming attention and in many cases satisfactory results were attained."[33] This interest intensified in 1933 when the United States price of gold was raised to $35.00 an ounce. The derived Canadian dollar price rose from $21.55 in 1931 to $35.19 in 1935, at which level it remained until 1939.

Although there was a great increase in prospecting activity throughout the Yukon after 1933, most of the actual increase in gold production came from more intensive working of known placer deposits. This increase did not come about immediately, however, partly because of the time required to increase productive capacity in the industry and partly because of difficulties within the Yukon Consolidated Gold Corporation itself. Charges of corruption and mismanagement in this organization were prevalent both in the Yukon and outside at this time. The company's labour policies especially were a source of complaint in the Yukon, with its Member of Parliament observing in the Commons, for example, that the living facilities furnished by the corporation "were not fit habitations for a well-bred dog."[34] In 1935, however, there was a change in the management of the corporation and a large expansion programme was undertaken. In 1936 the company began to improve its power and water facilities. The output of the old hydro-electric plant on the Klondike River was increased by two-thirds, new ditches were constructed and modern pumping plants installed to facilitate the stripping

---

[32]D.B.S., *Mineral Statistics 1931*, p. 51.
[33]Cited in D.B.S., *Mineral Statistics 1932*, p. 59.
[34]*House of Commons Debates*, 1936, p. 2696.

operations in advance of the dredges. The construction of new dredges continued and by 1939 the company had eleven of these plants in operation.

In addition to expanding its operating capacity after 1935, Yukon Consolidated also succeeded in increasing the utilization of its existing plant. This was achieved by devising ways of lengthening the operating season for the dredges. In 1938 two of these succeeded in operating until the 24th and 25th of December respectively, the latest dates ever worked by dredges in the Yukon. As a result of this increase both in plant and in its rate of utilization, the corporation succeeded in processing 10,141,189 cubic yards of gravel in 1939 compared to the 7,957,108 it was able to handle in 1936.[35] In 1939 the Yukon Consolidated Gold Corporation produced 84.6 per cent of the Yukon's gold output. The balance came from individual operators working the old placer sites, from a few larger operators such as the Holbrook Dredging Company, and from the lode mines.

The unusually favourable conditions confronting gold producers in the 1930s gave new encouragement to those seeking lode gold in the Yukon. Intermittent attempts to develop lode properties had been made since the days of the Klondike rush, but continuous production had never been achieved. In the early 1930s a strong attempt was made to develop such properties in the Carmacks district and, as a result of encouraging developments on Mount Freegold there, more than 600 quartz-mining grants were made in the district by 1935. As in the case of the copper mines, however, sufficient reserves of high-grade ore could not be maintained and by 1939 the mines had been abandoned.

From the foregoing account it will be clear that, even under the unusually favourable conditions confronting gold producers during the 1930s, attempts at extensive expansion were disappointing in both the alluvial and lode branches of the industry. Although there was a significant expansion of production under the influence of falling costs and rising prices, this was achieved through more intensive operations on existing properties. The only important discoveries of new mineral resources made in the Yukon during this period were not of gold, but of silver-lead deposits.

Although silver prices had been declining since 1920 and lead prices since 1925, by 1929 the Treadwell Yukon operations in the Mayo district appeared to be well established and yielding a satisfactory profit. In the early 1930s, however, when silver and lead prices were at their

[35]D.B.S., *Mineral Statistics 1939*, p. 59.

lowest levels in a decade, the company was confronted by a sudden deterioration in its reserve position. By the summer of 1932 the principal deposits on Keno Hill were exhausted and, in November the concentrating mill there had to be closed down. It is interesting from the standpoint of northern operating conditions to note that this mill, the most northerly on the continent, had operated for 94.05 per cent of the time between January 6, 1925, when it was opened and November 16, 1932, when it was closed.[36]

Once again the demise of the Yukon silver-lead industry appeared imminent. With low prices for lead and silver and the exhaustion of the main ore deposits on Keno Hill, most of those engaged in silver-lead operations in the Mayo district left to seek employment elsewhere. In 1933, however, the Treadwell Yukon Company undertook development work on several old workings on Galena Hill and, as a result of surprising ore discoveries there, resumed large-scale mining in 1935.[37] In that year a new 250-ton mill was installed on Galena Hill to concentrate ores from the previously abandoned Elsa and Silver King mines. And in 1936 it was announced that the company expected to expand its production beyond the levels previously reached.

These plans for a large expansion of production in the Mayo district were thwarted in 1937, however, when the British Yukon Navigation Company lost a steamer and had its carrying capacity reduced to 10,000 tons a season.[38] During the next two years the Treadwell Yukon company shipped ores to the extent permitted by the available river transport.

From the foregoing it is evident that despite the many difficulties which beset it between 1929 and 1939 the end of this period found the Yukon silver-lead–mining industry, if not expanded, at least no worse off than it had been at the beginning. The effects of falling prices and reserves had been offset by the discovery of new, high-grade deposits of ore. In the Yukon mining industry as a whole, the years from 1929 to 1939 were, in general, years of contraction because of decreasing silver-lead production and the delay experienced by the chief gold producer in expanding output in response to increased gold prices. After 1935, however, gold production expanded rapidly and surpassed all previous production since the end of the war. For the mining industry as a whole, therefore, the decade of the 1930s ended with a

[36]See D.B.S., *Mineral Statistics 1931*, p. 67.
[37]A. E. Pike, *Brochure on the Yukon Territory*, p. 16.
[38]Yukon Territory, *Report of the Territorial Controller*, March 31, 1937.

higher level of production than it began with. The period opened with a total average annual employment of 455 and closed with 728. Salaries and wages were up by $675,058 over 1929 and, during the last five years of the period, population in the Yukon actually increased by 25 per cent to reach a total of about 5,000 by 1939. This increase in population must be attributed to immigration associated with the revival of the mineral industries after 1935, for the Territory had a negative rate of natural increase from 1924 until 1937, at which time births exceeded deaths by the narrow margin of 0.4 per 1000 of population.[39]

Mineral Development in the District of Mackenzie

It has already been noted that in the late 1920s considerable interest was shown in the mineral resources of the District of Mackenzie when, through the use of aircraft, it became economically feasible to carry out extensive prospecting over the great distance involved in exploring such country.[40]

During the 1928 season, Gilbert Labine, with one of the several parties then prospecting in the Great Bear Lake area, noted an interesting mineral showing on the east shore of the lake. The following year he returned with a partner to stake claims on what turned out to be a major pitchblende-silver deposit. Capital was raised by incorporating the Eldorado Gold Mines Limited and development work on the property was begun. Although a number of other properties were staked near the original claim, only one of these was developed and it was eventually taken over by the Labine organization which thereafter dominated the entire development.

The chief problems encountered in establishing the mine at what became known as Port Radium on Great Bear Lake were associated with the complexity of the ore mined, the inadequacy of transport facilities and the absence of power supplies. Two distinct types of ore were mined at Port Radium, one containing mostly pitchblende and some silver, the other containing mostly silver along with copper and some other metals. In 1933 a concentrating mill was completed at the mine to concentrate both types of ore. The silver-copper concentrates were then shipped to custom smelters at Tacoma, Washington. The pitchblende-silver produced presented difficult processing problems,

---

[39]D.B.S., *Vital Statistics 1956*, p. 68.
[40]See J. A. Wilson, "The Expansion of Aviation into Arctic and Sub-Arctic Canada," *Canadian Geographical Journal*, XLI (September 1950), 136; see also *House of Commons Debates*, 1928, p. 1580.

but with the technical assistance of the federal Department of Mines, the company devised a process for separating the various elements and for extracting refined radium from the pitchblende. This process was carried out at a special refinery built by the company at Port Hope on Lake Ontario. The value of the radium and uranium compounds produced at Port Hope was so high that it justified the extensive use of aircraft for moving the more valuable concentrates over the remarkable distances separating the mine and the refinery.[41] (The problems of transporting equipment and supplies into Mackenzie District during the 1930s will be described in Chapter 7.)

The solution to the power problem at Port Radium was provided by the Norman Wells oil field. This operation was re-activated by Imperial Oil to supply diesel fuel to Eldorado which then generated its own diesel-electric power at the mine. Thus, by 1934, the mining of pitchblende-silver ores was successfully established only 25 miles south of the Arctic Circle. By 1936 the annual gross value of production from this mine was exceeding $1,000,000—and in 1939 reached $2,391,325. Of this total, well over $2,000,000 must have been attributable to the radioactive materials produced.[42]

The development of this mine at Port Radium had a marked effect on the economic character of Mackenzie District in so far as it encouraged the improvement of transport facilities, provided a market for local oil production and demonstrated, to government and industry alike, the possibility of large-scale mining operations under far northern conditions. These effects were reinforced after 1935 by the development of auriferous quartz-mining at Yellowknife.

Gold was discovered at Yellowknife Bay on Great Slave Lake in 1896 by miners on their way to the Klondike, but it was not until the great renewal of prospecting in 1933 that any interest was shown in the area. Large numbers of claims were staked there in that year and by 1935 it was reported that the entire shoreline of Yellowknife Bay had been staked to a depth of several miles. A number of large companies, including the Consolidated Mining and Smelting Company of Canada, began to sink shafts on the "Con," "Negus," and "Giant" claims in 1936 and 1937.[43]

Commercial gold production began in the Yellowknife district in

---

[41]D.B.S., *Mineral Statistics 1937*, p. 97.
[42]Estimated from D.B.S. data on silver production and pitchblende-silver ores mined in the years indicated.
[43]D.B.S., *Mineral Statistics 1937*, p. 83.

September, 1938, when a gold brick weighing 72½ lbs. was poured at the Con mine. The following year, when the Negus mine came into production, 51,914 ounces of gold with a value of $1,876,224 were produced.[44] Further development of the industry was halted, however, by the outbreak of World War II.

Taking these developments all together we see that under conditions highly favourable to the production of gold, the output of this metal in the Yukon was greatly expanded during the decade of the 1930s. The silver-lead–mining industry of the Territory made little progress during this period, for low metal prices and failing reserves restricted production during the first half of the decade and the expansion made possible by the discovery of new reserves on previously abandoned property during the latter half of the decade was restricted by the limited carrying capacity of the available transport system. But the combined effect of the two industries was to expand total mineral output considerably over the levels of the preceding period and to raise employment and earnings in the mining industry as a whole to much higher levels. During this period the population of the Yukon Territory grew by about 25 per cent as a result of this expansion of economic activity.

In view of the marked reduction in federal expenditures in the Yukon during this period, almost all this expansion was attributable to investments made by the very large operators already located in the Yukon. Despite the boom in prospecting activity throughout the Territory over these years, no important new mineral deposits were developed there. Virtually all the increase in actual production resulted from the redevelopment of existing deposits and the application of more capital-intensive methods of exploiting them. What large-scale development of virgin land resources did take place in the northwest during this period was located in the previously unexploited District of Mackenzie.

The central problem associated with the development of mineral resources in Mackenzie District was the inadequacy of the available transport facilities. This affected mineral development in two ways: by limiting the rate of development through lack of carrying capacity into the district and by keeping freight rates so high as to impose high operating costs upon those mines which were developed. Because of the latter effect, only those minerals which had a very high value per unit weight of product could be developed and only the very richest deposits of even these minerals could be successfully exploited. Under these conditions the mineral development in Mackenzie District was limited

[44]See Table 4.1.

to the production of gold and radioactive metals. By 1939, however, these minerals were being produced on a large scale from mines which appeared to be operating sufficiently above the margin of commercial profitability to have a reasonable chance of long-term survival. On this basis, permanent mining camps were established, transport expanded, and a small labour force imported into the district. Between 1921 and 1938 the population of the Northwest Territories increased by 37.5 per cent from 8,000 to 11,000, all of which was attributable to white migration into the mining camps of Mackenzie District. Admittedly, much of this development was stimulated by the unusually high returns to gold production under the conditions of the 1930s. Moreover, the soundness of this development from the standpoint of world demand for the district's output was not to be tested for some years because of the extraordinary changes wrought by World War II in both the market and the supply conditions affecting the industries of Mackenzie District.

THE MINERAL INDUSTRIES OF THE NORTH DURING WORLD WAR II AND THE IMMEDIATE POST-WAR YEARS

The economic development of the territorial north between 1939 and 1949 was greatly affected by the first rewakening of national interest in its problems since the 1890s. This interest was initially motivated not by any new recognition of the economic potential of the area but by considerations of continental defence. Indeed, the immediate effect of the war was seriously to disrupt the established forces of development in the north.

Despite the healthy condition of the Yukon gold-mining industry in 1939 and the further help it received in 1940 when the Canadian dollar price of gold rose from 36.14 to 38.50, like the rest of the industry it was thereafter afflicted with a growing labour shortage as men were lost in increasing numbers to the armed forces and to more essential employments. In the Yukon this was perhaps more serious than in most other areas because of the sudden creation there of alternative labour opportunities associated with the great defence projects carried out early in the war. Because of them, attempts to substitute local (native) labour for imported labour were less successful than they might otherwise have been. By 1943 only 175 men could be found to fill the 400 jobs normally available in the industry and Yukon gold production fell by 50 per cent both in 1943 and again in 1944.

Reconstruction in the Yukon gold industry took place only slowly after the end of the war. Because of a persisting labour shortage and a drop in the price of gold, by 1949 actual production (while four times the 1944 amount) was still 5,775 ounces below the amount produced in 1939. Despite the slow recovery in production, however, there was considerable prospecting and development activity in the Yukon associated with placer and quartz properties between 1945 and 1949. Several new placer mining companies appeared in 1945 and undertook the development of a number of placer sites, although the industry continued to be dominated by one larger producer, the Yukon Consolidated Gold Corporation. The latter regularly accounted for about two-thirds of the total production.[45] The net effect of the war upon the Yukon placer gold-mining industry then was simply to reduce production from established properties which returned to their normal operations once wartime restrictions on labour and supplies were removed.

The experience in the silver-lead–mining industry was again rather different. The Treadwell Yukon Company, which had been responsible for the successful re-establishment of the Yukon silver-lead–mining industry in the 1920s, by the end of the 1930s was producing at a very high level in relation to the apparent capacity of the industry. In the early 1940s, however, the company found that its ore reserves were near exhaustion and preparations were made to close the mines. Although the mill continued to operate through the 1940, 1941, and 1942 seasons, total production dropped rapidly and the final shipments were made in 1942. The following year the company was liquidated.

The Treadwell Yukon Company had achieved a remarkable production record at Mayo, particularly when its operating conditions are taken into account. It had produced 624,570 tons of ore which had yielded 44,338,696 ounces of silver and 96,023,566 pounds of lead. True, this ore had varied greatly in grade, but it was all relatively rich, ranging from about 54 ounces of silver per ton in some claims to a remarkable 102.4 ounces in the richest. During the twenty-one years of its operation, the company produced more than 21 million dollars worth of metals and was reported to have "returned a very handsome profit."[46]

---

[45]Canada, Department of Mines and Resources, Lands, Parks and Forests Branch, *Report of the Bureau of the Northwest Territories and Yukon Affairs 1946* (Ottawa, 1947), p. 91. This series of reports is hereafter cited as *Bureau of the Northwest Territories and Yukon Affairs* followed by the year covered by the report.
[46]Pike, *Brochure on the Yukon Territory*, p. 19.

Little further interest was taken in the base metal resources the Yukon until the end of the war. In 1945 the Yukon Northwest Exploration Company acquired claims on Keno Hill and the former properties of the Treadwell Yukon Company were taken over by a newly formed organization, the Keno Hill Mining Company.[47] These developments were part of a general post-war increase in mining activity throughout the northwest which was largely attributable to the high metal prices expected, and in large part realized, after the war. By 1948, for example, lead prices were three times the 1939 average. The rapidity with which prospecting in the Yukon boomed after the war was made possible by the opening up of large areas of previously inaccessible territory which occurred during the war.

The most significant of the base metal development projects in the Yukon at this time was that organized by the Keno Hill Mining Company on the old Treadwell Yukon properties. By 1947 this company had re-developed these properties and during that year produced over 1,000,000 pounds of lead concentrates.[48] The Keno Hill Company was reorganized in 1947 and its name changed to United Keno Hill Mines Limited. This reorganization was prompted by the need for larger capitalization which was attributed, in part, to the necessity of acquiring sufficient working capital to "finance production during the long period from September to June when the Stewart and Yukon Rivers are closed to navigation."[49] This seasonal transport problem has been characteristic of northern mining development dependent upon river transport. The subsequent annual winter hiatus in transport has tended to increase costs of operation by requiring larger investments in working capital and in inventories.

By the end of 1949 the United Keno Hill Limited was firmly established in the Mayo district. Within two years it had found at least temporary solutions to the most formidable problems presented by operating a sub-arctic silver-lead mine. The very high fuel costs associated with such an operation were reduced by replacing increasingly costly wood fuel with coal mined near Carmacks by a subsidiary company created for the purpose. The problems of transport were not to be solved for some years, but in the meantime a subsidiary agency was established in Whitehorse to expedite movement of supplies and outgoing shipments of concentrates and ore. Several other companies were

[47]*Bureau of Northwest Territories and Yukon Affairs 1946*, p. 92.
[48]*Bureau of Northwest Territories and Yukon Affairs 1947*, p. 95.
[49]United Keno Hill Mines Limited, *First Annual Report* (Toronto, 1947).

active in the Mayo district at this time, but they did not contribute a significant part of the total production from the area.

By the end of 1949 physical production in the Mayo mining industry had reached its pre-war level and, because of price increases, an even higher level of production in value terms. But, as in the placer gold fields, the post-war recovery was attributable to operations carried out on land resources first developed many years earlier and, despite the far-reaching prospecting boom in the early post-war period, no new properties had been brought into production by 1949. It will also be shown later in this chapter that the war had relatively little effect upon the underlying economic "problem" of the Yukon. This was quite unlike the experience in Mackenzie District between 1939 and 1949, for there the war delayed a vigorous new mineral development, altered significantly the basic transport and supply situation during the period of delay and, with its termination, released strengthened forces of growth.

Upon the outbreak of war, the Yellowknife gold-mining industry was just passing from the development to the production stage. This growth continued until 1942, in which year actual gold production amounted to about 100,000 fine ounces. Because of the same conditions previously noted in connection with the Yukon placers, the Yellowknife development was halted in 1942 when two of the six operating mines were closed. During the next two years the other mines were closed down as well and by the fall of 1944 gold production from the area ceased entirely.

With the end of the war, Yellowknife became a major mining and prospecting centre. Great interest was shown in the Yellowknife area itself where a major staking rush took place after extensive diamond drilling along the west side of the Bay revealed large bodies of auriferous quartz ore. The issue of new mining licences increased by almost ten times in 1945–46, by which time there were about 200 companies incorporated to conduct operations in the area.

A number of factors contributed to the Yellowknife boom in 1945. One of these was certainly the promise which had been indicated by the operations of the Negus, Con-Rycon, and other mines brought into production at the beginning of the war. This was supplemented by successful exploration on properties such as the Giant which was found to be located on an immense ore body. Another factor was the federal government's decision to undertake responsibility for the development of hydro-electric power in the area.[50] The transportation problem was

[50]As described in Chapter 8.

also alleviated by the agreement between the Alberta and federal governments to build an all-weather highway from the Grimshaw railhead to Hay River, just across the lake from Yellowknife.

When the Canadian dollar was established at par with the American in July, 1946, the capital sustaining the Yellowknife boom was withdrawn and the extensive development was halted. Nevertheless, work continued on a number of the well-established properties, several of which showed promise of becoming major producers. The Negus mine was re-opened early in 1946 and was joined in the fall of the year by the Con and Rycon mines. Great promise was shown in the same year at the Giant mine where shaft-sinking was in progress. Joint drilling undertaken on the Con and Negus properties confirmed earlier suspicions that they were located on extensions of the Giant ore body. Thus, the mines which formed the nucleus of the Yellowknife gold-mining industry seemed to be assured of a reasonably long productive life.

The development of these properties in the immediate post-war years was made under difficult general conditions. Labour continued to be in short supply, the Canadian dollar price of gold was down from $38.50 to $35.00 and operating costs were rising rapidly, thereby creating unfavourable conditions in the Canadian gold-mining industry generally. The resulting distress in the industry led to the federal Emergency Gold Mining Assistance Act, legislation establishing a federal subsidy to gold producers in Canada to compensate for increased production costs after December, 1947. The payments, to continue for three years, were to be determined by taking half the amount by which the mine's cost of production exceeded $18.00 per fine ounce and applying this to the amount by which production in the assistance year exceeded two-thirds of the production of a base year—the twelve months ended June 30, 1947.[51]

The estimated assistance payable under this arrangement in 1948 was $919,418 to the Yellowknife mines and $285,327 to the placer mines in the Yukon. In 1949 the payments were estimated at $968,846 and $366,693 respectively.[52] It might be noted here that the published net profit of the Giant Yellowknife mine in 1949 was $167,552.[53] The net profit before depreciation and other write-offs of the Yukon Consolidated Gold Corporation was $744,810 in 1949.[54]

By the end of 1947 three of the large producers were once again in

[51]*Statutes of Canada*, Geo. VI, c. 15.
[52]D.B.S., *The Gold Mining Industry 1954*, p. B-13.
[53]Giant Yellowknife Gold Mines Limited, *Annual Report 1949* (Toronto, 1949).
[54]Yukon Consolidated Gold Corporation, *Annual Statement* (Vancouver, 1949).

large-scale production. In that year the Consolidated Mining and Smelting Company produced 42,284 fine ounces of gold, the Negus Mines 17,118 fine ounces and the Thompson-Lundmark properties accounted for 3,062 fine ounces of the total.[55] Total employment had risen to 500 and the end of the following year found it at 649. Total production in 1948 was double that of 1939.[56]

This expansion continued through 1949. In part this was due to improved conditions generally in the industry throughout Canada. During 1949 the supply of labour and materials became somewhat easier, the mines were earning subsidies, and additional encouragement was given by the alteration in exchange regulations which brought about an increase in the Canadian dollar price of gold once again to $38.50 per ounce. A particular factor which assisted in the expansion of the Yellowknife field was the completion in 1948 of a hydro-electric power station on the Snare River which did much to alleviate the shortage of power which had previously hindered operations in the area. This power development will be described in more detail later in this study.

The other major industry of Mackenzie District during this period was the pitchblende-silver–mining industry located on Great Bear Lake and operated by the Eldorado Gold Mines Limited. By the fall of 1939 Eldorado had developed an extensive transportation system, a large and complex concentrating plant at the mine and a refinery at Port Hope, Ontario. With the collapse of radium markets as a result of the war, the Eldorado properties were closed down in June, 1940. Two years later the mine was reopened "with a minimum of publicity" to supply the uranium required for the United States atomic bomb project.[57] At that time a complete censorship was imposed upon the production data relating to the operations.

On January 27, 1944, all the property and assets of Eldorado Gold Mines Limited were expropriated by the federal government and put under the control of a crown corporation, the Eldorado Mining and Refining (1944) Limited and it was reported that the operations at Port Radium were "greatly expanded."[58] Very little information concerning the operations of Eldorado in the early post-war years is available. In

[55]D.B.S., *Mineral Statistics 1947–8*, p. 57.

[56]*Ibid.*, p. 72.

[57]See W. D. G. Hunter, "The Development of the Canadian Uranium Industry: An Experiment in Public Enterprise," *Canadian Journal of Economics and Political Science*, XXVIII (August, 1962) pp. 329–31.

[58]Canada, Department of Mines and Resources, *Industries of the Northwest Territories* (Ottawa, 1953), p. 10.

general, production appears to have increased, employment continued to exceed 200 and numerous improvements in the operation were made. Ore reserves were maintained and extensive exploratory operations were carried out on neighbouring properties.[59]

By appropriating the Eldorado properties in 1942 the government had, in effect, nationalized the production of radioactive materials in Canada. Orders-in-council passed in 1943 reserved all rights on radioactive minerals located on crown lands in the Yukon and Northwest Territories to the government of Canada. These provisions were extended by the Transitional Measures Act of 1947.[60] In 1948, however, the government, while retaining Eldorado and making it the official refining and marketing agency for radioactive materials, announced a policy which entrusted future development of radioactive ore deposits to private enterprise. Although the government had itself sponsored prospecting and development work for radioactive minerals with considerable success during the war, the new policy indicated that it intended to encourage private prospecting and development programmes in accordance with its belief that, in the words of C. D. Howe, "minerals in the ground should not be subject to control."[61] The basis for this latter judgment was never made explicit. In his study of the Canadian uranium industry, however, Professor Hunter has pointed out that in 1947 the government had to decide "whether to perpetuate its state monopoly or to permit private investment in the industry." He suggests that the reason for its choice was reluctance to commit public funds to a venture as risky as uranium prospecting.

While Canada has had a long tradition of government intervention in the economy, there are but few cases of government ownership in the mining industry. It was not simply a question of running an established mine, but of spending public money in an effort to find new commercial deposits. In view of the uncertainties of exploration it is not surprising that the policy-makers invited private industry to enter the field.[62]

Such an approach would be quite consistent with other aspects of federal policy in the north generally in the early post-war years as we will see when its policies with respect to investment in transportation and power facilities are examined in Part III.

[59]*Bureau of Northwest Territories and Yukon Affairs*, 1945, p. 66.
[60]*Statutes of Canada*, 11 Geo. VI, c. 16 (1947).
[61]*House of Commons Debates*, 1948, p. 2353.
[62]Hunter, "The Development of the Canadian Uranium Industry: An Experiment in Public Enterprise," p. 332.

In any event, the government's new policy of encouraging private enterprise to develop uranium resources did lead to extensive prospecting for radioactive ores both in the Territories and in other parts of Canada during the late 1940s and early 1950s.

THE METALLIC MINERAL INDUSTRIES AFTER THE POST-WAR RECONSTRUCTION

During the years following the end of World War II the value of mineral production in the Yukon and Northwest Territories increased markedly, leaving no doubt that the future development of the area would depend upon the continued performance of these industries. On the other hand, this post-war expansion of output was attributable more to the further development of known mineral resources, and indeed of established mining centres, than to major discoveries either of new kinds of minerals or of entirely new ore bodies.

Total metallic mineral production in the Yukon and Northwest Territories is shown in Tables 4.4 and 4.5 where it will be noted that the rate at which the total value of mineral production increased was about the same in both the Yukon and the Territories. Prior to 1954, however, the value of mineral output in the Territories is greatly understated due to the exclusion of the value of uranium production. Consequently, the Territories probably led the Yukon in terms of value of minerals produced throughout most of the post-war period.

The relative importance of each mineral industry contributing to these totals is interesting, partly because it indicates the extent to which the demand for the output of the northwest in an "administered" demand. Table 4.5 shows the composition of total metallic mineral output for the Territories from 1945 to 1961. It will be seen from the table that in 1954 uranium was the most important single export from the territorial north, accounting for 36 per cent of the total value of mineral production from the combined Territories. Gold production accounted for 30.9 per cent of the total in the same year. Thus, two-thirds of total mineral production from the north derived from the production of two minerals, uranium and gold. Virtually all the pitchblende ore was mined at Great Bear Lake in the Territories by the crown corporation, Eldorado Mining and Refining (1944) Limited. The entire product was bought at fixed prices by the same company acting as the government's purchasing agent for all radioactive ore mined in Canada. Gold production was also bought, almost entirely, by the federal government at the fixed price of $35.00(U.S.) per fine ounce. It follows from this that even after wartime price controls were removed, the largest part of the total mineral production of the northwest was not produced in response to price changes established in the market, but in response to changes in administered prices. This is not to say that the effective price to the producer for gold did not fluctuate during these years—it did vary in response to changes in the exchange rate between Canada and the United States as shown in Table 4.7. There is no doubt, however, that the chief industries of the northwest have been insulated from the market forces which would otherwise be assumed to determine the demand for these products. The market plays a relatively small direct role in determining the output of those industries which account for approximately two-thirds of the mineral production of the territorial north.

The most important part of the area's production which is more or less directly exposed to market fluctuations of demand is the silver-lead-zinc–mining industry, consisting for practical purposes of only one firm, the United Keno Hill Mines Limited. Total production of these three metals (including some silver produced by gold-mining companies) contributed 30.7 per cent to the total value of mineral production from the combined Territories. Lead and zinc prices were government controlled between 1939 and 1947, but this had no effect upon operations in the northwest because the existing mines there closed in 1942 and did not reopen until 1947. After controls were removed in June, 1947, the price of lead[63] rose sharply and, although it fluctuated considerably thereafter, it reached a record post-war level of $18.30 per pound in 1951. Thereafter it declined erratically and in the early 1960s hovered around 10 cents per pound. The initial post-war period of high lead prices doubtlessly assisted in the re-establishment of the industry in the Yukon. The subsequent fluctuations enabled that industry to demonstrate its ability to compete in a free market despite its location.

It must not be inferred from this that the other mineral industries of the northwest owe their existence to federal support. Although they produced at what was essentially an administered price, sold their product to the state and, in the case of gold, drew a direct subsidy on production, they enjoyed no advantages not shared by all producers of gold and uranium in Canada.

Looking first at the uranium-mining operations we find that at the

[63]Toronto and Montreal prices. See Table 4.8.

end of World War II an intensive development programme was undertaken on the Eldorado properties at Port Radium on Great Bear Lake. As a result of this work the ore reserves there were again built up after having been seriously depleted during the later years of the war. By 1949 these reserves were higher than at any previous time in the Eldorado mine's history. In 1952 the mine was provided with a new gravity mill and a leaching plant to treat reclaimed tailings. Although ore reserves began to decline both in quantity and in grade by 1953, these additions to plant made it possible to maintain production levels. Strenuous efforts to increase development underground in 1954 met with little success, although it did prevent the decline in reserves from becoming critical for several more years.

During the early 1950s, the prospecting and geological studies carried out under government direction in many other parts of Canada began to yield returns, as did the work of a number of private concerns which had entered the field after the federal government authorized private prospecting and mining for uranium in 1948.

The first discovery to be developed was the Ace mine, an Eldorado property located in the Beaverlodge region in northern Saskatchewan, an area in which the metal had been known to occur since the 1930s. This property came into production in 1953 and was joined by the large Gunner mine in the same district two years later. The latter mine was provided with a processing plant with an initial daily capacity of 1,250 tons, more than four times that of the Great Bear Lake plant.

This proliferation of uranium-mining properties continued during 1954. It was reported that, "During the years from about 1950 to 1954 more persons were prospecting for uranium than for any other metal in Canada, and more uranium prospects were being explored than those of any other kind."[64]

Some of this activity was located in the Northwest Territories, and the development of the Beaverlodge district in Northern Saskatchewan was in some ways related to development in the Territories. This was chiefly because of the remoteness of the Beaverlodge district and its integration into the Mackenzie River waterway transportation system which had been originally developed, in part at least, to serve the even more remote operation on Great Bear Lake. Despite this, developments in uranium mining after 1954 moved the centre of interest away from

[64]Canada, Department of Mines and Technical Surveys, *The Canadian Mineral Industry 1955* (Ottawa, 1959), p. 110.

the remote prospects of the north to less remote areas in Ontario and British Columbia. The greatest interest came to be centred on the Blind River (Elliot Lake) district in Ontario where large properties came into production in 1955 and 1956. It is significant that the Ontario uranium mines developed low-grade ores containing on the average about 0.1 per cent of uranium (U_3O_8).[65] The ores at Port Radium, on the other hand, were of a very high grade—in the neighbourhood of 0.6 per cent.

Although as many as 21 new radioactive properties were reported in the Northwest Territories during 1955, only one new mine was brought into production, a mine on the Rayrock Mines Limited property located in the Marian River region north of Yellowknife. This mine was developed as a small operation using high-grade ore and employing about 150 men in 1957 and 1958. Its mill capacity was only 150 tons per day. Production began during 1957 with grade averaging more than six pounds of U_3O_8 per ton of ore mined.[66]

Despite the Rayrock development, by 1958 the Northwest Territories had become a relatively minor source of Canadian uranium production, accounting for less than four per cent of it.[67] In that year the Northwest Territories produced 456 tons of U_3O_8 compared to almost 10,000 tons from Ontario and nearly 3,000 from Saskatchewan. By 1959 it was clear that in view of the collapse in world markets for uranium no new properties would be developed in the Territories, or in any other part of Canada in the forseeable future. And even the existing developments at Great Bear Lake and Marian River were doomed by this time. The Rayrock mine closed down in July, 1959, "Owing to failure to locate ore in economic quantities below the 500-foot level." And it was announced that the Great Bear Lake mine was finally exhausted. The last ore was hoisted there on September 16, 1960, and the mine closed down shortly thereafter. It had operated as a uranium mine for eighteen years.

The closing of Port Radium serves to mark the collapse of the phenomenal boom in Canadian uranium production which occurred between 1956 and 1959. But it also marked, temporarily at least, the disappearance of what in the 1950s had promised to be one of the

[65]Canada, Department of Mines and Technical Surveys, *The Canadian Mineral Industry 1957, Mineral Report Number 2* (Ottawa, 1961), p. 220. This series of reports is hereafter cited as *Mineral Report Number*, followed by the year to which the report pertains.
[66]*Mineral Report Number 5, 1959*, pp. 234–5.
[67]See Table 4.9.

leading points of resource development in the Northwest Territories.[68] (For data on the value of uranium produced in the Territories relative to the value of other metals produced there see Table 4.10.)

The other principal mining industry in the north during this period was, of course, the gold-mining industry. The dependence of the territorial economy upon gold was, however, greatly reduced in the post-war period by the development of silver- lead- zinc- and uranium-mining. In the Yukon Territory in 1945 gold accounted for 71 per cent of total mineral production. Alluvial gold production increased in absolute terms during the post-war period until the 1950s during which it remained more or less steady, running between 50 and 80 thousand fine ounces annually.[69] But because of the growth in silver-lead-zinc production during the same decade, this gold production came to account for only about 20 per cent of the total value of Yukon mineral production.

In the Northwest Territories gold production increased greatly throughout the post-war period, but it was probably exceeded in most earlier years of the period by the value of uranium production. Because of the continued growth in gold output and the decline in uranium production after 1953, however, gold regained its position as the chief industry of the Territories in terms of the annual value of production. Gold contributed 39 per cent of the total value of mineral production in the Territories in 1954, 54 per cent in 1956, 47 per cent in 1958, 52 per cent in 1960, and almost 80 per cent in 1961.

The physical volume of production and the value of production is shown against the Canadian dollar price of gold in Table 4.7. It will be seen there that the reconstruction of the industry in the northwest after the war took place despite the severe drop in the Canadian dollar price of gold consequent upon the establishment of the Canadian dollar at par with the United States dollar in July 1946. This was a difficult period for the entire Canadian gold-mining industry, for it was afflicted not only with the drop in price, but also with a continuing labour shortage and rapidly rising costs of production. Despite this, the Yukon placer operations were expanded and, in the Territories, Yellowknife was in the midst of a major boom in auriferous quartz development. The strength of this industry in the Territories under these conditions indicates that it has not been a marginal operation despite its peculiar

---

[68]In September, 1964, it was announced that Echo Bay Mines Limited, an Edmonton-based company, was re-opening the Port Radium mining camp to produce silver from known silver-bearing ores not previously worked because of low silver prices.

[69]See Table 4.1.

disadvantages relative to its competitors elsewhere in Canada. Physical production in the Yukon expanded steadily to a peak of 93,339 ounces in 1950. In the Northwest Territories expansion continued without serious interruption. In 1960 a record 418,104 fine ounces were produced. The general situation of the gold-mining industry was improved by 1949 through an easing of the labour situation, an increase in the Canadian dollar price of gold and the enactment of legislation to provide all gold producers with a direct subsidy.

As noted earlier, in 1947 the federal government introduced the Emergency Gold Mining Assistance Act which made provision for the Department of Mines and Resources to administer payments to gold mines to assist in defraying the increased costs of production for a period of three years. The payment, it will be recalled, was determined by taking half the amount by which the individual mine's cost of production per fine ounce of gold exceeded $18.00 and applying this to the amount by which output in the assistance year exceeded two-thirds of the production of the base year—the twelve months ended June 30, 1947. The provisions of this act were extended in 1950 and continued through 1954. In 1955 the government announced that because the economic situation which necessitated this assistance to gold mines still existed, the provisions would be extended through 1956 on a somewhat reduced basis. A new formula was introduced whereby the rate would be established at two-thirds of the amount by which the average cost of producing an ounce of gold from the mine during the year exceeded $26.50 per ounce. Under the new provisions this rate of assistance per ounce was not to exceed $12.33 and, instead of using production in a base year to determine the number of ounces upon which the subsidy was to be paid, payment was to be on the basis of two-thirds of total *current* production. Hence, maximum allowable cost of production qualifying for subsidy could not exceed $45.00. The purpose of the new provisions was reported to be to make possible greater assistance to higher cost mines, thereby assisting communities "which are dependent upon gold mines for their existence."[70] The effect of the change was not great in the Yukon, but in the Northwest Territories it resulted in a substantial reduction in the rate of assistance. A mild protest was made to the government by Yellowknife interests but the reduction in assistance there did not appear to affect production which, in fact, continued to increase. In 1960 the act was again amended to extend its

---

[70]See *House of Commons Debates*, 1955, p. 1570.

application for another three years,[71] but by this time the three operating mines at Yellowknife had reduced their operating costs to below the level which would qualify them for benefits under the act.

Activity in the gold-mining industry in Canada as a whole remained sluggish throughout the entire period from 1949 to 1960 despite the contribution the GMA Act made toward offsetting rising production costs. This was partly because of the relatively low gold prices of the period. Although the average Canadian dollar price of gold rose to $38.05 in 1950, it subsequently fell and remained at, or even below, $34.00 (Canadian) throughout most of the decade of the 1950s. Between 1949 and 1961 no large lode gold mine was brought into production in Canada and, in fact, many established mines ceased operations. Against this background the performance of the lode gold mines in the Northwest Territories during the period suggests considerable strength, for physical output continued to increase fairly steadily. In the placer fields of the Yukon, however, the steadily rising operating costs made it difficult to maintain the production levels of the late 1940s.

The Yukon alluvial gold-mining industry was relatively stable from the end of World War II through the 1950s. Output increased somewhat until 1950 and then declined to remain at an average of about 75,000 ounces per year over the next ten years. The Yukon Consolidated Gold Corporation continued to dominate the industry. In 1951, 69 per cent of the output came from this company, 11 per cent from two closely associated companies (Yukon Gold Placers and Clear Creek Placers), 9 per cent from Yukon Exploration Limited and the remainder from the usual very small operators. It was reported in 1951 that Yukon Consolidated had reserves for 20 years in the creeks, although the reserve situation would depend upon marketing conditions over that period.[72]

During the decade of the 1950s the relative importance of the Yukon Consolidated Gold Corporation Limited tended to increase, as it might have been expected to during a period of relative difficulty for the industry. Although it was not a particularly good year for the company, in 1961 it produced almost 80 per cent of the placer gold mined in the Yukon Territory. Most of this output was produced by five large dredges supplemented by some hydraulic and mechanical operations on

[71]See E. C. Hodgson, "Summary Review of Federal Taxation and Legislation Affecting the Canadian Mineral Industry," *Mineral Information Bulletin* MR 42, Department of Mines and Technical Surveys (Ottawa, 1961), pp. 20–1.

[72]Canada, Interdepartmental Committee on Territorial Financial Problems, "Report on the Yukon Territory" (Ottawa: undated mimeographed report in the library of the Dominion Bureau of Statistics, Ottawa), Appendix C.

"benches" near Dawson City. The remaining 20 per cent of the Yukon's alluvial gold production came from the usual small operators who, in 1962, numbered about thirty.

In view of the length of time the Yukon placer fields were worked it is interesting to note that the physical efficiency of the operations remained remarkably stable over a long period of years. Table 4.11 shows that the ounces of gold yielded per cubic yard of gravel handled had in fact increased in recent years.

Despite these satisfactory physical yields, however, the Yukon Consolidated Gold Corporation experienced a large decline in its published profits after 1950. Because there appear to have been no significant additions to the company's capital investment during this period (there was actually a small reduction), the chief causes of the decreased profits and restriction of output were probably the fall in the Canadian price of gold from $38.05 in 1950 to $33.57 in 1959 and the marked rise in labour costs during this same period.

Although it would appear that placer mining with heavy mining dredges would require relatively large capital inputs, placer mining of this type has actually been quite labour-intensive in the Yukon. The dredges themselves were operated by very small crews—perhaps six men on the largest units. Because the creek beds were permanently frozen, however, extensive thawing operations had to be carried out in advance of the dredges. These operations required large inputs of labour as shown in Table 4.12 where it will also be seen how the cost of these inputs increased in the post-war period. Labour costs absorbed almost 60 per cent of the total gross value of production in the post-war period as contrasted with the 30 per cent so taken up in 1939. The great rise in wage rates is indicated as the cause of this, for actual employment in the industry was declining. The average annual wage in 1960 was $5,740 compared to $1,993 in 1939.

Labour remained a major cause of the post-war difficulties of the Yukon placer industry, not only because of its increasing cost, but also because it was reported to be "difficult to obtain and equally difficult to hold."[73] The general implications of this labour situation will be considered later after the experience of industries operating in the Northwest Territories has been examined. But it may be noted here that productivity per unit of labour input was probably relatively low in the Yukon placer industry. The labour-gross product ratio in this industry

[73]Yukon Consolidated Gold Mining Corporation, *Annual Statement to Shareholders, 1951* (Vancouver, 1952).

during the 1950s was approximately half that in the auriferous quartz mining industry in the Northwest Territories.

The great difficulty in the Yukon placer industry was, of course, the seasonal nature of the operations and the absence of any significant local labour pool. Each year the employers had to import labour (usually from Vancouver) for the season and then send it back south at the onset of winter. This was regarded by operators as a major source of inefficiency and an obstacle to effective planning.

During the operating season the employees of the company were accommodated in semi-permanent camps located near the placer sites. The bulk of the labour force was relatively unskilled. Some effort was made by the company to hold supervisory staff over the winter by finding employment for it in its machine shops and other works, but a large part of even this class of labour left the area every fall. Employment opportunities in the Dawson area during the winter season were very limited.

Turning our attention to the auriferous quartz-mining industry of the Northwest Territories, we see that it was subject to the same cost-price problems as the Yukon placer industry in the post-war period. Nevertheless, output in the Territories continued to grow throughout the entire period. The auriferous quartz-mining industry in the Territories during this period consisted of four main mines, the Con and Rycon mines operated by Consolidated Mining and Smelting, the Discovery mine and the Giant mine. Of these the largest was the Giant which in 1954, for example, hoisted more ore than the other three combined.[74] By 1960 this mine was the third largest producer in Canada. In addition to these four large mines there were varying numbers of small operations.

The richest of the mines was the Discovery mine which has been ranked as the highest grade gold mine in Canada.[75] This mine, which began producing in 1949, was relatively small employing 150 men in its most active years. It remained, however, a remarkably efficient operation, and despite a slight drop in grade in 1958 (when it reached 1.78 ounces per ton) the mine was highly profitable. Its net profit in 1958, for example, was close to one million dollars.[76]

The Con and Rycon mines were actually operated as one, with most of the mining and all the milling done on the Con property. The grade

[74]D.B.S., *The Gold Mining Industry 1954*, p. B-9.
[75]*Mineral Report Number 1*, 1956, p. 78.
[76]Alberta and Northwest Chamber of Mines, *Annual Report 1962*, p. 19.

there was much lower than at Discovery. Daily production at the Con mine in the early 1960s ran about 500 tons and employment averaged about 200 to 250 men. By then the Con mine had become a fully developed operation producing at a fairly stable rate year after year. Along with the Giant mine, it was the chief reason for the growth and continued existence of Yellowknife—the most economically significant settlement in the Northwest Territories.

The Giant mine became a large operation giving employment to between three and four hundred men in most years during the 1950s. Its daily production grew steadily during the decade to reach more than one thousand tons in 1961. Between 1953 and 1961 it produced between five and nine million dollar's worth of gold per year and returned a profit frequently exceeding one million dollars per year.[77] The mine itself provided an excellent example of the problems mining in the far north presents and of the remarkable extent to which these problems can be overcome. Despite its proximity to Yellowknife, the Giant mine became a well laid out settlement in its own right—with considerable capital invested in social amenities seldom found on such sites.

Although gold production in the Northwest Territories continued to increase markedly during the decade of the 1950s, this was a consequence of the further development of properties which had been established either in the late 1930s or immediately after the war. The falling Canadian dollar gold prices after 1950 discouraged the prospecting for new gold properties in all the major gold-producing areas of Canada. Despite this, some exploration and staking activity was carried out in the Territories during the 1950s and there was reason to hope at the end of the decade that the rise in the Canadian dollar price of gold, which became apparent in 1960, would lead to the establishment of some new properties outside the Yellowknife district itself. Of these prospective developments the most promising, as well as the most interesting from the standpoint of regional development, was the Taurcanus property located well out in the Barren Lands 150 miles northeast of Yellowknife. This development, jointly controlled by Consolidated Yellowknife Mines and New Dickinson Gold Mines, was begun in 1956 and, using a great deal of air freight to supplement a hazardous winter truck freighting system, was scheduled to be brought into production in 1964 at a rate of 100 to 125 tons per day.[78]

This project was particularly significant in that it marked a new phase

[77]*Ibid.*, p. 18.
[78]*Mineral Report Number 9*, 1964, p. 266.

in the extensive development of the north. During the late 1950s the locus of mineral exploration in the Northwest Territories shifted away from the relatively well-known western edge of the Canadian Shield in Mackenzie District and moved both eastward into the remote and little-known Barren Lands toward Hudson Bay and westward into the perhaps even less familiar region of the Yukon-Northwest Territories boundary. This new orientation of northern mineral exploration was marked in the eastern regions not only by the Taurcanus development just noted, but also by the attempt to develop nickel-copper deposits at Rankin Inlet on the coast of Hudson Bay itself. The westward movement was marked by the Canada Tungsten development just east of the Yukon-Northwest Territories boundary, 135 miles north of Watson Lake. Both developments are described later in this chapter. But despite these new developments the most important production of minerals other than gold and uranium after 1949 was from the old Mayo district.

The initial redevelopment of the Mayo district ore deposits after World War II, like the earlier development which occurred in the 1920s, attracted a number of individuals and companies, of which the largest was United Keno Hill Mines Limited. The success enjoyed by this company in developing the old Hector claim on Keno Hill encouraged several others to explore the Mayo district intensively for similar prospects.[79] One of these, Mackeno Mines Ltd., was incorporated in 1951 to develop claims on Galena Hill. Between 1954 and 1957 when it was re-organized as Galkeno Mines Ltd. this firm produced substantial quantities of silver, zinc, and lead. Another firm, Bellakeno Hill Mines Ltd., undertook a similar development on Sourdough Hill between 1952 and 1954. The Bellakeno mill on Crystal Lake served as a custom mill for several other small operators. But of all these undertakings only the relatively large United Keno Hill operation had become securely established by the early 1950s. Its dominant position in the area was attributable to its relatively strong financial backing and the success of its extraordinary efforts to overcome the chief locational disadvantages of mining in the Mayo district.

In 1949 the old Treadwell Yukon Company 150-ton mill, which had been brought back into operation by United Keno Hill Mines Ltd. in April 1947, was destroyed by fire. Within a few months time a vastly improved 250-ton flotation mill was built and put into operation. In 1951 the capacity of this mill was increased to 500 tons and a 350-ton

[79]By the end of 1951, 13 companies and several individual prospectors were either developing or operating base metal holdings in the Mayo district.

cyanide plant was installed to treat "tailings." As a result of these investments silver production from the Mayo district rose during the early
1950s well above the former peak outputs of 1930 and 1937. In 1953
physical output exceeded 6,600,000 fine ounces of silver and during
the remaining years of the period stayed near that level.[80]

Zinc and lead concentrates can also be produced from the ores mined
in the Mayo district. But although they have been important sources of
revenue to the producer, they have remained a by-product of the silver
extracting operation. It was always the high silver content of the Mayo
district silver-lead-zinc ores which made its mining not only economically
feasible, but surprisingly profitable when account is taken of the high
operating costs imposed upon the company by the location. The net
profit of the company is shown, along with relevant production data in
Table 4.15.

Part of the success of this operation must be attributed to the nature
of the ore and its silver content already referred to. During the period
from 1949 to 1961 the average price of silver in Canada and the United
States remained fairly stable at a relatively high level (ranging from a
low of $ Canadian 0.7 in 1949 to over 0.9 in 1951 and 1961). The prices
of lead and zinc were less stable during this period. Because of the
variety of ores available to United Keno Hill it was able to maintain its
profit margins during periods of poor base metal prices by operating on
ores having relatively high silver content. In 1959, using high silver
content ores from the mine at Galena Hill, the company produced over
seven million fine ounces of silver, thereby becoming the largest silver
producer in Canada. The following year, in 1960, it produced more than
20 per cent of all the silver produced in this country. Because of
unfavourable prices base metal production lagged after 1954 when a
record production of almost 34 million pounds of lead and 24 million
pounds of zinc was achieved.[81] During the late 1950s and early 1960s a
substantial amount of cadmium was also recovered from the Mayo
concentrates.

In addition to the element of versatility introduced into its operations
by the nature of its ore deposits, the United Keno Hill Company's
success in operating a sub-arctic silver and base metal mine in this
recent period must also be attributed to its vigorous efforts to solve the
serious problem of high operating costs.[82] The basic cause of these high

---

[80]See Table 4.2.   [81]See Tables 4.13 and 4.14.
[82]The problem of high operating costs in this and other mines in the territorial
north is analyzed later in this chapter.

costs in the Mayo district, as at other mining centres developed in the northwest, has been the small scale of the mining operation itself. So long as a number of small operators tried to develop the ores in the area it appeared unlikely that suitable investments in more efficient industrial facilities such as transportation and electric power systems could be justified. But as we have seen, these smaller operations tended to disappear during the post-World War II period and the one large company, United Keno Hill Mines Limited, quickly came to dominate the lode-mining industry of the Mayo district in the same way that the Yukon Consolidated Gold Corporation had come to control activity in the Klondike placer region. This relatively large firm in the Mayo district was able to negotiate cost-sharing programmes with the federal and territorial governments for major highway and hydro-electric power developments which served greatly to reduce over-all operating costs in the Mayo area. Dependence upon river transport between Mayo and the railhead at Whitehorse was eliminated, along with the winter stock-piling it had entailed, by the construction of a highway from the mines to Whitehorse.

This Mayo-Whitehorse Highway was constructed by the federal government and opened to traffic in 1950. It completely freed the mining operators in the Mayo district from their dependence upon the river services formerly provided by the British Yukon Navigation Company.[83] Although trucking costs were higher than the direct costs of freighting concentrates by water to Whitehorse, the dependability and virtually all-season service offered by the highway led to the complete abandonment of the river services.

The terms of the agreement whereby federal participation in the construction of this important highway was secured included a provision that the United Keno Hill Company would assume 42.5 per cent of the cost of maintaining the highway and that it would also maintain at cost, and as the agent of the territorial government, the other roads and the air-strip in the vicinity of Mayo.[84]

The United Keno Hill Company operated its own highway freighting services. A fleet of heavy trucks was used to haul all the concentrates out of the mines to the railway at Whitehorse and on the return trip supplies were hauled back to the mines. The trucks, carrying about 24 tons of concentrates each, required about eleven hours to make the trip during the 1950s, being slowed in the summer months by three

[83]See page 205.
[84]United Keno Hill Mines Limited, *Sixth Annual Report* (Toronto, 1953).

river crossings by ferry.[85] These same crossings, which have since been bridged, forced a suspension of transport services during the freeze-up and break-up periods of the year during which urgent shipments of supplies to the mines had to be made by air (at a rate of thirty cents per pound!).

The second major post-war development in the Mayo district brought about by the United Keno Hill undertakings was the construction of a power plant on the Mayo River by the federal government. This development will be considered in some detail elsewhere. It should be noted here, however, that the Northwest Territories Power Commission negotiated an agreement with the company in 1950, two years before the plant was completed, binding the company to purchase "a minimum of 1600 H.P. for a period of twenty years at the initial rate of $125 per horsepower per year subject to revision as provided in the contract."[86] This contract was never ratified by the federal government, however, and its terms were not recognized by the Commission when the plant went into operation. In consequence the company was buying power at two and seven-eighths cents per kilowatt hour, or $187.88 per horsepower year, in 1953.[87] Even this rate enabled the company to reduce its power costs considerably, for when the mine was run on diesel power it cost the company three and one-half cents per kilowatt hour.[88] In 1954 the cost of primary power at the mine was reduced to two and five-eights cents per kilowatt hour or $171.54 per horsepower year.[89]

In addition to these major improvements in the transportation and power situations, the United Keno Hill Company developed its own lumbering operations in 1950. The company had its saw-mill and logging operations on a timber berth above Mayo on the Stewart River. Not all the company's lumber requirements were satisfied from this source, however, and the mine also provided a market for the products of independent lumber operators in the area. The establishment of the lumbering operation was reported by the company to have "guaranteed to its operations adequate lumber and timber at costs which compare favourably with lumber prices elsewhere."[90]

The company also operated its own coal mine at Carmacks. The coal,

[85]The Whitehorse-Mayo Highway crosses the Yukon, Pelly, and Stewart rivers.
[86]United Keno Hill Mines Limited, *Third Annual Report* (Toronto, 1950).
[87]United Keno Hill Mines Limited, *Seventh Annual Report* (Toronto, 1954).
[88]Personal interview with A. E. Pike, United Keno Hill Mines Limited, Elsa Camp, Yukon Territory, June 27, 1958.
[89]United Keno Hill Mines Limited, *Eighth Annual Report* (Toronto, 1955).
[90]United Keno Hill Mines Limited, *Third Annual Report* (Toronto, 1950).

used for heating at the mines, was picked up by the concentrate trucks on their "light" haul to the mines. The cost of mining the coal in 1957 was about seven dollars per ton to which was added a three-dollar payment to the federal government to reimburse it for assistance given in re-opening the coal mine.

Further consideration will be given to the question of operating costs in the Mayo district silver-lead-zinc–mining industry later in this chapter. The foregoing will serve to indicate, however, that much of the credit for the re-establishment of this industry in the Yukon must be given to the great enterprise shown by United Keno Hill Mines Limited in establishing an ingeniously integrated operation combining mining, concentrating, transportation, power development, and supply procurement. It undertook these developments with substantial government assistance. But the company itself provided the initiative and the guarantees which made this assistance possible.

Apart from this successful redevelopment of the silver-lead-zinc–mining industry in the Mayo district, no important new sources of these metals had been developed in the period 1949 to the time of writing. During this period a number of deposits were prospected,[91] but of these only one showed promise of becoming a major development. And even it was based upon showings of lead-zinc ore first examined at least as early as 1920.

Large deposits of apparently low-grade lead-zinc ores were long known to exist at what is now known as Pine Point on the south shore of Great Slave Lake in the Northwest Territories. Although claims had been repeatedly staked on this property since as early as 1898 and although development work done in 1929 indicated the presence of a deposit containing 500,000 tons of ore, no further work was done at Pine Point until 1946 when rising base metal prices, combined with a more positive development policy by the federal government, encouraged large mining companies to investigate the deposit. The chief operator was Consolidated Mining and Smelting Corporation of Canada Limited which was granted large concessions in the area in return for committing itself to a large-scale exploration programme.[92] The Consolidated Mining

[91]For example in the Pelly River and Hyland River areas of the Yukon Territory in the late 1950s.

[92]This concession system for encouraging further development of an area of known mining possibilities was subsequently used by the federal government in the Northwest Territories on at least two occasions in the 1950s. Once was in 1950 when it called for tenders for the exclusive right to explore and develop a block of 500 square miles in the vicinity of Ferguson Lake in return for an undertaking on

and Smelting Corporation concession gave that company exclusive rights to explore and to develop a tract of approximately 500 square miles during a period of three years.[93] Several other companies were also encouraged to do development work in the general area.

By the end of 1954 the work done in the Pine Point area had established the presence of what has been described as "one of Canada's and the world's largest known reserves of zinc and lead."[94] In the course of this work it was also discovered that large reserves of high-grade zinc and lead ore existed along with the low-grade ore bodies which had been outlined earlier. But despite the presence of this higher grade ore, and despite the fact that the ore was located in one of the most southerly and accessible parts of northern Canada, it was apparent that these base metal deposits could not be developed further unless heavy investments in transportation facilities were made.

This development was of great importance to the north not only because it was the first large-scale investigation of the possibility of exploiting purely base metal deposits in the Territories but also because of the questions of public policy it raised with regard to northern development in general. Despite the fact that the chief company interested in the development was a subsidiary of a national railway company, it did not decide to undertake the building of the necessary 400 to 450 miles of railway to link the Pine Point area to the Canadian railway system. Instead, it contented itself with delaying further development of its holdings in the area until public financing for this large capital undertaking could be secured. It was recognized, of course, that such a railway would overcome one of the main transportation difficulties facing the entire Mackenzie area in the Northwest Territories, eliminating as it would the need to rely upon the southern part of the Mackenzie waterway system for the shipment of heavy freight. Obviously, part of the economic benefits from an extension of the railway system to the south shore of Great Slave Lake would accrue to companies and individuals operating in northern Alberta and in Mackenzie District other than those developing the Pine Point lead-zinc deposits themselves. Whether or not a private railway to Pine Point could be operated in

---

the part of the successful bidder to spend a certain amount on exploration in the area over a four-year period. Again, in 1955, a similar concession was offered in the Coppermine River area.

[93]Canada, P.C. 1004, March 23, 1948.

[94]W. K. Buck and J. F. Henderson, "The Role of Mineral Resources in the Development and Colonization of Northern Canada," in Bladen, ed., *Canadian Population and Northern Colonization*, p. 93.

such a way as to recover (through its rate structure) earnings equal to these benefits conferred upon other private interests in the area must have seemed doubtful. And unless substantial revenues were obtained from "other business," engineering studies of the proposed railway suggested that it could not be a commercially profitable investment given existing base metal requirements. Further development of this project leading up to the official sod-turning for the new railway on February 12, 1962, is described and its implications considered in Part III. It may be noted here, however, that in 1961 it was reported that Consolidated Mining and Smelting Company of Canada Limited was by then "anxious for the commencement of construction because additional supplies of raw materials would soon be required to maintain refinery production at Trail" and because the "principal alternative to supply from Pine Point is the importation of zinc and lead concentrates from abroad."[95]

Other Major Mining Developments 1949–61

Only two other mining developments occurred during this period which actually reached or even approached the production stage. Both represented ambitious excursions of developers into areas which in earlier periods were almost entirely unknown or considered hopelessly remote. One of these was the nickel-copper mine at Rankin Inlet, 270 miles north of Churchill on the west coast of Hudson Bay; the other a tungsten mine in the Flat River area on the Yukon-Northwest Territories boundary.

In 1955 it was learned that North Rankin Nickel Mines Limited had outlined near Rankin Inlet on the west coast of Hudson Bay a body of nickel-copper ore containing an estimated 460,000 tons grading 3.3 per cent nickel and 0.81 per cent copper.[96] The following year a 250-ton concentrator was built on the property and production of nickel concentrates began in 1957. Concentrate was originally shipped to the Falconbridge smelter at Sudbury, but subsequent shipments were to the chemical-metallurgical refinery operated by Sherritt Gordon Mines Limited at Fort Saskatchewan, Alberta. By 1959 it was apparent that the known ore deposit would be exhausted in a matter of two or three years and a widespread exploration programme was initiated in the area. Prospecting was carried on as far as ninety miles from the mill, but without success. The mine completed its last full year of operation in

---

[95]Buck and Henderson, p. 93.
[96]Canada, Department of Mines and Technical Surveys, *The Canadian Mineral Industry 1955*, Publication Number 862, p. 76.

1961 and shortly thereafter the milling plant was dismantled and the townsite sold.[97]

This mining venture at Rankin Inlet is of particular interest to students of northern development in Canada, not because it contributed greatly to the mineral production of the north (see Table 4.9) but because it was the first truly "arctic" mine to operate in the northern Territories. It provided a testing ground for mining and milling techniques in an arctic environment (as distinguished from the sub-arctic environment of the Yukon and Mackenzie District operations) and also provided an opportunity to test the adaptability of Eskimos to modern industrial employment on a relatively large scale.

The other interesting development during this period began in 1959 with the announcement by the Canada Tungsten Mining Corporation that it had outlined an ore body on its Flat River properties containing over one million tons and carrying values of $37.00 per ton.[98] This valuable ore body was located, however, in a particularly remote area about 135 miles north of Watson Lake, lying just east of the Yukon-Northwest Territories boundary at approximately 61°57' latitude and 128°16' longitude. During the winter of 1959–60 equipment and supplies were hauled overland to the site and plans were made to build a road from Mile 65 on the Watson Lake–Ross River Road northeastward into the Mackenzie Mountains to connect with the tungsten deposits so that concentrates could be trucked out. The distance by road is about 200 miles to Watson Lake. Eighty miles of this road (from the junction with the Watson Lake–Ross River road to Hyland Valley) was to be paid for by the federal Department of Northern Affairs and National Resources and the remaining fifty miles into the camp site was to be financed jointly by the Department (two-thirds) and the Company (one-third).[99]

A 300-ton-a-day concentrating plant was under construction in 1961, and the mine at what was to become Tungsten, Northwest Territories, promised to become the sole domestic source of tungsten in Canada.[100] Although it would probably employ fewer than one hundred men, the project added a new mining centre to the north and its development served to open up to further intensive exploration and development one of the previously most inaccessible and remote regions in the northern

[97]"Mineral Report Number 9," in *The Canadian Minerals Yearbook 1962*, p. 411.

[98]Canada, Department of Northern Affairs and National Resources, *Annual Report 1959–60* (Ottawa, 1960), p. 40.

[99]Buck and Henderson, p. 95.

[100]"Mineral Report Number 9," in *The Canadian Minerals Yearbook, 1962*, p. 589.

Territories. And, along with the Taurcanus auriferous quartz mine north of Yellowknife and the short-lived Rankin development, it provided the only mineral developments based upon newly discovered deposits to even approach the production stage during the period after 1949. Although a great many new mineral deposits were located throughout the north during this period few, other than those already mentioned, showed promise of adding greatly to the existing mineral output of the area.[101]

SUMMARY OF THE DEVELOPMENT OF THE TERRITORIAL MINING INDUSTRY TO 1961

The purpose of this section is to summarize the available output data for the mining industry of the Territories from the turn of the century to 1961. The focus of attention here is upon that part of total territorial mineral production which may be thought of as constituting the output of a territorial mining industry producing for "export" to markets outside the Territories themselves. For this reason, the production of mineral fuels, specifically coal in the Yukon and petroleum in Mackenzie District, is excluded and considered later along with other "residentiary industries" which operate to supply only local markets within the Territories.

The range of mineral products exported from the Territories has been a narrow one to date. The only minerals exported more or less continuously have been gold, silver, and lead produced from silver-bearing ores. Radium concentrates were exported from the Great Bear Lake deposits from 1934 until 1942 after which time the mine was devoted to production of uranium concentrates and production data was "classified." From 1954 to 1960 data relating to this production are available but, by the latter date, production had ceased. There has also been an erratic production of copper from various mines in the Territories but, as Table 4.3 shows, this never became an established industry. Similarly, occasional shipments of other metallic minerals such as nickel have been made but these outputs have been short-lived.

It is correct to conclude, then, that the metallic mineral industry of the Territories has always depended upon the development of ores containing precious or rare metals. The sporadic production pattern for other

---

[101]The production of mineral fuels is examined in Chapter V, for this branch of the territorial mining industry has remained a purely local industry supplying territorial markets.

metals such as copper, tungsten, and nickel suggests that even rich deposits of these metals could not be exploited profitably enough to permit the establishment of mining industries based upon them. Because of this, the basic export mineral industry of the Territories from 1900 to 1961 may be thought of as consisting of mining operations devoted to the production of gold and silver. Lead production from 1915 to date is almost entirely attributable to the processing of silver-lead-zinc-bearing ores in the Mayo district, as is the zinc production recorded since 1949. Copper production from 1906 to 1920 and in 1928 and 1930 came from the Whitehorse area and the small amounts produced during the early 1940s, in 1951 and 1952, and since 1957, were from mines in the Northwest Territories.

The physical production of these metals is shown in the various tables in the statistical appendix. The total territorial production of gold shown in Table 4.1 consists of placer gold mined in the Yukon throughout the entire period plus continuous lode gold production from the Yellowknife area after 1938. The table shows the sharp drop in gold output from 1900 to 1907 associated with the collapse of the Klondike boom, the modest recovery in the early years of this century as large-scale mining techniques were applied to the placer deposits and the subsequent decline to the low reached in 1926. The rise in total output after the middle of the 1930s was attributable to the development of the Yellowknife lode deposits rather than to any great change in production from the Yukon. The reduction of the middle 1940s was attributable, of course, to wartime production difficulties and unfavourable economic conditions in the industry generally around the end of the war. The expansion of the 1950s was chiefly attributable to increased production from the Yellowknife area.

Table 4.1 also shows how changes in the output of gold in the Territories have been reflected in similar fluctuations in the percentage of total Canadian gold production attributable to territorial operations. As production from the Yukon placer fields declined through the first quarter of the century, the territorial share of the Canadian total fell from almost 80 per cent in 1900 to 1½ per cent in 1926. This percentage remained near that low figure until 1938 when the Yollowknife output began to have its effect. Because of the wartime set-back in the development of Yellowknife, however, territorial gold production did not again become a significant part of the total Canadian output until the decade of the 1950s during which it gradually rose to around 10 per cent, a level last recorded in 1920.

The production of silver in the Territories has rivalled gold production in terms of importance since the development of the Mayo silver-lead-zinc deposits during World War I. Although part of the silver output from the Territories has been produced as a by-product of alluvial gold-mining in the Yukon (see Table 4.16) and, in the Northwest Territories, in the process of refining gold and pitchblende ores, the major fluctuations shown in Table 4.2 reflect the fortunes of the operations at Mayo—hence the "peaks" of 1915, 1923, 1930, and those occurring in the late 1940s and during the 1950s. And, as in the case of territorial gold production, these periods of high output correspond to peaks in the percentage contribution of territorial silver production to total Canadian silver production. Although at the height of Yukon placer gold operations around 1900 the output of silver was large enough to constitute around five per cent of Canadian production, between then and the first effective development of the Mayo silver deposits in the early 1920s, the output was below one per cent of the Canadian figure. It subsequently reached approximately 18 per cent in 1931 and 1939, but fell to very low levels again during the 1940s. With the reorganization of the Mayo operations in the late 1940s output was expanded there much more rapidly than in the Canadian industry as a whole—with the result that since 1953 territorial silver production has regularly accounted for over one-fifth of total Canadian silver production.

Because virtually all the lead produced in the Territories has also come from the Mayo operations it is not surprising that the level of output has fluctuated in roughly the same pattern as the production of silver. What divergence from this pattern there has been can be attributed to the operators responding to market conditions facing lead producers. As noted earlier the operators at Mayo have been able to exercise some discretion in selecting ores for milling on the basis of prevailing lead prices—utilizing high silver-content ores during periods of weak lead prices. This is the chief reason for the continuous decline in lead output since the all-time peak reached in 1954 as shown in Table 4.13.

The relative importance of the territorial lead production in terms of national production is also shown in Table 4.13. As in the case of silver, the great fluctuation in the territorial share of total lead production in Canada has reflected the major changes which have occurred in the level of operations at the mines in the Mayo district. The periodic closing of the mines there and their subsequent redevelopment accounts for the fluctuation from zero to the maximum 8.2 per cent of national lead output realized in 1953. Previous peaks were recorded in 1939 (1.9 per cent), 1930 (2.7 per cent), 1923 (6.1 per cent), and 1916 (2.3 per cent). As was true of silver, in almost every instance these peaks correspond to the peaks in northern lead production in absolute terms. The implication is, of course, that the output of the northern mines has been governed by "local" influences affecting the cost or "supply" side and by a greater sensitivity to price fluctuations than was displayed by mines operating elsewhere in Canada. These related possibilities will be considered further in a later chapter.

The production of zinc concentrates began at the Mayo mines in 1949, aided by the rapid rise in world zinc prices which began in 1947. As in the case of lead, the price of zinc more than tripled between 1946 and 1951. Table 4.14 shows how the output of these concentrates increased rapidly after 1949 to reach a peak of almost 12,000 tons in 1954. Subsequent weakening of zinc markets, however, and increased emphasis on high silver content ores at Mayo led to a steady decline in zinc production from the Yukon.

Even at its peak levels, however, production of this metal in the Territories has been much less significant as a percentage of total Canadian zinc output than has been the case with silver and lead production. The largest annual contribution, of 3.1 per cent, was made in 1954. The importance of the Mayo production of zinc concentrates has been enhanced, however, by the recovery of significant amounts of cadmium from the concentrates produced. The cadmium production shown in Table 4.9 was from concentrates shipped from Mayo. This output has accounted for as much as eleven per cent of the total Canadian production of this metal. Annual contributions of over five per cent have been typical.

Turning to other metals also produced in the Territories in more recent years, Table 4.9 also summarizes the physical output data for uranium and nickel. Although radioactive ores shipped from Port Radium for the production of radium during the years from 1934 to early in World War II constituted Canada's only source of this metal, and although the re-working of these properties for uranium production made them the major source of that metal in North America during the war years, their subsequent output was of steadily declining importance during the post-war years. Physical production data is not available prior to 1956, but it may be assumed that territorial output accounted for a relatively large part of total Canadian output. In 1956, as shown in Table 4.9, over 19 per cent of Canadian uranium production was attributable to the Northwest Territories operations. But despite subsequent development of new properties in the Territories and a substantial increase in output there, major developments elsewhere in Canada proceeded to reduce greatly the relative importance of territorial uranium production to the level shown in the table. The disastrous market developments which confronted the Canadian uranium mining industry in the late 1950s quickly forced out of production the small mines whose production had just begun to augment that of the only large, but by then exhausted, mine, the Eldorado property at Port Radium.

The physical output of nickel is shown in Table 4.9 from which it will be seen that the Rankin Inlet mine remained a marginal and very small-scale operation. Nickel output averaged less than one per cent of the Canadian total annually and the Rankin copper output remained insignificant. The only earlier attempt to develop non-precious metal bearing ores that resulted in several successive years of measurable output was that made in the Whitehorse copper belt between 1906 and 1920. Even in 1916, the best year of those operations, however, territorial production accounted for little better than two per cent of the Canadian total.

The aggregate value of this territorial metallic mineral production (excluding radioactive ores and nickel) in current dollars is depicted in Table 4.4 for the years 1900 to 1961 inclusive. The falling total value from 1900 to 1907 reflects the decline in the output of gold (and silver) from the Klondike placers prior to the introduction of large-scale mining techniques. The subsequent application of these methods checked the decline in production and the value of total output was further augmented after 1915 by the production of silver and lead from Mayo. But despite the growth in the value of lode silver and lead production in the Yukon after 1921, the value of total metallic mineral production in the Territories continued to decline until lode gold-mining began at Yellowknife in the late 1930s. The percentage contribution of the Klondike placer gold production to the total value of metallic mineral production will be seen to have fallen to 23.8 per cent by 1926. After 1930, however, the value of silver and lead production declined greatly and allowed the total value of territorial production to fall, in 1935, to the lowest level since 1924. The increase in the value of total output after 1935 was attributable to rising gold production in the Yukon placer fields, renewed silver-lead production in the Yukon and, by the end of the decade, substantial gold production at Yellowknife in the Northwest Territories. In 1940, for example, almost 34 per cent of the value of territorial metallic mineral production came from the Yellowknife gold mines, 50 per cent from Yukon placer gold-mining operations, and approximately 16 per cent from the Mayo silver-lead mines. The great reduction in the total value of this production in the later years of the war is attributable to production difficulties associated with the war. The subsequent rise in total output from 1945 to 1960 resulted from increasing production of gold in the Northwest Territories, increased silver and lead production and the initiation of zinc (and cadmium) output at Mayo and, from 1947 to 1956, rising lead and zinc prices. Over this post-war period, the contribution of the Yukon placer output to the total value of territorial production declined steadily from approximately 78 per cent in 1945 to under 9 per cent by 1961. The lode gold mines of the Northwest Territories increased their share of the total to a high of 55.5 per cent in 1949 and from then until 1961 averaged around 46 per cent annually. The Mayo operations accounted for nearly all the remaining value produced after 1945, rising from 1.2 per cent of the total in 1945 to approximately 50 per cent by 1954. From 1954 to 1961 the Mayo output of silver, lead, and zinc provided annually around 40 per cent of the total value. This was made up of silver in excess of 20 per cent of total value throughout, lead declining from 17 per cent in 1954 to just over 6 per cent by 1961, and zinc declining from a high of 11.7 per cent in 1955 to 5.6 per cent in 1961. It will be noted from Table 4.4 that from 1900 to 1911 placer gold production accounted for more than 50 per cent of the value of metallic mineral production in the Yukon Territory itself. The value of the Mayo operations exceeded the value of the placer operations most years from 1922 to 1932. The latter became dominant again from 1933 to 1949 and from then to 1961 the Mayo production once again accounted for more than half the value of metals mined in the Yukon.

Similarly, in the Northwest Territories, two major mining industries—the Yellowknife auriferous quartz-mining industry and the radioactive ores mining industry historically have accounted for virtually all the mineral exports from that part of the north. As shown in Table 4.5, production of gold (and a small related silver output) developed more slowly than the radium mining operation at Great Bear Lake in the early 1930s with the result that until 1939 the latter accounted for more than 50 per cent of the value of mineral products exported from the Northwest Territories. In 1941 and 1942, however, only 12.5 per cent and 19.4 per cent respectively of this value was attributed to the radium mining operation. After value data became available for uranium mining in 1954, it was seen to be accounting for an average of around 40 per cent of the total value of minerals mined in the Territories for outside markets prior to the total collapse of the industry in the early 1960s.

From this over-all view of the historical development of the metallic mineral mining industries of the northern Territories it may be concluded that these industries have been very narrowly based upon four major groups of ore bodies from which nearly all of the value created by these industries was derived. These four major mining centres—the gold placers of Dawson and the silver-lead-zinc deposits at Mayo in the Yukon, the auriferous quartz gold mines at Yellowknife, and the pitch-blende ores at Port Radium in Mackenzie District of the Northwest Territories—have served as the backbone of the mining industry of the north. As noted earlier in this section, many attempts were made over the years to establish mining operations away from these centres but, prior to 1961 at least, these must be counted failures. Thus, not only did the realized production for export of the northern mining industries remain limited to products derived only from ores containing precious or radioactive metals throughout the period from the 1880s to the early 1960s, but these products were derived from a very limited number of geographic locations. Variations in physical output were primarily the consequence of more or less intensive exploitation of the deposits known to exist in these areas. The growth of the territorial mining industry in terms of its relative importance to the northern economy was consequently primarily attributable to more thorough development of these established centres. The net value of mining operations (which includes the value of fuels produced for territorial markets in addition to the metals produced for outside markets) rose from 62 per cent of the total net value of territorial production in 1948 to over 80 per cent during the decade of the 1950s as shown in Table 11.13. This same expansion even enabled the basic metal mining industry of the Territories to grow in terms of national importance as shown in Table 4.6. Territorial production of gold, silver, lead, zinc, and copper averaged 5.6 per cent of the national production of these metals annually during the 1950s, compared to 2.5 per cent annually during the 1940s, 2.1 per cent during the 1930s and 3.7 per cent during the 1920s.

5 The Residentiary Industries

THE INDUSTRIES WHICH SUSTAIN the economies of the Yukon and the Northwest Territories are those already described. In this chapter attention is directed to a number of other industries which produce goods and services, not for export from the north, but for sale in local markets. Our concern here will continue to be with privately sponsored activities. Consequently, we will examine the mineral-fuel-producing industries, the forest industry, agriculture, and manufacturing. The transportation and electric power industries will be considered separately in the next chapter and again in Part III where publicly sponsored activities are examined. Since World War II both transportation and electric power facilities in the Territories have come to be more or less publicly owned and directed—which means that their more recent development has to be considered in a rather different context.

THE MINERAL FUELS INDUSTRIES

The fuels available for heating and for the generation of steam and electric power in the Territories are wood, coal, petroleum, and natural gas. Throughout the entire history of the Territories wood cut from as near as possible to where it was to be used has constituted a major fuel for all purposes. It has heated dwellings and industrial buildings, fired boilers generating steam to move river-boats and, in the mines it has been used to hoist ore, to thaw placer-mining grounds, and even to generate electric power. In the Yukon especially supplies of fuel wood were often conveniently located and easily exploited without need for skilled labour or expensive equipment. As elsewhere, however, wood had many disadvantages as a fuel, mainly its bulkiness and low efficiency, in industrial applications. Because of the latter problem it is not surprising that even in the Yukon, as more accessible supplies of wood were used up and as large-scale mining developments got under way, efforts were made to locate local supplies of alternative fuels. In the Mackenzie area this was even more essential because of the lack of timber near the mining centres which grew up there. In the Yukon the alternative local fuel discovered and developed was coal. In Mackenzie District it was petroleum.

The Yukon Coal-Mining Industry

Several deposits of coal were discovered in the Yukon during the late nineteenth century. Surface outcroppings in most cases, they were easily worked with a minimum of equipment and were conveniently situated to satisfy local needs. The most important deposits were those at Rock Creek on the Klondike River, Coal Creek on the Yukon River in the Whitehorse-Wheaton area, and at Carmacks on the Yukon River. The coal found at Rock Creek and at Coal Creek was lignite and at the other two locations a good quality bituminous. Most of the recorded production has come from several mines near Carmacks which have, at various times, provided most of the fuel required in the silver-lead-zinc–mining and –milling operations in the Mayo district.

With the exception of a few years (1919, 1920, and 1934), coal was produced annually at the Carmacks mines from the turn of the century until 1939. Output fluctuated greatly during this period from a high of almost 20,000 tons recorded in 1913 to less than 100 tons in 1937 as shown in Table 5.1. The bulk of the output prior to the 1920s appears to have been used for domestic heating and in the generation of steam in some of the Klondike mining operations. The great decline in the population of the Yukon which occurred between the turn of the century and the beginning of the 1920s greatly reduced the local demand for all kinds of fuel.

During the 1920s and 1930s the decline in population was reversed, largely because of the development of the Mayo district lode-mining operations. The milling of the silver-lead-zinc ores there created a new industrial demand for fuel and consequently a small but fairly steady production of coal was maintained thereafter in the Carmacks area. The market for this coal was temporarily destroyed during World War II when the Canol project made possible the large-scale importation of petroleum into the Whitehorse area, but demand was restored in 1947 when United Keno Hill Mines Limited undertook the re-development of several mining properties in the Mayo district. Steam plants were installed at the "Elsa" and "Calumet" mines, and the company decided to use coal to fire them. It thereupon acquired coal properties at Carmacks and formed a subsidiary, the Yukon Coal Company Limited, to hold and operate these properties. The company negotiated with the federal government and secured assistance in the form of a loan which it used to finance the development of the coal mines. It was announced that coal would be produced not only to supply the company's own operations but for sale to other users in the Territory as well. Virtually the entire output was subsequently used for local industrial purposes—although small amounts were shipped to northern British Columbia from time to time.[1]

The level of output since production resumed in 1948 is shown in Table 5.1. The operation remained small and, compared to larger coal mines in Canada, costly.[2] Nevertheless, the product itself compared reasonably well with that produced elsewhere. Bituminous coal produced in 1962 in the Yukon yielded an average of 11,450 B.T.U.'s per pound compared with 11,900 for New Brunswick bituminous and 12,950 for Alberta bituminous. Its average value per ton in the same year was $15.06 compared to $8.28 for New Brunswick and $7.26 for Alberta bituminous coal.[3]

Employment provided by the Carmacks coal mining operations has been insignificant. In the early years of the operations, prior to World War II, the mines were operated only seasonally with employees working as few as two or three months in a year but after 1948 mining was done more and more continuously. In 1961 the average number of man-days worked per year reached a record 341.[4] The average number of employees, however, declined from 23 in 1948 to 7 in 1961.

By the early 1960s it was apparent that the high cost of alternative fuels and the transportation problems that had made the development of local coal supplies possible were breaking down. No serious efforts were being made to increase coal reserves and the future of even a nominal coal-mining industry appeared uncertain. In this respect the prospects of the other fuel industry in the Territories were quite different.

[1] In 1953, 1954, and 1956.
[2] See Chapter 6.
[3] Canada, Department of Mines and Technical Surveys, *The Canadian Minerals Yearbook 1962* (Ottawa, 1964), p. 197.
[4] All data on coal production is from D.B.S., *The Coal Mining Industry 1949*, and annually to 1962.

The Petroleum Industry of the Territories

It has been noted in earlier chapters that a number of mineral occurrences in the Northwest Territories were discovered by the early explorers. As early as the eighteenth century it was known that copper deposits existed in what are today known as the Coppermine River and Yellowknife areas. Coal was also known to exist on the Mackenzie River, having been noted by Mackenzie in 1789. Other mineral occurrences, including oil seepages on the Mackenzie River, were reported from time to time by fur traders, missionaries and other travellers. And during the rush to the Klondike in 1898, some rather casual prospecting was done in Mackenzie District by miners on their way to the Klondike via the Liard and Mackenzie Rivers. No attempt appears to have been made to pursue any of this work, however, until 1914. In that year a number of petroleum and natural gas claims were staked at two locations by gold prospectors from the Yukon. These were at Windy Point on the north shore of Great Slave Lake and at a location on the Mackenzie River about 45 miles below the trading post of Norman. No work was done at either of these locations, however, and although a small amount of prospecting and staking took place during World War I, no significant development occurred until 1919. In that year the Northwest Company, a subsidiary of Imperial Oil, obtained some of the property previously prospected and took drilling equipment and crews into Mackenzie District to test for petroleum at the Norman and Windy Point sites.

The first oil strike in the Territories was made on August 24, 1920, when the Northwest Company's Discovery well near Norman gushed at a depth of 783 feet. This was the first major mineral development to occur in the Northwest Territories and it was responsible for drawing national attention to the economic prospects of Mackenzie District for the first time. It also set off a minor prospecting and staking boom in Mackenzie District but, for at least two reasons, this boom was short-lived and of small proportions. The first of these reasons was that the operations involved in this industry were bound to be extremely costly due to the size and amount of equipment required and the extraordinary transportation difficulties involved not only in getting this equipment into the sites, but also in getting the product out to the existing markets. The risks involved were such, too, of course, to discourage those lacking very substantial financial backing. Drilling operations in 1921 and 1922 amply demonstrated the risks. One hole sunk a few miles up-river from the Discovery well by the Fort Norman Oil Company was abandoned after drilling for 1,512 feet. Another drilled at Windy Point by the Northwest Company in the winter of 1921 was abandoned at 1,806 feet. Yet another hole sunk by the White Beaver Oil Company near Hay River south of Great Slave Lake in 1922 was abandoned at 712 feet.[5] Several other holes drilled in the Norman area in the next few years resulted in only one more commercially productive well being established. And it, like Discovery, was capped due to the marketing problem.

The second reason for the rather modest extent of the Mackenzie District oil boom in the 1920s was the close regulation imposed on oil development there by a newly interested federal government. The regulation devised upon the discovery of oil at Norman Wells provided that prospectors could stake as much as 2,560 acres in four different areas if desired. A rental fee of 50 cents per acre would be required during the first year and $1.00 for each acre retained thereafter. A drilling outfit had to be located within two years. In the case of producing properties a royalty of 2½ to 5 per cent was imposed on output for the first five years and of 5 to 10 per cent for the next five years. One quarter of the staked ground could be retained by the developing company with the other three-quarters reverting to the Crown.

In a debate remarkably similar to that arising out of the federal regulations concerning the disposition of the Yukon placer gold lands, the territorial oil regulations were alleged in the House of Commons to be "detrimental to the development of the oil industry both in law and equity and the purport thereof is to unduly discourage private initiative and unduly protect large interests by allowing the same to take full possession of the oil fields of the Territories." It was suggested that the regulations were unduly onerous in view of the great obstacles to further development of oil resources in the Territories—that they were, in fact, based upon the assumption that facilities existed for getting oil out of the Territories to market. With respect to the other charge, that the regulations discriminated in favour of large developers, the government readily admitted that this was indeed the case.

The government's position was explained by the Prime Minister, Mr. Meighen, as follows:

Now I am quite free to admit that under the regulations that we passed only a few weeks ago there can be actual development in that district only by the investment of large sums of money. . . . These regulations . . . are different . . . from those that apply to the provinces. The reason is this: in the provinces

---

[5]Canada, Department of the Interior, *The Northwest Territories 1930* (Ottawa, 1930), p. 79.

there is no proven field as yet on any considerable scale; it is largely a matter of prospect and hope. . . . In this Fort Norman well, the flow is large. . . . undoubtedly it is a field of very considerable dimensions. The regulations, therefore, . . . fix definitely the royalty that can be charged, and they are such as not so much to encourage people to come in to look for oil, but to encourage people to go in who are going to bring oil out.[6]

It was to be some years, however, before it was established that there was a significant oil field at Norman and to this day no commercially feasible way has been devised for getting the oil from Norman Wells to outside markets.

It is not surprising that, under these conditions, further major development work was suspended in the Territories by oil companies. One more wildcat drilling venture was undertaken in 1930 in the Hay River area (with no success) but, otherwise, development remained at a standstill until well on in the 1930s. Late in that decade it became apparent that a small local market for petroleum products was being created by the pitchblende mining operations on Great Bear Lake and by the Yellowknife auriferous quartz-mining developments.

A very small refinery (with a daily capacity of 300 barrels of crude oil) had been erected by the Northwest Company at the Discovery location in the early 1920s. Although it was capable of producing gasoline and diesel fuel until 1933 the local market for these fuels was negligible. Domestic heating requirements in the Mackenzie Valley were satisfied by local wood and some small outcroppings of lignite coal located near Norman.

The development of the Port Radium pitchblende deposits by Eldorado Gold Mines Limited in 1933 created a major demand for diesel fuel and other petroleum products. The obvious source of supply was Norman Wells, conveniently located on the main river route which Eldorado planned to use for all its supplies and also for getting at least some of its product out. Barges propelled by diesel tugs were to be used to transport the products of the Norman refinery to Port Radium. To meet this demand, petroleum output at Norman Wells was stepped up from 910 barrels in 1932 to over 4,000 in 1933 and 1934, and to over 5,000 in 1935 and 1936. In 1937, with the creation of another major industrial demand for petroleum products in the Yellowknife area, output rose to over 11,000 barrels and in 1938 this was again doubled.[7] The rapid expansion in local markets for petroleum products led Imperial Oil

---

[6]*House of Commons Debates,* 1921, pp. 898–900.
[7]See Table 5.2.

to build a new refinery at Norman Wells in 1939 and to drill two more wells there, one in 1939, and the other in 1940. The new refinery was able to produce aviation and other gasoline, light and heavy diesel oils, and fuel oil. Its initial capacity was 840 barrels of crude per day and this was expanded to 1,100 barrels in 1943.[8] With the further development of economic activity in Mackenzie District in the early 1940s substantial sales of petroleum products were made to transportation companies such as airlines and river-boat operators as well as to mining companies. It is interesting to note how the development of the local market for these products encouraged investment in producing facilities which subsequently permitted larger scale and more diversified production which in turn permitted a reduction in the costs of these products to consumers. It was reported in 1940 that the erection of the new refinery at Norman Wells resulted in "a substantial reduction in the price of gasoline and fuel oil."[9] The price of aviation fuel was particularly affected for it had previously been shipped into Mackenzie District all the way from Vancouver, British Columbia. In the normal course of events it would have been expected that a substantial reduction in fuel costs in the area would have provided a further inducement to exploration and development there and the creation of a still larger market until truly efficient large-scale refining operations could have been established at Norman Wells. But the pattern of development in Mackenzie District was greatly disturbed in the early 1940s by an extraordinary military undertaking which directly involved the Norman Wells petroleum industry.

The outbreak of war in the Pacific in 1942 resulted in the sudden creation of a potentially large demand for petroleum products, especially aviation fuel, in Alaska and northwestern Canada. The loss of Hong Kong and Singapore, the invasion of the Aleutian Islands and the presence of enemy submarines off the west coast of North America created a military situation in the Pacific Northwest which aroused great anxiety in Washington and Ottawa. Confronted by the possibility of an interruption in the transportation of aircraft fuel by coastal tanker to United States bases in Alaska, the United States government sought Canadian co-operation in a project to develop a local source of supplies in the area. A subsequent exchange of notes between the two governments

---

[8]Canada, Department of Resources and Development, *Industries of the Northwest Territories* (Ottawa, 1953), p. 8.

[9]Canada, Department of Mines and Resources, *Annual Report 1940* (Ottawa, 1940), p. 66.

gave the United States authority to let drilling contracts to Imperial Oil at Norman Wells, to construct a pipeline through the virtually unexplored Mackenzie mountains area to connect Norman Wells to Whitehorse, to erect a refinery at Whitehorse, and to build storage facilities and distribution systems at Prince Rupert and Skagway.

The subsequent developments at Norman Wells proved conclusively that earlier development of the petroleum resources there had been limited not by the availability of the natural resource itself but by the narrowness of the local market. The same transportation difficulties which had preserved the small local market for the local petroleum industry had also, of course, prevented the industry from selling in "outside markets." Under the contracts let to Imperial Oil in accordance with the Canol agreement, 67 new wells, of which 60 were producers, were drilled on the company's existing properties and on new properties leased from the federal government. While this drilling was in progress, United States army engineers built a 580-mile pipeline and an accompanying service road through the Mackenzie mountains to Whitehorse. This astonishing undertaking was accomplished despite the necessity of learning how to build on permafrost, how to use mechanical equipment during a sub-arctic winter, and how to get this equipment and the necessary supplies into one of the least-known parts of the continent. Furthermore, the pipe itself had to climb from an elevation 300 feet above sea level at Norman Wells over a mountain range exceeding 5,800 feet—and this change in elevation occurred within the first 90 miles of the line. The Canol road was the first road built in the remote territory lying between the Mackenzie Valley and the southern Yukon.

The entire Canol project was completed in March, 1944. By that time the military need for a local fuel supply in the area had disappeared and the entire project was abandoned, virtually as soon as it was completed. The complete cost of the project is not, and perhaps never will be, known. But some indication of its magnitude is suggested by the report of a United States investigating committee which indicated that more than $134,000,000 had gone into it.[10] The effect on operations at Norman Wells may be inferred from the fact that gross output rose from 266,882 barrels in 1943 to 1,229,310 in 1944 and fell the following year to 353,117 barrels.[11]

It was apparent by the end of World War II that the Norman Wells

[10]Report of the Truman Committee, cited in *House of Commons Debates*, 1944, p. 3271.
[11]See Table 5.2.

industry would revert to its role of an industry producing for only a limited local market despite the pipeline link which made possible shipments of oil not only to the central Yukon market, but to tidewater and outside markets as well. There has never been a clearer demonstration of the fact that northern development has been paced by economic rather than physical or "engineering" difficulties. In the case of this industry, and several other "local" industries discussed below, the provision of a physical link with outside markets is seen to have done as much to limit the development of the industry as to encourage it. The pipeline from well-head to Whitehorse and from there to tidewater made it physically possible to export Norman Wells oil—but it also made it possible to import petroleum products produced in very large, highly efficient refineries outside. Given the scale advantages of these outside producers, it is always possible that their products can withstand transportation costs into the north and reach the consumer more cheaply than local products. Improvements in transportation facilities linking the north to the outside consequently often mitigate against the development of "secondary" local industry there—and quite properly so, of course, for the long-term development of the north will best be promoted by minimizing operating costs in the mining industries which may, depending upon ores, possess a natural advantage over some "outside" competitors.

The delicate balance of the economic forces which determine the position of secondary industries in the north was thoroughly demonstrated by what happened to Norman Wells after the War. Not only did it prove economically impossible to market Norman Wells oil outside the north, it was not even possible to retain the central Yukon market to supplement the "safe" market area of the Mackenzie Valley. The pipeline running along the White Pass and Yukon Route right-of-way was maintained after the war by private interests associated with the railway, not to export products refined in Whitehorse but, by operating it in reverse, to import petroleum products to Whitehorse from refineries on the West Coast. These products, shipped to Skagway and then overland via the pipeline to Whitehorse proved cheaper than products produced there from Norman Wells oil. Because of this the Canol pipeline and its service road were abandoned. It was estimated that approximately one million dollars annually would have been required to maintain and operate the pipeline and the road.[12] Thus, by the end of 1945 it was apparent that the Norman Wells operation would revert to its pre-war

---

[12]*North Pacific Planning Project*, p. 42.

role as a small local supplier for the Mackenzie Valley[13] market. Its subsequent development was determined, as it was before the war, by the rate of expansion in the mining and related activities in Mackenzie District. In the early post-war years the largest part of the output went to the Yellowknife area, with Port Radium as the next largest market. Relatively small amounts were marketed in centres along the Mackenzie from Hay River in the south to Aklavik in the north.

The level of output from Norman Wells after the end of the war grew slowly but fairly steadily as the local market expanded. As Table 5.2 indicates, however, by 1961 gross petroleum output had still not reached 50 per cent of the record level attained in 1944. It is perhaps surprising that under these circumstances exploration for new petroleum deposits in the Territories should have assumed major proportions in the post-war years. But this did happen.

The exploration for new oil resources in the Territories in the immediate post-war years was generally discouraging. New regulations governing exploration and development of these resources in the Territories were made by order-in-council of the federal government in 1944 and a leasing arrangement was made, effective in May, 1945, with Imperial Oil concerning the "proven field" area at Norman Wells.[14] Under these and other regulations approved in the summer of 1945, exploration permits were issued covering a total of 2,242,284 acres. Most of this area was in the vicinity of Norman Wells, but one permit covered 640 acres on the Hay River in the relatively accessible area south of Great Slave Lake. The work done under these arrangements during 1946 proved unsuccessful in the Mackenzie River locations and the permits there were abandoned. The following year the Hay River permit was also abandoned when drilling failed to locate oil.[15] Exploration continued in a new location near Fort Providence, however, where a permit covering 64,000 acres was issued in 1947. This area remained the focus of petroleum exploration in the Territories for several years despite rather discouraging results. In fact activity throughout the area increased and by the early 1950s was beginning to spread into other parts of Mackenzie District and even into the Yukon. In 1950, 31 petroleum and natural gas permits were issued in the Fort Providence area and 2 in the Fort Liard area to the west. When two wells in the Fort Providence area failed to

---

[13]In 1945 most of the producing wells were capped and only seven were used to produce the oil required by the territorial market.

[14]Canada, P.C. 2904, April 27, 1944.

[15]Canada, Department of Mines and Resources, *Annual Report 1948*, p. 185.

locate oil, attention shifted to the area west of Great Slave Lake and something resembling a major staking rush developed there in 1951. During the 1952 fiscal year 255 permits covering 15,000,000 acres were issued in the Northwest Territories and twelve wells were drilled—and abandoned. This type of activity spread into the Yukon about this same time where one permit had been issued by the end of the 1952 fiscal year. A public competition was held to dispose of the right to explore for petroleum and natural gas in two areas containing over three million acres, one of which was partly in the Northwest Territories.[16] Similar competitions were held under new regulations respecting oil and gas rights in the Yukon and Northwest Territories which came into effect in the spring of 1953.

The extent of the exploration programme for petroleum in the Territories during the early 1950s is suggested by the following summary of permits, leases, and reservations in good standing as of March 31, 1954.[17]

	YT		NWT	ACREAGE
Permits	67		396	26,928,326
Reservations	—	2	—	9,584
Leases			9	6,158
Surface Leases			2	892

Despite the fact that none of this activity had led to the discovery of new commercially significant oil reserves, the exploration programme in the Territories continued during the remainder of the decade and was, if anything, intensified. Although considerable attention continued to be given to the areas just north of 60°, the search for oil during the 1950s was pressed further and further north until, by the end of the decade, the frontier of exploration had moved off the mainland into the islands of the high arctic. In view of this it is not surprising that total expenditures on petroleum exploration in the territorial north increased greatly during the decade of the 1950s. Table 5.3 shows that these expenditures exceeded one million dollars annually for the first time in 1953 and grew tremendously thereafter to exceed twelve million dollars in 1961. By 1961 the total cumulative expenditure on this kind of work in the Territories since the beginning of the 1950s exceeded forty million dollars. The Department of Northern Affairs and National Resources reported in 1961 that "between 30 per cent and 40 per cent of this figure

---

[16]Canada, Department of Resources and Development, *Annual Report for the Fiscal Year Ending March 31, 1953*, pp. 66–9.

[17]Canada, Department of Northern Affairs and National Resources, *Annual Report 1953–4* (Ottawa, 1954), p. 16.

is estimated to have been spent on building and clearing roads, bridging, cutting trails and bringing in supplies."[18]

The total acreage held under permit continued to grow both in the Yukon and in the Northwest Territories from the levels reported above for 1954. By 1959, as shown in Table 5.3, the area under permit in the Yukon had reached approximately 20,000,000 acres and in the Northwest Territories more than 73,000,000 acres.

By 1961, although a great deal of geological information about the territorial north had been acquired in the course of these activities no significant petroleum resources had been discovered. Although over 100 wells were drilled between 1950 and 1960, the only producers were four development wells drilled in the proven field at Norman. Several gas wells were also brought in but they were either capped or abandoned because of the absence of transportation facilities for gas. But despite these negative results, at time of writing, the search for petroleum in the Territories continues. If major discoveries are made it is possible that the petroleum industry could eventually become established as an industry exporting from the area. Extraordinary transportation problems would have to be overcome, of course, although the Canol project described above demonstrated that no insurmountable engineering difficulty is likely to be experienced in providing the facilities required. But it also demonstrated that the effective limit to this kind of development is economic. And the seriousness of the economic difficulties involved is amply indicated by the fact that forty years after a sizeable field was tapped at Norman Wells, production has continued to be restricted to supplying a local market even after a pipeline to tidewater was built and abandoned. Furthermore, as noted earlier, the security of even this local market is threatened by every improvement in transportation facilities which reduces the cost in the Territories of petroleum products from the south. It would appear quite likely, for example, that the railway to Great Slave Lake could permit petroleum products from Edmonton to sell in the relatively large Yellowknife area market at prices below those of products produced at Norman Wells.

It will be apparent from the foregoing consideration of the mineral fuels industries of the Territories that they have been of relatively slight importance both in terms of national production of mineral fuels and with respect to the economy of the territorial north itself. The total output of coal in the Yukon and petroleum in the Northwest Territories

[18]Canada, Department of Northern Affairs and National Resources, *Annual Report 1960–1* (Ottawa, 1961), p. 42.

remained an insignificant part of the total Canadian production of these fuels. In the context of the territorial economy, their chief importance lay neither in the employment opportunities they provided, nor in the contribution they made to the total value of production there. In the early 1960s annual employment at Norman Wells averaged about a dozen men and in the Yukon coal mines about six. In 1961 only 2.4 per cent of the total value of mineral production in the Yukon and Northwest Territories was accounted for by the production of mineral fuels. The real importance of these industries lay in the fact that they probably permitted lower fuel and power costs for the metal mining and transportation industries located in the Territories than would otherwise have been possible. The significance of this contribution will be considered further in Chapter 7 below.

THE FOREST INDUSTRIES

It was noted in Chapter I that the forest resources of the territorial north, while not extensive, are probably greater than their northerly location might suggest. The eastern part of the Northwest Territories lying in or near the arctic climatic area is virtually devoid of significant tree growth, but in Mackenzie District to the west there are fairly substantial forested areas, especially in the river valleys. Further north in Mackenzie District the wooded areas become more and more scattered and the tree growth increasingly stunted. Nevertheless, in the valley of the Mackenzie, trees suitable for use as firewood are found as far north as the Delta. The chief varieties in the southern parts of the district are white and black spruce, white birch, aspen and balsam poplar, tamarack and jackpine. In the Yukon tree growth is extensive throughout the Territory up to about 65° north, beyond which latitude wooded areas become sparse, the varieties few, and the rate of growth extremely slow. Even below 65°, however, the relatively high elevation of the central Yukon, the lack of moisture and the short growing season combine to inhibit tree growth. As in Mackenzie District, major stands of trees which have attained a commercial size occur chiefly in the river valleys and other low places. In these stands, white spruce is the most important species. Other important species, often found in the same stands as white spruce, are the aspen and balsam poplar and birch.

Throughout the north these forests have always supplied the local population with building materials and fuel wood. But it was not until mining developed that a commercial market for forest products appeared. The chief products required were lumber for the construction of buildings in the mining camps, timber for use in the mines themselves, and fuel wood for both industrial and domestic heating purposes. The small local forest industry that has developed in the Territories has always been, and it remains today, a creation of the mining industries there.

The first major mining event to create a substantial demand in the north for forest products was, of course, the Klondike gold rush. Although useful statistical information concerning these operations is not available before the 1930s, it has been reported that for about 30 years after the gold rush of 1898, "nearly all lumber used in the Yukon was of local manufacture."[19] Very large amounts of lumber were used up quickly to construct the town of Dawson and many placer mining camps in the vicinity. Quantities of fuelwood were also consumed in the thawing operations at the placer mining grounds themselves. It is not surprising then that accessible stands of good timber were depleted within a very few years.[20] As the accessible timber disappeared, local forest products became increasingly costly. This not only encouraged local users to develop alternative sources of fuel in the form of coal, as already noted, but it also made imported lumber competitive in local markets. Such imported lumber tended to be of a higher quality than that produced locally, partly because of the superior tree growth from which it was derived, but also because of a higher standard of quality control exercised in its production. Because of this, and the relatively good transport facilities from mills in British Columbia to the central Yukon, after about 1930 a major part of the need for lumber in the Yukon came to be satisfied by products imported from outside. Since then local forest resources have continued to supply local needs and to sustain a certain amount of employment in the woods and in the sawmills of the Yukon. But the extent of these small-scale local operations has been dictated by the competition from outside large-scale producers. The local industry has continued to exist largely by virtue of the shelter afforded by a none-too-secure natural protective tariff—the cost of transporting products into the Yukon from "outside."

The situation in Mackenzie District has been similar to that in the Yukon, although the development of the mining market as a support for local operations in the woods did not occur there until the 1930s. As in

[19]Canada, Department of Mines and Resources, The Yukon Territory—Administration, Resources, Development (Ottawa, 1944), p. 20.
[20]See pp. 97–8.

the Yukon, small sawmills (usually equipped with planing facilities) were set up at suitable locations having access both to river transport and to good stands of timber. In both Territories the administration of the forest operations has been a federal responsibility. Commercial timber berths have been made available by licence and permits issued for cutting specified amounts of timber in both Territories. Throughout most of their history, however, the regulation exercised over forest operations there must have been rather casual in so far as little was known of the extent and characteristics of the forest resources themselves until after World War II. It was only when national attention was drawn to the area by the military undertakings there in the 1940s that systematic inventories and studies of these resources began. In the Yukon, for example, the construction of the Alaska Highway during the war greatly facilitated the investigation of forest resources through the southern and western parts of the Territory. One of the first reconnaisance surveys of the forested areas along the route of the highway, and along the Yukon River between Whitehorse and Dawson, was carried out in the summer of 1943 by the federal Department of Mines. As a result of such investigations it was estimated that the forests of the Yukon could sustain an annual cut of 50 to 100 million board feet under the conditions prevailing in 1945.[21] The actual amount reported cut annually in the Yukon will be seen in Table 5.4 to have never exceeded ten million board feet even in the peak years to 1961. From this it is clear that the exploitation of the timber resources of the Yukon must have been limited not by "physical" factors but by economic ones. The studies made by Holman in the Yukon showed that in the vicinities of larger centres such as Whitehorse and Dawson, practically all the reserves of standing timber had been exhausted. Consequently, that part of the demand for forest products which was satisfied by production from within the Territory was supplied from areas located a considerable distance from these centres—the Stewart River area in the case of Dawson and the Teslin and Marshall Creek areas for Whitehorse.[22] In each case the local products were transported 100 miles by road. Under these conditions British Columbia forest products were found to be highly competitive, especially in the Whitehorse market.

[21]J. L. Robinson, "Agriculture and Forests of Yukon Territory," *Canadian Geographical Journal*, XXXI (August 1945), 70.

[22]H. L. Holman, "Forest Resources of the Yukon," cited in *North Pacific Planning Project*, pp. 50–6.

Similar surveys were begun in the southern part of Mackenzie District in the late 1940s. These confirmed the existence there of at least two major areas possessing significant timber reserves: one along the Slave River between Fort Smith and Great Slave Lake and the other in the lower Liard River valley between Nelson Fork and Fort Simpson. A more detailed survey of the southern part of Mackenzie District and of Wood Buffalo National Park, which extends southward into Alberta, was made in 1949. It was subsequently estimated that almost 2 billion feet board measure of "excellent spruce saw timber" was available along the Peace River and its delta in Wood Buffalo National Park. A further 85 million feet board measure was estimated to be available along the Slave River from Fort Smith to its mouth in Great Slave Lake.[23] During the 1950s large-scale lumbering operations, by territorial standards, were established in these areas and these account for the very great increase in the amount of timber cut and attributed to the Northwest Territories in Table 5.4 for the years after 1950. Although much of this output came from forests located in northern Alberta, because it was from a park area under federal jurisdiction, it is included with territorial production. The figures shown are consequently somewhat misleading for this period. Furthermore, much of the output from this area was sold in markets outside the Territories. What is apparent, however, is that the potential output of these southern areas, supplemented by the much smaller local operations scattered northward along the Mackenzie Valley was more than adequate to supply the territorial market. The bulk of this market, as in the Yukon, was provided by mining operations and especially by major new mining developments with their attendant construction programmes.

The general condition of the forest industries in the Yukon and Northwest Territories after 1940 is indicated by the data set out in Table 5.5. Given even the very rough estimates of the amount of wood available in the Territories noted above, it is apparent that physical output in these industries was limited by the market rather than the availability of the natural resource. It will be noted that this market showed evidence of only modest expansion—judging by the total volume of forest production. The war years, and especially 1943, were unusual, of course, for the normal market for forest products in the Territories was enormously swollen by military needs at that time. The record output in 1956 was largely the consequence of the large-scale lumbering operations in Wood

Buffalo National Park and the Fort Smith area referred to above. The subsequent falling off in total output reflects a general weakness of lumber markets, including those "outside" markets upon which these larger commercial operations were depending for most of their sales. The total equivalent volume in merchantable timber produced for sawing in the Yukon and Northwest Territories in 1956 was 5,204,000 cubic feet. By 1959 it had fallen to 1,276,000 cubic feet.

The other main products of the industry were mining timbers and fuelwood. In the case of the former the demand was obviously a function of the amount of development work being done in the various underground mining operations and the fluctuations in output shown in Table 5.5 require no further explanation. But, in the case of fuelwood production, it will be noted that, despite population growth, physical output failed to increase during the 1950s and in some years actually fell to record low levels. Output in 1959, for example, was lower than that recorded in 1940. The explanation for this is to be found in the adoption of fuel oil in the place of wood for both domestic and commercial heating purposes throughout the north. As local supplies of fuelwood became increasingly expensive due to the exhaustion of easily accessible stands of trees in the vicinity of settlements, and as transportation facilities gradually improved, fuel oil became increasingly competitive in terms of price. But in addition to this, fuel oil has certain obvious advantages over fuelwood, especially in larger applications (such as central heating plants) because it lends itself to mechanical handling and automatic control. Even in smaller domestic applications, users who had become accustomed to this type of fuel "outside" naturally prefered it to "old fashioned" fuelwood. These points were well illustrated when the Northwest Territories Council considered the possibility of encouraging the use of locally produced fuelwood in Inuvik as a means of creating employment in the Mackenzie Delta area. The investigation of the relative costs involved indicated that only one federal government building in Inuvik was heated with wood and that this involved an annual outlay of $4,000 for 200 cords of wood plus $3,500 worth of labour used to carry wood, stoke the furnace, and remove ashes. Using fuel oil to heat this building, it was estimated, would require 17,800 gallons at 25.3 cents per gallon for a total of $4,500 and no additional labour costs. With respect to privately owned buildings in Inuvik, it was indicated that "unless there were a cost incentive (which, on the basis of the estimated costs for supplying wood for departmental buildings, would require a substantial subsidy), it is unlikely that the average householder now using oil would wish to convert to wood and give up the convenience and economy of oil."[24] Similar conditions apparently prevailed in other parts of the north and explain the failure of local fuelwood production to keep pace with the growth of population and economic activity throughout the Territories in the post-World War II years.

It is obvious then that both the main products of the territorial forest industries, logs and bolts for sawing and fuelwood, have faced strong competition from products produced outside. As we shall see in a later chapter, the protection afforded local forest industries by high transportation costs was steadily eroded during the 1940s and 1950s by the installation of new transportation facilities and by the improvement of existing ones. Consequently, the markets for local production were restricted and forestry declined in importance as a component of the territorial economies. As shown in Table 11.13, the percentage of the total net value of commodity production in the Yukon and Northwest Territories attributable to forestry declined from 8 per cent in 1947 to less than 4 per cent in the late 1950s. The actual decline was in fact very much greater than that indicated because of the inclusion of Wood Buffalo National Park timber operations in the totals attributed to the Northwest Territories since 1953. Actual lumber production from operations in the Northwest Territories outside Wood Buffalo National Park probably did not exceed two million board feet annually in the later 1950s, compared with the totals shown which are based on a physical lumber production of several times that amount. The actual amount of employment provided by the operations in the woods is difficult to estimate because of the casual nature of much of this employment and the irregularity of it. But in the Northwest Territories, Workmen's Compensation statistics indicate that lumbering operations in the woods during the 1950s did not exceed, and frequently fell far below, a monthly average of 43 employees. Similar small numbers were probably employed in the Yukon where comparable amounts of timber were cut. Closely associated with these operations, however, were the various sawmills which employed, during the 1950s, a maximum of 76 persons in the Territories. During the later years of the decade the number of mills declined and employment fell to only 21 persons in 1959.

As was seen to have been the case in the mineral fuels industries, by the early 1960s the forest industries of the territories had not become a significant source either of employment or income. Their importance

[24]Council of the Northwest Territories, *Votes and Proceedings, 1963*, Sessional Paper No. 14, pp. 180–1.

rested almost entirely upon the way they made supplies of wood products available to some local users who, given the poor transportation facilities at hand, would either have been unable to operate at all, or who would at the very least have been faced with higher operating costs resulting from the necessity of importing wood products from outside. It is interesting to note in this connection that mining companies, such as Eldorado Gold Mines, which developed Port Radium, and more recently Taurcanus Mines Limited, operating near Yellowknife, established their own lumbering operations in order to satisfy their requirements for various forest products. Nevertheless, it would appear that the importance of local forestry in the Territories was waning during the 1950s. One of the important reasons for this may have been the changes in transportation which will be described in Part III—a possibility which is strengthened by the experience of the small agricultural industry which had a role to play in the economy of the north similar in many ways to that of the forest industries.

AGRICULTURE

One misconception prevalent outside the north is that agricultural production is physically impossible there. In fact such production has been commonplace, at least in the western regions, since the first settlements were established there early in the nineteenth century. While it is true that local growing conditions are frequently not good even in the more favoured regions, the historical record of development suggests that northern agriculture has probably been limited more by factors operating on the demand side of the market than by those directly restricting supply.

Prior to World War II remarkably little was known of the agricultural possibilities of either the Yukon or of the Northwest Territories, although foodstuffs had been produced in Mackenzie District and in the central Yukon since the early days of the fur trade. In the Mackenzie Valley gardens had been established at all the Hudson's Bay Company's trading-posts as far north as Fort Good Hope by 1826.[25] Fort Good Hope is within a few miles of the Arctic Circle. Thereafter, traders and missionaries demonstrated that vegetables could be grown even further north— as far north indeed, as Aklavik in the Mackenzie delta. In the Yukon,

---

[25]Canada, Department of Northern Affairs and National Resources, *Industries of the Northwest Territories* (Ottawa, 1953), p. 27.

extensive cultivation of vegetables and the grazing of cattle were undertaken with the development of the Klondike in the 1890s. These activities
were initially concentrated in the Dawson area, but they subsequently
spread to Mayo and other centres in the central Yukon. That these
efforts in the Yukon were also reasonably successful is suggested by a
government report of 1909 which complained that "Up to the present
time . . . the number of agriculturists is not sufficient to supply the
local demand for farm produce, and the quality of some of the products
is not quite equal to the imported article." The report went on to say
that "Careful and systematic farming operations, with due regard to
the peculiarities of the climate, would abolish the importation into the
Yukon of many of the agricultural products required by the people of
Dawson and surrounding districts."[26] Thus, it appears that early in this
century there were many small agricultural operations established in
the Yukon and in Mackenzie District to supply at least part of the food
requirements of the population engaged in the fur trade, mining, and
other activities. One authority writing in the 1940s expressed the conviction that during the early years of the century there was a greater total
acreage under cultivation in the Mackenzie Valley than there was at the
end of the World War II.[27] Less surprisingly, given the great decrease
in population there, the same appears to have been true in the Yukon
where to this day visitors to Dawson City may see traces of large garden
plots on land that has not been worked for half a century.

It is not difficult to find the reasons for the proliferation of agricultural
activities throughout the Territories during the early years of their
development history. The lack of transportation facilities made it difficult
and costly to import supplies from the outside. What facilities did exist,
such as the river systems, were slow and operated only a few months out
of the year. Perishable commodities could seldom be imported at *any*
price under these conditions. Consequently, fresh vegetables and fruits
had either to be grown locally or done without. Furthermore, the Hudson's Bay Company itself encouraged its Factors to establish gardens
in order to reduce the effects of heavier food imports on the already
unbalanced volume of inbound compared to outbound freight on its
river transportation systems. Encouragement to local agriculture in the
Territories was also provided by the federal government which under-

[26]Canada, Department of the Interior, *The Yukon Territory: Its History and
Resources* (Ottawa, 1909), p. 124.
[27]J. L. Robinson, "Land Use Possibilities in Mackenzie District, N.W.T.," *Canadian
Geographical Journal*, XXXI (July, 1945), p. 37.

took a certain amount of agricultural experimental work in co-operation with religious missions in the Mackenzie Valley after 1911 and in the Yukon after 1915. The Dominion Experimental Farms Service participated in field studies with the Oblate missions at Fort Smith, Fort Resolution, and Fort Providence along the Mackenzie River from 1911 until 1940 and at Fort Good Hope from 1928 to 1940. In the Yukon a sub-station was established at Minto Creek in 1915 and two years later on an established farm at Swede Creek in the Dawson area.[28] Studies of crops cultivated by missionaries at Carmacks and Carcross in the Yukon were also made during the 1930s.

The agricultural experimental work done in the Territories before World War II appears to have done little more than confirm the belief that soils and growing conditions, while not good, at least did not prohibit the production of vegetables and even cereals in many scattered northern locations. The effectiveness of this early work was, unfortunately, severely limited by difficult problems of communication and the divided interests of the amateur horticulturists who did the field work. By the late 1930s the entire programme appears to have disintegrated and it was not until interest in the north was revived by the events of World War II that a more comprehensive scientific appraisal of its agricultural possibilities was undertaken.

In 1943 the federal government established the Interdepartmental Committee on Agriculture for Northern Canada in order to "encourage agriculture in the Territories and also in the Yukon."[29] This committee was responsible for a series of soil surveys carried out by various government agricultural experts over the course of the next several years. Surveys were conducted along the Alaska Highway in the Yukon, up the Liard River valley and throughout the Mackenzie Valley in the Northwest Territories.

These surveys, made in haste and with small staffs, were merely preliminary investigations but, even so, they provided the first serious descriptions of the agricultural resources of the northwest. They revealed the existence of considerable areas of soil suitable for cultivation and they suggested that, while growing seasons were short, the long hours of sunlight could offset this disadvantage to a sufficient degree to permit production of many early ripening cereals as well as of most vegetable

[28]Canada, Department of Mines and Resources, *Canada's Western Northland—Its History, Resources, Population, and Administration* (Ottawa, 1937), p. 74.
[29]Canada, Department of Northern Affairs and National Resources, *Industries of the Northwest Territories* (Ottawa, 1953), p. 28.

crops. In his 1945 survey of the Mackenzie,[30] Leahey reported that "drought is the most serious factor limiting crop production"—a conclusion supported by a subsequent study of evapotranspiration[31] rates in the valley. The latter reported as follows on the situation at Fort Norman.

When moisture reserves are exhausted, and in Fort Norman this occurs about the end of June in the average year, the crops must depend on current precipitation for their water supply. Usually the summer rainfall is not enough to meet the demand and a water deficiency, or drought, occurs.[32]

Similarly, in the Yukon an experimental farm sub-station established in 1944 at Pine Creek in the Takhini–Dezadeash Valley, one of the largest tracts of potential agricultural land in the Territory, found that the chief physical difficulty there was the shortage of moisture.[33] But, despite such difficulties, experience at these experimental farms and also at the few private farms established throughout the Territories indicated that it was possible to produce a considerable variety of agricultural products. Feeds successfully produced over the years from 1921 to 1961 included root crops such as potatoes, turnips, and carrots; cereals including wheat, oats, and barley; and cultivated hay and other fodder crops. Horses, cattle, swine, and poultry have been maintained at many locations. The number of cattle, it might be noted here, rose from 47 in 1921 to 72 by 1931 and then declined to 15 in 1951. By 1961, however, this figure had increased to over 200.

Unfortunately, estimates of the amount of land suitable for agricultural production in the Territories have varied so greatly as to make it difficult to attempt anything but the roughest guess as to what the potential might in fact be. The post-war surveys mentioned above suggested, however, that there might be something like one million acres of land suitable for mixed farming or ranching in the Northwest Territories and perhaps 250,000 acres in the southern and west-central parts of the Yukon.

[30]See A. Leahey, "Soil Survey of the Mackenzie and Liard Valleys," Dominion Experimental Farms Service Pamphlet, 1945 (mimeographed).
[31]The evapotranspiration rate is used in the Thornthwaite classification of climate to relate the water need of growing plants to the available moisture in a given area. The study quoted (see next footnote) states further that "It has often been said that although precipitation is low in northwestern Canada, the need for water is low and a humid climate results. Nevertheless, the Thornthwaite classification indicates that the water need . . . in the northwest is high and a subhumid climate results."
[32]M. Sanderson, "Is Canada's Northwest Subhumid?", Canadian Geographical Journal XLI (September 1950), 144.
[33]W. Dickson, "Northern Agriculture," in Dawson, ed., The New Northwest, p. 180.

Information relating to the amount of this land actually brought under cultivation over the years is equally conjectural. Canadian census data indicates that in the Yukon Territory the total number of acres included in established farms rose from 1,622 acres in 1921 to 5,197 acres in 1931. This figure thereafter declined to 2,781 acres in 1941, and to only 432 acres by 1951.[34] The total land under cultivation in the Northwest Territories in 1943 was reported by Robinson to be 252 acres.[35] Subsequent census data cover the Yukon and the Northwest Territories together and indicate a total farm area of 4,477 acres in 1956 and of 8,590 in 1961.[36] Of the total 8,590 acres of farmland reported in 1961 only 1,088 acres were described as improved land and of these only 526 acres were actually under crop. Crude as it may be, this information shows conclusively that only an insignificant part of the total potential agricultural land available and suitable for production in the Territories has been brought under cultivation to date. The data also indicate, of course, that agriculture, like forestry and the mineral fuels industries, has not been an important source of employment or income in the territorial economies. The total farm population of the Territories in 1956 was 56 and in 1961 it had risen to 65. No estimates of the value of farm production are available.

There is some evidence that the decline in agricultural activity in the Yukon and Northwest Territories which is apparent in the census data from 1921 to 1951 was checked and that during the 1950s a renewed effort to expand local food production got under way. The increase in farm area from 432 acres in 1951 to 8,590 acres in 1961 and the increase in the number of occupied farms from 4 to 26 have been noted. Data relating to the number of agricultural land leases in effect in the Yukon and in the Northwest Territories confirm this trend, although the numbers are so small that it is not possible to have any confidence in their significance. The number of leases in good standing in the Yukon Territory rose from 5 in 1953 to 13 in 1961 and in the Northwest Territories from a low of 8 in 1955 to 20 in 1961.[37] In the Yukon it was reported in 1961 that "growing interest in arable land" there had prompted the establishment of an "interdepartmental committee made up

[34]The figures used are those given for the Yukon Territory in the 1921 Census (Volume V, p. cxvii) and in the 1951 Census (Volume VIII, Appendix B) for 1931, 1941, and 1951.

[35]J. L. Robinson, "Land Use Possibilities in Mackenzie District, N.W.T.," *Canadian Geographical Journal*, XXXI (July 1945), p. 38.

[36]D.B.S., *Census of Canada 1956 and 1961*.

[37]Data from *Annual Reports* of the Department of Northern Affairs and National Resources.

of representatives of the Department of Agriculture and the Economics and Resources Division of Northern Affairs and National Resources."[38] But, at the same time, in the Northwest Territories concern was being expressed for the future of agriculture there. The commissioner of the Northwest Territories stated in a meeting of the Northwest Territories Council in 1961 that there "certainly appeared to be less agriculture in the north at the moment than in previous decades."[39]

In the absence of useful data describing the volume of farm output in the Yukon and Northwest Territories it is difficult to judge whether the industry, if we may call it that, has in fact been expanding or contracting during the last decade or so. While the data on farm acreage and number of agricultural leases in effect cited above might suggest an increase in agricultural activity there, they indicate that at best the long run decline in the absolute amount of this activity may have been checked. When account is taken of the extraordinary population increase in the Territories since 1951, however, it is likely that local agricultural production has continued to provide a *decreasing* share of the total amount of food consumed there. The total population of the Yukon and of the Northwest Territories more than quadrupled between 1951 and 1961. The farm population on the other hand increased less than one and a half times. Furthermore, when the economic classification of the farms is considered, it is apparent that most of the increase in the number and acreage of farms between 1951 and 1961 was attributable to the establishment (or reporting) of new non-commercial farms. The increase in the number of farms reported, from 4 to 26, was attributable to the reporting of eleven small-scale farms, six of which were "part-time" operations; seven "residential and other small farms"; and five "institutional farms," such as experimental farms and farms attached to training schools and similar institutions. The increase in the number of commercial farms was only from two in 1951 to three in 1961 although there was some increase in the size of the individual operations concerned. The two commercial farms reported in 1951 sold only between $1,200 and $2,499 worth of products annually whereas two of the three reported in 1961 had sales in excess of this. From this data it may be inferred that commercial sales of farm products in the Territories in 1951 could not have exceeded $5,000. In 1961 they could not have exceeded $12,000.[40] Assuming that

[38]Canada, Department of Northern Affairs and National Resources, *Annual Report 1961–2* (Ottawa, 1962), p. 39.
[39]See Council of the Northwest Territories, *Votes and Proceedings, 1961*, p. 21.
[40]D.B.S., *Canada Year Book 1963–4*, p. 479.

the approximately 30,000 white residents of the Territories in 1961 spent only the national per capita average of about $318 annually for food (and because of higher prices in the north they probably spent considerably more), total food consumption there must have approached 10 million dollars. It appears unlikely, therefore, that much more than one-tenth of one per cent of the food requirements in the Yukon and Northwest Territories in 1961 would have been produced locally.

No matter how inaccurate such a crude estimate may be, it is obvious that local producers have supplied only a very small part indeed of the food requirements of the population of the Territories. At the same time it has been shown that a similarly small part of the available arable land in the area has been brought under cultivation. Some of the possible reasons for the restriction of local agriculture will be considered in Chapter 6. Here our main concern has been to indicate the extent of agricultural development and to outline briefly some aspects of its evolution up to the early 1960s. Slight though this development was, it did serve to demonstrate that food could be produced at a great many places in the north despite the frequently unfavourable climatic and soils conditions. And, given the fact that only a very small part of the known arable land resources had in fact been utilized, even during the 1950s, it must be concluded that the level of agricultural output attained had not reached the point where it was being restricted by such physical factors directly. In fact we have seen that the level of output in the 1950s barely exceeded the levels attained earlier in this century when knowledge of the soils, climate, and suitable plant varieties was inferior to that subsequently available. In Chapter 6 it will be argued that the effective limit to agricultural development in the Territories has been determined by the fact that the local population has generally preferred imported to locally produced foodstuffs whenever a choice was available and that this preference was determined in turn both by considerations of price and "taste."

MANUFACTURING

The final privately undertaken commodity producing industry in the Territories to be considered is manufacturing. The greatest part of this industry has been closely related to the petroleum and forestry operations described earlier in this chapter, for the refining of crude oil at Norman Wells and the production of sawn and planed lumber in the sawmills scattered throughout the Territories were the most important sources of "manufacturing" output attributable to the Yukon and the Northwest Territories. Other manufacturing output consisted of bakery products, carbonated beverages, painting and publishing, art goods and novelties, salt, jewellery, and sheet metal products. With the exception of sawmills, however, the number of establishments producing these commodities during the 1950s did not exceed more than one or two, sometimes three, in each case.

The history of some of these manufacturing activities in the Yukon and Northwest Territories has been a long one, dating from the time of the earliest settlements. The local production of lumber and other wood products was begun during the nineteenth century at points both in the Yukon and in the Mackenzie Valley. The Klondike boom in the Yukon, of course, created a substantial local market there for manufactured goods such as newspapers and other local publications, bread and other bakery products, simple furniture, mill work, and a variety of other goods which it was difficult or impossible to bring in from "outside." Census of industry data for the Yukon between 1917 and 1922 indicate that in 1918 there were 14 manufacturing establishments in the Yukon (excluding laundries, shoe repair, blacksmithing and other "repair industries") employing a total of 59 persons. From then until 1922 the number of establishments declined steadily reaching 3 (employing a total of 10 persons) in that year. The population of the Yukon by then was roughly half of what it had been a decade earlier. Publication of manufacturing data for the Yukon ceased in 1923 and was not resumed until 1939 when it was combined with the Northwest Territories.[41]

The net value of manufactures for the Yukon and the Northwest Territories since 1939, as set out in Table 11.13, shows that this has been a small industry characterized by very slow growth up to the middle of the 1950s and by a declining absolute level of output in more recent years. The net value of manufacturing output in terms of current dollars rose quite steadily from under $100,000 in 1939 to a record $1,856,000 in 1954 and, by the early 1960s, had declined to less than half that figure. The relative importance of the manufacturing industry to the economy of the Territories is suggested by the fact that during the post-World War II period it often contributed more to the total net value of commodity production there than did forestry, fishing, or even trapping. In 1955, for example, manufacturing accounted for approximately 5 per cent of the total compared to 1.5 per cent for forestry,

[41]D.B.S., *Canada Year Book 1924*, Table 1, p. 388.

1.7 per cent for the fisheries, and 2.5 per cent for trapping. The subsequent decline in the absolute value of manufactured output thereafter, however, placed manufacturing roughly on a level with trapping and the fisheries in terms of the net value of production.

The general trend of the industry's development is further illustrated by the data in Table 5.6. The number of manufacturing establishments rose from 5 in 1939 to 12 in 1944. During the post-war years the proliferation of these establishments continued, the number rising quite steadily to a peak of 31 in 1954. Similarly, total employment rose from 55 in 1939 to a record 191 in 1954. But after 1954 the number of establishments and the number of employees declined rapidly, bringing the number of establishments by 1959 back to 12, the same number as in 1944. Figures for the early 1960s suggest that this downward trend may have been halted, but there was no indication that a major reversal was taking place.

A more detailed analysis of the manufacturing operations in the Territories shows that a major factor in the decline of manufacturing activity after 1954 was the reduction of sawmill operations. During most of the decade of the 1950s sawmills accounted for about half the total number of manufacturing establishments; but between 1954 and 1959 their number fell from 18 to 4. Employment in sawmills declined from 689 in 1953 to 260 in 1959.

It has already been noted in an earlier part of this chapter that large timber concessions made in Wood Buffalo National Park in 1956 permitted the production of far more lumber than even the entire Mackenzie Valley could absorb and that this would probably eliminate many small operators in that area. However, total sawmill output declined from a record $677,515 in 1953 to less than $260,000 in 1959. But important as the deterioration of this particular industry was as a cause of the over-all decline in manufacturing activity, it is significant that other activities, such as baking, also experienced a contraction during the 1950s, as is shown in Table 5.7.

The conclusion which must be drawn from this information is that despite continued, if erratic, growth of local markets in the Territories during the 1940s and 1950s, the local production of food, wood, and a small number of other manufactured commodities did not increase in relative importance. In the absence of direct information on the actual volume of manufacturing output, it is impossible to assess the extent to which local production supplied the local demand for these commodities; but employment statistics would suggest that while some increase in manufacturing employment relative to total population took place during the 1940s, just the opposite trend occurred in the 1950s. In 1941 approximately 0.4 per cent of the population was employed in "manufacturing." This increased to 0.6 per cent in 1951, but by 1961 the figure had fallen back to roughly the 1941 level. This, combined with the failure of new types of manufacturing activity to appear (or to survive more than briefly), despite a growing market suggests that the development of manufacturing, like the development of the other industries examined in this chapter, has been somehow discouraged or restrained, especially in the later post-World War II years. The obvious explanation is the same in all cases. If the total population was growing, but local production of fuel, food, lumber, and other supplies was not keeping pace in terms of quantity and variety of goods produced, the proportion of goods imported from outside the Territories must have been increasing. And if local producers found it difficult to expand, or even to retain, their share of local markets it must have been because imported goods were relatively more attractive to the population. The most likely causes of this, in turn, would be considerations of relative prices and the "tastes" or preferences of local users as between locally produced and imported commodities. These possibilities are considered further in the following chapter.

6 Factors Restricting the Private Development of Industry in the Territorial North

THE FIRST TWO chapters in this part have traced the development of various natural resources of the territorial north by private *entrepreneurs* from the early days of the fur trade to the beginning of the 1960s. In each of the industries established on the base of these resources we have seen that the level of output attained over this period of time was not *directly* limited by the availability of the natural resources themselves. That is, the production of furs, minerals, fish, forest products, agricultural products, and certain locally manufactured goods, was not in any instance carried to the point where further development was prohibited because of the exhaustion or rate of depletion of the necessary natural resources. But if the development of these industries was stopped short of this point where a direct physical limit would have become effective we must seek another cause. And the appropriate place to begin is by asking who in fact was responsible for making the decisions which restricted development in these industries to the levels which were attained. The answer is, of course, that all these industries were, with only temporary exceptions during and shortly after World War II, under the direction of private investors. If we may follow the traditional assumption that the business decisions of such agencies were motivated by a concern to earn a profit, we must conclude that the effective limit to the development of the northern resource-based industries has been the private investor's estimate of their probable profitability. This must in turn derive ultimately from the markets for the commodities produced and the costs of producing them. It is on the basis of the first of these factors, the markets, that the distinction was made which separated Chapters 3 and 4 above, dealing with the "export base industries" of the north, from Chapter 5 on the "residentiary industries." The former industries have sold their output in national or international markets outside the north. The latter industries have been oriented toward local markets within the Territories themselves. In both cases locally produced goods have had to compete with similar or identical goods produced outside. The extent to which they have been able to do this in a commercially profitable manner has depended upon the relative costs of producing these goods inside and outside the Territories.

The contention here is that the most obvious factor influencing the competitive position of territorial industries is also by far the most important—the simple fact that territorial producers are remote from the places where most consumption and most other production of goods takes place. This remoteness from major centres of economic life shows up in the costs of producing goods whether they are for "export" to outside markets or for consumption inside. The economic and political development in the Territories described in the first two parts of this discussion may be understood in terms of the struggle by producers operating on northern land resources to overcome the effects of remoteness. But such remoteness is not merely a spatial phenomenon. The distance factor, for example, may be offset by the provision of transportation facilities. Since the construction of the Mackenzie Highway Yellowknife is certainly much less remote than it was in the 1940s. The other cause of remoteness is the absence of local markets and supplies of productive resources. New York is just as far away from Dawson City as Dawson City is far away from New York, but only a person with rather unusual standards in mind would think of New York as the remote place. Consequently, a second approach to overcoming remoteness is to develop in the distant area some of the things which it was initially remote from. One of these things might be population. Migration into the remote area could be expected to provide both a local market for produced goods and services and a local supply of labour for local industries. The other main class of things which could be brought in would be capital goods and facilities of various kinds: electric power stations and hospitals. How are such "remedies" for remoteness to be brought about? Do they occur spontaneously and piecemeal as a consequence of "natural" economic forces or must they be deliberately organized and encouraged by some centralized agency? Some reliance has been placed on both methods in the course of territorial history. Prior to World War II the tendency was to rely on natural market forces to provide the appropriate (economically warranted) allocation of human and capital resources to the Territories. After World War II, as suggested in Chapter II, a more active policy of central administration of the transfer of labour and capital resources to the Territories was adopted.

The purpose of this chapter is to show how the phenomenon of remoteness as described above has been translated into cost of production levels which have in turn restricted the level of resource development in the Territories. And we will also see how the private *entrepreneurs* directing this development sought to overcome the effects of remoteness, on their own initiative, prior to the large-scale participation by government in territorial economic life after World War II.

PRODUCTION COSTS IN THE TERRITORIES

Although it is a commonplace that northern producers of goods and services of virtually all kinds must be confronted with "high" operating and overhead costs of production because of their location, very little is known of the cost differentials which do in fact exist between the Territories and other parts of Canada. One reason for this is the almost complete absence of statistical data relating to territorial production in official publications. Only within very recent years have the Yukon and the Northwest Territories begun to appear regularly in some basic publications of the Dominion Bureau of Statistics. The reasons for this are not difficult to find. The figures involved are frequently statistically insignificant, they are difficult to collect in the first place, and the fact that only a few producing firms are involved in each industry creates the possibility that published data might disclose information obviously pertaining to a particular firm or individual.

Quite apart from these practical difficulties are the usual technical difficulties involved in any inter-regional comparison of production data. Relative costs are determined by a great many factors, some of which are difficult to standardize; these will include the geographical factors such as climate and topography, economic factors such as the scale of operations involved, political factors such as relative tax burdens, and demographic factors including the nature and extent of available labour resources.

Under these circumstances it would obviously be desirable to undertake a serious direct study of relative production costs in the Territories so that these may be directly compared to those prevailing in relevant areas outside before attempting to draw conclusions as to the seriousness of the differentials involved. Such a study has been found to require resources beyond those available to the present writer. The following is presented in order to show that it would be rash to accept at face value prevalent popular assumptions concerning the extent and nature of the cost disadvantage at which northern producers operate.

Labour Costs

Attention here is focused upon costs of labour inputs employed by private producers in the Territories during the early 1960s. The chief industries for which useful data are available are gold-mining, metal-mining other than gold and iron, manufacturing (including sawmill operations) and, to a lesser extent, construction.

A simple comparison of hourly wage rates in the Territories with those prevailing in other areas at this time indicates that while territorial hourly rates were in some industries, such as gold-mining, generally higher than they were outside, in other industries they were sometimes relatively low. Table 6.1 compares average hourly wage rates (time work) of various underground and surface occupations in auriferous quartz-mining operations in the Territories (Yellowknife) with those in Quebec, Ontario, and British Columbia for 1961. Territorial workers were paid at a rate approximately 25 per cent higher than the industry average on a time work basis and, in the case of "miners," over 66 per cent higher in terms of straight-time earnings (basic rates plus bonus earnings). It appears that higher bonus payments were characteristic of northern operations. The effect of this upon operating costs may have been offset, of course, by greater productivity, a possibility considered later in this section.

Turning from auriferous quartz to other types of mining, the hourly wage rate differential between territorial and other mining centres disappears, or is even reversed. Unfortunately the data is also less revealing, for the territorial operations included in Table 6.2 were chiefly silver-lead-zinc–mining operations whereas that for the provinces included silver-cobalt, nickel-copper, and several other types of mining. But for the two occupations shown, "miner" and "miner's helper," the Yukon rates in 1961 were in fact lower than the industry average for

Canada and, in the case of "miners," lower than in Quebec, Ontario, and British Columbia.

The only other wage rate comparisons that can be made here are for certain occupations in the construction industry for the year 1961. Table 6.3 compares the rates for bricklayers, carpenters, electricians, plumbers and other tradesmen prevailing in territorial centres lying west of 110° longitude with those prevailing in a number of other centres located on the prairies, at the Lakehead, and in important mining areas of Ontario and Quebec. Again, the differences are not, perhaps, what might have been expected. The fact that rates in the Northwest Territories were almost identical to those prevailing in Edmonton probably reflects the fact that most of the labour in centres such as Yellowknife was drawn from Edmonton, largely through an effective placement service provided by the Alberta and Northwest Chamber of Mines located there. The other conspicuous element of the table is the fact that the rates in the Yukon and Northwest Territories were considerably lower than those prevailing at the Lakehead centres of Fort William and Port Arthur—centres closer to the heavily populated industrial region of Canada by more than 1,500 air miles.

It is obvious, of course, that local market conditions will exert a strong influence on such hourly wage rates as these, and that relative rates will fluctuate considerably over time. The value of such a comparison lies in the fact that it discourages the belief that northern labour markets are somehow unique, by virtue of incomparably high wage rates. For some types of labour these rates have tended to be higher in the Territories than in most of the more southerly parts of the country. But it is also true that if labour inputs were more costly for "northern" than for "southern" operators in mining and other industries, consistently higher wage rates alone can hardly be taken as the inevitable cause. Even the sketchy evidence presented above demonstrates that producers in other areas can be confronted by equally high, and sometimes even higher, market prices for this particular factor of production.

Even if hourly wage rates in the Territories have not always been as relatively high as might have been expected, however, labour costs for territorial producers may still have been relatively high in terms of costs per unit of output. In mining, for example, the cost of labour per ton of ore milled could be higher in one operation than another even if hourly wage rates were similar. Differences in the quality of other inputs such as land, capital, and *entrepreneur*-ship could cause great differences in the *amount and kind* of labour used to get a ton of ore out of the ground and through the mill. Obviously less labour expense will be incurred per unit of ore milled if the ore deposit is readily accessible, if it can be mined by workers with little training or experience, or if large amounts of sophisticated machinery and equipment are being used in the operation.

Again, because of limited statistical information it is difficult to assess the relative position of territorial producers with respect to labour costs in this wider sense and again only a rough impression of this position can be given until a more detailed study is performed. Some limited comparisons of direct labour costs per ton of ore milled in the auriferous quartz-mining and silver-lead-zinc–mining industries inside and outside the Territories may be made from data presented in Tables 6.5 and 6.6. Table 6.4 indicates that average salaries and wages in the auriferous quartz mines at Yellowknife, Northwest Territories, in 1961, for example, were about 45 per cent higher than those in Ontario and the average labour cost per ton of ore milled about 37 per cent higher. But in comparison with the old mines of British Columbia, while average salaries and wages were about 18 per cent higher in the territorial mines, the average labour cost per ton of ore milled was almost 80 'per cent *lower*.

It is even more difficult to compare labour costs per ton of ore milled in the silver-lead-zinc–mining industry because much less detailed statistics are available. From the estimates shown in Table 6.7, however, it appears that average salaries and wages in the Yukon operations were about 24 per cent higher than the average in other silver-lead-zinc operations outside—chiefly in British Columbia, but also in Ontario, Quebec, and the Maritimes. Average salaries and wages per ton of ore milled, however, appear to have been extremely high in the Yukon, exceeding the average level in the provinces by more than five times.

What reasons can be found to account for the fact, then, that the major mining operations established in the Yukon and Northwest Territories required larger outlays upon labour for each ton of ore milled than was the case in many, although not all, mining operations being conducted elsewhere in Canada? Was it because the physical productivity of labour was low due to the northern location, the quality of the labour employed, or the quality of the other inputs such as land, capital, or management? Or was it because wage and salary rates had to be kept unusually high in order to attract the necessary labour to the area?

With respect to the question of physical productivity in the two chief mining centres in the Territories, Yellowknife and Mayo, it is obvious that this is an important factor in one but not in the other. Physical productivity in the Yukon silver-lead-zinc mines has been very low compared with that in the silver-lead-zinc mines located elsewhere in Canada. A rough estimate for 1961, for example, would suggest that the physical output at Mayo was about 386 tons per worker (surface and underground) compared to an average of 1,493 tons per worker in the mines in the provinces. In the alluvial quartz-mining industry, on the other hand, the physical productivity of labour at Yellowknife compared well with that in many other parts of Canada. The tons of ore milled per employee (surface and underground) in the gold mines of the Northwest Territories in 1961 were 835 compared with 396 in British Columbia and 789 in Ontario. The reasons for such variations may be complex. They may include variations in the type of mining being done, the nature of the ore bodies, and certainly the scale of the operation itself. The latter point is particularly relevant, for the larger the mine (and its associated milling facilities), the more likely it is that extensive use will be made of capital inputs in the forms of machinery and equipment to perform operations which in a smaller operation would be performed by workers less elaborately equipped. The mines in the Territories have been relatively small compared with those in other parts of the country. Under these circumstances there is no reason to assume that the physical productivity of labour in the north has been necessarily low or that when it was low that this was necessarily because of the *northern* location of the mining operations concerned.

Turning to the possibility that high labour costs per ton of ore mined in the Territories could have been the result of unusually high wage rates being needed to attract labour to the area, it should be understood that most of the industrial labour force in the north normally consisted of more or less itinerant workers of European stock rather than of local natives. As noted elsewhere the many reasons for this would have included the cultural characteristics of the people, the lack of education and training facilities in the north, the preferences and, perhaps the prejudices of white employers there, and the pervasive influences of the clerical, police, and fur-trading "authorities" all of whom sought to insulate the native population against the supposedly corrupting effects of modern industrial employment.

It has already been shown that hourly wage rates were not inevitably higher in the Territories than in centres to the south. But there is some evidence to suggest that wages and salaries in territorial mining may have included amounts greater than a simple comparison of hourly wage rates would suggest. In one of the few studies made of northern mining costs, Dubnie found that a greater number of workers in northern mines were hired on a contract basis than was the case elsewhere and that this had the effect of increasing average earnings. Furthermore, bonus rates in the northern mines appeared to be higher than in southern operations by, according to Dubnie's estimates, about 20 cents per ton of ore mined.[1] Again it is difficult to establish the reasons for such higher labour outlays because they could reflect many factors, such as the characteristics of the particular mines involved, the absence of a local pool of labour in the particular mining area concerned, as well as the remoteness of the mining camps themselves. But what such attempts at estimating relative labour costs to northern mine operators do strongly suggest is that these direct labour outlays have probably not been as important as is generally assumed and that their significance as relative cost factors *attributable to the northern location* of the mines is over-shadowed by higher indirect labour costs in the form of expenses associated with providing workers with such things as transportation allowances, housing and recreational facilities. In the same category of indirect labour costs would be those expenses connected with an unusually high rate of labour turnover reported by many northern operators. All of these items have tended to be larger in the Territories than in most of the mining areas to the south and in one way or another this was the consequence partly of the northern winter, but also of the remoteness of the territorial operations. It is obvious that housing costs must be high in an area where heating is necessary for most of the year. And if firms have a policy of subsidizing transportation costs for holidaying employees they will be involved in greater outlays if they are a thousand miles from centres of population than if they are a few hundred. But again, "remoteness" implies more than this simple distance factor.

The indirect labour expenses mentioned above have been high in the Territories because of the facilities that simply were not there. And, for the most part, they were not there simply because the scale of economic activity did not, until very recently perhaps, warrant them. Thus, in so far as housing costs were high because of the fuel required for heating,

[1]A. Dubnie, *Some Economic Factors Affecting Northern Mineral Development in Canada*, Mineral Information Bulletin Number MR38, Department of Mines and Technical Surveys (Ottawa, 1959), pp. 40–1.

the fuel bill was large chiefly because of the cost of fuel oil, not so much because a remarkably large number of gallons were consumed. And the high cost of fuel oil was attributable to the fact that investment in efficient, large-scale distributing facilities had been discouraged by the smallness of the local markets. Similarly, high annual electric light bills, as we will see below, were to some extent the result of a long dark winter, but they were also the result of high electricity costs arising from reliance upon small-scale, inefficient generating plants. Thus, high costs associated with housing workers in the north may be viewed as having been the consequence, in some part, of the absence of efficient, large-scale facilities for supplying heat and light. Similarly, high overhead costs associated with the provision of recreational facilities are the consequence of the absence of such facilities as cinemas, sports arenas, dance halls, and even television in mining centres too small to attract *commercial* enterprises of this kind. The mining firm consequently had to provide such facilities itself or at least subsidize their operation. And to offset the inadequacy of these facilities, it also probably had to provide some subsidized transportation for workers going outside for holidays. The amount of subsidy required was often large because of the absence of large-scale, efficient transportation facilities linking a small northern mining centre to the outside. Such facilities as were available were usually the kind that required a minimum of investment in fixed capital—such as air services utilizing small aircraft needing little in the way of landing and other ground facilities. Obviously transportation allowances made by firms so served would exceed those of firms located on or near a transcontinental railway system.

Finally, there have been the costs associated with the unusually high labour turnover reported in territorial industries. Again these may in part be attributed to the small scale of the operations conducted in the Territories. Many workers have always been attracted to jobs in the Territories by prospects of unusually high earnings, prospects created by the frequently higher hourly wage rates, better bonus pay, and other wage benefits available there. But such prospects often proved illusory because of the extraordinarily high cost of living. It will be seen in Part IV that the cost of living differential between the Territories and other parts of Canada was certainly more general and remarkable than the money, wage, and salary rate differentials examined above. One experienced employer in Yellowknife has suggested that most of the people who came into that centre from other parts of Canada did so in the expectation of having to endure considerable hardship, but at the same time expecting to earn a larger income than they could elsewhere. His experience led him to believe that they usually over-estimated both the hardships *and* the income to be earned. Some tended to remain under these circumstances, but a large proportion returned to the outside world as soon as they could.[2] The result, of course, was a relatively high turnover of labour directly attributable to a cost of living which more than offset the higher money incomes. And it in turn was the consequence of the high prices of goods and services which, given the smallness of local markets, had either to be imported at high cost over relatively inefficient, small volume transportation facilities or produced locally in small-scale high-cost plants. These same fundamental influences which made the total cost of labour inputs higher in the Territories than outside also caused, even more directly, other production costs to be higher there.

Costs of Process Supplies

It will be seen in Tables 6.8 and 6.9 that the costs of "process supplies" both in the Yellowknife auriferous quartz mines and in the Mayo silver-lead-zinc mines were on average much higher than in similar mines located in the provinces. The cost of these items, which include explosives used in mining and chemicals used in treating ores, averaged $1.68 per ton of ore milled in the territorial gold mines in 1961, compared to $1.09 in British Columbia, $0.75 in Manitoba and Saskatchewan, $0.52 in Ontario, and $0.35 in Quebec and Nova Scotia. Again, it is difficult to account for these differences due to possible variations in the type of ore deposits involved, the difficulty in mining them and possible differences in the refining processes required. But part of the cost differential was undoubtedly attributable to higher transportation costs. Similarly, the extraordinary costs of process supplies in the Mayo operations compared with the outside average must have resulted from the fact that all such supplies had to be trucked in from Whitehorse, a distance of 300 miles after being carried there by rail from the coast. The freight rates involved in these operations will be examined in the next chapter.

Costs of Fuel and Electricity

Although not as large a cost item as labour in the mineral industries, fuel and power are important inputs contributing to production costs. In the auriferous quartz-mining and -milling operations in the Territories,

[2]Personal interview with J. Parker, Yellowknife, N.W.T., June 1958.

for example, we have seen that labour earnings have amounted to from $6.00 to $7.00 per ton of ore milled in the early 1960s. The cost of process supplies varies considerably from year to year, but in the same years averaged in the neighbourhood of $2.00 per ton milled. Fuel and purchased electricity inputs in the same operations approached $1.50 per ton for the gold mines of the Northwest Territories and over twice that amount in the Yukon silver-lead-zinc–mining operations. These fuel and electricity costs greatly exceeded those encountered by producers in the provinces. In the silver-lead-zinc–mining industry, for example, the outlays for fuel and purchased electricity during 1960 were $3.85 per ton of ore milled in the Yukon compared to an average in the provinces of $0.28. In the auriferous quartz-mining industry in 1960, as shown in Table 6.10, the $1.49 cost per ton milled for these inputs compared with $1.17 in British Columbia, $0.93 in Manitoba and Saskatchewan, $0.46 in Ontario, and $0.40 in Quebec and Nova Scotia.

The relatively very high outlays for fuel and purchased electricity in the Territories were attributable to two factors—the larger amount of heating required than in most southern mines and the generally higher prices for fuel. The relative disadvantage to territorial mine operators with respect to the *amount* of heating required varies throughout the Territories from location to location. And it is also difficult, of course, to find appropriate centres in the south to compare them with. Some indication of the general magnitude of the differences involved, however, may be gained from a comparison of climatic conditions at Sudbury, one of the major mining centres of northern Ontario with those at Yellow-knife, Northwest Territories. The number of annual degree-days of heating[3] required at Sudbury average 9,500 compared to 15,600 at Yellowknife. Thus, there are approximately 64 per cent more degree-days of heating required in Yellowknife than in Sudbury. Again, because of the great number of variables involved, it is difficult to assign a value to the cost of production disadvantage such climatic differences impose upon the territorial producers. The nature of the fuel available, the kind of building construction employed, the size of the plant being heated, and the types of heating systems installed will, along with many other factors, cause large variations between mining camps even when located in similar climatic regions. Consequently, until a highly detailed study of

[3]The difference between 65° and the mean outside temperature for a day (or other period of time) is used by heating engineers as an index of the fuel required for heating a building. Thus, a degree-day of heating is defined as a departure of one degree per day from 65°; see G. T. Trewartha, *An Introduction to Climate* (New York: McGraw-Hill, 1954), pp. 43–4.

the various mining centres is done, no conclusions may be drawn respecting the extent of the heating differential that exists.[4] But it is apparent that whatever this differential has been, it was not only the result of more heat being required in the territorial operations, but also of the considerably higher prices which producers had to pay there for the fuels (and electricity) required.

The prices actually paid by mining companies for fuel and purchased electricity in the Territories and in the various provinces during 1960 are calculated in Table 6.11. It will be seen from the table that the coal used for fuel in the Yukon mining operations was the most expensive per ton in Canada. Wood fuel in the Yukon was also the most expensive in Canada, followed by that used in the Northwest Territories. Some of the reasons for this have already been suggested earlier in this chapter. They included the smallness of the operations involved, the relatively expensive labour used, and, of course, the often expensive local transportation costs involved as a consequence of the small-volume, low fixed-capital transportation facilities which were used. The cost of petroleum fuels required in the Territories will also be seen to have been relatively high compared to the costs in the provinces. The comparison is complicated in this case, however, by variations in provincial and territorial taxes on such fuels. But again transportation costs must have been responsible for much of the difference shown. And once more it must be noted that these were not only influenced by the distance the product was shipped but by the efficiency of the shipping facilities available. The price of gasoline in the Northwest Territories in 1960 greatly exceeded the price in Ontario despite the fact that mines in Ontario were often more distant from the sources of petroleum than were the mines of the Northwest Territories. But the former were nearer the large markets for such products which are economically supplied with petroleum products transported at very low cost by highly efficient, large-volume, and specialized transportation facilities. The point is reinforced by the figures shown in Table 6.11 for Alberta which indicate that mining companies operating in Canada's major oil-producing region paid more for gasoline and fuel oil than did Ontario mining companies. The fact is, of course, that the price of petroleum products throughout the entire country is determined by the price of imported oil at tide water and by internal

[4]Dubnie, in the study already cited, estimates that at Yellowknife heating costs at the Giant Yellowknife and Consolidated Discovery mines in 1958 were responsible for adding from $0.20 to $0.27 to the per ton costs of production over what they would have been if the mines had been located in Edmonton, Alberta.

transportation costs from there to user. These costs depend upon the efficiency of the transportation facilities available and this in turn depends largely upon their size and degree of specialization. Where local markets are small, as in the Territories, it is not commercially feasible to provide such facilities, with the result that prices of petroleum products there tend to be relatively high despite the proximity of petroleum sources.

In the case of electricity costs, although the nature of the production and distribution problem appears to be different because of the technical differences involved, the fundamental economic reason for the relatively high cost per unit of the commodity in the Territories is the same—the smallness of the local markets. Again, as is also true of fuel inputs, some part of the greater total outlay made by territorial producers on electricity may have been attributable to climatic factors which made it necessary to consume more electricity (for lighting and heating) per unit of product turned out. But part of the reason for these higher production costs is also to be found in the higher prices which were paid for these inputs. It will be noted in Table 6.11 that in 1960 electricity costs were approximately the same in the Yukon and the Northwest Territories. But similarly high rates also existed in other parts of Canada where electric power was also generated on a relatively small scale—notably in the Prairies and the Maritimes. The prices paid for electricity by mining companies in all these areas were much higher than those paid by companies operating in Ontario and Quebec where very large-scale power generation has been warranted by large industrial and domestic markets.

When the development of power-generating facilities in the territories is examined in some detail, it will be seen that the electric power prices shown for the Territories in the table represent a marked improvement over the situation which prevailed there in earlier years. The chief reason for the improvement, and for the relatively favourable average power cost to territorial mines shown in the table, was the hydro-electric power plant constructed on the Snare River to supply power to the gold mines of the Yellowknife area. Prior to the construction of this relatively large facility by a public agency (and a similar, but less efficient one, near Mayo in the Yukon) most territorial mining operations relied upon very expensive electric power from small diesel generating plants. Given the inherent relative inefficiency of this type of generating plant (aggravated by high fuel costs) very much higher electric power costs plagued most northern mine operators. The same situation confronted newer mines

being established away from the existing centres of activity at Yellowknife and Mayo.

Capital Costs

The same difficulties which beset us above in considering the relative
costs of labour and material inputs in territorial mining ventures and
those located elsewhere in Canada make it impossible, given our existing
data, to estimate the relative costs of the capital inputs which were
involved. But again there are reasons to believe that these costs were
also generally higher in the Territories. The chief ground for such a
belief is not that the northern developments would necessarily involve
higher financial charges in the form of interest rates, but that they would
require larger capital inputs per unit of productive capacity. A number
of reasons for this have already been noted in connection with specific
developments and it may be useful to summarize them here.

There are at least four main reasons why larger amounts of capital
should have been required in territorial mining operations than elsewhere
in Canada. As with the relative costs of other inputs considered above,
they will be seen to have stemmed from both the peculiar physical
characteristics of the territorial environment and their economic remoteness. The four reasons which would lead us to expect higher capital
outlays per unit of output for the territorial operations are: first, that
pre-production outlays were probably higher; second, the inventory
problem required operators to hold larger stocks of "working capital";
third, larger investments in ancillary facilities were necessary; and
fourth, the territorial operations were generally not on as large a scale
as those in the south.

There appears to be a general consensus among mining engineers and
government geologists in the Territories that development costs tend to
be higher there than in most southern areas. The reasons most often
cited are the shortness of the operating season, perma-frost conditions
that make trenching and other prospecting operations unusually difficult
and, of course, the relatively high cost of transporting men, supplies, and
equipment.[5] As an illustration of the latter point it might be noted that
in the 1950s a "Beaver" aircraft chartered at up to $90.00 per hour in
Whitehorse, compared to a rate of about $65.00 per hour prevalent in
northern Ontario.[6] Such considerations as these may make the initial

[5]See, for example, A. E. Aho, "Mineral Possibilities of the Yukon Territory"
(Vancouver, 1958), mimeographed, p. 3.

[6]Whitehorse Board of Trade, *Submission to the Royal Commission on Canada's
Economic Prospects* (Vancouver, 1955), p. 58, mimeographed.

prospecting of a mine a relatively heavy investment in the Territories compared to what is involved in prospecting in areas better served with transportation facilities and where the effective season for exploration and development is long enough to permit more efficient operations in the field. Again it must be emphasized, however, that the force of these influences may vary greatly throughout the north, as everywhere else, due to extreme variations in the nature of the operations involved. By way of illustration it is shown in Table 6.12 that, in contract drilling for mining companies, the efficiency of the operations, in so far as that may be judged from the "labour cost per drilled foot" figures, appears to be as high (or even higher) in the Northwest Territories as in the country generally, whereas in the Yukon operations it has been very much lower. Once the property is taken into the stage of actual shaft sinking and building construction, additional relative capital cost increments may be encountered. These will, of course, vary greatly from property to property but, again, generally higher costs for such construction are likely to prevail in the Territories. Not only must construction of buildings often be of a more substantial nature to keep heating costs down but, as we have already seen, construction labour costs have been higher in the Territories than in most (but not all) other parts of the country.[7] Added to these extra costs will be the expense of transporting machinery and equipment required for the plant into the site. In 1960 Dubnie estimated that for various large items of typical mining equipment manufactured in Canada a transportation cost increment of under one per cent prevailed at Sudbury compared to an increment ranging from two to ten per cent at Whitehorse or Yellowknife.[8] Again, the chief determinant of the size of this increment would be the availability of suitable transportation facilities, for the cost to the mining company of moving heavy equipment for 50 miles over a bush trail may exceed the cost of shipping the same equipment many hundreds of miles by rail. This same transportation factor would also be the chief determinant of the extent to which territorial mining (and other) operators would be handicapped by the need to hold unusually large inventories.

The fact that mining operators in the Territories have generally had to hold large stocks of process supplies, fuel, replacement parts and, in the case of base metal producers, finished products, means that their total investment in the operation has had to be higher per unit of productive capacity than is required in other locations. Although a number of

---

[7] See Table 6.3—"Prevailing Hourly Wage Rates for Selected Occupations in Construction."

[8] Dubnie, p. 49.

factors will affect the size of any one firm's investment in inventories, such as management policy itself, the chief factor which has compelled producers of all kinds to hold larger inventories has always been the nature of the transportation facilities available.

Until relatively recent years territorial mining operations depended on river transport for inbound shipments of supplies and equipment and, in the case of base metal producers, for the movement of outgoing concentrates. Despite the advantages of river transport, chiefly the low level of investment in fixed capital, it could be relied upon for only a few months of the year. Consequently, it was necessary for producers to stockpile incoming supplies, and sometimes outgoing product, during the few months of the open navigation season. Thus, the Giant mine at Yellowknife during the early 1950s often held a supply inventory valued at approximately two million dollars. By comparison, the Kerr-Addison mine in Ontario, with a daily output almost five times as great as that of the Giant mine, carried an inventory worth only about $750,000.[9] Similarly, at the United Keno Hill silver-lead-zinc–mining operations in the Yukon, prior to the adoption of truck transport in 1950, supplies and concentrates had to be stockpiled for nine months of the year because of the short navigation season on the Yukon River and its tributaries. The importance of the inventory problem there is suggested by the fact that an alternative trucking system was adopted despite the higher per mile transportation charges involved because it permitted almost continuous shipping of concentrates. But even after the introduction of trucking, because of seasonal interruptions in service due to unbridged river crossings, a supply inventory valued at approximately one million dollars had to be maintained.[10]

The third factor which may have been responsible for higher capital inputs per unit of productive capacity in territorial operations is the simple fact that most of the mines established there have been relatively small. The Yukon placer mining operations were an exception, of course, for after the consolidation of producers in the 1920s, relatively large-scale techniques were employed by the major firm there. But the Mayo silver-lead-zinc mines, the Yellowknife auriferous quartz mines, the uranium mines in the Northwest Territories, and the Rankin Inlet nickel-

[9]Municipal District of Yellowknife, "Submission to the Royal Commission on Canada's Economic Prospects," mimeographed; see also L. S. Bourne, *Yellowknife, N.W.T., A Study of its Urban and Regional Economy* (Ottawa: Northern Co-ordination and Research Centre, Department of Northern Affairs and National Resources, 1963), pp. 74–6.

[10]See p. 121.

copper operations were not as large as many mines located south of the Territories, especially those in Ontario. As shown in Table 6.13, for example, in 1960 the average milling capacity of auriferous quartz mines in the Northwest Territories was 352 tons per day compared with 568 for Quebec mines and 825 for Ontario mines. In the larger mines there are certain to be economies associated with the plant construction, and the provision of ancillary services such as housing, recreational and various other facilities which involve investment spending on the part of the mining company. But not only have companies operating in the Territories found it difficult to provide such capital facilities economically because of the usually small size of their operation, they also have had to provide more capital facilities not directly connected with their actual mining and milling operations than have companies located in less economically remote parts of the country.

The fourth factor, then, which may account for unusually high capital outlays per unit of productive capacity in the Territories has been the need for mining companies locating there to invest in facilities which in many other locations have been provided by other agencies—either private or public. Many possible reasons could be found to explain why this should have been the case, but the most obvious of them must surely also be that the most important mineral development in the territorial north has occurred only in a very few widely scattered centres at which very high-grade ores could be developed. A second requirement was that these places could be linked to markets and sources of supply by transportation facilities which could be developed without heavy commitments of capital to immovable structures such as railway trackage or highways. The high-grade ore requirement was needed to overcome the various operating cost differentials surveyed in this chapter, for only in this way could capital, labour, and enterprise be attracted to the Territories in competition with opportunities elsewhere. The reliance upon the kind of transportation system described was necessary because an individual mining development in an otherwise undeveloped area cannot often justify the installation of heavy capital facilities such as railways which have to be amortized over periods of time which could easily exceed the operating life of a mine—especially one which relies upon the maintenance of very high-grade reserves for its profitability. This has meant that, until quite recent years, suitable mining sites were restricted to areas accessible by water transport—by the Yukon River and its tributaries in the Yukon, by the Mackenzie waterway system in Mackenzie District and by sea in the eastern arctic.

In view of this it is not surprising that the various mining centres to grow up should be both widely scattered and relatively small. This in turn has meant that the local markets for food, clothing, shelter, recreation, etc., created by the establishment of mining camps were too small to attract *entrepreneurs* who would make it their business to supply these needs. And so, the mining companies have had to do so on their own. Of course, there is nothing unusual about mining companies assuming such responsibilities. Mining firms throughout the southern parts of Canada also frequently provide housing, food services, medical centres, barber shops, recreation halls and similar facilities. But in many locations even these facilities are provided commercially in towns that have grown up around major mining operations or in towns which were located near them because of other economic development in the area which attracted population to it. The point here is that in the Territories the provision of such facilities was more generally the responsibility of the mining companies. But added to this was the requirement that they provide their own schools, hospitals, transportation facilities, electric power plants, fuel supplies, communication systems, sawmills and generally a wide range of social and industrial capital facilities that in more settled parts of the country could be provided commercially or publicly. This not only constituted an additional capital burden for territorial mining companies, but because of the small scale of individual investments of these kinds, they were highly inefficient to operate and this tended to keep the costs of such items as fuel, building materials, electric power, and transportation at the relatively high levels noted earlier in this chapter.

But why, one might ask at this point, did not the public agencies directly responsible for resource development in these areas undertake to provide such facilities? The answer to this has already been suggested in Part I where we saw that prior to World War II the federal government had little interest in subsidizing development in the Territories. The territorial "governments" either had similarly little interest in promoting change, as was the case in the Northwest Territories or, as was true in the Yukon, had been stripped of any power—political or financial—to do so.

In the following chapter we shall see how these circumstances shaped the pattern of development in the Territories prior to the intervention of government in the economic life of the area after World War II.

7 The Attempts by Private Enterprise to Overcome the Economic Effects of Remoteness

+

GIVEN THE OBSTACLES to northern resource development outlined in the preceding chapter, it is perhaps surprising that any commercially feasible activity was established there at all, especially during the years prior to the active intervention by the government in the process of northern resource development. How did privately owned firms overcome, or attempt to overcome, the effects of "remoteness" as this term was defined earlier?

The purpose of this chapter is to identify various forms of adaptation used by private *entrepreneurs* to cope with the specific economic environment they encountered in the territorial north. In very general terms, these forms of adaptation were, first, a deliberate reliance by primary producers upon high-grade natural resource occurrences and, second, a persistent pursuit of efficiency through integration of enterprise both in primary production and in the related processing, supply, and general transportation operations.

The history of mineral development in the Territories outlined in Chapter 4 showed that, with minor exceptions, the only minerals developed for export from the area were those derived from ores containing gold and silver. The major development at Yellowknife was based on auriferous quartz ores yielding gold and small amounts of silver. The long-established operations at Dawson in the Yukon were based entirely upon alluvial gold-bearing deposits. The Mayo development in the Yukon yielded substantial amounts of base metals in the form of lead and zinc concentrates but it owed its continued existence to the high silver content of the complex ores mined there. The only other major mining operation to exist for any length of time in the Territories was the mining of radioactive ores at Port Radium on Great Bear Lake; but again this operation depended upon a product, radium, of such value as to make even gold appear virtually worthless in comparison. Even so, the Port Radium operations also involved a substantial production of silver, for the ores mined there were of two distinct types—pitchblende-silver and silver-copper. Thus, the only exceptions to the rule that terri-torial mineral development be based upon ores containing precious metals were the several attempts, all unsuccessful, to develop copper mining near Whitehorse and the attempt to develop nickel-copper ores at Rankin Inlet on the west coast of Hudson Bay during the 1950s. The development of coal in the Yukon and petroleum at Norman Wells on the Mackenzie fell into a quite different category, of course, for those operations were designed to provide a local source of fuels rather than products for export from the Territories.

In addition to this reliance upon ores containing precious metals, territorial operators have been confined to operating upon unusually high-grade deposits of such ores. The best illustration of this is provided by the auriferous quartz-mining operations at Yellowknife. The gross value of production per ton of ore milled at these mines is compared with the average for the Canadian gold quartz-mining industry as a whole in Table 6.14. It is apparent that the grade of ore processed at Yellowknife has been consistently very high. Indeed, it will be recalled from Chapter III that the Discovery mine at Yellowknife has been one of the richest ever developed in Canada.

By operating upon such high-grade land resources, territorial mining firms have been able to overcome many of the cost disadvantages dis-cussed in the preceding chapter. The sometimes surprising consequences of this are perhaps best illustrated by reconsidering some of these operating costs in terms of costs per unit of the final product—in this case, per ounce of gold produced in a typical year during the 1950s. Thus, the productivity of labour in the territorial gold mines is seen to have been 422 ounces of gold per wage-earner in 1954 when the average for the auriferous quartz-mining industry in Canada as a whole was only 227 ounces. The remarkable consequence of this was that, despite an average annual outlay on labour 43 per cent higher in the Territories than in the industry as a whole, the cost of wages per unit of output was actually less. Although the amounts of capital used in the territorial operations were probably relatively higher than was the case elsewhere, for the reasons outlined earlier, it is not likely that the additional capital inputs were of the kind that would directly enhance the relative productivity of labour there. Nor would there be reason to assume that the technology employed was conspicuously different from that used generally in the industry. It must be concluded, therefore, that the greater physical productivity of labour in the territorial mines has been attributable to relatively larger inputs of land in the form of higher grade ore. Consequently, in 1954 for example, with productivity per worker as much as 86 per cent higher in the gold mines of the Northwest Territories than elsewhere, because labour outlays by firms there were only 43 per cent higher than in the industry as a whole, labour costs *per unit of output* were actually lower there than in the national industry. Similarly, it will be found that the costs of process supplies used in the production of refined gold in the Territories has been less per unit of output than the national average—and this too must be attributable to the higher grade of ore being processed.

The two other costs specified earlier, the costs of fuel and electricity inputs, have generally been higher in the Territories than in the industry as a whole. But, in the case of these factors, the relative price disadvantage has been so great that it has not been offset by the relative richness of the land inputs. Furthermore, a significantly larger share of total production costs has been contributed by outlays on fuel and electricity in the Territories than elsewhere because of the physical–locational disadvantages of the northern producers.

The second type of approach used by mining *entrepreneurs* in the Territories to overcome the economic disadvantages of their location is less obvious than the reliance upon high-grade precious metal bearing ore deposits. The general history of development in the area, however, reveals a persistent tendency toward integration of enterprise. This has taken both "horizontal" and "vertical" forms. It has been horizontal in that there has been a tendency for one relatively large firm to "take over" the development of primary resources in a particular area. And it has been vertical in that firms initially organized to exploit a particular natural resource have tended to become involved either directly or through subsidiaries in a variety of other activities such as water control, transportation, electric power generation, fuel production, and forestry operations.

Our hypothesis concerning this tendency is that *entrepreneurs* attempting to develop the land resources of the Territories had, in the absence of effective government participation in the development process, no alternative but to undertake, on their own initiative, the provision of a great deal of capital infra-structure which would elsewhere have been treated as social capital—in the sense that it would have been provided publicly. This helps to explain why total capital outlays tend to be higher in the territorial mining industries than elsewhere, as noted earlier. And it also helps to explain why small operators who have attempted to establish themselves in the Territories have tended to merge with, or sell out to, larger operators located near to them and why government policy, as outlined in Part I above, has sometimes been deliberately framed to discourage small operators from undertaking resource development. Only the larger organizations have been in a position to undertake the necessary investment in the "infra-structure" capital required, particularly the transportation and electric power facilities. Illustrations of this fact of territorial economic life may be drawn from the history of the fur trade there and, perhaps more usefully for its implications with regard to future development, from the history of the many mining ventures (both successful and unsuccessful) which were described earlier.

In the remaining part of this chapter some illustrations of horizontal integration will be recalled from the earlier survey of primary resource-developing industries presented in Chapters 3 and 4. Following this, the process of vertical integration will be considered in rather more detail, for it will involve examination of the investments made by primary-resource developing industries in transportation and power facilities and in the development of local subsidiary industries to supply fuel, forest products and other productive inputs which would otherwise have been imported from "outside." We will also consider the closely related investments made by private *entrepreneurs* in large-scale commercial transportation facilities in those few instances where certain unusual circumstances made such investments feasible.

HORIZONTAL INTEGRATION OF TERRITORIAL ENTERPRISE

In an almost totally undeveloped area where private concerns are interested in attempting to develop primary resources on an independent basis, the advantages of scale must be readily apparent. The chief reason for these advantages is the need for the resource-developing firm to provide, for its own use, whatever capital facilities are required by the nature of its operations and which are not provided publicly. Many of these facilities, such as those included under the term "infra-structure capital" (transportation devices and power systems, for example) and "social capital," are known to be facilities the efficiency of which increases greatly with size. Small resource-developing firms consequently find it difficult, if not impossible, to equip themselves with such facilities because the market they themselves provide for the services of such facilities is too small to justify the investment that would be entailed in constructing reasonably efficient facilities of this sort. Consequently, when the discovery of rich land resources has attracted a variety of *entrepreneurs*, large and small, to a remote area, it is inevitable that only the larger ones will succeed in establishing even the minimum facilities required to sustain their operation beyond the early development stage. Smaller operators must either abandon their operations or, possibly, associate themselves in some way with a larger operator in the area so as to avail themselves of his capital facilities. This association may be effected in various ways. The small operator might remain independent and merely purchase the services of the larger operator's facilities or, at the other extreme, he might sell out or merge his operation as a business with that of the larger concern.

The history of the fur trade in the Territories provided a classic illustration of this process. Only large organizations could establish the supply routes, operate the transportation services required, maintain the stable marketing arrangements with trappers over a large area and extend the credit required to maintain these trappers. Small operators could exist by making use of some of these facilities but the eventual result was, of course, the establishment of the monopoly organization apparently inevitable in that trade. In the history of mining development in the Territories sketched earlier, one of the best illustrations of a similar process was provided by the Klondike placer mining development. It began with the extraordinary influx of small, often individual operators, many of whom survived for some time as producers because the deposits could be worked with a minimum of capital inputs efficiently enough to provide a satisfactory return. But when the easily worked gravels began to disappear, larger operators—who could equip themselves with the dredges and other capital required for profitable working of the deposits—came to dominate the industry. As the process continued, still larger capital inputs, such as immense water supply systems and efficient hydro-electric generating plants were needed in order to reduce operating costs to a level commensurate with the increasing difficulty of extracting gold from the countryside around Dawson. When it developed that public investment in such facilities would not be forthcoming, the industry was reorganized to the point where a single large firm emerged and, in effect, took over operations in the entire area.

Examination of the long history of the silver-lead–mining district near Mayo reveals a similar process. There the chief device used for overcoming the transportation problem created by the nature of the product was the installation of concentrating mills to improve its value per unit of weight. The smaller operators in the district were unable to provide themselves with efficient mills or with the transportation facilities required to overcome the problem of getting the concentrates from the mines to the river, but were able to operate by selling their ore output to the largest operator, Treadwell Yukon, which was able to provide the necessary facilities. The result, as we have seen, was that the Treadwell Yukon organization came to control virtually all the production in the Mayo district in the late 1920s in much the same way that the Yukon Consolidated Gold Corporation came to control production in the Klondike. With the redevelopment of the Mayo district after World War II, a similar process was repeated and led to the domination of the area once again by the largest of a number of firms which were initially active, the United Keno Hill Company. Yet another illustration is provided by the development of the pitchblende-silver operations on Great Bear Lake in the 1930s. In the earlier description of that development it was seen that although a number of firms were attracted to the area by Labine's original discovery, the only other operator who developed a claim sold out to Eldorado Gold Mines Limited. The latter succeeded in establishing the elaborate transportation, fuel, power, and other facilities required to make the mining operations possible.

The only major mining area in the Territories which did not experience this concentration of production in a single dominant firm was Yellowknife. There, as we have seen, several firms have operated producing mines for a long period without any one of them assuming control over the area. Many factors may be found to explain this, but it is perhaps significant that the Yellowknife gold mines were developed at a time when large-scale *public* investment in basic industrial facilities, such as hydro-electric power and transportation systems, was becoming for the first time a factor in the economic life of the Territories. After the outbreak of World War II, it became unnecessary for private firms contemplating the development of mineral resources in the Territories to assume that the necessary infra-structure and social capital would have to be provided entirely or even substantially through their own organization. The nature of this new public investment in such capital facilities during and after World War II is considered in Part III of this study.

THE VERTICAL INTEGRATION OF TERRITORIAL ENTERPRISE

While it is not unusual for primary resource-exploiting firms to undertake considerable investment in social overhead capital as that term is broadly understood, we saw in the last chapter that the cost of providing such facilities and services has probably been relatively high in the Territories. And, given the organization and policies of government there, the possibilities of securing public assistance in providing these facilities were perhaps unusually slight prior to World War II. But we have seen, too, that private firms also often had to invest in what may be termed "public tertiary equipment" and "public tertiary construction." This would include roads, highways, waterways and landing fields and the related equipment such as trucks, river vessels, and aircraft.

It is common to think of these facilities as being provided by public agencies or by specialized private businesses because normally they serve not only specific users but the general public as well. A considerable measure of public investment in such capital is often thought to be justified because many benefits which it is difficult to price and charge to individual users accrue to the community at large. But in the Territories, because of the extraordinary dispersion of the small population and the dispersion of the centres of primary resource development, it was difficult to justify public participation, let alone public initiative, in creating such facilities. Consequently, many investments in transportation and power facilities which elsewhere might have been considered investments in social or public capital were treated as though they were investments in primary plant itself. And substitutes for investment in transportation facilities, such as investments designed to establish local supply sources for such things as fuel and building materials, were often made by primary resource-exploiting firms as well.

The implications of this are important enough to bear repeating: Investment by primary resource-exploiting firms in subsidiary operations involving housing, recreation, fuel, building supplies, transportation and power added to the total capital inputs they had to make and this helps to explain the relatively high capital costs per unit of primary output considered earlier in this chapter. But a further important implication of this method of supplying such facilities is that when they were provided even by relatively large single firms they were small in scale. Consequently, they lost the economies of scale which are so conspicuous in these fields—especially in transportation and electric power generation. The consequence was unusually high costs per unit of the commodity supplied—high costs of transportation per ton mile, high costs of electric power per kilowatt hour, high cost per ton of coal and high housing and servicing cost per worker employed. Because many of the attempts by primary producers to develop local sources of supplies (and even "social amenities") may be regarded as approaches to the transportation problem, particular attention must be given to their efforts in this area.

PRIVATE INVESTMENT IN TRANSPORTATION FACILITIES

It was noted in Chapter 3 that the commercial trading companies operating in the Yukon before the Klondike gold rush had depended for their transportation upon the long but unobstructed river route from St. Michael's, Alaska, inland to the central Yukon. By the late 1860s these private trading firms had several steamboats operating over the length of the river. With the Klondike strike in 1896, a sufficient volume of freight and passenger traffic was created to support a large number of commercial carriers on the Yukon River. So great a boom in river-boat construction occurred as to provide enough carrying capacity to satisfy the needs for river transportation in the Yukon for the next half century.[1] But this did not eliminate the need for other transportation facilities in the Yukon, for the river route from St. Michael's to the central Yukon was extremely long, roundabout, and seasonal. The river was open to navigation for only about four months of the year, during which time the river-boats were fortunate to complete even two round trips between St. Michael's and Dawson City.

Under the pressure of the gold rush, an alternative route into the Klondike was developed. Passengers and freight came up the Pacific coast to Juneau, Alaska, crossed over the difficult Taiya Pass and

[1]H. A. Innis, Problems of Staple Production in Canada (Toronto: Ryerson, 1933), p. 84.

travelled overland to Whitehorse at the *head* of steamer navigation on the Yukon River. Most of this traffic then proceeded by steamer downstream to Dawson. Although this route was much shorter than the long journey up the river through Alaska, it was much more difficult. Commenting on the two routes in 1896 William Ogilvie wrote:

Once let a railroad get from some point on the coast to some point on the river so that we can have quick, cheap and certain entrance and exit, and the whole Yukon basin will be worked. At present the long haul makes the expense of mining machinery practically prohibitive, for the cost of transport is often more than the first cost of the machine.[2]

The problems of constructing such a railroad were indeed formidable, for it had to cross a range of mountains that was difficult to negotiate even on foot. Although the federal government carried out plans for a number of public works projects in the Yukon, especially around the turn of the century, there were no large transportation projects such as a railway to the coast envisaged in them. In the fiscal year 1899–1900, when the Department of Public Works' expenditures in the Yukon were at their peak, the chief item of expenditure was $380,254 for work on an ambitious telegraph system to connect the Yukon with British Columbia, while $102,749 was spent for special road construction, $61,751 for clearing river obstructions and $9,386 on a trail leading from Edmonton in the direction of the Yukon. It was left to private capital to make the most significant investment in transport facilities in the Yukon, and in 1900 the White Pass and Yukon Route Railway Company constructed a narrow-gauge railway to connect the port of Skagway, Alaska, with Whitehorse on the Yukon River—a distance of 110 miles. When the railway was completed this company created two subsidiaries, the British Yukon Navigation Company and the "American Yukon Navigation Company," to operate steamships on the Canadian and United States sections of the river system. These well-organized companies quickly monopolized transport on the river so that the parent company obtained, in effect, a monopoly of almost all the transport in the Yukon Territory. Even the operation of the winter stage between Dawson and Whitehorse was secured by the White Pass and Yukon Route organization.

The White Pass and Yukon Route monopoly on transport in the Yukon was established when the economic activity associated with the Klondike placers was at its peak around 1900. With the decline in gold

[2]Canada, *The Yukon District 1897*, p. 53.

production, conversion of the placer operations to large-scale techniques and the subsequent loss of population from the Territory, there was no incentive for private enterprise to invest in transport facilities to compete with those already in operation. But because the decline in gold production was accompanied by a number of attempts to bring other kinds of mineral deposits into production, there was a persistent demand for road construction. However, for the reasons already considered in Chapter 2, neither the federal government, nor the territorial government was willing or able to make very substantial investments in major road or other transportation systems in the Yukon after the turn of the century.[3]

The dilemma of the firms attempting to develop mineral deposits other than gold in the Yukon early in this century was well illustrated by the experience in the Whitehorse copper belt where, despite the availability of rail and ocean transport from Whitehorse to southern smelting plants, the extraordinary costs of getting the ore to Whitehorse by road, combined with initially high rates required by the White Pass and Yukon Route Railway, prevented the development of all but a few very rich deposits in the area. Similarly, the basic problem confronting firms attempting to develop the silver-lead ores in the Mayo district was to get their product moved from the mines over a distance of about forty miles to the landing on the Stewart River from where it could be shipped by river vessels to Whitehorse. The best that they could do in the early years of the development was to haul the ore on horse-drawn sleds over a frozen "winter road" at a cost, as noted earlier, of approximately $20.00 per ton in 1914. With the further development of the Mayo district after World War I, private firms took the initiative in trying to provide improved transportation facilities in the area. When a private company organized for the purpose of building a railway along the Stewart and Mayo rivers collapsed, it was left to the mining companies to attack the problem on their own. They did so, it will be recalled, by introducing tractors to haul the ore to the river in 1922 and by building a concentrating plant to raise the value of the product to be shipped. In this way the Mayo silver-lead mines continued to operate until they closed down in 1942.

The closing of these mines meant that during the war the Yukon river system declined in importance as a transportation route. What new demands were created by the wartime developments in the Yukon fell on the White Pass and Yukon Route railway. Total rail traffic

[3]See pp. 24–5.

in the Yukon rose to a record 300,000 tons in 1943, an amount almost ten times the pre-war annual tonnage. The necessary additions to the railway's carrying capacity were made after the system was leased, in the fall of 1942, to the United States Army for the duration of the war. During the time it was held under this lease, the line was improved and large quantities of rolling stock were added to it. The number of locomotives, for example, was increased from 10 to 33.[4]

Traffic on the White Pass and Yukon Route railway was sustained after the war not only by the resumption of concentrate shipments from United Keno Hill mines, but also by shipments of asbestos fibre from the Cassiar Asbestos Company's operations just south of the Yukon–British Columbia boundary. The latter firm, affiliated with the Keno Hill Company, used a similar system for trucking its product north to Whitehorse for trans-shipment by rail to the sea.

Although the balance of traffic on the railway historically had always been heavily biased inbound because of the relatively heavy imports of foodstuffs and building materials, the post-war export of both silver-lead-zinc concentrates and asbestos fibre made it possible to overcome this imbalance and, by 1955, the back-haul to Skagway equalled the inbound traffic to Whitehorse for the first time.[5] By the early 1960s over 70,000 tons were being imported annually compared to about 50,000 being exported. The ocean services connecting Skagway and Vancouver have been virtually a monopoly of the Canadian Pacific Railway's west-coast steamship services until recent years. In the post-war period this company operated three major passenger-cargo vessels on the route. One ship was also operated by the Canadian National Railway's coastal shipping subsidiary.

In 1954 the White Pass and Yukon Route organized a new subsidiary, the "British Yukon Ocean Services Limited," to establish a service between Vancouver and Skagway. Upon completion of its first vessel, the *M. V. Clifford J. Rogers*, the parent company completely modernized its freight-handling services. The new motor vessel was a specially designed ship of 4000 tons which carried its cargo in 168 four-hundred-cubic-foot steel containers along with 2,500 tons of concentrates packed at the mine into standard pallets. The containers, which were handled by fork-lift trucks, were loaded with cargo for Whitehorse by the

[4]H. W. Hewetson, "Transportation in the Northwest," in C. A. Dawson, ed., *The New North-West*, p. 194.

[5]Whitehorse Board of Trade, "Submission to the Royal Commission on Canada's Economic Prospects," pp. 40–1.

shippers in Vancouver and sealed, fitted into the ship, taken into Skagway, loaded onto flatcars, hauled by train to Whitehorse, and then distributed by truck to their final destination. In this way the problems of breakage, theft and damage from extremes of temperature were overcome.[6] Handling costs were also reduced by minimizing the amount of labour required through implementing completely mechanical handling procedures. With its diesel-propelled rolling stock, this small railway, operating under the most difficult conditions of climate and terrain, has been one of the most efficient in North America. This is borne out by the very favourable ratio of operating revenues to expenses of this line. In 1955 this ratio was 73.6 percent whereas that of all Canadian railroads was 87.5 per cent.[7] The largest part of the White Pass and Yukon Route revenues have always been, of course, derived from freight traffic, which by 1955 had reached an annual volume of 98,929 tons. In that year, $900,055 were credited to freight revenue and only $51,194 to passenger revenue.[8]

An examination of the operating costs of the White Pass and Yukon Route reveal that they were often surprisingly low. The chief operating expense, the maintenance of way and structures, however, which accounted for only 20 per cent of total average operating costs on Canadian railways generally, comprised 33 per cent of the White Pass and Yukon Route expenditures in 1955. Expenditures on train crews, fuel, and maintenance of equipment, items which might have been expected to account for a disproportionate share of total operating expenses under northern conditions were, in fact, considerably less than the corresponding Canadian averages. There is no doubt that this reflected the efficiency of this small, but well-equipped and managed company. And this is one reason for the usually satisfactory net income of the operation. In 1955 the net operating revenue of this company, whose total capital assets were about six million dollars, was $316,152. But another reason for the profitability of the company was its high freight and passenger rates. In 1955 the freight revenue per ton mile was 10.18 cents on the Yukon railway as compared with the 1.46 cents per ton mile averaged by all Canadian railways. Similarly, the revenue per passenger mile travelled was 7.16 cents against a national average of 2.87 cents in the same year.

The freight carried on the White Pass and Yukon Route in the 1950s

[6]Information supplied by R. Winter, Public Relations Director, White Pass and Yukon Route, Whitehorse, Y.T., July 1958.
[7]D.B.S., *Railway Transport 1955*, Part II, p. 7.
[8]*Ibid.*, p. 8.

consisted principally of two types—mineral products being carried out of the Territory and the foodstuffs, fuels, and manufactured goods being imported from outside. A detailed break-down of these imports indicates that about half the total tonnage consisted of gasoline, after which the next largest item was cement, followed closely by food products in containers, iron and steel, forest products, and beverages.[9]

From the foregoing it is obvious that the White Pass and Yukon Route railway enjoyed a unique position as a transport facility. Not only did it possess a virtual monopoly in the movement of freight both into and out of the Yukon, but it handled such a variety of commodities essential to the economic functioning of the Territory that it was in direct contact with most of the economic units functioning there. Because of this, it was in a position to tax, by way of its rate schedule, most of the beneficiaries of its operation. In short, it was able to capture a large part of the total economic returns generated in the Yukon by its own investments in capital and maintenance. Upper limits to its rate schedule were set, of course, by institutional restraints and by the threat of competition from other types of transport services, but the fact that the rates and net revenues were maintained at the level they were during the 1950s suggests that the company enjoyed considerable latitude in this regard.

It is hardly surprising that such a situation should have given rise to some local feeling in the Yukon that the company enjoying such a strategic monopoly position was exploiting firms and individuals dependent upon its services. Indeed as early as 1910 we find in the minutes of the Territorial Council reference to the "large profits" accruing to the White Pass Route Company and a resolution urging "that the . . . Canadian Railway Commission at a very early date hold a session within this Territory to investigate the excessive charges of said Railway."[10] But such excess profits, if they existed, did not attract competitors, either public or private, although proposals for additional large-scale transportation projects have never been lacking in the Yukon. In 1907 the Yukon Council concurred in a committee report urging the federal government to assist in the construction of a railway from the Yukon by an "all Canadian route to connect with some transcontinental Canadian line." And reference has already been made to a more modest, but also unsuccessful, attempt to develop a railway within the Yukon to service the Mayo silver-lead mines in the 1920s.[11]

---

[9]*Ibid.*, Part V.
[10]*Journals of the Yukon Council* (1910), X, 74
[11]See Chapter 4.

But such proposals did not bear fruit and the White Pass and Yukon Route retained its ability to capture returns which in other circumstances would probably have appeared in the form of benefits external to the transportation company.

Apart from some local road construction, the only alternatives to the rail and river transportation system in the Yukon prior to World War II were the small-scale flying services established there during the 1920s and 1930s. These are of particular interest here in so far as they displayed the familiar patterns of adaptation to the problems of operating in a remote, undeveloped area with a minimum of governmental support.

Initially the development of aviation in northern Canada was actively promoted by the federal government. At the end of World War I the government had conducted an inquiry into the whole question of the development of aviation in northern Canada and apparently discovered a sufficient amount of interest on the part of mining companies and various government agencies to warrant the implementation of policies designed to encourage the development of this new field of transportation.

In June, 1919, the Canadian Air Board was created and made the regulatory body for all air services in Canada. Under its supervision, the development of air services in northern Canada was given direct encouragement through a programme of aerial surveys sponsored by the federal government. These surveys produced maps of water routes, promising mineral areas, and guides to navigation throughout the north. They also promoted the establishment of air bases, fuel caches and other facilities required for large-scale development of aviation in the north. Flights sponsored by private interests, such as the Norman Wells flight of 1921, demonstrated the potential of aircraft in northern development, but they also showed how difficult it would be to exploit this potential in the absence of refuelling stations, maintenance facilities and navigational aids in the north. Under the Air Board, it appeared that the federal government's policy was to promote actively the development of such facilities. But in 1923 this whole policy was altered, and, when the functions of the Air Board were absorbed by the Department of National Defence, direct government assistance to northern aviation ceased.[12] At the same time, general interest in the mineral resources of the Territories declined and there was a temporary stagnation in the development of all types of transportation facilities there.

Toward the end of the decade of the 1920s important advances in the

[12]See J. A. Wilson, "The Expansion of Aviation into Arctic and Sub-Arctic Canada," *Canadian Geographical Journal*, XLI (September, 1950), 132–3.

techniques of aircraft construction, combined with renewed interest in northern prospecting, created new opportunities for commercial air services throughout the north generally. In the more developed areas, such as the southern Yukon, there was also a demand for passenger and mail services between the more important settlements and the "outside."

Air mail service was provided for the principal centres of the Yukon as early as 1927 by Yukon Airways and Exploration Company, although it was not until 1937 that regular direct air services were established between Edmonton and Whitehorse. In 1937 United Air Transport (a charter service organized in Edmonton in 1934 by Grant McConachie) began flying scheduled services between Edmonton and the Yukon via Fort St. John, Fort Nelson, and Watson Lake. A connection between this and a Fort St. John service to Vancouver was effected a year later when United Air Transport and Ginger Coote Airways joined forces and subsequently developed the Yukon Southern Air Transport Company. Yukon Southern was itself absorbed in 1942 by the large Canadian Pacific Airlines organization, a subsidiary of Canadian Pacific Railway.[13]

The establishment of scheduled air services between western Canada and the Yukon had required the development of an extensive system of landing fields. The Yukon Southern Company had surveyed landing strips at Fort St. John, Fort Nelson, Watson Lake and at Whitehorse which were subsequently developed. The field at Whitehorse was built by Pan-American Airways with assistance from the Yukon territorial government. The Yukon Southern had undertaken to build fields at Fort St. John and at Fort Nelson, but progress had been very slow because of financial difficulties and the virtual impossibility of moving heavy grading equipment into the airfield sites.[14]

In 1939, the federal government, apparently convinced by the pioneering efforts of the private operators that the route was feasible, undertook a complete engineering survey for airfields at Grande Prairie, Fort St. John, Fort Nelson, Watson Lake and Whitehorse. These fields measured 3,000 feet by 500 feet and were to be equipped with radio ranges. With the outbreak of war the government decided to carry out the project as planned and by September 1941 the system was usable by daylight.[15] This route came to be known as the "Northwest Staging Route."

[13]See F. H. Ellis, *Canada's Flying Heritage* (Toronto: University of Toronto Press, 1961), p. 322.
[14]Wilson, "The Expansion of Aviation into Arctic and Sub-Arctic Canada," p. 138.
[15]*House of Commons Debates*, 1944, p. 979.

When war began in the Pacific in 1942 it was apparent that the Northwest Staging Route would be the only means of communication with Alaska and the North Pacific if the West coast shipping route should be cut by Japanese submarines. The immediate strategic necessity in 1942 was to strengthen this air route. Accordingly, in 1942 the Canadian government enlarged the fields, installed navigation facilities, fueling systems, and living accommodation. The following year the United States Army undertook further development and laid large concrete landing strips and made other improvements before handing back the fields to the Canadian government. The total cost to Canada of this air route by the end of the war amounted to about forty-four million dollars.[16]

The fields described lay about one hundred miles apart over virtually unbroken wilderness. The problem of supplying them and of maintaining fuel deposits at them required the construction of connecting transportation facilities on the surface. This connecting route was provided by the Alaska Highway. Because it was designed to service the airfields of the Northwest Staging Route, it was built through 1,500 miles of wooded, often swampy and occasionally mountainous terrain between Dawson Creek, British Columbia, and Fairbanks, Alaska, instead of up the relatively simple "Trench" route through northern British Columbia. The consequence of this choice of route was that the highway itself was unlikely to provide an economical alternative to the sea–rail route for carrying freight into and out of the Yukon. It did, however, serve to strengthen the air route into the far northwest and eventually it also provided a trunk from which an internal highway system could be developed for the southern part of the Yukon Territory. The subsequent development of these facilities was largely a matter of new kinds of public policy in the north, however, and it will be convenient to defer consideration of them to the next chapter.

In the Northwest Territories the first transportation facilities provided were those required by the fur trade. And these, like the first river transportation facilities developed in the Yukon, were provided by private trading companies themselves—and notably, of course, by the Hudson's Bay Company. Until the 1920s the Company carried on the navigation of the Mackenzie waterway with virtually no assistance from the public authorities. In his study of the waterway, Zaslow found that although it "had been utilized for 130 years before 1920 by fur traders their boats were so light that they had not been called upon to

16*Ibid.*

investigate or experiment with various channels, to dredge or remove boulders from channels, or build expensive break waters or wharves."[17] There was no demand for such improvements to the waterway until the discovery of commercial quantities of petroleum at Norman Wells in 1920. The ensuing flurry of activity in the area led the federal government to make a number of rather small investments in the system. In 1921 the estimates for the Department of the Interior included provision for the construction of floating wharves at Fort MacMurray to accommodate the increased river traffic and for the establishment of survey parties to chart the river.[18] It soon became apparent, however, that even the relatively large private firm developing the oil discoveries at Norman Wells could not cope with the problem of transporting the oil from the wells to outside markets and there was not, at that time, any significant local demand for petroleum. The only transportation facility available for shipping the oil over the first 1000 miles of this distance was a system of river steamers designed for the rather specialized needs of the fur trade. Because speed was not important in this trade the vessels employed were slow and low-powered and they provided only the infrequent service required by the fur trading-posts scattered along the river.[19] It was obvious that this fleet could not transport oil on a commercial scale from Norman Wells to railhead in Alberta. It was equally obvious that the Hudson's Bay Company would not revolutionize its river transport system to suit the requirements of an oil company. The only step taken by the Company to accommodate the north-bound volume of freight associated with the Norman development involved merely lashing barges to the steamers, an expedient which increased volume per trip at the expense of speed and reliability.

It was because of the slowness and limited operating season of the waterway that the early mining developments in the Mackenzie area were forced to take an interest in the development of costly alternative transportation facilities. In the initial development at Norman, for example, the first producing well was brought in in the fall of 1921 after the river had been closed to navigation. Imperial Oil thereupon acquired two Junkers float-equipped aircraft to fly urgently needed supplies into the camp from Edmonton, 1200 miles to the south. This novel adventure, for it was more that than an unqualified business

17M. Zaslow, "The Development of the Mackenzie Basin, 1920–1948," unpublished Ph.D. thesis, University of Toronto, 1957, p. 177.
18Canada, *Public Accounts* (Ottawa, 1922).
19Zaslow, "The Development of the Mackenzie Basin, 1920–1948," p. 164.

success, was neverthless the precursor of an important new factor in northern transportation. But the costs of such air-freighting of supplies were so high at the time that it had little immediate impact on the overall development problem of the area; nor did the even more visionary schemes, such as those aiming at the development of rail lines to link the Mackenzie to the continental railway system.

In 1921, for example, the "Edmonton and Mackenzie River Railway Company" was incorporated to build a four-foot-eight-and-one-half-inch gauge railway from Edmonton to "a point at or near where the Hay River empties into Great Slave Lake, in the North West Territories."[20] And, later in the decade, it was proposed to extend the existing railway system in northern Alberta to the 60th parallel in order to eliminate the need to use the unsatisfactory southern portion of the Mackenzie waterway for freighting purposes. The feasibility of this project was enhanced in 1929 when the existing rail lines in northern Alberta were acquired jointly by the Canadian Pacific and Canadian National Railway Companies and organized to form the "Northern Alberta Railways" system. But with the general economic collapse of that year, the proposed northern extension to the system was "postponed" and it became clear that, at least for the duration of the Depression, the transport needs of mining companies in Mackenzie District would have to be met by further development of the existing facilities either by commercial transportation companies or, failing that, by the mining companies themselves—just as had been the case in the Yukon.

It was not until late in the 1930s that interest in the mining potential of Mackenzie District was revived. Largely because of the rapid prospecting made possible by the introduction of aircraft for this kind of work early in the decade, a considerable expansion of facilities for shipping supplies and heavy equipment into the District was required.[21]

As a result of the increasing mining activity incoming freight carried by the Mackenzie River Transport Company[22] in 1929 was almost four times as high as the volume carried in 1921.[23] This expansion continued into the 1930s and encouraged MRT to invest $100,000 in

[20]See *Statutes of Canada*, 11–12 Geo., c. (1921).

[21]During the late 1920s and early 1930s claims had been staked over large areas in Mackenzie District, ranging from the south shore of Great Slave Lake to Coppermine on the arctic coast; see D.B.S., *Annual Report on the Mineral Production of Canada* (Ottawa, 1933), p. 67.

[22]The name of the Mackenzie River Transport Company is hereafter abbreviated to MRT.

[23]Zaslow, "The Development of the Mackenzie Basin, 1920–1948," p. 166.

additional floating equipment between 1930 and 1935.[24] As in the case of the White Pass and Yukon Route, there is reason to believe that this Company also passed on the costs of this investment, through its rate structure, to the mining companies, government departments, and other customers dependent upon its services. Because of a virtual monopoly over the entire length of the waterway, MRT was in a position to set rates high enough to capture many of the "social" returns to its investment in increased carrying capacity. In a competitive situation some of these returns might have been expected to pass to the various users of the system. Indeed, when competition did appear on the Mackenzie in the later 1930s, a marked reduction in freight rates did occur. The following comparison of rates is from the Minutes of the Northwest Territories Council where it appeared in conjunction with a resolution to the effect that "it is in the public interest that there should be at least two transportation companies providing freight service by water from the end of steel at Waterways to points served by water transportation in the Mackenzie district."[25]

MACKENZIE RIVER FREIGHT RATES

Waterways to:	DOLLARS PER CWT	
	1930	1939
Fort Smith	2.50	1.25
Hay River	4.50	1.75
Norman	7.25	2.50
Aklavik	9.75	2.50
Yellowknife	5.50	2.00

This combination of high rates and a mode of operation which, despite the addition of some new equipment to the system, remained unsuited to the needs of a growing mining community, had indeed led some exploration and development companies to establish their own transport fleets on the Mackenzie system. Thus, in 1929, for example, the Commercial Airways Company acquired a fleet of boats to haul aviation fuel to the small air bases it maintained in the Mackenzie valley; in 1932 the Great Bear Lake Mines Company bought equipment with which to transport supplies north to its mining properties; and two years later, the White Eagle Silver Mines Company built several vessels for the same purpose.[26] Late in 1934 two of these fleets were merged to form the "Northern Transportation Company" which carried the freight

24*Ibid.*, p. 174.
25*Minutes of the Council of the Northwest Territories*, October 15, 1940, X, 2405.
26Zaslow, "The Development of the Mackenzie Basin, 1920–1948," p. 171.

required to establish the large Eldorado Gold Mines Company's operation on Great Bear Lake.[27] In 1937 the latter Company acquired the Northern Transportation Company and operated it as a transport subsidiary.[28]

As a result of such investment in new equipment (and of partly successful attempts to improve the annual rate at which this equipment could be utilized), a large expansion of freight movement was accommodated by the Mackenzie waterway in the late 1930s. Records of freight traffic in the early part of the decade are unreliable, but it is unlikely that the north-bound volume exceeded 5,000 tons annually. In 1938, by comparison, 19,003 tons moved north from Waterways, 13,474 tons of which were for delivery in the District of Mackenzie.[29]

Despite the substantial increase made in the carrying capacity of the Mackenzie River system during the 1930s the demand for transport services into Mackenzie District continued to exceed the available supply. The inadequacy of the waterway at that time is attested to by the fact that many mining and exploration companies had recourse to alternative types of transportation despite their relatively high cost in terms of ton mile rates. The two alternatives to river transport at the time were the tractor-train and the aeroplane.

The use of aircraft was promoted in the 1930s by the establishment of permanent mining camps at Yellowknife, Norman Wells, and at Fort Radium which presented opportunities for regular, scheduled flights into the area. This, in turn, encouraged the consolidation of small independent air services into larger operating units which were better able to provide the ground and other facilities needed for the operation of heavier aircraft. Although the federal government gave some encouragement to these developments by way of its airmail contracts to commercial aviation companies, only small amounts of direct assistance were given in the form of landing and navigational facilities.[30] The inadequacy of these facilities restricted the extent to which larger, more efficient, aircraft could be substituted for the small, float-equipped craft otherwise used in the north. Although costs remained very high in consequence, by the end of the decade a number of commercial companies were carrying passengers, mail, and small amounts of freight in the area and some mining companies were operating their own aircraft for similar purposes.

[27]*Minutes of the Council of the Northwest Territories*, May 8, 1935, III, 661.

[28]Personal interview with Gilbert Labine, Toronto, February 18, 1958.

[29]J. L. Robinson, "Water Transportation in the Canadian Northwest," *Canadian Geographical Journal*, XXXI (November 1945), 254.

[30]Wilson, "The Expansion of Aviation into Arctic and Sub-Arctic Canada," p. 134.

In 1937, for example, Eldorado Gold Mines transported 90,000 pounds of freight in its own aircraft.[31]

But such measures as these were very costly alternatives to water transport and while it is true that some use might have been made of them no matter how much water transport was available, the extent to which they were used suggests that they were at least in part supplementing an inadequate source of cheaper transport. Subsequent developments on the Mackenzie in the 1940s were to demonstrate, however, that given additional investments in fixed and movable capital facilities, the carrying capacity of the river system could be enormously expanded. Unlike the experience in the Yukon described earlier in this chapter, the river transportation system in Mackenzie District was called upon to handle most of the freight associated with the Canol project and other military undertakings of World War II in the central part of the territorial north.

Although data relating to the volume of freight moved on the Mackenzie waterway are most unreliable prior to 1945, it is possible to infer from some of the information available that the initial effect of the war was to reduce the amount of freight carried on the river because of the disruption of the gold-mining developments which had just got under way in the late 1930s. According to Robinson, the total volume of north-bound freight from Waterways, the southern terminus of the system, declined from 19,003 tons in 1938 to 15,108 tons in 1940.[32] The development of military activities early in the war, however, reversed this trend. The Canol project alone was estimated to have provided 29,400 tons of freight to the system in 1942.[33] Freight for military purposes continued to dominate traffic on the system throughout the war and it was not until 1944, when development at Yellowknife was resumed, that civilian freight again accounted for more than half the total being moved north from Waterways.

The boom in military traffic during the war subjected the existing system to an unprecedented strain and although a large part of the increased volume was handled by craft operated by the military authorities themselves, the capacity of the system was expanded through the improvement of portages, handling facilities and some increase in the floating equipment of the private organizations operating on the system.

[31]D.B.S., *Annual Report on Mineral Production 1937* (Ottawa, 1938), p. 97.
[32]J. L. Robinson, "Water Transportation in the Canadian Northwest," *Canadian Geographical Journal*, XXXI (November, 1945), p. 254.
[33]Hudson's Bay Company, *The Beaver*, September, 1943, p. 5.

The competitive position of the various commercial companies operating on the river during the war is suggested by the data shown in the following table:[34]

AVERAGE ANNUAL FREIGHT TONNAGE CARRIED OVER MACKENZIE RIVER
SYSTEM BY COMMERCIAL FREIGHTING COMPANIES 1938–44

Operator	North from Waterways	North into NWT	Point to Point in NWT	South to Waterways
MRT	13,909(67%)	7,322(60%)	3,454(45%)	1,089(27%)
NTC	5,789(28%)	3,741(31%)	3,502(47%)	2,824(71%)
Other	1,135(5%)	1,029(9%)	578(8%)	61(2%)

A significant change was made in the organization of these services on the Mackenzie in 1944 when the federal government expropriated the property of Eldorado Gold Mines Limited.[35] Along with its other assets, the government acquired this Company's river transport subsidiary, the Northern Transportation Company, which had become the chief competitor of the Mackenzie River Transport Company as a commercial freight carrier on the waterway. Indeed, the end of the war found the Northern Transportation Company handling more freight than the Hudson's Bay Company's transport subsidiary. Several smaller companies were also involved in carrying freight on the waterway. The most important of these was the Yellowknife Transport Company which was incorporated in 1938, but which did not become an important carrier on the Mackenzie until the Canol Project boom in the early 1940s. By the end of the war this Company was operating five diesel tugs, one motor vessel, and eleven barges. The old Mackenzie River Transport Company fleet consisted of three steamers, twelve tugs and fifty-two barges. The more modern Northern Transportation Company fleet was composed of fourteen diesel vessels and forty-one barges.[36]

The subsequent development of the Mackenzie system after World War II was dominated by the NTC operating as a crown corporation and by government policy concerning roads. Because of this new level of public involvement in northern transportation it will be convenient to consider further developments in the next chapter. It may be noted at this point, however, that unlike the river carriers established during the 1920s and 1930s in Mackenzie District, the commercial air carriers operating there were subsequently to remain almost entirely under private ownership during and after World War II. As in the Yukon, the

---

[34]J. L. Robinson, "Water Transportation in the Canadian Northwest," p. 254.
[35]See Chapter 4.   [36]*North Pacific Planning Project*, p. 102.

tendency toward concentration of ownership and control once again showed up in the subsequent development of this industry.

Regular commercial air services were first provided in Mackenzie District by Commercial Airways which began flying down the Mackenzie valley in 1929. In 1933 these services were taken over by Mackenzie Air Services which operated them during the 1930s in conjunction with several smaller charter firms to provide mail, freight and passenger facilities throughout the western part of the Northwest Territories and as far north as the Arctic coast. In 1941 Mackenzie Air Services joined with General Airways and Wings to form a new firm, United Aircraft Services. The latter had a short separate existence, however, for a year later it was swallowed up in a new series of amalgamations which brought the main regional air carriers together in Canadian Pacific Airlines.

The commercial air services made available by these private firms in the Northwest Territories before World War II depended almost entirely upon float- or ski-equipped aircraft and the limitations of such equipment became apparent with the beginning of major defence projects in the area early in the 1940s.

Although the relatively low-speed and small cargo capacity of float-equipped aircraft were not great disadvantages when their primary task was simply to gain access to remote areas, these limitations made freighting and large-volume passenger flying very costly—perhaps twice as costly as when wheel-equipped aircraft could be used.

When the Canol project began there was not one landing field in the Northwest Territories. In order to fly in men, supplies and equipment, the United States built fields at Fort MacMurray, Embarras, Fort Smith, Fort Resolution, Hay River, Fort Providence, Mills Lake, Fort Simpson, Wrigley, Norman Wells, and at Camp Canol. All these airfields were capable of landing the larger cargo planes of the time. In 1944 a small field was built at Yellowknife by the Canadian government. This field was enlarged in 1945 and a second strip was built in 1947 as part of the federal government's new policy of giving assistance in airport construction to mining communities.[37] The Mackenzie Valley landing fields built by the United States were taken over by the Canadian government and maintained by the Department of Transport after 1944.

By making use of these new landing fields and some float-equipped aircraft as well, the newly organized Canadian Pacific Airlines organization was able to provide regular, scheduled flights between Edmonton

[37]*North Pacific Planning Project*, p. 128.

and Yellowknife and less frequent services further down the Mackenzie valley during the later years of the 1940s. The actual routes and schedules were frequently altered in response to the marked fluctuations in traffic loads which took place in those years.

As on the water routes of the north, scheduled air services have been subject to unusual diseconomies of operation due to heavy traffic imbalance. While on the river system this appeared chiefly in the form of a continuous inward imbalance, the airlines have tended to experience a seasonal reversal in traffic flow, with the spring and early summer volume peak having a northward bias and the fall peak a southward bias. Hence, even in periods of peak traffic flow, either the north-bound or the south-bound flight was made at less than capacity. A comparison between CPA and other North American airlines made by Hewetson in 1946 showed that the CPA operating revenue per mile flown was seventy-five cents compared to $1.10 for Trans-Canada Air Lines and representative United States lines. It has been suggested that this was largely due to the traffic imbalance, although it was also to some extent the result of the large number of miles CPA was flying with float-equipped aircraft at that time. It should also be noted that in the immediate post-war years CPA was deriving nearly half of its gross earnings from passengers, less than 25 per cent from air mail, and nearly 30 per cent from express and freight. TCA, by comparison, derived about the same percentage of its revenues from passenger fares but only two and a quarter per cent from express and freight, with air mail making up nearly 40 per cent of its total revenue. Of even greater significance is Hewetson's finding that the operating costs of CPA compared "very favourably" with those of TCA. This was accomplished by virtue of unusually low sales and publicity expenditures, and low passenger service costs. Meals and stewardess services were considerably less important on CPA services than on southern services and economies on these items were sufficient to off-set the higher costs of flying and aircraft maintenance on the northern services. These high costs, as would be expected, were chiefly attributable to the inadequacy of facilities for moving gasoline and oil to the northern airfields. Fuel, oil and spare parts had often to be flown in—which was not only costly in itself, but it reduced the operating revenues of the aircraft so employed.

CPA fares by 1946 were essentially the same as those established in the 1930s, except for a 15 per cent government tax added.[38] Although these fares and rates were widely held to be excessive and discriminatory

[38]Hewetson, "Transportation in the Northwest," p. 223.

because they were considerable higher than those in effect on southern services, an investigation by the Air Transport Board resulted in its approval of the existing rate schedule in February, 1947. Only three months later, however, possibly as a result of pressure from the federal government, CPA made a large reduction in its northern fares and rates. Statistics for passenger traffic carried by Canadian Pacific Airlines and Pacific Western Airlines, and by some mining company aircraft flying north from Edmonton, are given for the years 1957 to 1961 in Table 7.1. It will be noted that the reported volume of passenger traffic handled by mining company aircraft was relatively small compared to the volume carried by the commercial airlines. But, as shown in Table 7.2, the relative volume of freight handled by the former was much more significant. The great reduction in the volume of this traffic after 1960 is explained by the closing down of the Port Radium operations of Eldorado Mining and Refining. As noted in Chapter IV this operation made extensive use of aircraft both for shipping uranium concentrates out of the area and also for bringing in supplies on the "back-haul." Eldorado formed its own air transport subsidiary, Eldorado Aviation Company, in 1953. Equipped with relatively large, wheeled aircraft (initially a DC-3 and a C-46) this organization demonstrated that where a sufficient volume of inbound and outbound freight could be concentrated, surprisingly low unit costs of air shipment could be realized. Although commercial air freight charges in the Territories during the 1950s ranged from about 40 cents per ton mile to well over $1.00 when small aircraft were used, mining companies having a large enough volume of their own freight available to permit efficient utilization of larger cargo aircraft have been able to operate at less than 20 cents per ton mile.[39] Eldorado Aviation provided an interesting demonstration of the economics of such operations by flying lumber and other wood products from the Company's own sawmill at Peace River into the mines.[40]

The direct costs of air transportation to shippers in the Territories have remained, of course, generally higher than for those located further south. Air freight and passenger rates both on scheduled and on charter flights have traditionally been higher in the north than elsewhere and commercial aircraft operators do in fact set rates on the basis of "zones"

[39]See A. Dubnie, *Some Economic Factors Affecting Northern Mineral Development in Canada*, Mineral Information Bulletin Number MR38, Department of Mines and Technical Surveys (Ottawa, 1959), pp. 30–1.

[40]Eldorado Mining and Refining Company Limited, *Annual Report 1953* (Ottawa, 1954), p. 8.

with the rate schedule rising with the latitude of the zone. The justification for this has generally been found in the higher operating costs encountered in northern operations. With fuel costs ranking second only to labour outlays as direct operating expenses for air transport firms, the relatively high cost of gasoline in northern centres must have been a major factor contributing to the high cost of northern flying.[41] But an even more fundamental factor, and one which brings us once again to a familiar economic fact of life, is the matter of "scale." As we have now seen many times in many different contexts, the simple fact that so little production has been realized in the territorial north, and that even this has been scattered widely in a geographic sense, means that it was seldom possible to realize a concentration of freight or passenger traffic large enough in absolute terms to justify private investments in the larger and more efficient types of transportation facilities there.

Physical principles dictate that large aircraft can carry freight and passengers at lower unit costs than can small ones. Just how significant these advantages of scale may be is suggested by the fact that one airline operating in the north during the early 1960s charged about $100 an hour for a Cessna-180 capable of carrying approximately 1000 pounds but only $247 an hour for a C-47 with a carrying capacity *nine* times as great as that of the small aircraft.[42] But few mining or other centres of production in the Territories were large enough to warrant (at least on a commercial basis) investment in large-capacity aircraft and the related ground facilities required. Even such a relatively large settlement as Yellowknife, in the early post-war years, proved to be a marginal centre for scheduled commercial air services for this reason. Complaints against the rates charged by the main commercial operator there were met by a catalogue of arguments attesting to the high costs arising from the lack of adequate facilities and markets. These included references to the capital costs sustained by the carrier for ground facilities along the route, wear and tear on aircraft from using unpaved run-ways, lack of surface transportation for equipment, the poor load factor resulting from the lack of outbound freight from Yellowknife to Edmonton, and the limited utilization of equipment arising from the absence of night-time and bad-weather navigation and landing facilities at Yellowknife and along the route. Many of these

[41]A. Dubnie, *Transportation and the Competitive Position of Selected Canadian Minerals*, Mineral Survey 2, Department of Mines and Technical Surveys (Ottawa, 1962), pp. 87–8.
[42]From data shown in Dubnie, p. 90.

difficulties were subsequently alleviated by an increase in the volume of air traffic into and out of Yellowknife, for this made possible the large investments in ground facilities required for the continuous operation of larger, more efficient types of aircraft.

Summarizing the development of transportation facilities in the Yukon and in Mackenzie District to the late 1940s, it is apparent that the experience in Mackenzie District differed considerably from that in the Yukon. But the basic economic patterns are seen to be quite similar, for in both cases a major river system was involved and it was necessary to make heavy investments in it if it was to serve as a satisfactory source of transportation for the same basic industry—mining. Although some public funds were made available for this purpose they fell short of what was required during the peak periods of resource-developing activity in both areas. The resulting deficiency in the supply of transportation services was partly made up by private enterprise organized either as specialized transportation companies where the volume of business appeared to be adequate or as transportation divisions of primary resource-developing firms. In either case an apparently inexorable tendency toward reduction of competition sooner or later made itself evident. On the Mackenzie, by the 1940s the water transportation system had come to be dominated by two large firms, Mackenzie River Transport and Northern Transportation—both subsidiaries of primary resource-developing firms.

In the Yukon, the extraordinary opportunities presented by the Klondike gold rush had attracted private enterprise in the form of a specialized transportation company which quickly established a monopoly position which enabled it to set rates which no one in the Territory could escape. It was in a position to "tax" businesses and individuals in the Territory for any transport services or other benefits rendered by the company's operations. In return the company provided the central Yukon with an efficient connection with the outside world and with a less adequate central transportation system based on the Yukon river system. The inadequacy of the highly seasonal river operations for many mining developments could be overcome only by either an internal railway system, which was projected and abandoned as being not commercially feasible, or by a system of trunk roads. But the provision of such a road system has never been attractive to private investors for the obvious reason that the collection of revenues commensurate with the benefits created by such an investment is technically difficult. A government could, of course, have effected such a recovery of revenues from a community through its taxing powers. In the case of the Yukon, however, while the territorial government recognized the need for a trunk road system, its ability to provide such roads was impaired by the federal government's reluctance to provide the necessary revenues. And so it was left to mining companies to provide many of the subsidiary parts of the transportation network in the Yukon on their own initiative.

In Mackenzie District, private enterprise failed to provide the railway link needed to establish an adequate connection with the outside. This was not so much due to a failure of private enterprise to recognize the demand for the services of such a facility as to its inability to raise the necessary capital in a time of general economic collapse. In consequence, the extent to which mineral resources could be exploited there was limited by the inappropriateness of the Mackenzie waterway as a source of the transport services required. Although the federal government made some investments to improve the waterway, these were not sufficient to alter significantly its fundamental weaknesses as a transport system. Because of this, and the high rates charged by the major carrier on the waterway, many mining companies were obliged to accept the high rates associated with expensive alternatives to the water route or, in some cases, the overhead costs connected with providing their own small-scale transport services.

In addition to the small-scale water transportation systems they established, some mining and exploration companies also provided themselves with private air services, and there was even some specialized commercial provision of air services in areas where sufficient traffic could be found. In both cases a perceptible tendency toward concentration of ownership and control was observed as small, private operators struggled to achieve some of the economies of geographic concentration and of larger scale operation.

These same fundamental economic (and political) forces which shaped the development of transportation facilities in the territorial north may also be observed in the history of electric power generation there. This is not surprising, for both the transportation and the electric power generating industries have many of the same economic characteristics. Both tend to be heavily capital-intensive, and the electric power industry especially involves large investments in fixed capital the returns or benefits of which are forthcoming as a flow over a considerable period of time. And because of the technology involved in these industries important economies of scale may be realized in them. Consequently, where the market is large enough to make it economically feasible to invest in a large plant, the commodity produced may be made available relatively cheaply because of the efficient use of resources thereby realized. But where the market is small, or fragmented, such large capital investments cannot be justified (at least on a "commercial" basis) and the commodity produced, if it can be produced at all, will be made available at a high per unit cost reflecting the relative inefficiency of a small-scale installation. In the two situations one would also expect, of course, that the specialized producing organization would be attracted to the former, but not to the latter—leaving would-be consumers of the commodity to produce it themselves on a piecemeal basis.

ELECTRIC POWER GENERATION IN THE TERRITORIES BEFORE WORLD WAR II

The generation of electrical energy in the Yukon during this period was almost entirely in the hands of mining companies whose primary interest was in providing power for their own needs, although domestic power was supplied to adjacent communities when it was convenient to do so. Despite the scarcity of suitable hydro-electric sites in the central Yukon, because the chief mining operations were of the placer type it was convenient to incorporate hydro-electric power generating facilities into the extensive water control systems used in these operations. The first major electric power plant built in the Yukon was the Yukon Gold Company's plant located on the Twelvemile River. First established with a generating capacity of 1650 horsepower at a cost of $200,000 in 1909, it was subsequently expanded to 3180 horsepower.[43] The efficiency of this installation was considerably impaired by the need to supply it with water by way of an elaborate ten-mile-long system of flumes which could function only during the summer season.[44]

A second hydro-electric plant was constructed in the Klondike area in 1911 by another large placer-mining firm, the New Northwest Corporation. Equipped with two 5000 horsepower generating units this plant was capable of supplying power not only for its owner's dredges but for sale to other users in the area as well.[45]

[43]Canada, Department of Mines, *Annual Report of the Division of Mineral Resources for 1909* (Ottawa, 1911), pp. 20–1.
[44]*North Pacific Planning Project*, p. 84.
[45]D.B.S., *Mineral Statistics 1922*, p. 154.

Thus, by the outbreak of World War I, the Yukon placer gold fields had two hydro-electric plants with a rated horsepower of over 13,000. The annual output of power approached ten million kilowatt-hours, most of which was consumed by the dredges and pumps of the placer gold operators, but some of which was supplied to other commercial and domestic users in the Dawson area. Dawson City itself was supplied with light and power by a distribution company which bought power wholesale from the plants. It is interesting to note that complaints concerning the price of such power became a matter of record from the earliest days of the industry. In 1913, for example, the Yukon Territorial Council investigated the rates being charged and conducted negotiations with the various companies concerned in an attempt to have them reduced. With unwarranted optimism the Council subsequently reported that "The result of these negotiations so far has been that the rate charged for electric light in the Town of Dawson has been reduced by about 50 per cent."[46] This reduction, as it turned out, lasted less than one year, however, for in 1914 the Dawson City Electric Light and Power Company restored the rates to their original level. The rather hard line that some of the utility companies were prepared to take is suggested by the fact that when the residents of Dawson voted against a proposed increase in the rates for hydrant service, the Dawson City Water and Power Company simply cut off the water.[47]

The electric power generating capacity installed in the Yukon during the years between the turn of the century and World War I proved to be adequate for the needs of the placer gold-mining industry for almost a quarter of a century thereafter. The only other significant industrial user of electric power was the silver-lead–mining industry at Mayo. One of the companies operating there, the United Keno Hill Company, generated a small amount of power from a thermal plant which actually used wood as its basic fuel. This small plant was acquired by the Treadwell Yukon Company during the concentration of ownership in the Mayo operations which took place in the early 1920s.[48] Small amounts of power were also generated for their own use by firms and individuals using small internal combustion plants.

It was not until 1935 that a major addition was made to the large-scale generating capacity installed in the Yukon and this took the form

[46]*Journals of the Yukon Council* (1913), XIII, 9.
[47]*Journals of the Yukon Council* (1914), XIV, 10.
[48]D.B.S., *Mineral Statistics 1924*, p. 158. See p. 108 above.

of expansion of the old "North Fork" plant in the Klondike. In that year the Yukon Consolidated Gold Corporation, which had taken over most of the major installations in the Klondike by that time,[49] installed a third 5,000 horsepower generating unit thereby raising the total generating capacity of the North Fork plant to 10,520 kilowatts. This was to be the last major investment in electric power generation by a private company in the Yukon.

In the Northwest Territories the first major mineral development, the Port Radium operation, was established using diesel-electric power. Drawing upon the fuel available from the small petroleum refinery at Norman Wells, Eldorado was able to supply its own power needs in this way despite the relatively high operating costs associated with this inefficient method of generating electricity.[50] The same technique was used by the developers of the first operations in the Yellowknife auriferous quartz mines later in the 1930s. The great advantage of the internal combusion generating units for such purposes was, of course, their small size which made them suitable for individual mines no matter how modest their power requirements. They were also easily installed and, if the venture failed, easily removed. On the other hand, if the venture succeeded additional capacity could be added without disturbing the original installation. All these characteristics meant that unlike alternative sources of electric power, the internal combustion generating units did not require heavy investments in fixed capital. Consequently, even small individual firms could use them to obtain electric power.

Investments in more efficient thermal or hydro plants, on the other hand, could be justified only under conditions such as those which prevailed in the Klondike where both the market and the kind of productive organization required were present. The demand for energy had to be large enough to justify investing in a large-scale power generating facility and, in the absence of public financing of such a facility, at least one user of the power would have to be in a position to finance the development itself and to recover the commercially necessary revenues from its operations. As the Yellowknife area gold boom developed in the late 1930s these necessary conditions for a large-scale power development came to exist. As noted in the earlier description of the mining operations there, four of the six properties brought into

[49]See Chapter 4.
[50]See p. 117.

production before development was interrupted by the war were owned or controlled by a single operator—the Consolidated Mining and Smelting Company of Canada, a subsidiary of the Canadian Pacific Railway and one of the largest mining companies in Canada. With its four properties located in the area it appeared feasible for this Company to undertake the necessary investments to acquire lower cost power than it could generate with diesel-electric units. Using stream-flow records which had been kept by the Dominion Water and Power Bureau the Company built a dam at the outlet of Bluefish Lake, impounding water which was fed through a half-mile long conduit to a power-house located on Prosperous Lake. The initial installation completed in 1941 consisted of a single 4,700 horsepower turbine driving a 4200 k.v.a. generator.[51] The output, which reached 21,733,000 kilowatt-hours in 1942, was sufficient to supply the Company's mines and to provide power to a distribution company which re-sold it to the town of Yellowknife.

This was the last large-scale private power development in the Territories. Its completion brought the installed hydro-electric generating capacity of the Territories up to 22,899 horsepower by 1942, although the following year the old 3180 horsepower plant on the Twelvemile River in the Klondike was taken out of service and dismantled, thereby reducing the total capacity to 19,719 horsepower. There was no further large-scale power development there until after the war, but by that time the great change in public and government attitudes toward the Territories described in Chapter II had taken place and the responsibility for making investments in large-scale electric power generating facilities (as well as for major transportation developments) was taken out of private hands and made a function of government. Subsequent developments in both kinds of facilities are examined in Part III which is concerned with public investment in the Territories.

[51]Canada, Department of Mines and Resources, "Report of the Dominion Water and Power Bureau 1941," in the *Annual Report* of the Department for 1941, p. 124.

III. PUBLICLY SPONSORED ACTIVITY IN THE TERRITORIES

8 Public Investment in Basic Industrial Facilities

DURING THE DECADES of the 1940s and 1950s, the economic environment of the north was fundamentally altered by the sudden commencement of large-scale publicly-sponsored investment programmes. These undertakings were associated with two main types of federal government programmes—one involving investments in basic industrial facilities such as transportation and electric power installations, the other in public health and welfare facilities. The first of these is examined in this chapter, the second in the next.

DIRECT PUBLIC INVOLVEMENT IN NORTHERN TRANSPORTATION

The belated large-scale involvement of government in northern transportation during the 1940s and 1950s was initially most apparent in the policies relating to roads and highways. This is not surprising for these are by their economic nature the kind of facilities private investors are generally least able to provide on a commercial basis. However, the initial large-scale public investments which provided the trunk routes for future highway systems to be built out from both in the Yukon and in Mackenzie District were justified more by military than by economic considerations.

In the Yukon, most of the roads built prior to World War II were local mining roads, such as the fifty-two miles built in the Dawson placer fields and the thirty-five miles in the vicinity of Mayo. Other roads, while often shown on maps, were seldom regularly usable by ordinary vehicles. Although some federal assistance for road-building in the

Yukon was furnished in the late 1930s as part of a national public works programme to create employment, this was offset in the Yukon by reductions in the normal federal road grant to the Yukon Territorial Council.[1] Given the federal government's general attitude toward the Territories in the pre-World War II decades and given, too, the low level of economic activity in the Yukon at that time, the best chance the Territory had for getting a major highway development lay in the possibility that the United States would seek to develop a land route through Canadian territory to Alaska. Such a scheme was indeed being promoted as early as 1929 by interests in the United States and in 1930 an international commission had been appointed to study routes and to estimate costs for such a project. The official Canadian response to these proposals was not enthusiastic. Nevertheless, in 1938 the United States War Department lent support to the project and surveys of two alternative routes, both running through British Columbia, were contemplated.[2]

From an economic and engineering standpoint, the obvious route for a highway to Alaska was one which would take advantage of a remarkable natural feature, the so-called "Rocky Mountain Trench" which provides a relatively easy route from a point on the Canadian National Railway line near Prince George, British Columbia, north into the Yukon Territory.[3] However, in 1940, the choice of a route was referred to the newly formed Permanent Joint Board on Defence which decided against the trench route in favour of a route lying far inland and running from Dawson Creek near the British Columbia–Alberta boundary via Whitehorse to Fairbanks, Alaska.

The 1,523-mile-long highway was built in little more than a year and at the peak of the construction programme more than 40,000 men, using the most highly mechanized equipment available, were engaged in the operation. The road was opened for military traffic in November, 1943. Of the 1,220 miles of the road which lie in Canadian territory, 554 are in the Yukon. About twenty-five miles west of where the highway passes through Whitehorse, it is joined by the Haines Cut-off, another military road 140 miles in length, built to connect the Alaska Highway with the Pacific coast port of Haines, Alaska.

There can be no doubt that the Alaska Highway as constructed did

[1]In 1931 the grant was increased to $160,500, but it was reduced again in 1934 to $70,000 and remained at this level during the rest of the decade; *Public Accounts* data.

[2]*Report of the Alaska Highway Commission* (Ottawa, King's Printer, 1942).

[3]*North Pacific Planning Project*, p. 119.

help to open up much of northwestern Canada. Along with its parallel telephone line and its emergency landing strips it provided ready access to thousands of square miles of territory which had previously been accessible only by canoe or small pontoon-equipped aircraft. Its direct effect upon the economy of the north was, however, little more than could be expected from any highway thrown across 1,500 miles of virgin lands without regard to existing or potential resource deposits or to costs, whether of construction or of maintenance.

Until the end of the war the highway was maintained by the North-west Service Command of the United States Army, and was closed to most civilian traffic. At the end of the war it was taken over by Canadian authorities. Although bus and commercial trucking services were established on the highway after the war, its importance as a means of moving freight in and out of the Yukon Territory proved to be strictly limited. The cost of hauling freight by truck over the route was so high that it could not compete with the sea and railway route from Vancouver to Whitehorse via Skagway. In the early post-war years it was estimated that it was economical to truck freight only as far as Watson Lake from the southern terminus of the Highway at Dawson Creek. For points further north it proved cheaper to ship by sea and rail to Whitehorse and then truck the freight from there to points within the Territory.[4]

The costs of maintaining the highway at the end of the war were assumed by the federal government. Because of the necessity of replacing more or less temporary bridges, culverts and other construction on the route during this period, the highway proved to be an expensive facility to maintain. Maintenance expenditures on the Alaska Highway increased from $110,107 in 1946 to $2,085,309 in 1951. Despite these costs, however, the highway was maintained and even improved during the decade of the 1950s. This is all the more remarkable in view of the fact that the inappropriateness of the road as a surface freighting facility had been recognized even by the military authorities responsible for its construction, for even while it was being built, the United States Army surveyed a light railway line northward up the Trench from a junction with the continental rail system near Prince George, British Columbia. The cost of this line was estimated at 112 million dollars.[5] Had the military situation persisted it is probable that the railway would have been built, but with the American victory at Midway the project was abandoned. The significance of the plan itself lies in the support it gives

[4]Ibid., p. 118.
[5]House of Commons Debates, 1949, p. 1933.

to the view that the Alaska Highway was never regarded as a satisfactory freight-moving facility.

Further proposals for an Alaska railway were plentiful in the post-war period. In 1947 the North Pacific Planning Commission expressed the opinion that:

There seems little doubt . . . that ultimately a rail connection will be established through British Columbia and Yukon to Alaska, primarily for defence purposes but looking also to its economic significance in the development of both Canadian and United States territory.[6]

By 1949 United States interest in such a project had reached the point where the President was authorized to undertake an agreement with Canada for the construction of a railway from the United States to Alaska. The Canadian government, however, was still not enthusiastic. Mr. Pearson, then Secretary of State, held that "largely financial" difficulties prevented the government from supporting the project although it was "of course interested in any transportation development in the northwest which would bring that part of our country in closer contact with Alaska, not only for strategic reasons, but for development reasons as well." He justified the government's attitude to an Alaska railway at that time on the grounds that "existing transportation facilities are not overtaxed . . . so there would undoubtedly be a substantial deficit for many years, running possibly to fifty million dollars per year."[7] Apparently the federal government still accepted commercial profitability as a dependable guide for public action—at least where investments in northern transportation facilities were concerned.

The great defence projects of the war years were, of course, exceptions to this rule. As we have seen, the Alaska Highway was not designed as a major transportation facility and, consequently, its peacetime usefulness was limited by its location. If the decision to maintain it had been based upon its economic justification, as this phrase was understood by the government during this period, it would have been abandoned. Instead, it was maintained as a defence measure.

Part of the final significance of the Alaska Highway for the Yukon and for the north in general derived from the way it drew attention to the area's economic possibilities. Unlike other defence projects carried out in the area, the Alaska Highway and the system of airfields it serviced were never kept secret for any length of time, even during the war. Indeed, from the moment the highway was begun its progress

[6]North Pacific Planning Project, pp. 124–5.
[7]House of Commons Debates, 1949, p. 1933.

was widely reported in the press throughout North America and it seems likely that the post-war conversion of the Canadian government from a passive regulatory agency in northern affairs to a supporting force in the development of the area owed something to this publicity.[8] In so far as this new government activity subsequently led to more support for road construction in the Yukon during the 1950s the Alaska Highway contributed directly to these developments by providing a trunk road from which branches could be extended into adjacent areas.

The only other major road development in the Yukon during the war was the Canol road built through the little-known country lying between the southern Yukon and the Mackenzie. But, like the pipeline it was built to service, the Canol road was abandoned at the end of the war. Although a private mining company subsequently attempted to restore part of the road for its own use, no serious effort was made to maintain it as a through road.

It is interesting to note that the once important highway leading from Whitehorse to Dawson was also allowed to deteriorate at the end of the war.[9] The neglect of such roads as this was partly attributable to the policy of the federal government in connection with air-transport— which it sought to encourage by granting airmail contracts to the airline companies. This meant that some of the internal roads and trails dating from the early phases of development in the Yukon were no longer needed for this purpose and many of them consequently disappeared. Most of the expenditures which were made on road maintenance in the Yukon during the 1940s were confined to the important mining roads of the Territory. Such expenditures increased considerably after the war as improvements and extensions of the road system were resumed, but even so the amounts remained relatively small. In 1947 for example, territorial road expenditures amounted to little more than $200,000.[10]

Turning to the Northwest Territories, we find that there was no internal road system there at all in 1939. The pioneer pattern of transportation development was still clearly apparent with mining and other industrial developments clinging to the water routes. The earliest roads built were those designed to supplement and to improve these routes. Such roads were of two types—the portage roads at Fort Smith and on the Bear River and the longer winter roads used to transport freight

[8]R. Finnie, "The Epic of Canol," *Canadian Geographical Journal,* XXXIV (March, 1947), 138.
[9]Much to the distress of some of the residents of the area; see *House of Commons Debates,* 1947, p. 1207.
[10]*Bureau of Northwest Territories and Yukon Affairs,* 1948, p. 167.

after the water routes had been closed for the season. These roads were fundamentally different from those of the Yukon which were typically *communication* routes rather than integral parts of the freight and passenger transporting facilities. This is reflected in their competitive role with respect to air transport, which in the 1930s began to replace them as communications channels. The roads of the Northwest Territories were fundamentally freight-moving facilities and, as such, were able to compete with the freighting function of the aircraft. Aircraft had always monopolized the communications function in the Northwest Territories, for most of the mining development there was undertaken after the advent of the aeroplane. Consequently, road transport in the Northwest Territories competed with the aircraft in the function least suited to it—the handling of heavy freight. Because most of the freight handled was north-bound freight, typically heavy mining equipment and supplies, there was no question of roads being developed to the point where they would eliminate water transport, as they eventually did in the Yukon. In the Yukon the nature of the freight was quite different, for the placer mining industry did not require large importations of heavy equipment and the silver-lead–mining industry's chief transport requirement was for shipping *out* its heavy products. Such requirements were better satisfied by more expensive, but faster and year-round highway freighting. In Mackenzie District, however, ninety per cent of the traffic was *north-bound* and, during the decades of the 1930s and 1940s, consisted of freight destined for newly developed mines—heavy machinery and equipment, building materials and supplies. There was no large export of material from the area because its export product was refined gold. Hence, the highways or roads could only complement the water system, which, despite more serious limitations than the Yukon system, could not be rivalled in view of the particular transport requirements of Mackenzie District. Even when a highway was built to duplicate the water route, the latter was little affected by it. The chief inadequacies of the Mackenzie waterway which the roads of the District were designed to alleviate were the two long portages and the shortness of the navigation season.

As noted in Chapter 1, the only complete interruption in the Mackenzie waterway between the head of steel and the Arctic Ocean is a 16-mile portage between Fort Fitzgerald and Fort Smith. Frequent attempts were made by private companies to improve this portage, but it was difficult for a private company to make such an investment profitable. The possibility of public investment was complicated by the fact that part of the portage lay in Alberta and the other part in territory under federal jurisdiction. Although the two governments worked out a plan for sharing the costs of maintaining a portage road in 1930, the Alberta government leased its part of the road to a private operator—whose monopoly position enabled him to levy a tariff of $1.00 per 100 pounds on freight crossing the portage.[11] The absurd result was that a second, parallel, road was built by another private operator. In 1935 this road was acquired by the Northern Transportation Company, which forced rates on the portage down to 55 cents per 100 pounds.

The federal government was eventually more successful in helping private operators to overcome the portage on the Bear River, which connects Great Bear Lake with the Mackenzie system. In response to "insistent" requests from mining companies,[12] the federal government built a portage road around the rapids in the Bear River and, between the years 1932 when the project began and 1936 when it was completed, spent approximately $28,500 on it.[13] A large part of the tonnage hauled over the road initially was fuel oil bound for the pitchblende-silver mine on Great Bear Lake. In 1937, however, the Imperial Oil Company built a pipe-line over the portage route so that oil could be pumped directly from barges at one end of it to barges at the other end. In the same year the Northern Transportation Company acquired new equipment specially designed for operation on the Bear River and for the transport of oil and other commodities on Great Bear Lake. It would be difficult to find a better illustration of the strong inter-dependence between certain kinds of investments in a previously undeveloped area than this.

The most immediately available practical means for overcoming the effects of the short operating season of the river system was to provide a temporary winter alternative to the river. Thus, in 1938, the province of Alberta approached the federal government with a scheme to build a "winter road" from railhead at Waterways north to Lake Athabaska to provide a means of freighting heavy materials into the north when the river was closed to navigation. The Northwest Territories Council appears to have responded with some enthusiasm to this proposal which,

[11]This put the Northwest Territories administration in a difficult position, for it was under considerable pressure from both its own field officers and the Hudson's Bay Company to operate its section of the road as a public utility; see *Minutes of the Council of the Northwest Territories*, September 3, 1931, I, 200–1 and July 10, 1931, I, 204. For a full discussion of this development see M. Zaslow, "The Development of the Mackenzie Basin 1920–48," unpublished Ph.D. thesis, University of Toronto, 1957, p. 180.

[12]*Minutes of the Council of the Northwest Territories*, September 21, 1931, p. 208.

[13]*Ibid.*, January 7, 1936, IV, 769.

it was told, "would serve equally for outbound freight (principally concentrates); it would extend the season of navigation of the Mackenzie River; it would provide for movement of agricultural produce from the Peace River country to Great Slave Lake and the Yellowknife country."[14] Nevertheless, the federal government rejected the proposal on the grounds that it "would incur very heavy expenditures and, in our judgement, was not the best method of proceeding with the development of transportation facilities into that area."[15] In the fall of that year, however, a large shipment of goods, urgently needed at Yellowknife, was caught by an early closing of the river and the Alberta government announced that it would build a winter road from Grimshaw in northwestern Alberta north to the south shore of Great Slave Lake. The federal government thereupon decided to participate in the construction of this type of facility and during the winter of 1938–9 federal and provincial crews completed the basic clearing of a roughly 400-mile route providing a winter connection between Mackenzie District and northern Alberta.[16] This road was extensively used to haul supplies into the Yellowknife area during the short period of rapid development there before the outbreak of World War II disrupted the development.

The cost of hauling freight on sleds propelled by heavy tractors over this type of road proved to be relatively high. Although rates varied from one contract to another, they ranged between 25 and 35 cents per ton mile depending upon the difficulty of the terrain.[17] When the alternative was to delay development by two-thirds of a year, however, mining operators were often willing to accept these charges.

At the end of the war the original Grimshaw-Hay River route was improved to highway standards. The total cost of this improvement was almost four and one-half million dollars and it marked the first large public investment in a major transportation facility in the area. There is some evidence that the great increase in mineral exploration and development in the southern part of Mackenzie District in the early post-war years was stimulated by this development, but the immediate importance of the road as a freighting facility was not great.

Before going on to consider later publicly sponsored developments in

[14]*Ibid.*, December 16, 1938, p. 1646.

[15]*House of Commons Debates*, June 30, 1938, p. 4499.

[16]*Minutes of the Council of the Northwest Territories*, Memorandum dated May 11, 1939, p. 1869.

[17]H. W. Hewetson, "Transportation in the Northwest," in C. A. Dawson, ed., *The New North-West*, p. 219.

transportation in the Territories it should be noted that the expansion of transportation facilities during the war and in the early post-war years emphasized the importance of the distinction between the needs of particular areas and the variety of ways in which different types of transportation could be used to satisfy these needs. The general development of roads and highways, for example, had quite different effects in the Yukon and in the Mackenzie area. In the Yukon, the growth of public interest in the needs of the area eventually led to the construction of a highway system which usurped the traditional function of the great Yukon water route as a freight-carrying facility and caused its abandonment in 1952. In the Mackenzie area, a similar road had little immediate effect on the existing river system. Indeed, as we will see below, the latter continued to expand the scale of its operation. The experience of the post-war period demonstrated that highways and roads can have several entirely different functions which, under frontier conditions, are perhaps more easily distinguished than may be the case elsewhere. Highways and roads may serve as aids to exploration, as freight-moving facilities or as means of communication. In the history of northern development all these functions have been described at one time or another. Similarly the aircraft may operate as an aid to exploration, or as a passenger- or freight-transporting facility. It has already been shown that when organized for the first function it is characteristically operated by a small-scale organization using float-equipped aircraft and operating with a minimum of investment in such ground facilities as surface transport, landing fields, and fueling stations. When it is organized for the second and third functions it tends to be operated as a large-scale, often monopolistic organization using wheeled aircraft and requiring extensive investment in ground services. Water transportation systems, in their turn, have also served the functions of exploration and their organization and equipment has reflected the function of primary importance at a given time.

Roads and Highways after 1949

The most important highway development in the Yukon in the 1950s was the completion of the highway from Whitehorse to Mayo in 1951. The effect of this highway upon the operations of the silver-lead-zinc mines at Mayo has already been described in Chapter IV, where it was noted that the chief immediate beneficiary of the project, United Keno Hill Mines Limited, secured federal support for the project by agreeing to assume a major part of the cost of maintaining the road and to maintain, at cost, and as the agent of the Yukon territorial government, the other roads and the air-strip in the Mayo area.

Most of the traffic on the Mayo-Whitehorse Highway consisted of the concentrates being hauled from Mayo to Whitehorse by the trucks of the United Keno Hill Company and their return hauls of supplies and materials for the mines. There was also some movement of local lumber products over the road. The road was greatly improved after the original construction by bridging the various river crossings, which were originally provided only with ferries, and by construction of an extension to the road from a junction at Stewart River Crossing to Dawson City in the placer gold fields and on through the old Sixtymile area to Alaska. Thus, during the 1950s it became possible to travel from either Mayo or Dawson City to Whitehorse and from there either north to Fairbanks or south to Edmonton via the Alaska Highway. The result of this highway construction was consequently to duplicate the Yukon River water route through the central and southern part of the Territory. This resulted in the abandonment of the latter system altogether during the 1950s.

In some respects the highway north from Whitehorse to Mayo and Dawson may be viewed as a re-routing of the Alaska Highway through the Yukon. Had the Alaska Highway originally been constructed with regard to its contribution to the economic development of the Yukon Territory it would obviously have been routed in such a way as to link the main existing centres of economic activity in the Territory, such as Whitehorse, Mayo, and Dawson, and also, perhaps, to provide a basis for projecting branch roads to prospective development areas. The Whitehorse–Mayo Highway came to serve both these purposes. Both it and the Alaska Highway have provided a basis for development roads leading, for example, north from Dawson into the Eagle Plain area, northeast from Whitehorse to Ross River, and north from Watson Lake to the tungsten development on the Yukon-Northwest Territories border.

Similarly, in Mackenzie District, the highway from Grimshaw, Alberta, to Hay River, Northwest Territories, served as the first step toward developing a highway system there, despite the fact that like the Alaska Highway, this road did not initially prove to be very important as a freighting facility. During the 1950s the most important road-building project in the Territories was the extension of the highway, now referred to as the Mackenzie Highway, from Hay River around the west end of Great Slave Lake to Yellowknife. This extension suggested the beginning of a trunk road network in the District of Mackenzie. In the early 1960s construction of a highway east from Yellowknife was under way and it was expected that this might eventually develop into a route circling around the east end of Great Slave Lake to join with the Mackenzie Highway again to the south. Such a route would provide a basis for projecting a series of development roads into the potential mining regions in the undeveloped eastern parts of the District. The Hay River–Yellowknife extension of the Mackenzie Highway also suggested the possibility of a main road being continued north along the Mackenzie to provide a highway connection for the various settlements along the river and to provide the trunk for branch roads to specific mining sites to the east.

The remarkable thing about these highway developments just described is that they were in large part financed by the federal government. This is perhaps not surprising in the case of the original Mackenzie Highway or even the Whitehorse–Mayo road, for both served to connect areas of known economic value to the outside world. Furthermore, the Mackenzie Highway had considerable strategic value as a military road and, from the outset, was not expected to serve as a major freighting facility.[18] In the case of the Whitehorse–Mayo road, as we have seen, a private company was prepared to participate financially in the project and, through its operation, give it a considerable economic justification as well. But, when we turn to the various projections extending from these trunk roads into apparently blank spaces on the map, we recognize a new kind of development in the history of territorial road construction. None would appear to be justifiable on military grounds and none led to established mining areas. For an explanation of this and the associated increase in public spending on roads in the Territories shown in Table 8.1, we must look at the development of the federal government's policy with respect to such road construction in the 1950s in more detail.

Federal policy with respect to financing roads in the Territories appears to have passed through two stages during the decade of the 1950s. The first stage was marked by a cautious acceptance of the fact that federal participation was warranted in the construction of roads which would support economic development in the north. This was in keeping, of course, with the awakening of the federal government to the possible economic value of the northern territories which was described in

---

[18]W. G. Scott, "Economic Report on the Mackenzie River Transportation System," in *Minutes of the Council of the Northwest Territories*, December 17, 1947, XIV, 342–3.

Chapter 2. The second stage occurred in 1957 when a new administration adopted a policy which went somewhat further than that of assisting in the construction of roads which were *currently* economically justifiable by undertaking to build roads into areas which had a known economic *potential*.

The policy prior to 1957, as applied initially in the Yukon Territory, recognized three types of roads. First, the "trunk roads" which connected major settlements. These were built and maintained by the territorial government. The funds available for this purpose came largely from the federal grant to the Territory and, although about one-third of the territorial budget was devoted to road construction and maintenance in the 1950s, it was not possible for the Territory to do much more than meet the most immediate needs for maintenance and improvements to existing facilities, except when special federal allowances were made for the development of these trunk roads. The second type of road, the "secondary roads," were those lying within the settlements themselves and these were also the responsibility of the territorial government. The condition of the roads through the territorial capital long served to attest to the inability of the territorial government to carry out this responsibility. The third type recognized by the federal authorities was the "resource road," a road servicing a specific mine or other land-exploiting operation. Both capital and maintenance costs of such roads were treated as a federal responsibility, although this did not preclude, of course, the participation in them by private companies directly benefitting from them.

The government attitude implicit in these arrangements was made explicit by the Minister-in-charge in the following statement of May, 1954:

. . . since the transportation problem is one that we have to cope with mainly for economic development it is one to which I have given and will give the highest priority. . . . Of course, we have to be careful, for there have been instances in the past where we have built or participated in the building of roads which were later abandoned because the mines in which there had been placed a high degree of confidence turned out to be uneconomic to operate I agree that some risks have to be taken and I do not mind taking a few risks, but a balance must be kept and a certain amount of care exercised.[19]

Critics of the government road programme at this time argued that, in practice, government appraisal of the potential returns to specific projects tended to be so cautious as to render government assistance a

[19]*House of Commons Debates*, 1953–54, pp. 4681–2.

post facto phenomenon. It was alleged that the government, when approached by mining operators for assistance in road-building, demanded proof that the project was profitable before government assistance would be considered.[20]

Mining interests in the north point out that the most difficult problem of financing a new mineral operation occurs at the initial development stage when the attempt is made to "prove" the deposit. The element of risk is, of course, very high at this stage and financial sources are reluctant to advance funds to the mining company. And it is at this time that the company must construct some means of access to the property. Once the initial development has shown the deposit to be capable of profitable operation there is no great difficulty in obtaining financial support. Hence, it is argued, the government resource road policy tended to withold assistance when it was most needed and to make it available when it was no longer essential. One mining engineer consulted in the north held that because of this, his operations were always planned on the assumption that federal aid would not be a factor—if it was forthcoming it was desirable but not essential.[21]

Late in 1956 the federal government appears to have reformulated its policy respecting northern road development, for in January, 1957, the member for the Yukon announced that the government had decided to implement a new road policy for the Yukon Territory in April, 1957. Under the new policy the entire cost of constructing "development" roads in the Territory was to be assumed by the federal government. The maintenance of these roads was to be shared by the federal and territorial governments in the proportions of 85 and 15 per cent respectively.[22]

This policy was expanded in 1958 when the new federal administration implemented a nation-wide programme of building roads to potentially valuable natural resources. The "Roads to Resources Programme" initiated in 1958 provided for federal-provincial cost-sharing in such road projects with the federal government making available to each province a contribution of up to $7,500,000. The territorial counterpart of this was the "Development Road Programme" in the Yukon and District of Mackenzie which provided that the federal government would assume total responsibility for constructing resource roads and would share

[20]*House of Commons Debates*, 1957, p. 266.

[21]See also Whitehorse Board of Trade, "Submission to the Royal Commission on Canada's Economic Prospects," p. 53.

[22]See N. Gritzuk, "The Role of Transportation in the Development of the North," *Western Miner and Oil Review* (April, 1959).

maintenance costs on an 85–15 per cent basis with the territorial government concerned. Under the scheme about 900 miles of road were to be built in the Yukon at an estimated cost of $36,000,000 and 1,300 in the Northwest Territories at a cost of $64,000,000.

It is this "development road" policy which accounts for such roads as the one north of Dawson to the Eagle Plain area, the road to Ross River (actually located on the Pelly River) from Whitehorse, and the road from Yellowknife to MacKay Lake, which were referred to earlier. These, like some of those built in the provinces under the Roads to Resources Programme were, at first sight, remarkable in that they appeared to lead nowhere. It is not surprising, then, that when the extraordinary costliness of some of these projects was taken into account, considerable controversy arose in connection with this policy. Although it is tempting to dismiss this controversy as merely representing the difference between persons who are more prone to gamble than their fellows, the issues involved are in fact more complex. Some of the complexity emerges when an effort is made to distinguish between the functions of different types of transportation facility in specific circumstances. As noted earlier, a road can be conceived of as an aid to exploration or as a means of moving freight, whether this consists of plant to be installed in the site or, in the case of low-value mineral deposits, of the product itself. Whether or not a road is an effective investment in terms of either function depends upon the alternatives available in a given situation.

The usual alternative to a road as an aid to exploring unknown territory is the aircraft. In the initial stage of exploration the problem is to get prospecting parties into the area. The next stage, if these parties have found resources warranting further development, is to transport the equipment, supplies and men necessary for proving up the deposit into the site. In the Canadian north, the aircraft has been used extensively for both these tasks. In fact, as shown earlier, northern air services originated in connection with such undertakings. In the later post-war period, however, the new federal road policy led to the construction of "development" roads to serve these same purposes.

The advantages claimed for this approach are, of course, that it opens up large areas of country rather quickly, it provides cheaper transportation for inward freight, and it may provide a sufficiently cheap means of getting shipments of the product out of the area if resources are successfully developed in it. There can be little doubt that in terms of operating costs per ton mile, road transport, even over rather primitive roads, is usually considerably cheaper than air transport for development purposes. Although costs vary from one part of the Territories to another, in the late 1950s it was probably reasonable to assume a cost in the vicinity of one to two dollars per ton mile for air transport connected with developing mineral properties. This would compare with about seven to twelve cents per ton mile for trucks operating on a highway such as the Mackenzie or Alaska Highways or up to about 30 to 35 cents per ton mile on unimproved trails.[23] Thus, for exploration and development of "land-locked" resources there is no question but that roads enable those undertaking the development activities to do so at much lower cost than if they were forced to rely upon air-transport.

But useful as such comparisons of costs may be, they normally do not take into account the capital costs associated with the two types of transport. And it is here that the problem appears to defy analysis. Very little capital must be risked in using light aircraft to explore and develop resources areas, for little fixed capital is committed to the area. But highway construction involves the commitment of considerable amounts of fixed capital to the area concerned. Again it is difficult to specify the amounts involved, for they vary tremendously from place to place depending upon the terrain and the standard of construction. A road suitable for moving heavy equipment into a remote area in Mackenzie District during the late 1950s may have cost at least $8000 per mile. More permanent roads with a gravel surface have run from $30,000 to $50,000 per mile.[24] Thus, even a rudimentary road into an unproven area represents a considerable investment which is not recoverable if the area should prove economically barren. How then can such investments be justified? This problem will be considered in some detail in Chapter 11, for it will be encountered several times again in this and the next chapter. But it must be noted at this point that opposition to a development road policy came not only from those who saw it merely as an unwarranted gambling with public funds, but also from those who believed that more economical alternatives to development roads existed. In 1955, for example, a brief submitted to the federal government urged reconsideration of plans to build development roads in Mackenzie District in favour of airfield construction to facilitate exploration and development by air. It was estimated that for the cost of ten miles of highway a landing strip capable of handling relatively large freight-carrying aircraft could be constructed. The feasibility of development of precious metal mines by air was demonstrated by the owners of the

---

[23]See A. Dubnie, *Transportation and the Competitive Position of Selected Canadian Minerals*, Mineral Survey Number 2, Department of Mines and Technical Surveys (Ottawa, 1962), p. 77.

[24]*Ibid.*, p. 67.

Taurcanis property in the Northwest Territories who used a Bristol aircraft to move 350 tons of freight into the mine site within two months. The obvious advantage of this type of development is, of course, the avoidance of heavy commitments of fixed capital to an area before it is proven.

It appears, however, that federal policy remained committed to the use of roads for such development purposes. In the spring of 1962 the policy was further extended to permit an increase in the amount of federal government assistance to mining companies engaged in development work in the Territories. Provision was made for federal aid in building access roads to mine sites so that development supplies could be transported to them. Up to two-thirds of the cost of such roads could be assumed by the government. It was also provided that the governments of the Yukon and Northwest Territories would each be provided with a fund of $50,000 which they could use to finance up to 50 per cent of the cost of "tote-trails" built by private companies developing minerals in the Territory. And finally, provision was made for the federal government to assume all the costs of building a road to a mineralized area being developed by two or more companies.

Turning to another function of highways, the transportation of freight (and passengers), it is apparent that the roads built in the Territories during the 1940s and 1950s remained relatively unimportant in this role compared with alternative forms of transport. In the Yukon Territory, despite the availability of the Alaska Highway for inward and outward shipments to the interior of western Canada, or, via the Haines Cut-Off Road, to the port of Haines, Alaska, the main freight movements were over the White Pass and Yukon Route railway to Skagway for transfer to coastal vessels sailing to Vancouver. One important reason for this is the remarkably low freight rates made available to the shippers of silver-lead-zinc concentrates from Whitehorse to Vancouver. It has been reported that a combined rail and water through-rate for such shipments amounted to about 1.4 cents per ton mile including all handling charges.[25a] It was the movement of this same traffic, of course, which made the Whitehorse–Mayo road the exception to the statement that roads were minor freighting facilities in the Territories, for the chief justification for this road was as a means for getting concentrates from the mines near Mayo to the rail terminal at Whitehorse. Subsequently, this road eliminated the alternative river freighting services despite the fact that the freight charges to the shipper were higher by road than by

25a*Ibid.*, p. 106.

the river. The choice of road transport under these circumstances was dictated by the virtually all-year transportation made available with attendant savings resulting from greatly reduced inventories both of supplies and product.

Air Transport in the 1950s

Public participation in the provision of facilities connected with territorial air transport in the 1950s appears to have been governed by the same general policies which prevailed in earlier periods. There is no evidence to suggest that this form of transportation, despite the arguments noted earlier, was viewed as a suitable instrument for more direct government participation in the economic development of the territorial north. While public expenditures on landing fields, access roads, and navigational aids have been made in the Territories, as elsewhere in Canada, the air services themselves have remained in the hands of private owners. It is obvious, however, that government policies with respect to the provision of surface transportation facilities in an undeveloped area must have an important effect upon the amount and kind of work left to the providers of air services.

Air transportation, as we have seen, has been used extensively in the Territories, not only for prospecting and exploration work of various kinds, but also for the movement of passengers and freight. In each case, the apparent direct cost to the user of such air services was higher than the cost of surface transportation when the latter was available. But users did not always choose the form of transportation which was "cheapest" in the sense of the cost per mile travelled, for often, especially where seasonal operations were concerned, speed of movement was highly valued. This was particularly true in the handling of passenger traffic, and the air services in the Territories have remained the chief passenger-carrying facility there despite the considerable improvement in road access to many communities. Nevertheless, as we saw in the last chapter, these air services were expensive relative to those available elsewhere in Canada. Among other reasons for this, it was noted that high costs were imposed upon northern air services by the use of small, inefficient aircraft to service most northern communities. In the context of our present discussion, therefore, it is appropriate to acknowledge the possibility that large-scale air services could have been provided to such communities even in the absence of an adequate volume of traffic to make such facilities commercially feasible. If the organization providing such services were in fact large enough to be operating on a national or international basis, it is possible that the financial difficulties associated with operating unprofitable services might be overcome by the simple expedient of using a surplus on profitable parts of its operation to subsidize the unprofitable parts. In Canada, the federal government operates such an organization, of course, in the form of Air Canada. But despite evidence of a growing willingness to use public funds to speed up economic development in the north during the later post-war years, the government showed no inclination to use the national airline as an instrument for developing the hinterland. The colours of Canada's national airline were certainly better known in the West Indies than in the Canadian north. Although a large network of air fields and terminal facilities were maintained throughout the Territories by the federal government, the use of these facilities was left strictly to the privately owned aircraft of such commercial air carriers as Canadian Pacific Airlines, Pacific Western Airlines, and Trans-Air, and the aircraft of mining companies and other private concerns.[25b] This is perfectly consistent, of course, with the "traditional" Canadian policy of leaving the initiative for investments in such undertakings to private enterprise in the uncertain economy of a slowly developing north.

It is necessary to qualify in only one respect the statement that the federal government did not participate in the air transport business in the Territories. As noted above, Eldorado Mining and Refining did establish its own (wholly owned) air transport subsidiary during the 1950s and, in so far as Eldorado was by then a Crown corporation, this enterprise could be considered a public venture in the provision of northern air services. But Eldorado Aviation was operated only as a mining company's air transport division much as several privately owned mining companies have operated such subsidiaries in the north. Consequently, this merely confirms the impression created by the absence of Air Canada from the territorial north that the government was not interested in providing northern air services publicly. That it might have done so through Eldorado Aviation is suggested by the fact that while this transport subsidiary of Eldorado's was restricted to the role described, another transport subsidiary of the same crown corporation was used to develop water transportation services on the Mackenzie

---

[25b]In 1959 CPA divested itself of some domestic Canadian routes including several northern services. These included the Mackenzie River route, subsequently operated by a rapidly growing firm, Pacific Western Airlines, and the central and eastern arctic routes which went to Trans-Air and Nordair.

river system in direct, and, after 1949, in devastating competition with private carriers.

Water Transportation in the 1950s

The operations of the Northern Transportation Company since World War II were notable for three main reasons: NTC steadily moved toward a monopoly position on the waterway, a position it gained while operating strictly on a commercial basis without subsidization from its owner, the federal government; and it relied upon current revenues to finance the large increase in its carrying capacity needed to accommodate increasing business.

It has already been explained how the ownership of the Northern Transportation Company passed into public hands with the expropriation of Eldorado Gold Mines Limited in 1944. Thereafter the Company was operated as a proprietary crown corporation with all its shares being held by the parent company, Eldorado Mining and Refining, the crown corporation which has controlled uranium production in Canada. Close contact between the parent firm and its subsidiary was established through overlapping of executive positions and close financial administration, but it appears that much responsibility for the daily operation of the transportation company was delegated to the general manager in the Edmonton office.[26] The apparently large degree of autonomy enjoyed by the management "in the field," as it were, may be explained by the highly specialized skills involved in operating a fleet on the difficult waterway and by the fact that, especially in more recent times, most of the freight carried by the Northern Transportation Company belonged to private shippers rather than to the parent company or the government. In 1960, for example, about two-thirds of the tonnage carried by NTC was for private customers.[27]

In view of our earlier findings with respect to the tendency for private resource-developing firms in the Territories to make extensive use of various kinds of integration of enterprise[28] in order to cope with the "remoteness" of their operations, it is important to notice that in the history of the Mackenzie waterway all the major firms involved in carrying freight on the system were in some way or other associated

---

[26]G. G. Thiessen, "Transportation on the Mackenzie River System," unpublished M.A. thesis, University of Saskatchewan, 1962, pp. 42–3.

[27]*Ibid.*, Table V, p. 46.

[28]See pp. 200–204 above.

with a large resource-developing firm. The Mackenzie River Transport Company was a subsidiary of the Hudson's Bay Company; the Northern Transportation Company was, and is, a subsidiary of Eldorado Mining and Refining (or Eldorado Gold Mines before 1944); Yellowknife Transportation Company was closely associated with the Imperial Oil Company for which it transported petroleum products (amounting to as much as 70 per cent of its tonnage in post-war years). Thus, the organization of the common carriers on the Mackenzie reflected the tendency toward "vertical" integration which has been one of the most persistent characteristics of territorial economic activity.

The parallel tendency toward "horizontal" integration was equally apparent, for despite their reliance upon a major "customer" for part of their business, the transportation companies sought additional business from other customers. Those which were successful in attracting such business would consequently be able to justify investments in larger and more efficient kinds of capital, such as boats, barges, and handling facilities, than would have been warranted by their volume of freight provided by their parent company or other chief customer. And such transportation companies would then be in a position, of course, to offer "cheaper" transportation than their less successful, less efficient, competitors. We have already seen, however, that the level of development in the region served by the Mackenzie waterway was such that except in a few periods of "boom" induced by new mineral discoveries or by military projects, the absolute amount of freight to be moved over the river system was small compared with that which would be carried on most other river systems in North America, such as the Mississippi, which would come to mind. Yet the Mackenzie system is long, the physical obstacles to efficient operation are immense, and relatively large capital outlays were necessary per unit of freight-carrying capacity. It would not be surprising, therefore, if it was found that in its pursuit of volume to justify investments in equipment a single firm could require all the traffic available. The evidence available suggests that this was indeed the case, for the Northern Transportation Company, during the later 1940s and through the 1950s, steadily improved and expanded its freight-handling facilities, offered better and better service to customers, and acquired a larger and larger share of the total volume of freight available to it. Its competitors, unable or unwilling to make similar investments in their own facilities, withdrew from competition as common carriers. But was this realization of a monopoly position on the waterway by the Northern Transportation Company the result of such general economic forces as described or was it the result of a publicly supported organization having an "unfair" advantage in competition with private firms?

Because of the significance of this question for our interpretation both of the evolution of government policy with respect to territorial development and of the more fundamental economic forces involved in this development it is worth examining this question in some detail. Why, first of all, should we regard investment in equipment as the critical factor determining a firm's competitive position on the waterway? Secondly, if such investment was so important, how was it financed?

The importance of investments in equipment by firms operating on the Mackenzie system stems from the fact that costs of shipping freight on any natural waterway are fundamentally dictated by the physical characteristics of the waterway itself. The use of such systems for transporting freight in the first place derived from the fact that fewer units of labour and capital were required to move freight on water than on land. And in so far as substantial capital inputs were still required on waterway systems, these were less "fixed" than those associated with alternative land systems. That is, they were largely in the form of floating equipment which could often be transferred to other locations if necessary. This "removability" of river transportation equipment has been well illustrated in the history of water transportation in the Territories. Many of the early vessels used on the Yukon system in the central and southern Yukon were brought there from the United States in the late nineteenth century. And on the Yukon, when the Canol project necessitated an immediate increase in carrying capacity, various kinds of floating equipment migrated there from great distances away.

In at least the early stages of the development of a natural waterway as a freight-moving facility, then, the principal investments required are in floating equipment. But the effectiveness of such investments, the efficiency with which the capital item such as a boat does its job, is largely dependent upon the size of the unit. If reasonable rates of utilization of the equipment can be assumed, it would appear that the chief factor affecting the cost per ton of freight moved by water is the cargo-carrying capacity of the vessel. But in the navigation of river systems the depth and width of the channel at its shallowest and narrowest point impose a direct physical restriction on the size of vessel which can be utilized on the system.

Thus, natural waterways limit, by their very physical dimensions, the efficiency of capital invested in floating equipment to be operated on them. It is of course possible that ways may be found for improving the natural waterway by deepening or widening the channel at critical points and by building canals to by-pass rapids or other obstructions to navigation. But such undertakings constitute the commitment of economic resources to the particular river channel concerned and these investments, unlike those made in floating and other types of equipment, are "fixed" in the sense that they are committed for as long as they last to a particular location. Where there is no certainty that the waterway concerned will remain in use or be used intensively enough to make a reasonable return from such investments likely, there would be little incentive for either private investors or the community as a whole to undertake such works. A further problem is that when such investments would have the effect of opening up an undeveloped area the benefits of these investments would be widely dispersed among enterprises already established or subsequently becoming established in the area. This could make it difficult for the investor to collect revenues commensurate with the benefits generated by his investment, a possibility which will be considered in some detail in the next chapter.

In the case of the Mackenzie waterway, it might be thought that many of the difficulties associated with making improvements in the system would have been overcome after World War II when a publicly owned company became the chief operator on the waterway and when a generally rising trend in freight traffic appeared to be developing. But, although the federal government continued to sponsor after 1949 the type of routine maintenance of the channel that was described above as having been carried on during earlier periods, no major capital projects were undertaken or, indeed, appear to have been contemplated.

The modest dredging programme initiated by the federal Department of Public Works in 1938 and augmented by the efforts of the United States Army during the war was continued and expanded during the years after the war. Most of this work was confined to the southern part of the system in northern Alberta where the Athabaska River creates a chronic dredging problem by silting-up its delta into Lake Athabaska. Total annual outlays on this type of work increased considerably after the end of the war, rising from about $20,000 in 1946 to almost $280,000 in 1960.[29] But these were relatively small amounts compared to what would have been needed to eliminate such major obstacles to navigation as the series of rapids on the Slave River which necessitated the twenty-two-mile portage from Fort Fitzgerald to Bellrock. The latter

[29]Canada, *Public Accounts 1946 and 1960.*

involved, as we have seen, an expensive and time-consuming transshipment of cargo, although in 1959 a new portage road built to highway standards replaced the two old portage roads and permitted large trucks to be used to move cargo over the portage. The effect of this was to reduce the time lost in traversing the portage by about fifty per cent. Neither the transportation companies using the Mackenzie system, nor the federal government proposed more fundamental improvements to the system. Indeed, in its annual report for 1952 the Northern Transportation Company reported that:

. . . the Company's studies have indicated clearly that a complete solution of the portage problem would involve capital expenditures out of all keeping with present levels of traffic. The amortization of such expenditures on any reasonable basis would impose a cost burden which would more than offset the probable savings in operating expenses.[30]

That others using the waterway concurred in this judgment is indicated in the findings of the Board of Transport Commissioners for Canada in its 1951 hearings into the matter of freight rates on the Mackenzie.[31] And the absence of any initiative in this respect by the federal government may not be surprising in view of its experience with the Yukon river system in the late 1940s. There, the operation of riverboats had always been impeded by a late break-up of the ice on the southern part of the system. The White Pass and Yukon Route Company had consequently built a dam on the Lewes River for the purpose of impounding a head of water in the fall and winter which was then released early in the season to speed the break-up of ice in the navigation channels below. In 1948 the federal government agreed to take over this dam, which by then had fallen into dis-repair, to rebuild it at a cost of $125,000 and to maintain and operate it. The government made it clear that this project was "strictly in the interest of navigation" on the Yukon waterway. As we have seen, however, the road-building programme in the Territory undertaken at the same time led within only a few years to the complete abandonment of navigation on the river system there.

The alternative to making a major improvement in the Mackenzie waterway was for the companies using it to invest in specially designed types of floating equipment which would permit the most efficient use to be made of what capacity the waterway's physical limitations would

[30]Northern Transportation Company, *Annual Report 1952* (Ottawa, 1953), p. 4.

[31]Canada, Board of Transport Commissioners for Canada, *Judgement in re. of Tolls of Licensed Water Carriers within the Mackenzie River Watershed*, April 6, 1951 (Ottawa: King's Printer, 1951).

permit. And it was because of this that the firms which could make the necessary investments in such floating equipment found themselves in a preferred competitive position.

We have already seen that despite its historical claim to a dominant position as a common carrier on the Mackenzie, the Mackenzie River Transport Company found it difficult to adapt its facilities and mode of operation to the new demands of mining companies for freight services in the late 1930s and again after World War II. With the acquisition by Northern Transportation of a modern fleet of steel-hulled, diesel-engined tugs and steel barges, the Hudson's Bay Company subsidiary found that it could compete as a common carrier only if it undertook similar improvements in its own fleet. Instead of attempting to do so, it withdrew as a common carrier in 1948 and restricted its operations to supplying the Hudson's Bay Company posts along the river and a few other settlements not otherwise served. Nine years later, in 1957, the Company gave up even this limited participation in the operation of the waterway, sold its equipment to the Northern Transportation Company, and became one of its customers. This left only one significant competitor for the Northern Transportation Company as a common carrier, the Yellowknife Transportation Company. As re-organized in 1946 this Company's operations were based upon contracts for carrying petroleum products for Imperial Oil Limited to various settlements along the waterway and, as noted earlier, these contracts provided the largest part of the Company's business. With the construction of the Mackenzie Highway in 1949, Yellowknife Transportation moved its terminus to Hay River and began to specialize in carrying package freight (shipped to Hay River by truck) to destinations on Great Slave Lake and on the Mackenzie River proper.[32] This, however, threw the Company into closer competition with the Northern Transportation Company which had come to depend upon the northern part of its route for most of its profits. Subsequent improvements to the truck route to Hay River and the extension of the highway northward to Yellowknife, combined with the collapse of the uranium mining activity in northwestern Saskatchewan, resulted in a declining level of business for the waterway after 1959. The resulting increase in competition for business eventually led to the apparently inevitable reduction in the number of firms operating on the waterway once again.[33]

[32]Thiessen, p. 39.
[33]In 1965 NTC took over the operations of the Yellowknife Transportation Company.

It is impossible to assess with any accuracy the extent to which the competitive strength of the Northern Transportation Company throughout this period was enhanced by its status as a crown corporation. Like other carriers on the Mackenzie it had one major customer, in this case, its parent company, Eldorado Mining and Refining, which provided a substantial part of its freight volume. In addition to this it derived some business from various government departments operating in Mackenzie District. But the latter business provided only from about two to seven per cent of the total volume of freight carried by NTC during the 1950s. It would consequently appear that there was little to distinguish the operations of NTC from those of a private transportation company, an impression which is heightened by the fact that unlike other crown corporations in the transportation business in Canada, it was completely self-supporting financially. Throughout the period from 1945 to 1961 the Company operated at a profit and required no subsidization by the federal government either on current or on capital account. Its net operating revenues were large enough, in fact, to enable the company to carry out a large capital expansion programme during this period with no more external aid than a promptly repaid loan obtained from its parent company at the end of the war.

In so far as the NTC served as an instrument of government policy in the north during this period, its role was to provide transportation services in the Mackenzie basin on a strictly commercial basis. That it was able to provide these services as efficiently as it did appears to have been the result of its ability to raise the financial capital required to equip itself with the most modern and specialized facilities available. And this was made possible by its ability, in the absence of serious competition from other water transportation companies operating on the Mackenzie or from alternative forms of transportation in the area served, to set and maintain prices for its services which were high enough relative to its operating costs to produce a substantial surplus (as well as a large depreciation reserve) in its annual accounts. Had the Company been privately owned, it is possible, of course, that these net earnings would have been paid out in dividends to its owners and, in view of the criticism which has been made of the NTC's policies (and those of the government from which they were presumably derived) during this period, it is worth noting that the NTC paid no dividends to either its parent company or to the federal treasury. Instead, it used its surplus to expand and to improve the quality of its capital assets.

The general level of freight rates on the Mackenzie waterway has generally been considerably higher than that prevailing on other inland waterways in North America such as the Mississippi and St. Lawrence. This is not surprising in view of the very short season of operation possible on the Mackenzie, the extreme imbalance in the upstream and downstream volume of traffic on the system, and the lack of improvements in the natural waterway, compared with these other systems.

With the type of equipment in use after World War II the operating season on the Mackenzie River proper and Great Slave Lake was about 120 days per year and on the southern part of the system approximately 150 days. This compared with about 260 days on the Missouri–Mississippi system and 235 days on the St. Lawrence at Montreal.[34] The result of this relatively short operating season was, of course, a low rate of utilization of equipment and inefficient use of labour resources as well. These operating difficulties were aggravated by a chronic imbalance of traffic on the system. Throughout the history of the system far more freight moved north than south during the typical navigation season. Although this did constitute a downstream imbalance, the modern equipment used on the system after the war was capable of carrying cargo against the current almost as efficiently as with it. Consequently, there was a great deal of excess capacity on the southward journey. The actual ratio of northbound to southbound traffic varied from year to year, but during the 1950s it ranged from as little as 3 to 1 to as high as almost 14 to 1. On the St. Lawrence the ratio of downstream to upstream traffic was 2.1 to 1 in 1960.[35]

Reference has already been made to the policy with respect to channel improvements on the Mackenzie. The effect of this policy was to cause users of the waterway to sustain high operating costs as an alternative to private or public capital outlays to improve the system. The level of public investment to aid navigation on the Mackenzie throughout the years following World War II was much lower than that on other water routes in Canada. Lessard estimates that 21.7 per cent of the total cost of water transportation in Canada in 1953 was in the form of government spending. A similar estimate for the total outlays on water transport on the Mackenzie would put the public share at about one-half that level in most years since the end of the war.[36]

For all of these reasons, then, it is not surprising that rates on the Mackenzie should have been higher than on other waterways with which it might be compared. Nevertheless, because of the lack of competition in the provision of water freight services, and in the absence of competi-

[34]Thiessen, p. 64.   [35]*Ibid.*, pp. 77–8.   [36]*Ibid.*, pp. 110–11.

tion for heavy freight from highways, railways, or aircraft in the area, many users of these services in the post-war years suspected that the rate schedule was higher than warranted. Although freight rates at the end of the war were considerably lower than they were before, an increase in its rates by the Northern Transportation Company in 1945 provoked many serious complaints. It also set in motion a chain of events which led to implementation of a nominal public regulation of rates on the waterway, a rationalization of the rate structure and the establishment of the NTC as the effective price leader for the various firms providing freighting services on the Mackenzie.

Following the protests received by the federal government from mining companies in the Mackenzie basin in 1945, the Transport Act was amended to place the operations of the Mackenzie waterway under the jurisdiction of the Board of Transport Commissioners.[37] The Board's first act was to bring some uniformity into the rate schedules of the various companies operating on the Mackenzie and it chose to do this, in the first instance, by requesting them to establish common rates corresponding to those being charged by the Northern Transportation Company at the time. It was subsequently discovered, however, that this schedule itself contained a number of inconsistencies and the Board undertook an investigation into the entire structure and level of rates on the system.

It was not until 1950, however, that the Board got around to holding hearings and to making its report. When it did announce its findings, those shippers in the area served by the Mackenzie waterway who expected major rate reductions were seriously disappointed—for the Board's judgment was, in effect, that with the exception of rates for refrigerated cargo, the general level of existing rates was *below* that which the Board considered warranted.[38] Thus, although the Board established a "Standard Tariff," which amounted to stipulating the maximum permissible rates, these rates were in fact higher than those actually in effect. Under these circumstances it is rather surprising that the following year, in 1952, the Northern Transportation Company lowered its rates still further. Additional rate reductions and adjustments on various parts of the route served by the NTC were subsequently made in 1955, 1956, and 1958. With the smaller companies operating on the Mackenzie forced by competition to adjust their rates correspondingly,

---

[37]*Statutes of Canada*, 2 Geo. VI, c. 53 (1938), and 9–10 Geo. VI, c. 32 (1945).

[38]Board of Transport Commissioners, *Judgement in re. of Tolls of Licensed Water Carriers within the Mackenzie River Watershed.*

it becomes evident that throughout this period the level of freight rates on the Mackenzie waterway was regulated not by the maximum tariffs established by the Board of Transport Commissioners, but by the pricing policy of the Northern Transportation Company.

The reasons for the price reductions made by NTC during the 1950s remain obscure. The Company's own explanations suggest that they were the consequence of "improvements in costs resulting from a larger volume of business and improved handling techniques."[39] Given the fact that physical limitation of the river channel prohibited economies arising from the use of larger vessels, and with a continuing imbalance in downstream and upstream traffic volume to limit the effectiveness of simply adding more vessels to the system, it is difficult to imagine how very substantial increases in operating efficiency could arise from an increase in the volume of business. But there is no doubt that very extensive improvements were being made in the Company's operations as a result of the introduction of mechanical freight-handling techniques during this period. And a larger volume of business may have encouraged the Company to adopt these more efficient techniques and to invest in the equipment necessary to implement them.

The volume of freight handled by the NTC increased steadily from the end of the war until the late 1950s. In 1945 NTC's volume totalled only 14,252 tons, compared to just under 190,000 tons in 1958. The largest part of this increase was not attributable so much to development in the Northwest Territories, however, as to developments in northern Saskatchewan, where large-scale uranium-mining operations were being developed on the northeast shore of Lake Athabaska. Because this lake forms part of the Mackenzie waterway system, these developments depended upon that waterway for heavy freight movements. In 1953, for example, 70 per cent of the freight shipped north from Waterways by NTC was bound for Lake Athabaska. However, there was also a large relative increase in traffic over these years into the Territories, although on a smaller absolute scale than the increase to points south of the sixtieth parallel. In 1957, for example, northbound freight moving through Hay River into the Territories was eight times greater than even the 1952 volume. This was a proportionately greater increase than the increase in total freight moved northward through the southern terminus of the system at Waterways, Alberta, although in 1957 it comprised only one-quarter of this total. The increase in the volume of freight moved over the northern part of the system in this period was only partly due

[39]Northern Transportation Company, *Annual Report 1954* (Ottawa, 1955), p. 5.

to increased mining and prospecting activities in the Territories; a considerable part of the increase was associated with the construction of the Distant Early Warning radar system in the north. As a result of this defence work, the new uranium developments in Saskatchewan, and increased economic activity throughout the north generally, the volume of freight handled on the Mackenzie waterway increased every season from 1949 to 1958.

During this period of the 1950s, the NTC made heavy investments in equipment and converted the Fort Smith portage and other terminal facilities to use mechanical freight-handling techniques. This substitution of capital, in the form of freight-handling equipment, for labour in an area with a surplus of unskilled native labour would at first sight appear anomalous. In fact, it offered the transportation company a solution to a chronic problem in its operations, for it, like similar firms in the Territories, had come to accept the direct costs of importing labour from the south to meet its seasonal requirements rather than utilize local native labour. The chief objection to the use of native labour for such work was its "unreliability."[40] Thus, after World War II, the NTC had made a practice of flying in its crews to work during the shipping season and flying them out again in the fall. This, combined with the costs of housing and maintaining this transient labour force, raised the labour costs to an estimated eighty per cent of the total costs of operating the portage.[41]

By replacing manual handling of freight with the mechanical "pallet board" system the NTC not only reduced the labour inputs required in its operations, but also the heavy breakage costs once characteristic of Mackenzie River water transport. It speeded up deliveries as well. The latter improvement also permitted more efficient utilization of floating equipment. Use of this equipment was further improved during this period by the introduction of more powerful tug-boats and the use of radar for navigation.

It would appear then that the most likely *economic* reason for the freight rate reductions made by NTC after 1951 was the reduction in operating costs made possible, despite rising prices for labour and other productive inputs, by the introduction of new and more efficient types of equipment. It should also be noted, however, that these rate reductions

[40]See *Minutes of the Council of the Northwest Territories*, October 15, 1949, XVII, p. 3723.
[41]*Minutes of the Council of the Northwest Territories*, March 24, 1949, XVII, pp. 3632–3.

may have been prompted by pressure exerted upon NTC by the federal government, for the government was under a more or less continuous attack from opposition critics and from residents of Mackenzie District for the rate policy of its crown corporation. Some critics felt that the Company was entirely too profitable an operation and that it should use its pricing policy as a means of "encouraging" economic development in the area it served. The Leader of the (Conservative) Opposition in the House of Commons pursued this line of argument in a debate in 1953 as follows:

This company should have regard to the fact that this is an essential service and that a reasonable profit would be the wise course rather than seeking to make large profits which impose burdens not only upon Eldorado Mining and Refining Limited, which by virtue of the nature of its activities can well support them, but also upon all individuals and smaller organizations which use the system and find it vital to their activities within the area.[42]

That the NTC was itself not unaware of the significance of its rate structure for the development of resources in the area served by it at this time is easily demonstrated. With reference to its services to the Beaverlodge developments in northern Saskatchewan referred to earlier, the Company reported in 1952 that "by maintaining an abnormally low rate, considering the distance involved, the Company has made a valuable contribution to the development of the new uranium field at the eastern end of Lake Athabaska."[43] It made no secret of the fact, however, that it was able to assist this development on the southern part of its system by virtue of the high rates it was able to command on services to the more northern regions. In the same report just referred to it noted that since 1945 it had derived the major part of its new revenue from the relatively small amount of freight shipped north of Great Slave Lake.[44] This discrimination against the northern users of its services was greatly reduced by the rate adjustments of 1955 and 1956.

Even these rate adjustments failed, however, to save the federal government from criticism for the way NTC was conducting business, for to the complaints of those who felt that the Company should reduce its rates in order to encourage resource development in the north were added the complaints of those who saw in the rate reductions NTC was making a deliberate attempt by this crown corporation to eliminate what

[42]*House of Commons Debates*, 1953–54, p. 777. For further criticism of the NTC rate policy during this period, see *House of Commons Debates*, 1955, p. 3743 and 1956, p. 1702.

[43]Northern Transportation Company, *Annual Report 1952* (Ottawa, 1953), p. 3.
[44]*Ibid.*

little competition private transportation companies serving the area were able to provide. Thus, in 1956 we find the Minister of Trade and Commerce (the Honorable C. D. Howe) defending the NTC rates against the criticism that they were excessively high by pointing out to his critics in the House that "there are competing services in the area which have a hard time getting along and each time there is a reduction in the rate by Northern Transportation there is a good deal of hardship caused among the competitors."[45]

Unlike its smaller competitors NTC found that its rate reductions during the 1950s did not prevent it from earning a substantial net income each year even after making generous allowance for depreciation. Although the Company's initial expansion of equipment and facilities at the end of World War II was financed by borrowing from the parent company, Eldorado Mining and Refining Limited, by 1950 this liability had been retired and over the next decade NTC financed a capital expansion programme which tripled the value of its capital assets (from $4.1 million in 1950 to $12.3 million in 1960) entirely out of current income.

The effect of NTC's financing during this period was to impose the capital burden of the improvements to its facilities upon those using its services. In so far as this permitted the Company to provide cheaper and also better quality service to its customers it must be credited with facilitating the development of the area served by the waterway. Although, as we have seen, some funds from the federal treasury were made available for maintenance and minor improvements to the waterway itself, an unusually large part of the full economic cost of providing water transport services in the area was undoubtedly borne by those who were directly served by it. In this respect, and in view of the role played by the state in providing transportation facilities in some other parts of the country, it would appear that despite its formal status as a crown corporation, the NTC was not regarded by the federal government during this period as a device for subsidizing private resource development in Mackenzie District. It was used instead as a device for collecting revenues from those operating in the area so as to finance the development of a large-scale and, under the circumstances, undeniably efficient transportation facility to carry heavy freight into, and from point to point within, the area.

In performing this function it was probably only incidental that the organization involved was a public enterprise rather than a private one

[45]*House of Commons Debates*, 1956, p. 1712.

like the Yukon and White Pass Route which, as we saw earlier in this chapter, performed a similar function in the Yukon Territory. Both of these large-scale transportation facilities were "commercially feasible" undertakings which required little support from the national treasury. They were largely self-sustaining out of revenues collected from those benefitting directly from the services they provided. Their ability to function in this way owed much to the monopolistic positions they were able to achieve. And from what we have seen of the history of the federal government's policy with respect to economic development in the northern Territories this type of organization, and this approach to the problem of providing transportation in the little-developed north, was compatible with what we might identify as the "traditional" attitude of the government—that is, the view that what development took place should be proven to be economically feasible before public funds were diverted from alternative uses and applied to the Territories. But in our earlier examination of federal participation in road construction in the Territories during the 1950s we noted some evidence of a different general approach to the matter. Epitomized in the Roads to Resources Programme and in its territorial counterpart, this policy was one of using public funds to finance the development of transportation facilities into areas where no commercial justification for such undertakings had already been demonstrated by the efforts of private *entrepreneurs*.

One of the strongest arguments against applying this same principle to the improvement of the Mackenzie waterway so as to permit lower charges to those using it must always have been the tendency for water transportation facilities serving a developing area to be rendered obsolete by the construction of highways and railways when traffic volumes developed to the point where the inescapably heavy fixed investments required for such facilities finally seemed to be commercially justifiable. Certainly, as we have seen, this happened in the Yukon in the early 1950s. And in the Mackenzie area, although the Mackenzie Highway did not immediately have so marked an effect as the Whitehorse–Mayo route had in the Yukon, its further development in the 1950s did break the waterway's monopoly on surface transportation into the southern part of Mackenzie District. The adequacy of this highway as a freighting facility to replace the difficult southern portion of the Mackenzie waterway was called into doubt, however, when the possibility of developing large-scale base metal mining at Pine Point on the south shore of Great Slave Lake was revived in the late 1950s.[46] Such a development would

[46]See Chapter 4.

generate a large volume of southbound freight from Mackenzie District for the first time in its history. Could such freight be handled by the existing waterway or the highway paralleling it? Or, taking into account the benefits that a railway line would confer upon Mackenzie District as a whole by providing it with year-round freight services and by paralleling the most inefficient part of the waterway, should a railway be built from the existing head of steel at Grimshaw or Waterways in Alberta north to Hay River on the south shore of Great Slave Lake?

The Great Slave Lake Railway

The proposal to build a railway to Great Slave Lake raised a number of questions concerning the entire process of territorial development. It is interesting in the light of the predilection of "authorities" on northern development to emphasize the physical or engineering obstacles to development there that these questions were economic and, perhaps more important in this case, political ones. In any event, as we shall see, the economic and political aspects of the proposal proved to be inseparable and, in fact, were probably indistinguishable. Because they were so fundamental, however, we will not examine these questions in detail at this point, but merely describe the project and indicate what the main issues arising in connection with it were. The latter will then be considered in more detail in Chapter 13.

The "proving up" of the remarkably large lead-zinc deposits at Pine Point in the late 1940s as described in Chapter 4 stimulated speculation that a major new industry for Mackenzie District was about to be established. In fact, as we saw, the owners of the property, Consolidated Mining and Smelting Company Limited, showed no inclination to go into production. The impression was subsequently created that the Company was not interested in bringing the Pine Point properties into production so long as it could keep its large smelter at Trail, British Columbia, supplied from its lead-zinc mine located nearby at Kimberly. It appeared that the Company was unwilling to incur the costs associated with developing a new and remote source of concentrates until necessary. With existing market conditions and the reserves at Kimberly being what they were, it seemed doubtful that Pine Point would be developed in the near future after all. At the same time it was tempting to wonder if an improvement in the transportation facilities available for shipping concentrates out of the area might not alter the costs of Pine Point concentrates enough to make them competitive at the smelters with concentrates being produced at existing mines. That is, the cost disadvantage of the Pine Point property, in so far as it was a remote property, was the consequence not only of its distance from processing plants and markets, but also of the relatively inefficient types of transportation facilities available over part of the distance involved.

In fact, of course, the Pine Point ore deposits were far better served in this respect located where they were than they would have been in most other parts of the territorial north, for they were located in an area served not only by an established water transportation route but by a good quality highway as well. Only short distances had to be traversed to connect the site of the mining operations to either the waterway, which could have moved the concentrates to railhead at Waterways, Alberta, or to the Mackenzie Highway for shipment by road to the rail terminal of Grimshaw, Alberta. Judging from the experience of the relatively small operations in the Mayo district, truck transportation of base metal concentrates in the north can be both technically and economically feasible under certain conditions. The direct cost to the shipper of such transportation would probably have been in the neigh-bourhood of 5 cents per ton mile. During the 1950s the rates on the Whitehorse–Mayo Highway ranged from 5 to 7 cents per ton mile and on the Mackenzie Highway freight moved at from 7 to 12 cents per ton mile. Considerably lower rates would have prevailed for the water route. Bulk commodity rates in effect on the Mackenzie for petroleum and sulphur in 1959 were as low as 2.73 cents per ton mile on the former (Norman Wells to Yellowknife) and 5.1 cents per ton mile for the latter (Waterways to Bushell). But in the case of water transport this advantage was offset by the short season of operation and would have entailed heavy stock piling of shipments during most of the year.

The Pine Point Company, a subsidiary formed by Consolidated Mining and Smelting to develop the Pine Point properties, took the position that neither of these facilities were adequate and that development of the property at Pine Point would have to wait until a railway was built extending the northern Alberta railway system to Great Slave Lake. But neither the Consolidated Mining and Smelting Corporation nor its parent company, the Canadian Pacific Railway, appeared to have any interest in building such a railroad in the present or near future. The only alter-native was for the federal government—or perhaps its crown corpora-tion, the Canadian National Railways, which shared ownership of the Northern Alberta Railway system with the Canadian Pacific Railway— to undertake construction of the line. But certainly the traditional policy of the federal government with respect to northern development would have prevented it from using public funds to finance a major transportation facility which private *entrepreneurs* judged to be not commercially feasible.

But, as indicated by the road development policies discussed earlier, this traditional approach was beginning to break down during the 1950s even before the national political upheaval of 1957 brought to power a government committed to the positive policy of speeding up northern development as a national objective. The new attitude which was developing in Ottawa during the 1950s is reflected in the brief prepared in the Department of Northern Affairs and National Resources and submitted by the Commissioner of the Northwest Territories to the Royal Commission on Canada's Economic Prospects in 1955.[47] A large part of this brief was devoted to elaborating arguments designed to justify immediate construction of the railway to Great Slave Lake. Although the total capital cost of the project was then being estimated at only 50 to 55 million dollars, it was understood at the time that the Northern Alberta Railways would consider undertaking such an improvement only if they could be sure of having 800,000 tons of outbound concentrates to carry each year. But the Pine Point Mines Company indicated that only about 157,000 tons of concentrates per year would be produced initially. With only this volume of concentrates added to the other traffic which would be foreseen for the railway it appeared that even if the capital cost of building the line was assumed by the government, the railway companies operating it would require an operating subsidy of as much as $750,000 a year until a larger volume of traffic became available.

It appeared, consequently, that the proposed railway could not be justified on the grounds that it was a commercially feasible project. But the brief went on to argue that the project was warranted because of the returns to the national economy (represented as increases in the Gross National Product) which would result from the development of economic activity in the regions served by the railway. In fact as the brief's argument developed it became clear that it was an attempt to extend the old arguments for a national railway policy to the new northern mining frontier in so far as this frontier was partly located in the remaining federal lands. The resemblance of the brief's argument to this traditional Canadian policy was heightened by references not only

[47]R. G. Robertson, *The Northwest Territories—Its Economic Prospects, A Brief Presented to the Royal Commission on Canada's Economic Prospects* (Ottawa: Queen's Printer, 1955), p. 28.

to "immense benefits" the new railway would make to the national economy, but also to its "implications for national and continental defence." The argument concludes with the following eloquent appeal:

In the 1870's Canada was at the point where a national decision had to be taken that determined whether the west would or would not be opened and developed. The costs were enormous and the risks were staggering, but the decision was taken. The people of the Northwest Territories feel that we are today at the point where a comparable decision has to be taken about our northland. The costs are much less, their magnitude in relation to our national wealth is nothing in comparison with those of the 1870's. Fundamentally, however, the question is the same. I respectfully submit that this Royal Commission should consider whether this is not a case where the nation should undertake the task in order to insure a greater national development in the future.[48]

It was not until two years after the election of the new government in 1957, however, that tangible evidence of the acceptance of this approach by the federal authorities was forthcoming. In June, 1959, a Royal Commission was appointed "to inquire into and report upon the respective merits of the alternative routes which might be followed by a railway line to be built from northern Alberta into the southern portion of the District of Mackenzie, Northwest Territories, for the purpose of providing access to and contributing to the development of that portion of the Territories tributary to Great Slave Lake."[49] Only two routes were considered by the Commission, one leading north from Grimshaw, Alberta, to the south shore of Great Slave Lake, the other from Waterways, Alberta, to the same destination. The former roughly paralleled the existing Mackenzie Highway while the latter followed the general route of the Mackenzie waterway as far north as Fort Smith and then turned northwestward toward Pine Point. Two of the three commissioners concluded in favour of the west or Grimshaw route, while the third, an economist, favoured the eastern route.

The advantages ascribed to the western route were that it would be cheaper and easier to build because it passed through well-known country and could be supplied during construction from the existing highway. It also passed through agricultural country and promised to serve the existing farm areas north of Peace River and to open up new farming areas still further north. The eastern route was seen to be more difficult to build because of the lack of experience with constructing surface transportation facilities in the area it would traverse. But it

48*Ibid.*
49Canada, P.C. 705, 1959.

promised to be of great value as a trunk line from which complementary facilities such as roads of various kinds and some water routes could push eastward into potential mining areas—and it was seen to offer greater benefits in terms of connecting with both existing and future routes down the Mackenzie.

The commissioner who favoured the eastern route argued that in view of the greater contribution which could be made both to regional development and to the Gross National Product by mineral development than by agricultural development, a route which would promote opening up the potential mining areas between Lake Athabasca and Great Slave Lake should be preferred over one which would open up only additional agricultural land in northern Alberta.[50]

In 1961 the federal government announced that the proposed railway would be built, following the western route and that a maximum subsidy of $86,250,000 would be provided to Canadian National Railways for construction of the line by the federal government and that $12.5 million would be provided by Pine Point Mines Limited.[51] This announcement appeared to confirm the change in the federal government's general development policies in the north which was first suggested by the northern roads programme described earlier, for it represented a major public investment in social overhead capital for the Territories, which would not be justified on the grounds of current commercial profitability, but only on the grounds that it would make a contribution to the national economy by accelerating the rate of development in a part at least of the northern Territories. No serious effort was made publicly to justify the project on the grounds of national or continental defence although, as we have seen, such an element could conceivably have been involved.

Thus, we see that federal policy with respect to *economic* development in the northern Territories appears to have gone through three distinct stages during the period with which this study is concerned. Prior to World War II public investments in capital facilities were kept to a minimum by encouraging private enterprise to undertake such investments—a policy which led, sometimes deliberately, to the establishment of monopoly conditions or at least a high degree of concentration of ownership in those few activities which did develop under these circumstances. During and shortly after the war public participation in the

---

[50]Canada, *Report of the Royal Commission on the Great Slave Lake Railway* (Ottawa, 1960), I, pp. 55–66.
[51]*House of Commons Debates*, 1961, p. 6528 and p. 7319.

provision of such facilities became more direct with airfield construction, more vigorous support of road and highway building, and through ownership of the dominant transportation company on the Mackenzie River system. But when this participation was not based upon military considerations, it was limited in most cases to undertakings which promised either to be self-liquidating, as was the case with the Northern Transportation Company, or justifiable because of an established need, as was the case with the Whitehorse–Mayo Highway. Finally, in the 1950s, it appeared that a tentative approach was being made in the direction of public investments which could be justified only in terms of the rather general, not specific, economic benefits which they promised for the country as a whole. But when we turn from transportation to the other conventional public utility area, electric power generation, we find the same policies being applied as were implicit in the operation of the Northern Transportation Company. By the 1960s the principle of "developmental" public investment in electric power for the territorial north had still not emerged. Public investment in this industry continued to rest upon a form of commercial feasibility and to be largely self-liquidating.

THE DEVELOPMENT OF ELECTRIC POWER GENERATING FACILITIES

We have seen in earlier chapters that the two chief sources of power in the Territories prior to World War II were hydro-electric generating plants and diesel-electric plants. Because of the lower initial investment involved, individual mines tended to rely upon diesel-electric plants in the absence of large-scale power supplies. Except in the Yukon, where the principal placer operators had been combined in one company large enough to operate an efficient hydro-electric plant, the demand for power was too widely dispersed to make such investments commercially profitable. The mine at Port Radium and the gold mines in the Yellow-knife area were all established on diesel power utilizing the local oil supply at Norman Wells.

In the Yellowknife area, however, four of the six properties brought into production before development was interrupted by the war were owned or controlled by a single firm—the Consolidated Mining and Smelting Company of Canada, a subsidiary of the Canadian Pacific Railway. With four producing properties in the area, this Company's operations provided a sufficiently large market for electric power to warrant the establishment of a small hydro-electric plant. Located on Prosperous Lake, the initial plant installed in 1940 consisted of a single

4,700 horsepower turbine driving a 4,200 k.v.a. generator. The output, which reached 21,733,000 kilowatt-hours in 1942, was sufficient to supply the Company's mines and also the small settlement at Yellowknife.[52]

There was no further investment in hydro-electric power facilities in the Territories until after the end of the war. In the later years of the war, however, the improved access to many parts of the territorial north and the re-awakening of interest in the area generally, led the government to establish a serious programme to study the water-power resources of the area. In 1944 and 1945 a number of new stream-flow recording stations were established throughout the Yukon and the Northwest Territories.[53]

With the revival of the interrupted development of the Yellowknife gold-mining industry after the war, it became apparent that companies other than Consolidated Mining and Smelting were considering the development of their own hydro-electric power. The small plant already in existence was operating at capacity to supply the needs of Consolidated's own operations. Consequently, the Giant Yellowknife Gold Mines Company, whose property promised to become one of the largest producers in the Yellowknife area, approached the federal government in 1946 with a proposal to construct a hydro plant on the Snare River. The subsequent action of the federal government was of the greatest significance, for it not only reflected the new official (and public) attitude towards the north, but it provided a guide to the content of the northern policy which the government was to adhere to until its defeat a decade later.

The reaction of the federal government to the Giant Yellowknife proposal suggested that the time had come when a federal government was prepared to enter the field and give direct encouragement to northern development. The Minister of Mines and Resources described the situation in the following words:

The matter was discussed fully with the Minister of Reconstruction and myself, and we came to the conclusion that if any hydro-electric power plant was to be built in that territory, the dominion government should do it. We therefore decided we would enter into that project and harness the power there for the benefit not only of the mines now existing but also for the townsite of Yellowknife. . . .[54]

---

[52]Canada, Department of Mines and Resources, "Report of the Dominion Water and Power Bureau 1943," in *Annual Report of the Department for 1943*, p. 116.

[53]*North Pacific Planning Project*, Table III, pp. 88–9.

[54]*House of Commons Debates*, 1946, p. 5481.

Following the decision of the federal government to assume responsibility for power production in the Territories, an order-in-council in February, 1946, was passed on the joint recommendation of the Minister of Mines and Resources and the Minister of Reconstruction and Supply authorizing the construction of a power plant on the Snare River if the preliminary engineering surveys were satisfactory. The transmission line from the power house to the mines was to be built by the Giant Yellowknife Gold Mining Company. The construction of this 90-mile transmission line was expected to create considerable difficulty, as was its operation. The line had to traverse muskeg, rock, and many small lakes. During the winter of 1948–49, temperatures as low as −62° were recorded. Although these low temperatures, combined with the rough terrain, made inspection of the line difficult, it was found that the transmission of power was not seriously hindered.

As the project neared completion the government created the Northwest Territories Power Commission which was to consist of a chairman and two other members all appointed by the government.[55] This was the first power commission organized at the federal level in Canada. It was given all the powers necessary to enable it to carry out its task, which, as interpreted by the Minister of Mines and Resources, was "to develop, operate and administer electric power in the territories" and "to plan and correlate as much as possible power needs in the mineral area."[56] During the passage of the Bill through the House, it was explained that "The objective is to supply ample power at a low cost and thus assist substantially in the development of the mineral industries in the Territories."[57] The Act itself defined the rate policy of the Commission in the following way:

The Commission shall, with the approval of the Governor-in-Council, establish schedules or ranges of rates for power supplied by it under this Act, but the rates to be charged for power within the said schedules or ranges shall not be less than the estimated cost to the Commission, as determined by it, of supplying the power.

The Act then went on to ensure that this estimated cost of the Commission "should include all interest charges; operating, maintenance and repair costs and the cost of establishing and maintaining a contingency reserve fund in the amount considered necessary by the Commission to meet unforseen or emergency expenditure."

[55]*Statutes of Canada*, 11–12 Geo. VI, c. 64 (1948).
[56]*House of Commons Debates*, 1948, p. 5171.
[57]*Ibid.*, p. 5172.

That the Northwest Territories Power Commission was designed to encourage northern development without subsidizing it is shown clearly in the first annual report of the Commission in 1949. Referring to the plants which it intended to construct, the Commission's report stated that power from such plants would be sold at "as low a rate as possible subject to the plants being on a self-sustaining basis from the standpoint of over-head, operation and maintenance." The report went on to state that "with power made available in mineral areas as soon as its need is definitely established, the development of mining properties will be greatly encouraged and the mining and processing of ore made easier and more economical." The important words from the standpoint of assessing the policy underlying the formation of the Commission in this statement are those which refer to the need for power *definitely established.*

The consequence of this conservative policy was that the first rate estimated for power from the Snare River plant was approximately $112.86 per horsepower, or approximately 1.73 cents per kilowatt-hour. As we will see when we examine these rates in more detail later, this relatively high price for hydro-electric power was only partly the result of the high operating costs attributed to the small scale of the plant and other factors associated with its location. It was in part attributable to a fifteen-year amortization period assigned the plant by the government. Strong protests were made by the users of the power, including Giant Yellowknife which was bound to a long period of guaranteed consumption as a prerequisite of government construction of the plant. As a result of such protests the amortization period was increased to twenty years.[58] The relatively short amortization period favoured by the government was undoubtedly a reflection of its lack of certainty about the future prospects of mining in the area.[59] It should be noted in this connection that the economically feasible range for the transmission of Snare River power was recognized by the government to be about one hundred miles.[60]

By March 31, 1949, the Snare River plant had been completed at a cost of $4,485,292. The installed capacity was 8,350 horsepower. A

[58]J. Parker, "The Northwest Territories 1945–1965," in *Proceedings of the Northern Development Conference* (Edmonton, May 1, 1957), mimeographed, p. 77.

[59]Although periods as long as forty years had also been proposed, it was argued by some officials that if the objective was to ensure full recovery of the capital expenditure, the period should be less than twenty years; see *Minutes of the Council of the Northwest Territories,* May 20, 1948, p. 3532.

[60]*House of Commons Debates,* 1948, p. 5171.

major reason for the relatively high cost per installed horsepower of generating capacity was the cost of transportation during the construction of the plant. The only transportation facilities available for bringing in supplies, equipment, and personnel were air transport and a winter road built from Yellowknife to the site over frozen lakes and muskeg. Some use of water transportation was also made over part of the distance during the summer months. It has been estimated that transportation costs totalled some $600,000 and amounted to roughly 13 per cent of the total cost of the project.[61]

While the Snare River project was still under construction, other sites for central electric stations were investigated. Although the only other established mining operations were those at Port Radium in the Northwest Territories and at Mayo and Dawson in the Yukon, there were a number of settlements scattered throughout the territorial north which could be considered potential markets for the output of a central electric station, especially when military or other government operations were being conducted in or near them. Investigations conducted by the Commission in 1949 led it to consider two additional projects, one, the construction of a hydro-electric plant on the Mayo River to serve the Mayo mining district in the Yukon, the other, a diesel-electric plant for Fort Smith, the administrative centre of the Northwest Territories. In both cases, the Commission was satisfied that a sufficiently large demand for electric power already existed and that any investment in the kind of installation proposed could be made self-liquidating. Furthermore, it appeared that in each case this demand could be guaranteed through arrangements with the chief customers to be served. The chief consumer served by the Mayo plant was, of course, United Keno Hill Mines Limited, and it was willing to enter into long term contracts with the Commission for hydro-electric power. At Fort Smith the major consumers would be the various departments and agencies of the federal government located there. It is interesting to note that the Commission suggested that in other settlements not already served by central generating stations operated by military forces, the federal government departments most concerned should build such plants themselves. But the Commission itself was able to consider undertaking such installations only where the load was such that the plant could operate on a self-sustaining basis.[62] One such self-sustaining plant was subsequently

---

[61]Canada, Northwest Territories Power Commission, *Annual Report 1949* (Ottawa, 1949), p. 13.

[62]Northwest Territories Power Commission, *Annual Report 1951*, p. 70.

constructed by the Commission at Fort Smith and was opened in the spring of 1950. The initial plant consisted of three diesel-driven generators with a total capacity of 520 horsepower. The original investment was 138,254 dollars.

A much larger undertaking by the Commission at this time was the hydro-electric plant on the Mayo River. Similar in design to the Snare River project, the Mayo development involved damming a natural reservoir, Mayo Lake, twenty miles upstream from the generating plant. The maximum capacity of the site was estimated to be 8,000 horsepower of which 3,000 were to be developed initially. The electricity generated was to be delivered over a 66,000 volt line 25 miles to the Keno and Galena Hill mines and 6 miles over a 6,900 volt line to the settlement of Mayo Landing. The initial construction was completed in the fall of 1952 despite unexpected construction difficulties which caused the capital cost of the project to rise to $4,306,218, considerably more than the original estimates.[63] The immediate effect of the operation of this plant was to reduce the cost of power in the United Keno Hill operations from approximately 3.5 cents per kilowatt-hour to 2.8 cents. Power was also supplied by the commission to the Army radio station at Mayo and to a private distribution company, Mayo Light and Power Company, for retail distribution in Mayo Landing at a price of 5 cents per kilowatt-hour. The latter service was taken over in 1956 by the Commission and rates in the settlement were considerably reduced at that time.

Despite these major power developments in the Yellowknife and Mayo districts, the quantity of power demanded, even at the Commission's prices, rose much more rapidly than the supply during the decade of the 1950s. One reason for this was the Commission's policy of waiting until an adequate future demand for power could be guaranteed before it committed itself to plant construction in any particular area. Even when it did undertake a hydro project it tended to build in stages rather than to the maximum capacity of a site. Consequently, the operations of the Northwest Territories Power Commission in the 1950s provide a classic illustration of the process whereby privately generated demand for the services of a public utility are made to *lead* investment in that utility. Because of this policy, many parts of the territorial north experienced periodic and, in some cases, virtually chronic shortages of power. And this led, in turn, to the undertaking in some areas of new investments in electric power facilities by private enterprise. In the Whitehorse area, for example, the rapid growth of the

[63]Northwest Territories Power Commission, *Annual Report 1954*, p. 8.

settlement after World War II had led to the construction in the late 1940s of a small hydro plant on Porter Creek by the Yukon Electrical Company which supplied Whitehorse and vicinity with electric light and power. This plant consisted of two units installed in 1949 with a total capacity of 1,000 horsepower. In 1954 this company, by then reorganized and known as Yukon Hydro Company (a subsidiary of Canadian Utilities Limited), opened at second hydro plant which added 800 horsepower to the Company's capacity. A smaller private power development involved the installation of a diesel-generating plant to supply the settlement of Hay River in Mackenzie District in 1952, a development which led the NWTPC to report in 1952 that it had "abandoned its plans for the establishment of a power plant at this point."[64]

Despite the construction of generating capacity at Fort Smith, and in the Yellowknife, Mayo, and Whitehorse areas, it was apparent by the middle of the 1950s that capacity was inadequate to meet the demands in these centres. In 1955 the capacity of the Fort Smith diesel plant was increased by the addition of a fourth generating unit and a more adequate storage system for the fuel which was obtained from Norman Wells was installed. Further improvements were subsequently made in this plant's generating equipment in 1957, 1960, and 1961. In the Yellowknife area the primary load on the Snare River plant had risen to 90 per cent of plant capacity in 1956 and secondary power supplies had to be rationed in the area. In the Yukon by 1956, it was also apparent that additional generating capacity was urgently needed both at Mayo and Whitehorse. The total load on the Mayo plant actually exceeded the plant's capacity during the winter of 1956–7 and emergency generating units had to be operated daily to meet the demands. Faced with these conditions, the power commission undertook to develop additional capacity both in the Yukon and in Mackenzie District. The Commission's ability to undertake such developments was enhanced by a revision of the NWTPC Act assented to in August, 1956. The new provisions changed the name of the agency from the Northwest Territories Power Commission to Northern Canada Power Commission in recognition of the extension of the agency's activities outside the Northwest Territories; they enabled it to operate in any province as well as in the Territories; and they empowered it to provide public utilities such as central heating, water and sewerage, and telephone services. The amended Act also provided the Commission with a fund which could be used to finance the investigation of projects. The latter

[64]Northwest Territories Power Commission, *Annual Report 1952*, p. 10.

provision enabled the Commission to finance preliminary studies of proposed projects, charging the cost of such studies against the capital cost of the project if it was proceeded with—or against a fund maintained by parliamentary appropriations in the event the project was rejected. Finally, the revised Act made it possible for the Commission to use surplus funds to improve plants "to which such funds accrued"— but no provision was made for the transfer of surplus funds from one plant to another.[65]

The further development of the Mayo site involved the installation of a second 3,000 horsepower generating unit in the existing plant. As before, the Commission continued to insist upon a guaranteed market for its generating capacity and the expansion at Mayo was approved only after United Keno Hill Mines Limited signed an agreement to purchase the output of the second generating unit at rates which would enable the Commission to meet the additional annual cost associated with the expansion.[66] It was further provided that the additional investment of $457,652 would be amortized over a fifteen-year period. By the 1960–61 operating year the entire plant was being used at full capacity, with the United Keno Hill Company using up secondary power to heat its boilers.

Additional generating capacity was provided in the Yukon by the Commission's first hydro project in the Whitehorse area—the most expensive single power development it had undertaken to that time. The important inter-relationship between apparently distinct types of investment was a conspicuous feature of this particular project. The site chosen for the plant in 1956 was at the Whitehorse Rapids, about two miles upstream from Whitehorse on the Yukon River. Despite the construction problems foreseen at this site, it was chosen over the several alternative sites for two main reasons. One of these was proximity to the main load centre. The other was that this site permitted the development of a larger capacity than did the others. In view of the Commission's tendency to "underbuild" in such projects this is perhaps initially surprising, until it is noted that at the time this plant was being planned, a large federal hospital was being built in Whitehorse. Because the federal government was ultimately responsible for both these large projects it was possible to consider them together. The result was that studies of heating costs in the hospital, combined with estimates of the cost of a continuous supply of electric power for heating purposes

[65]*Statutes of Canada*, 4–5 Eliz. II, c. 42 (1956).
[66]Northern Canada Power Commission, *Annual Report 1957*, p. 8.

generated as part of the output of the Whitehorse Rapids plant, showed that the hospital could be heated electrically more cheaply than by using fuel oil, the main alternative. Consequently, the Whitehorse Rapids project initiated in 1956 involved the installation of two generating units with a combined capacity of 15,000 horsepower and provision for the installation of an additional 7,500 horsepower in the future. The total capital cost of the project when completed in 1958 was $7,200,000. And, for the first time, the Commission adopted a more lenient depreciation policy by undertaking to amortize this investment over a forty-year period. An unusually broad market for the output of this plant may have been a consideration in this respect. Power from the Whitehorse Rapids plant was supplied to a number of large government installations in the area and also to the Yukon Hydro Company which purchased power to supplement that produced in its own plant for sale to domestic and commercial consumers in Whitehorse.

The expansion of the Commission's generating capacity in Mackenzie District took the form of a new dam and generating unit downstream from the original plant on Snare River. The new installation (referred to as the Snare Falls plant to distinguish it from the Commission's Snare Rapids plant) consisted of a single 9,200 horsepower turbine set up for automatic remote control from the old plant. The new installation, which cost $4,558,811, came into service in December, 1960.

In addition to these major hydro projects the Commission also built several diesel-powered central generating stations in the Territories during the decade of the 1950s and in the early 1960s. These were located in smaller settlements lacking the mining operations which created the market for power in the Yellowknife and Mayo areas or the population which existed in the Whitehorse area. Reference has already been made to the Fort Smith plant and the additions which were made to it. Similar plants were subsequently built at Fort Simpson, Fort Resolution, Frobisher Bay, and Inuvik. Details of these installations are shown in Table 8.2. The most interesting of these projects was that undertaken at Inuvik, for it illustrated at least two points of general importance to an understanding of this type of development. One of these is a technical matter with important implications for economic and administrative policy in the north. Specifically, the Inuvik project recognized the technical or physical advantage to be derived from combining electric power, water, sewerage, and heating distribution systems in a single physical unit in locations where soil conditions made underground installation of such facilities difficult. The second aspect of the Inuvk undertaking of importance here is that Inuvik itself was designed as the showplace of the new federal policy in the north. So far we have seen something of this policy as it developed in connection with government participation in the provision of large-scale transportation and electric power facilities. But important as these developments were, they present a rather drab appearance in comparison with the sometimes sensational public undertakings in the area of public welfare measures which were initiated during the decade of the 1950s.

The conservatism of the federal government at this time in the areas of electric power policy and, with the exceptions noted earlier, in transportation policy, contrasts with its efforts to solve some of the serious short-run problems of health and education discussed in the following chapter. The two areas of government policy came together, however, in the matter of electric power facilities, for the large federal expenditures on central residential schools and on relatively large medical centres created substantial demands for electric power in a number of centres previously too small to attract either private or public investments in central generating systems. Inuvik, a "model" town created by the federal government to replace the old settlement of Aklavik in the Mackenzie Delta, was the prime example of this kind of development, although it was also to be perceived at Fort Smith, Fort Simpson and even, as we have seen, at Whitehorse.[67]

The Inuvik installation of the Northern Canada Power Commission consisted of a power plant costing just over one million dollars and other utilities, including central heating and water services for the settlement, costing over seven million dollars. The electric power plant contained a 1,500 KW generating unit installed in 1958, which was later expanded to 2,500 KW. The other utilities included a central heating plant with a capacity of 90,000 pounds of steam per hour, a water pumping and treatment plant, and an integrated above-ground system of conduits (termed "utilidors") to distribute heat, water, and sewerage services to the central part of the town site.

Assessment of Northern Canada Power Commission Policy to 1961

As an instrument of government policy in the territorial north, the NCPC must be considered a reasonably successful agency of its kind.

---

[67]How striking the change in attitudes reflected in the Inuvik project was is suggested by the fact that in 1937 a proposal to provide Aklavik with electric power was opposed by a member of the Territorial Council on the grounds that if such facilities were made available the government could end up by providing electric power to the hospitals and schools there free of charge! See *Minutes of the Council of the Northwest Territories*, March 23, 1937, IV, p. 887.

Like the Northern Transportation Company examined earlier, it is apparent from the constitution and operations of the NCPC that it represented a specific type of federal participation in the economic life of the Territories. This type of participation became significant only after World War II and, as we have seen before, it consisted of much more positive measures to support private *entrepreneurs* in their attempts to develop the natural resources of the area than when the role of the government had been limited to maintaining law, order, and a minimum social capital structure.

The NCPC was the best illustration, perhaps, of what the federal government saw its more active role in the Territories to be in the decade following the war—at least in so far as it saw itself being involved in resource development at all. The policy was not to initiate such development but to *centralize* the supply of certain important industrial services, such as power and transportation—for example, within the limits imposed by physical and economic factors, to build central generating stations to supply electric power to a number of private consumers rather than to leave them to satisfy their own requirements. As we have now seen, prior to the appearance of the NCPC, the latter policy had prevailed and individual firms sometimes did succeed in providing themselves with such facilities. In the case of electric power this had been possible for relatively small, isolated operators because of the availability of small diesel-electric plants, although this made their power inputs extremely expensive. Because these factors in turn varied with the cost of transporting fuel and with the size and type of the equipment used to burn it, costs per unit of such power varied tremendously from one operation to another. It has been estimated, however, that when capital, operating, and maintenance costs of diesel-electric plants in northern mining applications are all considered, the cost of electricity so generated could have ranged from three to ten cents per kilowatt-hour.[68] In larger operations, however, as at the Eldorado Port Radium establishment where reasonable transportation facilities for fuel were available, the cost of diesel power, excluding depreciation of generating plant, was as low as 1.79 cents per kilowatt-hour.[69] In the case of even larger operations, it was feasible for individual firms to invest in small hydro-electric plants, and we have seen how this was done by the

[68]E. W. Humphrys, "Possibilities of Light and Heat from Atomic Energy and Other Sources," in Bladen, ed., *Canadian Population and Northern Colonization*, p. 119.

[69]See Dubnie, *Some Economic Factors Affecting Northern Mineral Development in Canada*, Mineral Information Bulletin Number MR38, Department of Mines and Technical Surveys (Ottawa, 1959), p. 36.

larger operators in the Klondike and by Consolidated Mining and Smelting at Yellowknife.

The difficulty with this policy of leaving it to individual firms to satisfy their own power requirements was that it favoured the large private operator, who could finance such investments, over the small. And in the case of all such undertakings the historical evidence, some of which has been noted above, suggested that the result was almost invariably the effective domination of a mineralized area by a single large firm. So long as local populations in the territorial north had no effective voice in the determination of resource development policy, this tendency toward concentration of ownership and control in particular areas posed no serious political difficulty for the federal government and, as we have seen, offered certain economic benefits in so far as a policy of encouraging large operators to develop resources permitted the federal authorities to avoid undertaking large-scale public investments in those areas. But with the growth of population in the Territories and the appearance of more effective political representation for this population during the 1930s and 1940s, opposition to such a policy became increasingly possible. Furthermore, there was no certainty that even large firms would undertake the type of investments required for the development of a region under circumstances where they were unlikely to realize returns from such investments commensurate with the sum of private and public benefits ultimately generated by them. The establishment of a public power authority in the Territories was one method available to the federal government for overcoming such difficulties.

At present too little is known of the background to the formation of the territorial power commission to indicate what combination of economic and political influences produced it. Debate in the House of Commons elicited from the government the explanation that the policy was not aimed at eliminating private investments in power facilities but was intended to make lower cost power available to smaller users and to ensure more effective utilization of the territorial water-power resources. A government spokesman further asserted that:

> ... at the present time mining companies may develop individual power sites under the Dominion Water Power Act ... but the smaller mining companies are often unable to finance a hydroelectric power development. There is also the tendency to have scattered water power plants in a mineral area rather than a larger development which would serve the whole area at a cheaper rate. The bill [to establish the Commission] reduces the danger of smaller power plants prejudicing the development of a large plant on the same river.[70]

---

[70]*House of Commons Debates*, 1948, p. 5175.

In short, the Commission was expected to make the economies of scale in electric power generation available to mining firms and other users who could not individually undertake the large investments involved. And it appears to have been taken for granted that private power companies would not be interested in undertaking such large investments even where the established demand was such as to make the investment potentially profitable, for there was no question of the Commission operating *any* individual plant at a loss. The benefits to power users in the Territories would appear in the form of lower cost power than they would otherwise be able to provide themselves with, although the rates charged by the Commission would be such as to cover all operating and capital costs. It is apparent, then, that the idea behind the NCPC was to use a public agency to undertake the kind of large-scale investments in efficient generating facilities which private investors would not undertake. Thus, the Commission's customers would receive the benefits of lower cost power at no cost to the federal taxpayer living elsewhere in Canada. The latter provision was zealously safeguarded, at least until the late 1950s, by the Commission's adherence to conservative practices for evaluating the feasibility of projects, by its high rate of amortization for established plants, and by its policy of guaranteeing markets in advance, as well as by its general rate policy. In no way, did it seem, was the Commission intended to serve as a means of promoting territorial development through subsidizing the users of its services. Indeed, it was even prevented from using profitable parts of its operation to subsidize other parts, unlike the Northern Transportation Company which, as we saw earlier in the chapter, had been allowed to do this.

Because of these conservative practices public investment in power tended to lag appreciably behind private investment in such activities as mining, thereby leaving many operators dependent upon high-cost diesel power. They also meant that, as a rule, plant was built to a minimum capacity initially and then expanded as further demand could be confirmed by long-term contracts with new customers. It is not surprising then that costs of even the hydro power provided by the Commission remained relatively high compared with that produced elsewhere in Canada. This was especially true where the future prospects of a particular area were particularly uncertain, as in the case of the Mayo district in the Yukon where the United Keno Hill operations seemed to offer the only market for the output of the hydro plant on the Mayo River. There the fifteen-year amortization period (for the plant expansion of 1957) and the long-term purchase commitments were combined with a rate of approximately 2.63 cents per kilowatt-hour. Even at Yellowknife in the late 1950s mines were paying approximately 1.5 cents per kilowatt-hour or more than twice the rate paid by mining companies in many other parts of Canada. This relatively high cost of power to the consumer in the Territories was even more striking in the case of domestic power rates. Throughout the 1950s the price of domestic power in the Yukon and Northwest Territories exceeded 5 cents per kilowatt-hour compared to approximately 1.6 cents per kilowatt hour in Canada as a whole.[71]

Thus, we see that although the NCPC made it possible for many consumers of electric power in the Territories to obtain lower cost electric power than they might otherwise have had access to, the general level of power costs in the Territories remained much higher than elsewhere in Canada. The reasons for this are not difficult to discover, although it is difficult to estimate their relative importance.[72] First of all it may be noted that the proportion of total power generated in the Territories by hydro plants was somewhat lower than in Canada as a whole. In 1961, 91.4 per cent of Canadian electric power was generated from water power compared to 83.5 per cent in the Yukon and Northwest Territories. This is even more important than the apparent difference in these figures would suggest, however, for the 16.5 per cent of output generated in thermal plants in the Territories often represented small diesel generation whereas the 8.6 per cent of output in Canada generated in thermal plants was produced in relatively large and efficient steam units.

When we examine detailed statistics for the electric power industry for a typical year in the 1950s, we find that in the Territories the costs of operation, maintenance, and administration were higher than in the Canadian power industry as a whole. In 1956 these items amounted to 0.34 cents per kilowatt-hour of electricity made available to final users compared to a corresponding figure of 0.28 cents for the national industry. Almost one third of these operating costs were attributable to labour outlays, which in these employments were running about 20 per cent higher in the north than elsewhere in Canada. This, then, was one reason for the high cost of power in the north. An even stronger factor,

[71]D.B.S., *Central Electric Stations*, annually 1950–55; *Electric Power Statistics*, annually 1956–59.
[72]The usefulness of published statistical data relevant here is affected by a major change in the basis for reporting electric power information by D.B.S. in 1956.

however, was the depreciation cost per unit of output, which in the case of the north in 1956 exceeded total operating, maintenance, and administration costs as a component of total costs of production. In 1956 0.35 cents per kilowatt-hour were attributable to depreciation charges—which were four times higher than the national average of 0.09 cents per kilowatt-hour for this industry. It must be concluded that while costs of operation, maintenance, and administration were 20 per cent higher in the north than in Canada as a whole, depreciation charges have been four times higher in the Territories. Because the latter charges were responsible for slightly more than half of total operating expense, they were a considerably more important reason for the high cost of northern power than those usually put forward.

It should also be noted that capital costs, in the form of interest payments, were considerably higher for power plants located in the Territories than for those located elsewhere in Canada. It would not be expected that this was attributable to higher borrowing rates—in view of the fact that most plants in the north were constructed with public funds. The relatively high interest payments in terms of cost per unit of output were, rather, attributable to the relatively low productivity of capital invested in these northern plants, which, in turn, was largely attributable to their small scale and high construction costs. Even the larger developments, such as the plant at Whitehorse Rapids, yielded only about 0.002 horsepower for every $500 of capital outlay in contrast to very large-scale hydro plants which could yield double this capacity. This high capital outlay per unit of generating capacity was reflected in relatively high interest payments, which, in 1956 for example, amounted to 0.203 cents per kilowatt-hour produced in the Territories compared with the national average of 0.120 cents. Despite this relatively high capital charge on operating income, however, the electric power industry in the Territories returned a net income (after tax, interest and depreciation) in 1956 of 0.0029 cents per kilowatt-hour produced, considerably more than the industry average of 0.0012. This is consistent, of course, with the requirement imposed upon NCPC to operate all its plants on a self-sustaining basis. In this regard, however, it is interesting to note that in 1954 the Commission was relieved of the need to pay federal corporation income tax. The reason given for this concession was that unless such relief was provided the Commission would eventually find it impossible "to meet all obligations without substantial rate increases" and that this would be inconsistent with its "special nature and function."[73]

[73]Northwest Territories Power Commission, *Annual Report 1955*, p. 8.

If this tax concession seemed to suggest a loosening of the very strict requirements which had ensured the operation of the Commission on a strictly commercial basis, by the later 1950s the significance of such a development was probably less than it would have been even a few years earlier. For, as we saw on examining the plant construction programme of the Commission above, the federal government was itself becoming one of the Commission's chief customers in the Territories. Thus the original conception of the Commission as a public utility supplying remote private mining centres with central power facilities was somewhat altered during the decade of the 1950s by the development of very large-scale public welfare programmes throughout the Territories. So long as its capital programme and operating policies had been based upon demand created by private investments in natural resource-based industries, the Commission's investments could be justified economically in terms of the most conservative understanding of the investment criteria applicable in a more or less free enterprise economic environment. But when the demand came to be created by government itself through an elaborate system of welfare facilities, it would seem that a new set of criteria for the Commission's investment programme (and operating policy) might be called for. The implications of this will be considered further in the concluding chapter of this part. But first we must examine the somewhat delayed application of the principles of the welfare state to the territorial north which resulted in the establishment of the facilities just referred to.

9 Public Investment in Educational, Health and Public Welfare Facilities in the North

In all measures adopted for the furthering of the development of the country, the welfare of the native and resident population is given primary consideration. Humanitarian reasons, of course, demand this, but it is felt by close observers that the successful development of the North will depend to a large degree on the co-operation of a healthy and contented native population. [F. H. Kitto, in Department of the Interior, *The North-west Territories 1930* (Ottawa, 1930), p. 64.]

PRIOR TO THE END of World War II direct federal investments in health and educational facilities were virtually non-existent in the territorial north. The smallness of the population there precluded the establishment of locally supported municipal schools and hospitals. In the Yukon Territory, despite its declining status after the turn of the century, the locally influenced but federally dominated territorial administration assumed much of the responsibility for providing such facilities, many of which have consequently always been operated as government-owned institutions. In the Northwest Territories, however, the absence of local influence in territorial government was reflected in a virtually complete absence of such institutions until very recent years.

EDUCATIONAL FACILITIES IN THE TERRITORIAL NORTH

Early in the history of the Yukon Territory the maintenance of public schools came to be regarded as a territorial responsibility. The origins of this system are to be found in a petition presented by a number of residents of the Yukon to the Commissioner-in-Council in 1898 asking that a school be established. It is interesting to note, because it appears to have established the approach of government to such matters for most of the subsequent history of the Yukon Territory, that the Commissioner reacted to this request by organizing a meeting of various clergymen in Dawson to discuss the establishment of a non-sectarian public school. Such a policy was approved by the meeting over the dissenting voice of a Father Gendreau who proposed the establishment of government-assisted separate schools. The apparently inevitable Canadian school issue did not, however, develop into a serious controversy in the Yukon, for in 1900 the Council adopted a resolution approving the establishment of a public school system in the Yukon but providing also that "in the meantime the Council should be prepared to make a liberal grant towards the maintenance of any school which may be established, in which the teaching and general carrying on of such school is made along the lines of the North-West Territories Ordinance."[1] Thereafter, the Dawson "public" school and Saint Mary's school in Dawson, as well as a number of smaller schools operated by the territorial government at centres such as Whitehorse and Carcross, were all maintained through grants from the Council. In 1908 the Dawson public school had 241 pupils enrolled, Saint Mary's had 65, and the school at Whitehorse had 62.

As the placer mining operations became increasingly centralized and converted to large-scale operations, the outlying camps were abandoned and the smaller schools closed down.[2] By the end of World War I school enrolment had fallen to 371 pupils, most of whom were in the two Dawson schools, and the total number of schools in the Territory had been reduced to 6.[3] There was little change between then and World War II, during the early years of which we find around 270 pupils in five schools, the two at Dawson and one each at Whitehorse, Carcross, and Mayo.[4] The schools continued to be supported by territorial grants (with the territorial administration being reimbursed by the federal government for Indian students who were served by them).

Thus we find that in the Yukon Territory, the heavy initial influx of white population at the time of the placer gold mining boom late in the

[1]*Journals of the Yukon Council* (1912), XII, 47.
[2]*Ibid.* (1908), VIII, 17.
[3]*Ibid.* (1920), XX, 10–11.
[4]"Annual Report of the Controller of the Yukon Territory, March 31, 1942", in D.B.S. *Mineral Statistics 1942* (Ottawa, 1944), p. 126.

nineteenth century created an immediate demand for educational facilities and that this was met by what was at the time a fairly strong territorial administration. Despite the tendency noted in Part I for the federal government to ignore the existence of this administrative machinery (or even to dismantle it) the provision of educational facilities in the Yukon remained a territorial governmental function. And despite the poverty of the territorial administration after the early years of the century, the provision of these facilities remained a function of *government*—for even the denominational schools operated by the Roman Catholic Church were in practice treated as part of the territorial public school system. This continued to be the case even when the system began expanding in the later years of World War II. During the years from 1943 to 1953 the annual student enrolment in the Yukon schools rose by almost five times, from 283 in 1943 to 1,415 ten years later. To accommodate this increase in enrolment the territorial government constructed a large new school at Whitehorse in 1952. Although it opened with 531 pupils, within two years it had to be enlarged by the addition of ten new classrooms. That the traditional territorial schools policy was still being followed in the Yukon is shown by the fact that a new Roman Catholic school was also constructed in Whitehorse during this period and, while it was built and supported like any other "territorial school," it was operated on a fee basis by the "Sisters of Providence." In the Mayo mining centre the United Keno Hill Company provided school buildings (and utilities) but the territorial government provided staff. As shown in Table 9.1 by 1962 the territorial school system consisted of 23 schools, staffed by 142 teachers, providing instruction for 3,123 pupils.

It will be seen from the foregoing that the basic elements of the school system in the Yukon were unlike those of the provinces in Canada in so far as the territorial system was organized and financed by the territorial government rather than by municipal governments. But the role of the federal government in this area of territorial affairs in the Yukon was quite similar to that which it played in the provinces. Although federal grants in support of education (and other government functions) in the Yukon have probably been more important there than in most of the provinces, the school system of the Yukon has been a territorial operation as separate from the federal administration as the general constitutional position of the Yukon Territory could allow it to be. In the Yukon Territory, for example, the federal government has made a practice of "farming out" the field of Indian education to the territorial school system. In addition to remaining free of direct federal control the Yukon school system remained free from the domination of religious organizations, and, as we have seen, managed to contain within itself the Roman Catholic "separate" schools. In both respects the school system developed in the Yukon could be distinguished clearly from the one established in the Northwest Territories.

Schools in the Northwest Territories

Lacking the large influx of white population early in its development which so influenced the establishment of the institutional structure of the Yukon, the Northwest Territories failed to develop its educational facilities either at the municipal or territorial levels. Indeed, it may be said that prior to the years after World War II, the provision of such facilities was not undertaken by government at any level in the North-west Territories, for the federal government avoided the necessity of making such investments by leaving the entire field of education there to religious bodies, and chiefly to the missionaries of the Church of England and the Roman Catholic Church. Because the white population of the Northwest Territories was so small and scattered before World War II, the system of mission schools that was established was primarily designed for the education of natives. Because both the Indians and the Eskimos were formally the responsibility of the federal government the mission schools were given direct financial support by that government. The initiative in providing these facilities came, however, from the churches, for their efforts to convert the heathen in the area that became the District of Mackenzie began well before the federal government entered into any agreements with native people residing there. Missionaries of both churches began their labours in the Mackenzie River area in the middle of the nineteenth century, but it was not until 1899 that the Canadian government got around to "making treaty" with the natives south of Great Slave Lake and not until 1921 that settlement was effected with the various bands living north along the Mackenzie and on the northern side of the lake.[5]

The schools provided by the missionaries were usually small day schools located in centres of Indian population, although some boarding schools were also operated. Thus, in 1925 the Church of England was operating day schools at Aklavik, McPherson, Simpson, and Norman Wells and a boarding school at Hay River. Roman Catholic boarding

---

[5]Canada, Department of the Interior, *The Northwest Territories 1930*, by F. H. Kitto (Ottawa, 1930), p. 65.

schools were located at Resolution and Providence and a Roman Catholic
day school was in operation at Fort Smith.[6] Similar schools were
established at other points in the Northwest Territories during the late
1920s and during the decade of the 1930s, so that by the beginning of
World War II there were thirteen day schools and five residential schools
in operation. At some of the larger centres, such as Aklavik and Fort
Smith, schools of both denominations were provided side by side. As
will be seen from Table 9.2 most of these schools had very small
enrolments.

As a result of the considerable increase in the number of white
children in Mackenzie District during the late 1930s, the shortcomings
of this mission school system became increasingly apparent. As early as
1927 the territorial administration received requests from at least one
of the larger settlements for assistance in providing a local public school,
but at that time the territorial council appeared quite unwilling to
consider such a development.[7] In the absence of such schools, it became
the practice of many white parents in Mackenzie District to rely upon
Province of Alberta correspondence courses for the education of their
children.

The chief objection to the mission schools appears to have been the
quality of the instruction rather than their denominational aspects. The
teachers were usually the missionaries themselves and they were not
necessarily (or customarily) professionally qualified to teach the variety
of subjects usually considered appropriate to a general elementary
education. Furthermore, there was no required curriculum and there was
no provision for inspection of the schools or supervision of the teaching
by public authorities.[8] Consequently, it appears to have been generally
believed that the quality of education being provided in these schools
was inferior to that available both in the public and Indian schools of
the provinces to the south. But it was not until after World War II that
the federal administration undertook a general revision of its policies
with respect to education in the Northwest Territories. When it did
come, this change in policy was partly the consequence of the pressure
created by the great expansion in the white population of the Territories
which followed the mineral developments of the late 1930s and the
activity indirectly associated with the military developments in the area
during the early 1940s. During these years a form of municipal public

[6]*Minutes of the Council of the Northwest Territories*, June 23, 1926, I, 45.
[7]*Ibid.*, December 28, 1927, I, 49.
[8]Memorandum on Education in *ibid.*, 1939, VII, 1654–5.

school system was tentatively established in Yellowknife and in the government's administrative centre of Fort Smith. Both of these schools were operated by local boards with financial support from the territorial administration.

In 1944, the federal government sponsored an extensive survey of the educational facilities and conditions in the Northwest Territories. One of the first consequences of this investigation was the appointment of an inspector of schools for the Territories in 1946. The following year the Northwest Territories Council approved an entirely new policy for schools in the Territories, the main elements of which were as follows: that the territorial administration would henceforth build and control all school facilities to be provided in the Territories; the Northwest Territories Council should have responsibility for the control of all education, including that of Indians, in the Territories; until the settlements had developed to the point where they could provide all or part of the cost of operating local school districts, the Northwest Territories Council would bear the full cost of educating all the children in such settlements; and that the territorial government would not build or operate residential schools.[9]

The main principles of this new policy were gradually implemented over a period of several years. Large public non-denominational schools were provided at Yellowknife and Fort Smith and a number of new schools to be operated by the federal territorial administration were established at smaller centres during the late 1940s and early 1950s. All the teachers in these schools were federal civil service employees. By 1954 the most important schools of this type were located in Mackenzie District at Fort Smith, Hay River, Fort Resolution, Fort Simpson, and Aklavik. During this same period federal funds were used to construct smaller schools, chiefly in Indian settlements, and these were operated by the Indian Affairs Branch of the federal Department of Citizenship and Immigration. This construction programme, as carried out between 1949 and 1954, provided such schools at Arctic Red River, Fort Franklin, Fort Good Hope, Fort Norman, Rocher River, Fort McPherson, Coppermine, Fort Rae, and Marie River. Roman Catholic day schools continued to operate at Fort Smith and Fort Simpson and residential schools at Aklavik, Fort Resolution, and Fort Providence. An Anglican residential school also operated at Aklavik. In addition, government assisted schools were provided by mining companies at Port Radium and Yellowknife and the local public school at Yellowknife was supplemented by a local

[9]*Ibid.*, November 17, 1947, XIV, 3408.

separate school in 1953. The latter received financial support from the territorial administration on the same basis as did the Yellowknife public school.

The next stage in the implementation of the new education policy in the Northwest Territories began in 1955. This was marked by a further integration of educational programmes in the Territories by bringing Indian (and Eskimo) education under the control of the territorial administration and through the adoption of a new policy aimed at bringing the children from the scattered settlements into large central schools.

As of April, 1955, responsibility for the education of Indians in the Northwest Territories was transferred from the Indian Affairs Branch of the Department of Citizenship and Immigration to the Department of Northern Affairs and National Resources. All the schools formerly operated by Indian Affairs were incorporated into the territorial school system which was being administered by the Department of Northern Affairs and National Resources on behalf of the Northwest Territories Council.

The new policy of providing a few large central schools instead of numerous small ones located near the natural centres of population in the Territories represented an imaginative (and controversial) approach to the problems of northern education, for it involved the removal of children from their home environments for the period of the school year, transporting them often many hundreds of miles to the educational centres, and maintaining them at the centres for the same period of time. Of course, denominational residential schools had used the same approach for many years, but not on the scale contemplated by the government programme announced in 1955. Quite apart from its educational and social implications, this scheme was remarkable in that it entailed massive investments by the federal government in what were, by earlier northern standards, elaborate capital facilities. The construction of these facilities was to be spread over a period of six years. Work began in 1956 with the construction of a hostel capable of sustaining two hundred pupils, a school, and an administration building at Fort Smith. The following year two hostel buildings and a school building were begun at Aklavik and contracts were awarded for high school, hostel, and dormitory buildings at Yellowknife. In 1958 a similar project was undertaken at Fort Simpson. And in 1959 two new hostels were built for the Yukon Territory at Whitehorse.

Because of these and related building projects, some of which are described later in this chapter, federal outlays on new public buildings in the territorial north as shown in Table 9.3 exceeded two million dollars in each of the years 1959, 1960, and 1961. This stands in sharp contrast to the record for most years prior to 1946 when nothing was spent for such purposes. Added to these unprecedented outlays of public funds for buildings associated with the new education policy was a very considerable annual operating charge upon the territorial and federal treasuries, for the total costs of maintaining children in the new hostels was to be borne by the two levels of government sharing in proportion to the children each was responsible for—that is, native and non-native. No means test was employed because of the "administrative difficulties" it would have created, and the position taken by the government was that "in establishing student residences the Administration was trying to take account of the physical circumstances of the Territory and parents should not be penalized by this policy."[10] By 1961 such residences could accommodate 1,236 students. Of this total, 1,100 spaces were available in Mackenzie District and 136 were in the arctic areas to the east.[11]

The effect of these new educational policies on the percentage of school-age population actually receiving schooling in the Northwest Territories was remarkable. Table 9.4 shows that in 1950–51 only 23 per cent of the total population in the 6 to 16 year age group was in school compared to 75 per cent in 1961–62. The improvement was most remarkable in the case of the Eskimo population, for one of the chief advantages of the policy was its appropriateness as a means of ensuring the attendance at school of children whose parents tended to move from place to place. Another advantage of the policy was that it permitted the provision of more specialized types of instruction than could be given at small local schools. Thus, at the Sir John Franklin School in Yellowknife, for example, various types of vocational training were made available in the hope that the potential native labour force could be equipped with skills which would enable it to find employment in such industries as mining, transportation, construction, and clerical work. In 1960 a mining course was being developed at Yellowknife to supplement courses already being offered in carpentry, auto and diesel mechanics, heavy equipment operation, and food service. In the 1961–62 academic year 34 Eskimos, 66 Indians, and 29 "other" students were enrolled in this school's regular programme.

This kind of programme, combined with efforts to develop a general

[10]Statement by the Commissioner of the Northwest Territories; see Council of the Northwest Territories, *Votes and Proceedings, 1961*, p. 47.
[11]Canada, Department of Northern Affairs and National Resources, *Annual Report 1961–2*, p. 27.

curriculum tailored to the post-war northern environment, was an integral part of the new conception the federal government had acquired of its proper role in the territorial north during this post-World War II period. Just as the creation of the Northern Canada Power Commission described in the last chapter represented a reversal of the federal government's policy of *laissez-faire* with respect to the industrial development of the Territories, so did the creation of a *public* school system constitute a similar abandonment of the earlier policy which left education to the voluntary efforts of the missionaries. The latter policy had been satisfactory so long as the purpose of education was only to fit children for life in an area left dependent upon hunting and trapping for a living, the church for social welfare, and the police for day-to-day administration. And like the other activities initiated by the government in the area after the war, the provision of this new school system involved the commitment of fairly large amounts of public money to the area for non-military purposes for the first time in history. Although the public schools established at Yellowknife and Fort Smith were partly financed through local taxes and partly through grants from the Northwest Territories Council, the great part of the programme was made possible only because of the expenditure of federal funds on it.

HOSPITAL FACILITIES IN THE YUKON AND NORTHWEST TERRITORIES

With few exceptions the development of hospitals in the Yukon and Northwest Territories paralleled the development of schools. In brief, hospitals in the Yukon were supported by grants from the Territorial Council and part of the hospital facilities were always owned by the territorial government. In the Northwest Territories, provision of such facilities was left to the churches (and to the mining companies) until late in the 1950s when large government-sponsored hospitals made their appearance and, like the central public schools described earlier, showed signs of replacing the church and privately operated facilities there.

Hospitals in the Yukon Territory

As in the case of its school system, the general pattern of hospital facilities in the Yukon was set during the period of the placer gold-mining boom with both public and church-owned facilities being provided. The hospital at Whitehorse was a public hospital, owned by the territorial government and managed by a board of trustees elected annually by the citizens of Whitehorse. In the larger centre of Dawson, however, both hospitals operating in the early years of the century were owned and operated by the churches. Saint Mary's hospital was a Roman Catholic hospital operated by an appointed board of managers. The other, the Good Samaritan Hospital, was managed by a board consisting of the Session and Board of Managers of Saint Andrew's Church and seven other members elected annually, five of whom were nominated by citizens of Dawson and the surrounding region, one by the Yukon Council, and one by the Commissioner of the Territory. All received operating grants from the territorial administration.

This system persisted in the Yukon without significant change for the next fifty years, although the relative decline of the Dawson area and development of mining at Mayo led to the closing of one hospital (the Good Samaritan) at Dawson and the opening of a new one at Mayo. Throughout the inter-war period the largest and most active hospital in the Territory was Saint Mary's at Dawson, much of its work arising out of the care of aged indigents. In the late 1930s Saint Mary's provided annually as many hospital-days of care to indigent patients as the total days of care provided to all patients in the two other hospitals combined.

No significant expansion of hospital facilities took place in the Yukon until after World War II. The effect of the war itself was to increase activity in the Whitehorse area and this led in turn to an expansion, financed by grants from the territorial council, of the old hospital there during the early 1940s, but the effect of this on the total supply of hospital beds in the Territory was offset by the closing of the Mayo hospital between 1942 and 1946. It was not until the 1950s that any marked change occurred in the provision of hospital facilities in the Yukon. When it did come it took the form of greatly increased participation by the federal government in the provision of this type of facility. This was done both through the provision of assistance to the territorial administration for hospital construction, and also through direct federal investment in a large modern hospital at Whitehorse to be operated by the federal government's newly formed Northern Health Services organization.

The system of hospital construction grants to the Yukon administration shows up as an annual item appearing in the federal estimates for the first time in 1953 and this reflected the extension to the Territories of arrangements made by the federal government with the provinces. Over the following decade the size of the grant grew steadily, rising from $8,582 in 1953 to $112,649 in 1962 as shown in Table 9.5. In 1956 the old hospital at Mayo was replaced by a new fourteen-bed hospital. The capacity of the Whitehorse General at this time was seventy-three beds and Saint Mary's in Dawson had forty-five beds. All continued to operate with grants from the territorial administration, the total amount of which for all three hospitals ran at about $60,000 annually during the 1950s.

The entry of the federal government into the direct provision of hospital facilities in the Yukon occurred in 1956 when contracts were let for the construction of a medical complex at Whitehorse consisting of a 120-bed hospital, nurses' and nurses' aides' residences, and related facilities. This subsequently became the principal public hospital in the Yukon and, in so far as its administration was primarily the responsibility of the federal Department of Health and Welfare, it represented a major departure from the federal policy of minimizing its direct responsibility for the provision of such facilities and services in the territorial north. This change of policy is even more conspicuous when the development of hospital facilities in the Northwest Territories is examined.

Hospitals in the Northwest Territories

The federal government's hospital policy in the Northwest Territories prior to the post-World War II period was succinctly described by a member of the government speaking in the House of Commons in 1938:

> We do not ourselves operate hospitals in the Northwest Territories; they are built either by the Anglican or by the Roman Catholic missions. In some cases we give a grant to assist in construction. For Indian patients and indigents who receive treatment in the hospitals we pay a per diem charge to the hospital.[12]

The direct participation by the government in the field of health generally during the pre-World War II years of the history of the Territories was limited to stationing government medical officers at various points throughout the Territories to be responsible for the health of the native population and to supervise the various mission hospitals, residential schools, and "industrial homes" maintained by missions to care for the indigent aged and chronically ill at various centres. Throughout the 1930s the number of these mission hospitals grew and their number was supplemented by the appearance of hospitals operated by mining companies at Yellowknife, Port Radium, and at Norman Wells.[13]

---

[12]*House of Commons Debates*, 1938, p. 3077.
[13]The mission hospitals in the NWT in 1940 are listed in Table 9.6.

During the war years it was reported that hospital facilities were also provided "by private enterprise at points throughout the Territories to care for those engaged in defence projects."[14] The only federally operated hospital in the Territories during this period was a small Indian hospital at Norman.

In 1944 the re-awakening of public and government interest in the north was reflected in the undertaking of a survey of medical and hospital services in Mackenzie District similar to the educational survey referred to earlier in this chapter. The hospital facilities then available were found to consist of nine mission hospitals, two mining company hospitals, and one Indian Affairs Branch hospital. The following year, in 1945, a general reorganization of government health arrangements in the Territories was initiated beginning with the transfer of responsibility for the medical care and hospitalization of Indians and Eskimos from the Department of Mines and Resources to the Department of National Health and Welfare. The health of other residents of the Territories remained a responsibility of the Department of Mines and Resources which provided, as we saw in Part I, the general territorial administration.

Aided by government grants, the missions and the Red Cross continued to expand the hospital facilities in the Territories during the years following the war. A new, forty-bed hospital was put into service by the Red Cross at Yellowknife in 1948, the Aklavik and Fort Smith mission hospitals were improved in the early 1950s, and between 1951 and 1956 nursing stations were built by the federal government at Cape Dorset, Coppermine, Fort McPherson, and Fort Rae. The result of all this activity was to provide the Territories with a remarkably extensive and even more remarkably inefficient system of hospitals. The total number of hospital beds (in terms of "rated capacity") in the Northwest Territories grew from 159 in 1932 to 774 in 1954. Although this number had declined to 579 by 1956, even then it represented 30.47 beds per one thousand of population in the Territories. This compared to 9.17 per one thousand in the Yukon and a Canadian average of 5.46.[15]

Because of the problems of transportation involved, the extraordinary prevalence of tuberculosis, and the use of hospital facilities to provide shelter for what would elsewhere have been treated as welfare cases, the benefits of this high ratio of bed capacity to population were illusory. The rate of utilization of these beds both in the Yukon and to an even greater degree in the Northwest Territories was usually well below the

---

[14]Department of Mines and Resources, *Annual Report 1944*, p. 64.
[15]All data from D.B.S., *Hospital Statistics 1962*, Volume I.

ratios achieved in the provinces. In 1955, when separate data were published for each of the Yukon and the Northwest Territories the "percentage occupancy" figures for *reporting* hospitals in the Yukon was 57.7, for the Northwest Territories 60.5 and for Canada as a whole 78.7. Given the low state of health among the territorial native population commented on by independent visitors to the north, it would appear that difficulty was experienced in getting the sick into hospitals for treatment. The male infant mortality rate in the Northwest Territories in 1959 was 140 per thousand births compared to a national average of 32. But those patients who were brought into hospital tended to remain there for long periods of treatment and care. Again, taking the hospitals reporting to the Dominion Bureau of Statistics in 1955, the mean stay of "separations" (those dying in the hospital or discharged from it) in the Northwest Territories was 52.9 days compared with 18.3 in the Yukon and a Canadian average of 10.9. At the same time deaths per thousand patients under hospital care in the Northwest Territories were only 11.2 compared with 24.1 in the country as a whole.

It was, consequently, apparent that there was room for improvement in the organization of hospital services in the Northwest Territories and the federal government took the initiative in this regard during the 1950s. The reorganization began in 1953–54 with the establishment of a new division within the Department of National Health and Welfare to be known as "Northern Health Services." Its purpose was to co-ordinate existing health services in the territorial north generally and to plan their future development. Although it was responsible for dis-charging the duties of the federal government in the Yukon, where it operated the new Whitehorse hospital as described above, for example, Northern Health Services was primarily designed as a kind of depart-ment of public health for the Northwest Territories. Initially operated as an agency organized and financed by the federal government, during the first few years of its operation attempts were made to turn it into an organ of the Northwest Territories administration. Thus, in 1957, the government of the Northwest Territories began sharing with the federal Department of National Health and Welfare the cost of operating the facilities of Northern Health Services in the Territories by assuming a part of the total cost of operating such facilities as nursing stations, health centres, and hospitals in a proportion equal to the non-native population being served by them.

In 1959 the Northwest Territories Council approved in principle the establishment of a hospital insurance plan similar to the plans operating in the various provinces. Such a plan, financed from general tax revenues and a *per diem* co-insurance fee, was subsequently implemented. The additional expenses incurred by the territorial government thereby were met by means of an increase in the territorial tax on fuel oil and liquor. The further "modernization" of health services in the Northwest Territories in the early 1960s took the form of increased public investments in new hospitals combined with a reduction in the extent of the nongovernmental hospital facilities previously relied upon. Although this replacement of church-organized facilities by governmental facilities did not proceed as rapidly in the case of hospitals as it did in the case of schools, such a development was perceivable during the late 1950s and the early 1960s. In 1961, for example, a new eighty-bed hospital was opened at Inuvik to replace the two mission hospitals operated in the old settlement of Aklavik. At the same time the rated capacity of the hospital system in the Northwest Territories was greatly reduced, being 248 in 1962 compared to 607 in 1959. "This reduction in rated capacity," the Territorial Hospital Services Board reported at the time, "is in accordance with the general Health Plan for the Northwest Territories, which proposes an eventual reduction in the number of beds to a more realistic level in comparison with the rest of Canada, having regard to the sparsity of population and the inherent transportation and economic problems."[16] The rated capacity of hospitals per one thousand of population in the Territories in 1962 was 10.33, compared to 2.40 in the Yukon and 5.75 in Canada.[17]

PUBLIC WELFARE AND SOCIAL SECURITY PROVISIONS IN THE YUKON AND NORTHWEST TERRITORIES

Prior to the appearance of large-scale public welfare measures in Canada during the 1940s, the task of caring for the disabled and indigent in the Yukon and Northwest Territories was left largely to private charity, the fur-trading companies, and the police. As already noted, the missions provided a few "industrial homes" for some of those unable to support themselves and the mission hospitals often provided shelter of this kind

[16]"Annual Report of the Territorial Hospital Insurance Services Board for the year Ending December 31, 1961," in Council of the Northwest Territories, *Votes and Proceedings*, 1963, p. 116.
[17]D.B.S., *Hospital Statistics, 1962*, Volume I, Table 13, p. 62. These data show large annual fluctuations even in the number of operating hospitals reporting. The N.W.T. rated capacity reached a record low of 4.26 beds per 1000 of population in 1961.

as well as medical care for residents of the area. The trading companies at one time operated elaborate systems of "credit" which, during hard times, served an important "relief" function as well, for it was in the interest of the trading company to keep its combined suppliers and customers through the periodic "seasons of distress" to which they were subjected by the vagaries of nature and the uncertainty of the white man's demand for furs. Formally, of course, the Indians of the northern territories were entitled to the same welfare benefits as their relations in the provinces under the provisions of the Indian Act, but in practice their needs were easily overlooked in the remote and unorganized areas of the territorial north. Much of the administration of Indian affairs fell to the police in such circumstances. Nevertheless, public funds were made available for the relief of Indians (and Eskimos)[18] in these areas. So far as the white and Métis population of the north was concerned, both the administrative provisions and the money were lacking until after World War II. Formally, indigent "white status" residents of the Yukon and Northwest Territories were the responsibility of the territorial councils and special arrangements were made from time to time in individual cases by these councils. But, especially in the Northwest Territories, only token appropriations of public funds were made for such purposes, even as late as the 1930s. The police apparently attempted, under these circumstances, to ensure only that persons not otherwise provided for not be allowed "actually to starve."[19]

With the creation of more extensive federally supported welfare programmes in the rest of Canada during the 1940s, an entirely new order of benefits became available to the native and "white" population of the territorial north. This threatened to precipitate, of course, a general upheaval in the economic and social arrangements in the area. As we have seen, a large part of the territorial population had a traditional material standard of life which hovered around a rather primitive subsistence equilibrium point determined by the income (cash and credit) derived from the fur trade, the uncertain proceeds of the hunt, the charity of the missions, and the judiciously administered supplies of emergency rations doled out by the representatives of the state in the area. The application of major national social welfare schemes, such as the system of family allowances introduced in Canada during the

[18]The legal judgment of the Supreme Court of Canada not withstanding, the welfare of the Eskimo population has traditionally been administered by the federal government's northern administration agencies rather than by its Indian affairs agency.

[19]See *Minutes of the Council of the Northwest Territories,* June 26, 1931, I, p. 199.

1940s, to such an economically backward community immediately created the possibility that such unearned income would come to be regarded as a substitute for the small income to be earned in such an area.[20] Although much more information is required before any serious assessment of this possibility can be made, the existence of such fears in the minds of government policy-makers and administrators responsible for the application of these programmes in the north does help to explain the surprisingly modest *per capita* outlays made under these schemes in the northern Territories.

It appears that government policy during the first decade or so after the introduction of these programmes was to administer them in such a way as to restrict the amount of assistance actually made available to certain groups in the area. But apart from a more paternalistic and perhaps less liberal administration of the schemes during the early stages of their implementation in the north, the main federally supported welfare programmes—the family allowance and old age security programmes—were, by the early 1960s, being conducted in the territorial north much as they were in the rest of Canada. The family allowance programme was administered in the Territories by the .Department of National Health and Welfare through its regional director for the Yukon and Northwest Territories located in Ottawa. In 1961 the *per capita* family allowance payments, as shown in Table 9.7, were higher in the Yukon and Northwest Territories than in most other provinces. This was largely due, of course, to the relatively large part of the territorial population in the age groups eligible to receive family allowances although it will be noted that, in that year, the *per capita* rate in the Territories was approximately the same as in New Brunswick and considerably lower than in Newfoundland. The payments were received by all persons in the Territories—those of white status, Indians and Eskimos alike. The federal old age security programme provided a pension of $65.00 a month payable by the federal government to all persons 70 years of age and over and, like the family allowance programme, this scheme was administered and financed in the Territories by the federal government in the same way as in the provinces. The payments made under this scheme in the Territories were, however, very much lower in total amount than in any of the provinces. It will be seen in Table 9.7 that in 1961 the *per capita* old age security payments in the Yukon and Northwest Territories were $10.95 compared to the highest provincial *per capita* figure of $47.09 for Prince Edward Island. The

20See, for example, the discussion in *ibid.*, August 9, 1950, XIX, p. 3856.

reasons for this discrepancy may be found in the age distribution of the northern population and in the fact that many residents of the Territories may have been either unaware that they were eligible for such benefits or unable to provide acceptable proof of their eligibility.

The principal welfare programmes which have been jointly administered by the federal and provincial governments elsewhere in Canada were also provided in the Territories by the agreements made between the federal government and the two territorial councils. These arrangements provided old age assistance, allowances for blind persons, allowances for disabled persons, and unemployment assistance. The total *per capita* costs of these programmes have been considerably lower in the Yukon and Northwest Territories than in the provinces. For the fiscal year ending in March, 1962, for example, the *per capita* cost of these programmes in the Yukon and Northwest Territories was approximately one-half the cost of the programmes in all the provinces.

During the 1950s all of the federal and federal-territorial programmes just referred to were applied more or less equally to all the ethnic groups living in the northern Territories. In addition to such welfare programmes as these, a number of measures were also implemented for different ethnic groups and these were administered by different agencies. Thus the territorial councils provided child welfare services, rehabilitation services, and social assistance or "relief" measures for white status residents of the Territories. Similar programmes were provided for Indians by the Indian Affairs Branch, and for Eskimos by the Northern Administration Branch. Details of these programmes varied somewhat, but in general they provided this type of welfare service fairly equally to the various ethnic groups living in the Territories—although there were charges of unfairness in the administration of them from time to time.[21]

In addition to these welfare programmes which provided direct benefits to residents of the Territories, a number of programmes were also designed to provide benefits indirectly by creating income-earning opportunities, especially for Indians and Eskimos. Although administered by different agencies, the programmes of this type for Indians and Eskimos were essentially the same. Often referred to as "economic development" programmes, these measures sought to create employment for natives by encouraging the development of native enterprises of various kinds. This was done by making available easy credit facilities

[21]See, for example, Council of the Northwest Territories, *Votes and Proceedings* 1962, p. 26.

for individuals and co-operative organizations. The funds were relatively easy to obtain, the terms for repayment were generous, and the interest charges were generally very low. As they were applied in the Territories, however, these measures were not unique, for similar assistance was available to natives in the provincial parts of Canada as well. The specific programmes involved tried to encourage natives to develop agricultural activities where this seemed possible, to stimulate the growth of home and handicraft industries, to instruct and interest natives in the economical management of fur, fish, and other wildlife resources, and even to operate retail stores. At time of writing the majority of these programmes were of very recent origin and, especially where the Indian population was concerned, this approach to the problem of low native income had not been much developed. Of particular interest in the context of this discussion, however, is a programme of this general type which was pursued over a long period of time—the attempt to develop reindeer herding in the northern part of Mackenzie District.

The Reindeer Project

Suggestions that reindeer be established in northern Canada may be traced back to early in the century. In 1913, for example, the Yukon Territorial Council, influenced by successful experience with reindeer herding in Alaska, requested the federal government to "cause to be procured and established in Yukon Territory a herd of reindeer and to cause to be made from time to time provision for the care and herding of same until the same shall become self-sustaining."[22] No official action on such proposals was taken, however, until the federal government appointed a Royal Commission in 1922 to enquire into the feasibility of establishing reindeer herding in the north.

During the late 1920s a reconnaissance of possible range areas suitable for reindeer was made and, in 1929, three thousand reindeer were purchased from an Alaska reindeer company. These reindeer were driven overland to Canadian territory in 1933 and were successfully placed on a reservation lying east of the Mackenzie delta in 1935. The object of the experiment was apparently to interest Eskimos in the herding of reindeer so that they would be able to provide themselves with income from the sale of reindeer hides and reindeer meat, to provide themselves with an additional direct source of food and clothing, and even, perhaps, transportation, for the reindeer were capable of being used as draft animals. The government's procedure was to acquire the services of experienced

[22]Yukon Territory, *Journals of the Yukon Council* (1913), XIII, 81.

Laplanders to help manage the herd and to train young natives in the techniques of reindeer herding and management.[23] Each year the herd was thinned out by slaughtering unneeded animals and the meat and hides were distributed and sold to religious missions or turned over to natives in the area. It was found that the physical conditions of the reindeer range were satisfactory and the herd increased in size very rapidly during the late 1930s rising from a total of 2,370 animals in 1935 to 4,500 in 1938.[24] In that year the herd was split and 950 animals were moved to Anderson River 150 miles east of the reservation and placed under the management of Eskimos, one of whom had been trained as an apprentice herder.

It was intended that this and subsequent native herds could be developed from the main herd with the natives paying back the breeding stock which they had initially been provided with. This first native herd developed satisfactorily despite the difficulties encountered in providing the necessary amount of constant supervision of the animals while at the same time permitting them to range over a sufficiently large area to prevent overgrazing of the mosses upon which they lived. In 1940 a second native herd was separated from the main herd and established near Horton River about 250 miles away from the main herd. In the spring of 1943 the first large sale of reindeer meat from a native herd took place when over 300 of the best animals were slaughtered and the carcasses sold for over $7,000.

The programme appeared to be developing well at this time with the number of animals rising to over 9,000 in 1942 and the programme of training native herders and establishing additional native herds continuing to expand as well. In the war years, however, the problem of interesting a sufficient number of natives in the reindeer industry was aggravated by the appearance of alternative employment opportunities in the northern areas. It was admitted in 1943 that with high fur yields combined with good prices natives were not only reluctant to become involved in the reindeer programme but many of those who had been

[23]From the outset it was evident that it would not be easy to induce the Eskimos to take up the new way of life associated with reindeer herding; see "Report of the Inter-departmental Reindeer Committee," March 6, 1935, in *Minutes of the Council of the Northwest Territories*, IV, p. 704.

[24]Data in this section is from the reports of the Inter-departmental Reindeer Committee (set up to advise the government on the reindeer project) found in the *Minutes of the Council of the Northwest Territories* for the period from 1935 to the late 1940s. Data for subsequent years is from the annual reports of the Department of Resources and Development for the years 1951–53 and the Department of Northern Affairs and National Resources for the years 1954–60.

employed in it deserted it for the more attractive income possibilities of the fur trade. The following year in 1944 the programme received a serious set-back with a tragic wreck of a native schooner during a severe storm which caused the death not only of the government supervisor of the two native herds but also of the two native proprietors of these herds. The native herds became scattered before new arrangements for their management could be made and the entire programme appears to have fallen into confusion. Many of the remaining animals of the native herds were subsequently rounded up and placed under government management. The total number of animals reported in 1946 had fallen to approximately 6,500 and continuing difficulty in interesting natives in herding was reported by the government, but despite these discouraging circumstances the government persisted in its policy of attempting to involve natives in the reindeer industry. After the end of World War II the government undertook to improve its management of the herds, to recruit young natives for training, to improve its herding procedures, and to develop more up-to-date marketing and processing facilities for the products of the industry. Revenues from the sale of these products remained very small, however (around $3,000 to $4,000), although some additional use was made of the industry by shipping reindeer skins to the eastern arctic for use by Eskimos there.

By the early 1950s enough progress had been made once again to place branch herds under native management and, by 1952, in addition to the main government herd there were three smaller herds under native control once again. Retailing arrangements were made at this time to improve the economic benefits available to the native herders and the Hudson's Bay Company was enlisted as a wholesaling agency which purchased reindeer meat and sold it through its retail outlets under a meat-marketing plan sponsored by the federal Department of Resources and Development. The gross revenue from the sale of reindeer meat for the fiscal year 1952–53 exceeded $15,000. Refrigeration facilities were provided at Aklavik which became the central storage depot for reindeer meat and portable freezing equipment was made available for the storage of meat at other locations in the reindeer region. The expansion of native herds continued and by 1956 there were four native herds in addition to the main government herd.

The policy of developing native herds in this way appears, however, to have encountered serious difficulties which showed up in the deterioration in the reindeer population during the later years of the decade. Although the total number of reindeer had risen to almost 8,500 by 1951 this number declined thereafter and reached a low of approximately 5,300 by 1958. The reasons for this were apparently connected with mismanagement of the native herds. Heavy losses of animals were incurred as a result of straying, injury, and disease. Consequently, in the late 1950s, the government retreated from its policy of encouraging the development of native herds and adopted a new policy of consolidating the herds and bringing them under centralized and more efficient management. In 1960 the government turned over management of its main herd to a private contractor from Edmonton who undertook to develop it on a commercial basis. A second herd was placed under Eskimo management and supervised by the professional Lap manager employed by the operator of the main herd.

Despite the apparent failure of the reindeer experiment, at least in so far as it had not become a significant source of native employment and income, the federal government was not deterred from undertaking similar programmes, especially for the benefit of the Eskimos, during the later 1950s. Indeed, in 1958 when the prospects for the reindeer industry looked most dismal, the Department of Northern Affairs and National Resources was acquiring six yak to serve as the nucleus for a pilot study designed to interest Eskimos in yak herding. At the same time a variety of other projects were being implemented. These included the establishing of an arctic char fishery in the eastern arctic, the manufacture of fur garments at Aklavik, and the development of Eskimo handicraft co-operatives throughout the north.

The proliferation of these new employment-creating projects, combined with the increased public spending on the more general welfare programmes and the massive investments in educational and health facilities described earlier in this chapter, points to a remarkable change in the policies of the federal government relating to the problem of welfare in the territorial north. When these new undertakings are compared to those relating to the provision of industrial facilities, such as electric power stations and transportation systems essential to the promotion of the long-term economic development of the area, it is difficult to avoid the conclusion that the federal authorities felt much more at home in the provision of welfare measures than in the provision of those forms of social overhead capital connected with economic development. Why this should have been so will be considered in Chapter 12 where the whole question of public policy is discussed in some detail.

IV. THE PROBLEM OF TERRITORIAL DEVELOPMENT

10 The Development Problem Re-stated

THE FIRST THREE parts of this study have examined the geographic and institutional backgrounds against which development in the territorial north has taken place, the activities of private agencies which have attempted to initiate this development and, finally, the main activities of the public agencies involved in the process. The reader acquainted with the extensive literature now available on the subject of economic development will have been struck, perhaps dismayed, by the simplicity of the approach used here to explain the process of development as it has occurred in the territorial north of Canada. Our approach has viewed the emergence of economic (and political) institutions in these areas in terms of the simplest elements of the so-called Canadian "staple theory" of economic development. This has seemed appropriate here simply because the northern areas of this country have constituted one of the most economically backward, but habitable, areas of known natural resource potential in the world during the twentieth century. Unlike most other economically *undeveloped* areas of the world, it has possessed so small a native population that throughout its history it has been one of the least densely populated land areas on earth, comparable perhaps with western and northern regions of Australia. But it has possessed natural resources and this fact alone accounts almost entirely for what economic, political, and social changes have occurred in the area during the past one hundred years.

The principal exceptions to the above generalization are the roles played by the religious and military agencies in the process of territorial development. The small native population was large enough to attract the missionaries and they were responsible for bringing some social overhead capital into the north in the form of churches, schools, and hospitals. Military operations, especially those undertaken during and after World War II, also on occasion caused labour and capital resources to be transferred from other parts of North America to the north. The most recent large-scale example of such a military undertaking was the construction of the Distant Early Warning radar "fence" across the top of the continent. There is reason to believe, however, that like the Alaska Highway and the Canol Project, the DEW line and various other smaller military ventures in the north had a relatively small effect on the long-term economic development of the area.

This suggestion is of enough importance to our interpretation of the development problem in the north to warrant a short digression at this point to illustrate, by means of some further discussion of the DEW line, the way such unusual undertakings have, and have not, affected the main course of development.

Like the Alaska Highway and the Canol Project, the DEW line was conceived as an instrument for continental defence. Like them, it entailed the performance of prodigious engineering feats; the expenditure of enormous amounts of public money (perhaps more than $500,000,000); and the establishment of facilities in the far north possessing little direct economic value for the area itself. The similarities are further enhanced by the possibility that the DEW line may well have been obsolete, at least in terms of its intended function as a defence against the manned bomber, almost as soon as it was completed.

The DEW line project grew out of the alarm created in the United States by the successful testing of an atomic bomb by the Soviet Union in 1949. Following a number of technological advances, both in the design of a radar warning system and in techniques of radio communications, it became technically feasible in the early 1950s to consider the installation of a series of radar stations in the high arctic for the purpose of providing several hours warning of an enemy bombing attack from the north. Despite the general lack of enthusiasm which greeted the first proposals for such a system, one of the last acts of the Truman administration in 1952 was to authorize its construction. Planning of the project went ahead slowly under the new Eisenhower administration until late in 1954, when a "crash" programme was undertaken in an attempt to complete the system by July, 1957.[1]

The basic elements of the programme were the 50-odd radar stations to be strung out along the arctic coast of North America from Alaska to the east coast of Baffin Island—a distance of some 3,000 miles. These

[1]C. J. V. Murphy, "The Polar Watch," *Fortune*, LVI (December, 1957), 246.

stations consisted of large electronic installations, structures to house the equipment and the men to operate it, electric power generating units, heating plants, fuel storage systems, and an air-strip. The main stations were staffed by about forty civilian workers and a number of military men. The creation of these stations involved the designing of suitable structures to withstand the arctic climate; the transportation of these buildings, the necessary personnel, the equipment, and stores of operating supplies from the south into the arctic; and, finally, the erection of the stations on what were often extremely difficult building sites. The actual construction was undertaken by a large United States firm which built the stations in the western arctic, and two Canadian firms, which built the eastern two-thirds of the system.

The type of building devised for the DEW line stations was a "modular" system of prefabricated wooden units sixteen feet wide, twenty-eight feet long, and ten feet high, mounted on low stilts (to prevent drifting snow from building up around them) and fitted together end to end in a kind of stationary "train." The radar antennae themselves were housed in fifty-five foot plastic domes. Because of permafrost conditions encountered at most locations, it was necessary to lay thick "pads" of gravel beneath the buildings, air-strips, and connecting roads at each site. It was estimated that ten million cubic yards of gravel were used in the project.[2]

Various modes of transportation were used to construct and to service the DEW line stations. The first stages of surveying and construction were carried out by air, using a great variety of aircraft ranging in type from the single-engined bush planes chartered for the project to the enormous "Globemasters" of the United States Tactical Air Command. The latter made over seven hundred landings on temporary ice landing-strips in the spring of 1955 to bring in the construction equipment and supplies needed to begin work at the main sites.[3]

The main task of moving heavy equipment and supplies into the construction sites was allotted to fleets of ocean-going ships, some sailing from Seattle for the western arctic and the others from Halifax and other Atlantic ports for the eastern arctic. Despite unusually severe ice conditions during the summer of 1955 a total of eighty-eight such vessels transported 129,000 tons of freight into the arctic. The following summer another 80,600 tons were shipped. Adding to this the estimated 140,000 tons transported by air during the construction phase of the

[2]H. La Fay, "DEW Line," *National Geographic Magazine*, DXIV (July, 1958), 136.
[3]*Ibid.*, p. 139.

project, the total freight moved north to build the DEW line would have totalled nearly 350,000 tons.[4]

The effect of this project upon the established economy and life of the far north is difficult to assess. Certainly the initial effect was to create "boom" conditions throughout the entire area and to raise the levels of employment and income there to unprecedented levels. Direct employment opportunities were created for Eskimos at some locations and employment for other residents of the Territories was generated by the boom in transportation and various other local industries throughout the whole area of the territorial north. Much of the labour used directly to build and subsequently to operate the system was, of course, brought in for the purpose from outside. One estimate of the number employed by the various contractors in this way during the peak of construction was seven thousand.[5] Some indication of the amount of continuing employment created by the DEW line in the Northwest Territories is provided by the following data derived from the records of the Northwest Territories Workmen's Compensation Administration:[6]

YEAR	TOTAL AVERAGE MONTHLY EMPLOYEES (number)	TOTAL PAYROLL (dollars)
1953	13	42,519
1954	288	796,146
1955	1751	11,216,611
1956	4140	32,935,579
1957	1245	5,855,670
1958	1011	8,167,614
1959	1197	9,746,168
1960	1807	13,904,976
1961	1429	10,897,954
1962	1575	11,857,424

Comparing these figures with the employment and labour income created in the Northwest Territories by the mining industry during the late 1950s and early 1960s, it may be noted that the DEW line provided twice as much labour income and almost double the amount of employment that the mining industry did. It would be easy to exaggerate the importance of this to the economy of the Territories, however, for the

[4]Data after Murphy, "The Polar Watch," p. 255.
[5]H. La Fay, "DEW Line," p. 141.
[6]*Tenth Annual Report of the Northwest Territories Workmen's Compensation Administration*, printed as Appendix "G" in Council of the Northwest Territories, *Votes and Proceedings*, 1963, pp. 179–96.

DEW line operations were kept separate from the established economic (and social) life of the north both by their location and by deliberate government policy. The latter was prompted, not only by the obvious military considerations which gave the United States government an interest in isolating the DEW line activities, but also, in the case of the Canadian government, by the traditional concern for the welfare of the native people in the area. An apparent dilemma confronting the Canadian authorities in its policy in this regard was that of minimizing the potentially harmful effects of a sudden exposure of the Eskimo to modern life as represented by the DEW line outposts while at the same time allowing him to take advantage of an unprecedented opportunity to earn a money income—especially when it came at a time when the fur trade could no longer provide such an income.

Because of this isolation imposed on the DEW line, its chief significance in the context of northern development, as was the case of the great military projects of World War II, is to be found not so much in its direct effect on the territorial economy as in its contribution to our knowledge of the area. Like Canol and the Alaska Highway, it demonstrated that what could be built and done in the south could be built and done in the north, although it would cost more to do it. In addition to such general lessons, however, the DEW line project also made a number of specific contributions to our knowledge of the arctic. One of these was that a newly developed system of radio communication could be used to provide, for the first time, radio transmissions which would not be affected by the difficult atmospheric conditions often encountered in northern regions. Another was the final charting of a Northwest Passage which would permit navigation of the arctic coast from the Atlantic to the Pacific by deep-draft ships.

One of the prerequisites for the effective operation of a distant early warning system was a reliable means of communication between the radar stations and the defence headquarters far to the south and among the various stations comprising the "fence" itself. Orthodox radio communication systems have often proved unreliable in the north because of interference created by intense "magnetic storms" which can at times completely obliterate short- and long-wave radio transmissions in the area. At the time the DEW line project was first being considered, however, a government sponsored research programme had just yielded a technique for bouncing high frequency radio signals off the troposphere and ionosphere. This "forward scatter" technique proved to be unaffected by atmospheric disturbances and thereby permitted the design of a radio communication system for the DEW line. Further military and civilian applications of this technique subsequently greatly improved communications throughout the territorial north.[7]

The second specific contribution of the DEW line project which may, eventually at least, prove valuable for the development of the arctic part of the continent was the charting and navigation of the arctic coast in much more detail than had previously been attempted. If the DEW line project was to utilize ocean-going ships to transport equipment and supplies to the proposed stations, it was necessary to obtain much more specific hydrographic information relating to the arctic coast than was then available.

A number of surveys were subsequently carried out during the summers from 1954 to 1957 by Canadian and United States vessels in these waters surrounding the arctic islands of Canada. These, and the voyages of the supply ships themselves, added not only to the knowledge of water and ice conditions in specific areas such as the hazardous Foxe Basin area, but led to the completion, after centuries of exploration, of the charting of a practical northern sea route from the Atlantic to the Pacific.[8] Whether or not such a sea-route along the arctic coast of North America will ever be economically valuable or not remains to be seen. Once again, however, comparison with the Alaska Highway is invited, for the arctic sea-route traced out in the summer of 1957 may yet open up the arctic north to further exploration and development in much the same way that the Alaska Highway and its associated air-fields opened up the sub-arctic northwest—even though it did not provide an immediately useful transportation facility for civilian purposes.

It would appear then that the large-scale military projects carried out in the north, such as the DEW line and the projects of the early 1940s described earlier, may have contributed indirectly to the long-term processes of economic development there. Nevertheless, attention in this study has been focused mainly on the economically more fundamental process whereby capital and labour were transferred to the northern Territories because of the natural resources discovered there. The subsequent establishment of productive activity in the northern Territories, which involved production both for "export" from the region and for the satisfaction of local needs within its boundaries, depended upon the

[7]At time of writing, tropospheric scatter systems were being constructed to connect Hay River in the southern part of the District of Mackenzie to Cambridge Bay in the high arctic.

[8]See C. J. Marshall, "Operation Bellot," *Canadian Geographical Journal*, LVII (September, 1958), 104–11.

quantity (and quality) of these inputs of labour (including the skills of managers as well as of technicians and the various grades of trained workers required) and capital goods of various kinds. The quantity of such inputs available in the Territories naturally depended upon the relative attractiveness of the alternative uses to which these versatile and mobile factors of production could be put. Thus, in so far as private *entrepreneurs* have been responsible for such resource-allocating decisions, we should expect that, normally, labour and capital were applied to northern land resources when it appeared more profitable to do this than to apply them to the development of resources located elsewhere. But this understanding of the relative profitability of such undertakings must rest upon some estimate of the returns to be expected from them and the outlays required prior to the realization of these returns—that is, upon the relative revenues and the relative cost expected to be associated with each unit of the product produced.

In our examination of the various resource developments which have been undertaken in the territorial north, attention was focused primarily upon the cost (supply) factors involved. Although ample evidence was found in our study of the development of specific industries in the Territories to attest to the great importance of revenue or demand influences as determinants of the level of activity in these industries, no effort was made to analyze these factors in detail. In the development of mining, for example, we noted how fluctuations in world metal prices were responsible for the opening-up or closing-down of operations on known deposits of minerals and also how they affected the level of exploratory work. But we have assumed that such factors affected equally the *alternative* employments for the labour and capital resources involved. High gold prices, for example, encouraged *entrepreneurs* not only to press more vigorously to develop mineralized areas on the geographic frontiers of the industry, including the territorial areas, but also to put more resources into the further development of known areas. Obviously this was not invariably the case, but it does not seem likely that major differences in the relative attractiveness of, let us say, northern and southern mining properties were greatly affected by differentials in the impact of demand changes upon them. Such major and *general* differences would seem to have been the result of differentials in the various cost factors involved on the "supply" side of the analysis. These were examined in the context of the historical record of industrial development as set out in Part II of this study and, in Chapters 6 and 7 of that part, some attempts to analyze these factors were reported and considered. Although much more detailed analysis of this kind is required before any unchallengeable conclusions can be drawn in this regard, our examination suggested that throughout the history of the Territories, the relatively high costs of production in all the activities carried on there were possibly more the consequence of the relative lack of investments in large-scale and efficient "social overhead capital" facilities than they were the consequence of such factors as distance and climate which have hitherto been emphasized in popular, and even in "scientific," discussions of the north.

One reason for the scarcity of such overhead capital facilities throughout the Territories has been the simple fact that the demand for the services of such facilities there was always small because of the low absolute level of investment in directly productive activities such as mining, and because of the wide dispersion of these activities over an immense geographical area. Such conditions seldom permitted a sufficient concentration of demand for the services of social overhead capital facilities to become established in a particular location. It is not surprising, then, that private *entrepreneurs* were not in many cases willing to invest in large-scale facilities to provide such services on a commercial basis. The few notable exceptions, such as the White Pass and Yukon Route system, arose from circumstances which made possible a form of monopoly operation through which the firm could use its price policy to recoup returns on its investments from a wide range of firms and even individuals benefitting both directly and indirectly from its operations. More commonly, however, and this phenomenon is not restricted to northern Canada, such facilities have been provided by governments rather than by private *entrepreneurs*. The reasons for this are complex and well-discussed in the extensive literature devoted to public utilities. But of particular interest to students of the processes of development in undeveloped areas is the great advantage government enterprise has over private enterprise in financing investments in such facilities. That we speak of the facilities created by such acts of investments as constituting "social overhead" capital suggests that their benefits are conferred rather generally upon the community at large and, consequently, not only the users (customers) of the utilities but also the general public might be expected to assist in financing the undertakings. The former contribute by means of the prices paid for the services directly received, the latter through the general tax system.

Whether or not such an approach is thought justified, one aspect of the development process in the territorial north which we have noted was the absence of such publicly sponsored undertakings during most of the area's economic history. The reasons for this, as is apparent from our examination of the area's history, were not only to be found in the lack of demand for such investments, but also in the policies and, indeed, in the very *structure* of government in the north. Enthusiasm for public initiative in providing social overhead capital facilities, both of the welfare type (schools, hospitals, recreational facilities) and of the natural resource-developing type (transportation and power facilities) has always been, not surprisingly, more conspicuous at the territorial level of government than at the federal level, whenever the territorial level of government contained some representation of local interests. As we saw in Part I, however, the system of territorial government devised for the northern part of Canada not only minimized the influence of local interests upon policy at that level, but the financial arrangements made it virtually impossible for the territorial government to implement measures arising out of such influence whenever it did make itself felt. This weakness of the territorial government arose largely, as we have also seen, from the constitutional provisions which removed control over natural resources from the jurisdiction of the territorial administration. This not only served to transfer the responsibility and the initiative for the development of such resources from the territorial government to the federal government, but it also eliminated the only major source of revenue which might have been available to the territorial government for financing the investments it might have undertaken in resource-developing capital.

When we examined the policies of the federal government with regard to its sponsoring or initiating of these social overhead capital facilities we found a remarkable lack of interest in providing them. Indeed, the characteristic attitude of that level of government could until recently have been described as a policy of "developmental *laissez-faire*" so far as the remaining federal lands were concerned.

At least three explanations for this traditional federal attitude can be identified. One of these was the concern of the federal government for the welfare of the native population of the Territories. It has been suggested that at one time it was believed that the welfare of the natives of the area could be best promoted by leaving them in the modified "state of nature" created by the fur traders and the missionaries.[9] If such a notion had any influence this would have stood in marked contrast to the federal government's policy with respect to the native

[9]See pp. 55–6 above.

population located elsewhere in Canada. But if the northern Territories were thought of as being devoid of economic potential in relation to the national economy, it may have seemed economical to treat it as a single immense "reservation" within which the influence of the outside world would be restricted to that exerted by the fur traders, the missionaries, and the nominal force of national police stationed there to maintain order and to represent the state. Such an interpretation of federal policy seems especially plausible in the case of the Northwest Territories prior to the 1930s.

A second and perhaps more general explanation sometimes offered for the absence of federal participation in the development of the territorial north was the preoccupation of that government with more pressing items on the nation's agenda. These would include, in historical sequence, the opening of the prairie west, waging World War I, the Depression of the 1930s, the pursuit of World War II, and "reconstruction" during the later 1940s.[10] But again, acceptance of this rather facile interpretation of events seems inconsistent with the federal policy in general over these long periods of time and would commit one to the belief that some absolute limit on the quantity of public thought and action exists for any point in time. Furthermore, it could well be argued that much of the federal involvement in territorial life which did occur was the *consequence* of such events as World War II and even of the preceding Depression. For example, much road construction in the Yukon occurred during the 1930s as a result of public works programmes sponsored by the federal government to create employment. And we have also seen how World War II was the direct cause of a great deal of similar work throughout the Yukon and the Northwest Territories.

A third possible explanation of the federal government's policy of developmental *laissez-faire* emerges from our survey of territorial development and would seem to be more fundamental than those just cited. Even if federal policy had been totally unconcerned with preserving the hegemony of the fur traders, missionaries, and police in the north, and even if no wars or depressions had occurred to distract the federal government from its work of promoting development of the national economy, it seems unlikely that a substantially greater effort would have been made to promote the development of the remaining federal lands by means of public investment in large-scale social over-

---

[10]See, for example, p. 52. Also F. H. Collins, *The Yukon Territory, A Brief Presented to the Royal Commission on Canada's Economic Prospects* (Ottawa: Queen's Printer, 1955), p. 6.

head capital facilities. By the time the question arose, let us say by the 1920s, the earlier enthusiasm for forcing extensive development in this way had disappeared in Canada. And this was the consequence not only of disenchantment with railways which had not magically proved to be self-justifying, but also by the growing influence of economic science on public servants. As we have seen, there is direct evidence that a knowledge of "sound economics" could be invoked thereafter to condemn public investments in social overhead capital facilities (or in anything else except in weapons of defence or destruction) in advance of a commercially produced demand for their services. That is, the orthodox economics of the day suggested (to some minds "proved") that the system of competitive markets would effect an optimum allocation of resources among alternative employments so long as these markets were allowed to function freely.

Anomalous as such an approach might seem in Canada, where the state has long had the responsibility for regulating such markets internally and externally, the analysis offered a convenient guide to those responsible for undertaking public investments in those facilities which, for one reason or another, private *entrepreneurs* would not or could not be allowed to undertake. If private investors in directly productive activities created by way of their efforts an adequate "effective demand" for the services of, say, a public utility, the latter would be able to operate without loss. This would indicate in a rough sort of way that the resources being committed to create such services were being efficiently used. But it would remain uncertain, of course, whether they were being used in the most effective way possible, for this would be ensured only if the profits of the utility were larger than they could be in any alternative use. And, given the context here, it would hardly be politically feasible to use a publicly owned firm to exploit a monopoly position to the point of maximizing its profits. But despite this limitation, the criterion of commercial feasibility provided the public investor with a useful guide to the application of public funds for the creation of such facilities.

That such a policy with respect to public undertakings in the Territories did exist is demonstrated not only by the various statements of policy noted in earlier chapters, but also by the observed tendency for investment in social overhead capital to lag behind investment in directly productive activity, especially in the cases of electric power and certain of the transportation facilities which we have examined. This lag, in turn, was revealed by the initiative taken by private *entrepreneurs* to provide themselves with such facilities, often on a surprisingly large scale, but always at great difficulty and expense in terms of operating efficiency and usually, sooner or later, leading to concentration of ownership and control of enterprise both in the particular and related areas of activity.

The ultimate effect of this must have been to reduce the efficiency of these operations relative to what could be achieved in competitive operations conducted in areas where circumstances permitted utilization of existing, large-scale, and often publicly financed housing, hospitals, schools, recreational and other community facilities. Although this disadvantage did not prohibit all private investment in directly productive activities it undoubtedly restricted it. The ventures which did succeed under these circumstances were those which overcame the simple lack of such facilities. This was done, as we saw in Part II, by attempting to develop only certain types of resources, by operating only on very high-grade occurences of these resources, and by trying to minimize the inefficiency of their own investments in social overhead capital. The latter effort was reflected in a high degree of integration of activities, both horizontally and vertically, as described in Chapter VII. But there were, of course, limits to the effectiveness of such measures. The individual privately owned firm developing land resources in an undeveloped area is not well suited to the provision of services which are able to confer widely dispersed benefits upon a larger community. Although these benefits accruing to the various enterprises, and even to individuals, in a given area might in *total* justify the use of resources to produce the capital facility required to generate these benefits, a private firm (especially one primarily concerned with operating a mine or other natural resource-exploiting business) is likely to be unwilling to finance such an undertaking even if it is large enough to consider doing so in the first place.

The simple reason for such a reluctance is that, especially in a remote, undeveloped area, many of the benefits generated by certain acts of an investment are apt to be realized by organizations other than the one undertaking the initial investment—and the latter may find it difficult or even impossible to levy charges against these beneficiaries of its enterprise commensurate with the service being provided. In other words, the individual firm in such a situation is likely to evaluate the feasibility of an investment in terms of its cost relative to total realizable returns. While it is true that this phenomenon exists everywhere, it is particularly significant in an undeveloped area where almost *any* act of investment, whether in directly productive activities or in social overhead capital makes subsequent development easier and cheaper and where, as we saw in Chapter 9, the scale of operations is so critical a factor influencing operating costs.

The first firm to begin operating in a virgin area must import from "outside" all the labour and equipment required to conduct its own operations. This will normally entail construction of some kind of transportation facilities, a camp-site, the producing plant, and related facilities. It will also have to arrange for the supply of fuel, food, and water. The establishment of such facilities and services in a previously *completely undeveloped* area will inevitably facilitate future developments there in many ways. It provides a basic system of facilities which will reduce the "remoteness" of the area for other firms which may locate there whether they are engaged in the same or in some other kind of activity.

It is true that in so far as such new firms rely directly upon facilities such as roads or power plants owned by the initial developer, the latter may be in a position to levy charges upon them equal to the benefits they are provided with. But there are many such benefits which may be too "indirect" to permit this. For example, the establishment of a local pool of labour by the original developer in an otherwise uninhabited area is something which may benefit other firms coming into the area without the original firm being in a position to charge them for these benefits. In Yellowknife, for example, the mining companies brought in a large "secondary" labour force made up of the married women and other dependants who accompanied the primary labour force of male mine workers. This secondary labour force provided remarkably cheap labour to local retailers who could not be charged for this benefit conferred upon them by the mining companies. Similarly, if there was native labour in the area which was trained and adapted to industrial employment by the original firm entering the area, this labour could be utilized by other firms subsequently establishing operations there.

The initial importation of capital goods may confer similar benefits upon other operators in an area. Suppose that the diesel-electric installation by one firm creates a local market for fuel oil. If local supplies of fuel oil are consequently developed, these will be available to new firms coming into the area and they will consequently be able to avoid the initial costs associated, for example, with flying fuel oil in from distant sources of supply. A great number of such pioneering works by early developers of an area will yield benefits to other private firms without cost to them. The effect of this may be to deter individual firms from taking the initiative in opening up such an area. But even more important than such considerations as these is the likelihood that individual firms, if they do decide to proceed with a venture in such an area, will undertake to develop sources of supply, transport, power, and other facilities only to the extent that is dictated by their own needs.

If subsequent development then takes place in the area, with other firms following the same kind of policy, the total resources committed to the provision of such facilities may exceed those which would have been required had the investments been made on a collective basis. This inefficient use of resources would show up, of course, in relatively high operating costs for each operation. This would be particularly true in the case of those facilities such as transportation and electric power which, as we have seen, are notable for the economies of scale realizable in them. If each firm operating in the area installed its own electric power plant and operated its own private transportation system the unit costs of such small-scale operations would inevitably exceed those attainable using facilities large enough to serve the several users collectively. But if such large-scale facilities were to be provided privately by a firm primarily concerned with directly productive activity, it would have to be willing to assume at the outset of its work in an area the heavy risk burden associated with "over-investing" in terms of current needs in the type of industrial facilities we have been discussing.

Only in rather unusual circumstances is it likely that a firm would accept such risks and responsibilities. More likely, judging from the history of such development in Canada, the individual firm would choose to minimize such investments by building only to meet its own requirements even if this meant accepting high operating costs. The latter could, of course, be so high as to make the entire investment unattractive, in which case the development would not take place. Thus, one disadvantage of this system of development in which those creating the demand for such services in an area are left to provide the means of satisfying them is that the most likely means to be employed will usually entail high operating costs which will, in turn, restrict the level of investment in directly productive activities based on the area's natural resource endowment. But an undesirable circular effect is thereby created, for this restriction on investments in directly productive activities in turn militates against the development of even a potential demand which could justify other types of investment, such as could be made by a public agency, in the kind of large-scale facilities which would reduce the level of operating costs. This dilemma is considered more fully in Chapter 12 below. Its effect in the Territories was, however, to restrict the level of development and to force what development did take place into the particular patterns which were described in Part II. At this point it will be convenient to sum up the development processes described earlier by drawing together some data to indicate more precisely just how limited the development in the territorial north had been to the early 1960s.

11 The Level of Development Attained

PER CAPITA INCOME estimates provide a rough indication of the level of economic development a country or area has attained. Such estimates are made by measuring the production of goods and services in the area during a specified period of time and by relating this total output to the size of the population among which it, or the proceeds from its sale, must be distributed. In this chapter we examine the growth of population in the northern Territories, the growth of production there, and the changes which have consequently taken place in territorial *per capita* income. It must be appreciated that our measurements here are extremely crude and that they deal only with those types of economic activity which involve commercial transactions, that is, transactions which show up in the operations of some "market." They exclude those activities, often important in the life of the aboriginal population, which are conducted on a production-for-use basis or which involve barter transactions in which money exchanges never do occur. Despite the significance of this non-commercial activity in the territorial north for the household economy of many of its natives, it would not appear to be useful to try to analyze the economy of the area in terms of a "native" or "domestic" sector and a "European" or "export" sector. As we saw in Part I the effect of the fur trade was to "commercialize" the native sector so far back in the history of the northern Territories that the entire economy had a commercial, export, basis for the whole period with which we have been concerned in this study. If the early modern history of the area's aboriginal population is understandable, as seems beyond question, in terms of its adaptation to the fur trade, its more recent history must be seen to have been dominated by the problem of adapting to the decline of that trade. The recent economic problems of

the native population of the north have been the consequence of the ✓
markets and technology of the twentieth century impinging not upon
a primitive native economy, but upon a native economy which had
adapted all too thoroughly to the markets and the technology of the
nineteenth century.

GROWTH OF THE POPULATION

Reasonably reliable population data for what is now the territorial north
as a whole goes back only to the National Census of 1921. As shown
in Table 11.1, in that year the total enumerated population in the Yukon
and Northwest Territories was 12,300, with 4,157 in the Yukon and
8,143 in the Northwest Territories. Separate data for the Yukon Territory are available from 1901. In that year the effect of the Klondike
boom is still evident in the cenus figure of 27,219. The collapse of the
boom and the conversion to large-scale techniques of placer gold-mining
led to a great reduction in population and by 1911 the census report had
only 8,512, a reduction of almost 69 per cent. Between then and 1911
the population of the Yukon was more than halved again as new mineral
developments failed to provide an adequate offset to the continued
concentration and mechanization taking place within the placer gold-
mining industry. This decline was not halted until later in the 1920s
when, as we saw earlier, developments in the Mayo district and in some
other mineralized areas created new employment opportunities in the
Territory.

The first flurry of mining activity also struck the Mackenzie in the
early 1920s, and these events are reflected in the census figures for 1931
which show a slight increase over the preceding decade of almost 2 per
cent in the Yukon and of over 14 per cent in the Northwest Territories,
most of the latter occurring in the District of Mackenzie. The next
three decades, the decades of the 1930s, 1940s, and 1950s, were marked
by continued population growth in the territorial north and the rate of
this growth, as shown in Table 11.2, greatly exceeded the national
average. Between 1931 and 1941 the population of Canada rose by
about 11 per cent but the territorial population rose by over 25 per cent
(from roughly 13,500 to almost 17,000). This was largely attributable to
growth of the white population in Mackenzie District where the rate of
population increase was over 29 per cent in this decade. In the Yukon,
the increase in activity in the placer gold-mining industry after 1935

was largely responsible for drawing additional population into that Territory and the overall increase there between 1931 and 1941 was a rather surprising 16 per cent to bring the total to almost 5,000 in the later year.

The great increase in activity through the territorial north during the years of World War II and of post-war reconstruction is reflected in a 50 per cent population increase between 1941 and 1951. This was chiefly attributable to a remarkable 85 per cent growth in the population of the Yukon Territory, although the Northwest Territories population grew by almost a third during this decade as well. These rates of growth in both of the territorial areas greatly exceeded the approximately 22 per cent rate achieved by the country as a whole between 1941 and 1951.

The extraordinary rate of growth in territorial population recorded during the 1940s continued undiminished throughout the 1950s. The total population of the territorial regions rose from about 25,000 in 1951 to roughly 38,000 in 1961. Thus, in 1961, the population of the territorial north was roughly half as large again as it was in 1951, although the population of Canada as a whole was only 30 per cent larger in 1961 than it had been ten years earlier.

We see then that the total territorial population increased by about three times between 1921 and 1961, growing from a total of 12,300 to 37,626, while the population of Canada roughly doubled during the same period, rising from less than 9 million in 1921 to over 18 million in 1961. While this more rapid rate of population growth in the territorial part of the country gave it a greater share of the total Canadian population, this share remained virtually insignificant as a part of the total. As shown in Table 11.1 the territorial population constituted 0.15 per cent of the national total in 1941 and by 1961 this had risen to only 0.21 per cent.

Analysis of the population growth of the territorial regions is difficult before 1941 simply because little effort was made to collect even reasonably accurate vital statistics or other population data for those regions until the re-awakening of interest in the north that took place after World War II. The available data do suggest, however, that what expansion of population did occur between the turn of the century and the beginning of World War II was entirely the consequence of the net migration of non-native persons attracted to the area by the development of resources there or sent to serve in the area by churches or by the federal government.

There is no evidence of growth in the native population of the area during this period. Indeed, the Indian population of the Yukon and of the Northwest Territories appears to have experienced an absolute decline during this period of time and it was not until 1954 that the census of Indians (conducted by the federal government every four years) shows a reversal of this trend. As shown in Table 11.3, the total Indian population of the Yukon and Northwest Territories declined from 6,456 in 1914 to 5,215 in 1949. If we assume that the reporting of this population improved over this period of time the decline in its size would be even greater than that indicated. The total Eskimo population of Canada was recorded, in a survey undertaken in 1927, as 7,103 and probably about 5,000 of these were located in the Territories. Again, difficulties in collecting data were such that the information reported must be viewed only as a more or less well-informed guess for these early periods; but it appears that the Eskimo population at least held its own until the early 1940s by which time it was showing signs of achieving a more positive rate of growth. The National Census of 1941 recorded 5,404 Eskimos living in the Northwest Territories.

Because of this decline or, at best, stagnation of the native population in the Territories, we may attribute the growth of territorial population before World War II to the expansion of the non-native population of the area. And this, in turn, must have been chiefly attributable to net migration into the Territories from other places in Canada or from abroad, for the rate of natural increase in the territorial population as a whole (native and non-native) was extremely low during this period. As shown in Table 11.4 the annual rate of natural increase in the Yukon Territory was actually *negative* most years during the 1920s and 1930s because of the aging of the white population which remained there after the boom of the 1890s and because of the high death rates which characterized the declining native population (which constituted about one-third of the Territory's population during the 1920s and 1930s). In the Northwest Territories, with the non-natives constituting an insignificant part of the total population before World War II (as shown in Table 11.5), a birth rate which approximated the Canadian average (of about 20) was offset during this period by a crude death rate much higher than the national average. As will be seen from Table 11.6, the crude death rate (deaths per thousand of population) in the Northwest Territories averaged 21 between 1926 and 1930 compared to 11.2 for Canada as a whole and this pattern remained typical throughout the remainder of the period. The result of this was a low rate of natural increase in the order of 4 to 5 per thousand of population.

After 1940, the causes of the population growth in the territorial north became more complex, for an extraordinary acceleration in the rate of natural increase was thereafter combined with greatly increased net migration to give the rapid population growth described above. It will be seen from Table 11.7, however, that the relative importance of these two factors in population growth differs greatly between the decade of the 1940s and the decade of the 1950s. During the 1940s, natural increase was responsible for adding less than half as many people to the population of the Territories as were added by net migration. Taking the territorial north as a whole, natural increase added 2,638 to the population between 1941 and 1951 compared to 5,520 added by apparent net migration (which included 750 immigrants from abroad). This pattern was completely reversed during the decade of the 1950s during which natural increase added 9,034 to the population of the Territories compared to an apparent net migration of only 3,492. It would appear, therefore, that the continuation of the rapid rate of population growth in the territorial north that was achieved during the war and early post-war period, largely as a result of people being attracted to the area from elsewhere, was sustained during the later post-war period by an extraordinary rate of natural increase within the Territories themselves.

The source of this increase in the rate of natural increase in the territorial north is to be found in a rather abrupt rise in the birth rate which began in 1940 in the north as it did elsewhere in Canada. But in the north, and especially in the Northwest Territories, as will be seen from Table 11.8, the rise was much more rapid than in the country as a whole. Even in the Yukon, where the birth rate had reached a low of 7.6 in 1936 compared to a national average of more than 20, the increase during the 1940s quickly put it up to levels ranging above the national average which, by the late 1940s was itself in the high 20s. Between then and 1961 the national rate never exceeded the 28.9 recorded in 1947 but the rate in the Yukon moved above 30 in the late 1940s and above 40 in the early 1950s to reach a peak of 47.6 in 1955. The Yukon birth rate subsequently declined somewhat, as did the national rate, but in 1961 was still much above it at 38.1 compared to 26.1. In the Northwest Territories the pattern was similar except that the birth rate there was considerably higher than the rate in the Yukon when the acceleration began, with the result that the rate in the Northwest Territories surpassed the national rate in 1941 (when the rates were 26.3 and 22.4 respectively) and remained greatly above it thereafter. While the national rate remained in the 20s, the rate in the Northwest Territories exceeded

40 for the first time in 1945 and hovered around that point for the next ten years. Unlike the Yukon rate (and the national average), however, after 1955 it showed a tendency to rise still higher instead of declining or levelling off. In 1960 the birth rate in the Northwest Territories reached a record 49.7 compared with 38.4 in the Yukon and 26.8 in Canada as a whole.

Although less spectacular than the change in the birth rate, it will be seen from the tables that changes in the death rate also contributed to the rise in the rate of natural increase in the territorial north during the 1940s and 1950s.

In the Yukon the death rate began an erratic but perceptible decline about 1943, although it was not until the middle 1950s that it became established at a level comparable to the Canadian average. In fact, in 1955, the Yukon rate, which had previously been as much as double the national rate in some years, fell below it and remained below it. In 1961 the Yukon death rate was 6.4 compared to the national average of 7.7. In the Northwest Territories, the death rate, like the birth rate, was generally higher than in the Yukon during the 1940s but because it declined after the war at about the same rate, it remained considerably above the rate in the Yukon and, consequently, very much above the national rate. The gap between all these rates showed signs of narrowing in the late 1950s and early 1960s, however, because the Northwest Territories rate continued to fall substantially (from 17.1 in 1957 to 11.4 in 1961) while the other rates seemed to be levelling off—with the Yukon's falling from 7.8 in 1957 to 6.4 in 1961 and the national rate from 8.2 to 7.7 in the same years. This, taken in conjunction with the absence of any falling off in the birth rate in the Northwest Territories, naturally invited speculation about the ultimate extent of the rise in the rate of natural increase which was possible in the Northwest Territories.

The prospects were made particularly interesting by the obvious possibility of further major reductions in the death rate occurring as a result of new health and welfare programmes in the Northwest Territories. For, in addition to the fact that the crude death rate in the Northwest Territories in 1961 was still much above the level achieved in the Yukon and elsewhere in Canada, it appeared certain that it was the absence of modern health and welfare facilities that was responsible for this rate remaining so high. This was supported by the barely credible infant mortality statistics set out in Table 11.9. The evidence on this point can be summarized by noting that while the infant mortality rate in Canada as a whole fell fairly steadily from over 90 (per thousand live births) in the late 1920s to a low of 27.2 in 1961, the rate in the Northwest Territories not only remained over 100 throughout this period but it was as high in the 1950s as in the 1930s. The rate of infant mortality in the Yukon, on the other hand, did decline during the thirty years between 1930 and 1960.

Appalling as it was by the standards of the western industrialized countries, the Yukon infant death rate appeared almost "civilized" compared with the rate in the Northwest Territories. The latter rate was exceeded only by the rate displayed by such primitive countries as Chile, which had a rate of 127 in 1960, and it compared unfavourably with the rate in the reporting districts of India, which was 100 in 1961. If such a high infant mortality rate as this does indicate the lack of adequate (by present standards) medical, educational, and related facilities, it was difficult in the early 1960s to avoid the conclusion that if such facilities were provided and the birth rate did not simultaneously decline sharply, the rate of natural increase in the Northwest Territories would reach a level seldom realized in human history. In 1961 the crude fertility rate in the Northwest Territories was 253.6 compared to 187.2 in the Yukon and 127.6 in the Canadian provinces.

In view of the tendency to associate such population phenomena as these with the aboriginal population of the territorial north, it is worth noting that the group officially designated as "natives" was a declining part of the territorial population during the period of rapid population growth which began in 1941. This is not surprising for the period 1941–51 during which, as we have seen, net migration accounted for twice as much of the decade's population growth as did natural increase. As shown in Table 11.5, during that decade those classed as natives fell from 30.7 per cent of the population to 17.2 per cent in the Yukon, from 78.6 per cent to 66.6 per cent in the Northwest Territories, and from 64.7 per cent to 48.7 per cent in the territorial north as a whole. But in the next decade, during which population grew mainly as a result of natural increase, the "native" population again declined, although to a lesser extent, falling to 15.1 per cent in the Yukon, 57.5 per cent in the Northwest Territories, and to 41 per cent of the population of both Territories taken together. Taken in conjunction with the fact that the rate of population growth in Mackenzie District was even more rapid than in the almost totally native-populated eastern arctic regions of the Northwest Territories, this suggests that the "non-native" (white and Métis) population of the north may also have been responsible for much of the natural increase recorded there after 1941.

If we assume that this non-native population was the part of the total population most likely to have benefitted from the higher income and from the access to modern health, welfare, and educational facilities made possible through industrial employment, it might be possible to explain their contribution to a high rate of natural increase in terms of low death rate. If the rest of the population had a higher death rate, this might account for whatever evenness in the rate of natural increase we might find throughout the population as a whole. But this leaves to be explained the remarkably high fertility rate, which would have to characterize the native population if this were true. While the advent of even slightly improved living conditions might lead us to expect a rapid rise in fertility in a native population once ruthlessly held in check by such elementary Malthusian factors as famine and disease operating to reduce the potential for giving birth as well as operating on the survival of those born, it is difficult to explain why fertility in such a population should subsequently have risen to such extraordinary levels as those shown in Table 11.10.

The investigation of the possible cultural and biological explanations of this phenomenon is beyond the scope of this study and must await more detailed and fundamental studies of the pattern of living in this economic hinterland of Canada. It seems likely, however, that the explanations, if they are found, will not be the most obvious ones. While it is true, for example, that (as shown in Table 11.11) the age composition of the territorial population is typically youthful, the effect of this on fertility was probably offset by other characteristics of a frontier population—notably the heavy excess of males and the fact that many of these males would be temporary residents of the area without much intention of "settling down" in it. Again, while the development of the country may have weakened such offsets to fertility, thereby explaining why the fertility rate should have risen in a developing frontier region, it does not help us to understand why, in absolute terms, fertility should have risen far above the level realized in even the most developed parts of the country. In view of the important implications of future population developments in the territorial north for economic policy and for the organization of public institutions there, further study of these demographic phenomena should receive the highest priority.

The geographical distribution of the population of the Territories has been remarkable, even by Canadian standards. The fact that the small total population of the northern regions has been located in such a number of small and widely separated communities underlies and, in the case of the native population, probably *reflects* many of the serious economic and political disadvantages of the northern Territories which have been referred to in earlier parts of this study. Such a population must face the greatest difficulties in obtaining any of the immense technological advantages embodied not only in such obvious types of industrial capital facilities as the transportation and power systems examined earlier, but also in the perhaps less obvious devices of modern life such as retailing and public welfare programmes. A system of health insurance may just as much depend on having a large number of participants to achieve low unit operating costs as a hydro-electric plant may depend upon having a minimum demand for its output to achieve the same objective. And the low unit operating costs of the supermarket or department store presupposes some minimum potential turnover. No one is surprised to hear that the Hudson's Bay Company has a different retail pricing policy in its fur-trading outlets in the Territories than in its city department stores to the south.

It will be seen from Table 11.12 that in 1961 over 60 per cent of the population of the territorial north resided in communities too small to be organized as units of local administration. The oldest organized communities in the territorial north are Dawson, founded during the Klondike rush at the end of the nineteenth century, and Whitehorse, formally organized in the first decade of the new century. The population of Dawson declined, of course, due to the change in the placer gold-mining industry after 1900, reached a census-year low of 819 in 1931, and remained thereafter at about the same level (except in 1941 when it was reported at slightly over 1,000). The population of Whitehorse declined from 727 in 1911 to a low of 331 in 1921, but then more than doubled over the next twenty years. Between 1941 and 1951 Whitehorse replaced Dawson as the chief centre of population in the Yukon Territory. The population of Whitehorse more than tripled between 1941 and 1951 and, partly because of incorporation of suburbs, doubled between 1951 and 1961. By 1961 Whitehorse contained more than one-third of the population of the Yukon Territory. The only other important organized community in the Yukon has been Mayo, a long-established centre near the silver-lead mines east of Dawson which was incorporated as a town following re-development of these resources in the late 1940s. Mayo remained a small centre, however, with its population rising from 241 in 1951 to only 342 in 1961. It should be noted, however, that all these settlements in the Yukon experience so large a seasonal fluctuation in population that these census figures provide only a rough indication of the actual size and importance of the settlements concerned.

The 30 to 40 per cent of the population of the Yukon which did not reside in the organized settlements of Whitehorse, Dawson, and Mayo was located chiefly in small settlements, many of which were established during the early years of the fur trade, or in the few mining camps such as those in the Mayo area, or along the route of the Alaska Highway. With the exception of Old Crow on the Porcupine River in the northwestern part of the Territory, most of these settlements were located in the relatively well-known southern part of the Territory and especially in the southwestern corner along the old river transportation route on the Yukon and its tributaries and along the modern route taken by the Alaska Highway. Many of these settlements were occupied primarily by natives and by Métis still living on trapping, hunting, and casual paid employment, supplemented by a few agents of the church or the state stationed in the community to provide educational, health, and administrative services of various kinds.

In the Northwest Territories there were no "organized" communities before the 1950s and most of the settlements located there were of the type just described in the Yukon, that is, largely native communities located in accordance with the dictates of the fur trade during the nineteenth century. Such settlements were most prevalent, of course, in the District of Mackenzie which has, since the data first became available in 1921, always held more than half the total population of the Northwest Territories as we know them today. The settlements which acquired some measure of local administrative organization in more recent years were all located in Mackenzie District and they all, for one reason or another, were centres to which unusually large numbers of white immigrants to the north were attracted. Yellowknife remained a predominantly white settlement after its inception as a servicing centre for the auriferous quartz mines in the vicinity in the late 1930s. Its census population grew slowly after 1951, rising from 2,724 in that year to 3,245 in 1961. Hay River was also first organized (like Yellowknife, as a local administrative district) during the period 1941–51 largely as a result of the white settlement occurring there in connection with the centre's importance to the Mackenzie river transportation system and the development of the Great Slave Lake fishery which was described in Chapter 3. The population of Hay River rose from approximately 800 in 1951 to over 1,300 in 1961. Both settlements were reorganized as "municipal districts" in 1953. Fort Simpson and Fort Smith were added to the list of organized communities in Mackenzie District in 1954 when they were created Local Improvement Districts. Fort Smith's white population derived largely from the centre's administrative function as the field headquarters of the federal government's Northwest Territories administration. The settlement's population grew from about 1,200 to almost 1,700 between 1956 and 1961. Fort Simpson differed from the other organized settlements in Mackenzie District in that, unlike them, its population remained predominantly native and, while the settlement acquired some importance as a transportation centre, it continued to resemble the other "trading-post" native settlements strung in a chain down the Mackenzie than centres such as Yellowknife, Fort Smith, or even Hay River. Its cenus population in 1956 was 495 and it had grown to 563 by 1961. The only other settlement treated as an organized community for census purposes in 1961 was the new model community of Inuvik in the Mackenzie delta, with a census population of 1,248 in that year, about 80 per cent of which was "non-native."

The result of this development of at least rudimentary municipal institutions in Mackenzie District during the post-World War II period was to bring the proportion of the population living in unorganized communities in the Northwest Territories as a whole down from 78 per cent in 1951 to 65 per cent by 1961. This part of the population, as in the Yukon, remained in widely scattered and predominantly native communities such as the important Indian settlements at Fort McPherson, Arctic Red River, Fort Good Hope, Fort Providence, Fort Franklin, Wrigley and Fort Norman along the Mackenzie and the Eskimo settlements such as Cambridge Bay, Perry River, Bathurst Inlet, Tuktoyaktuk, Cape Perry, Aklavik, and Coppermine along the arctic coast of the Northwest Territories. With the "non-native" population of the Territories concentrated in the few organized communities in Mackenzie District referred to earlier, we find that in 1961 roughly half the population in the District was native Indian or Eskimo and the other half was white and Métis. In the eastern arctic districts of Keewatin and Franklin, the native part of the population had a majority of 5 to 1, if the personnel stationed at DEW line posts is excluded.

The rate of population growth in the three districts of the Northwest Territories was similar enough over the thirty years from 1931 to 1961 to prevent any major shift of population from occurring among them, although between 1951 and 1961 the population in the arctic islands District of Franklin grew more rapidly than the population in the mainland District of Keewatin. Considering these arctic regions together, however, and comparing them to Mackenzie District, we see that the latter grew proportionately more rapidly. The population of Mackenzie was 57 per cent of the total for the Northwest Territories in 1931 and this proportion rose gradually but steadily over the next thirty years to reach 65 per cent in 1961. Thus it would appear that the Mackenzie area has not only dominated the Territories in terms of the absolute level of its development as this is reflected in its ability to support population, but also in terms of the rate of increase in this level of development.

THE LEVEL OF PRODUCTION

Physical measures of the production of the basic export commodities and of the main commodities produced in the territorial north for local consumption have been given in Chapters 3, 4, and 5. Here the various output data are collected on a net value of production[1] basis so as to provide some indication of both the level and the composition of commodity production in the Yukon and Northwest Territories since such data were first collected in 1920. Table 11.13 summarizes the current dollar net value of production for the primary (natural resource based) industries of the Territories as a whole.[2] The use of current dollar values means, of course, that the data reflect price changes as well as changes in the physical volume of the goods being produced. However, the latter has already been discussed for the few industries, chiefly trapping and mining, which are involved here. What is apparent from even the crude value data set out here is that the end of World War II marked the beginning of an unprecedented growth of output in the territorial north and that the source of this growth was the mining industry. The end of World War II was also marked by an abrupt and fundamental alteration in the composition of the territorial economy whereby the traditional trapping industry declined not only in relation to the growing mining industry but in absolute terms as well. It will be seen from the table that the recovery in the value of fur production from

---

[1]The "Net Value of Production" or "census value added" is obtained by deducting the cost of materials, fuel, electricity and process supplies used up in the process of production from the gross value of output (as measured by total sales or shipments adjusted for inventories) in various commodity-producing industries; see D.B.S., *Survey of Production*, annually.

[2]"Current dollar" values are values expressed in terms of the prices existing at the time indicated.

the low levels of the Depression continued throughout the years of World War II but that after the war a perceptible weakening developed, with the value of output falling during the late 1940s and throughout the 1950s to levels lower than those realized during the 1920s and the Depression. The effect of this collapse of the trapping industry, combined with the rapid development of mineral production, was to reduce the relative importance of trapping in the territorial economy during the late 1950s to about the same status as was held by those industries such as forestry and manufacturing which produced primarily for local markets only. Indeed, during the 1950s the trapping industry contributed less to the value of primary output in the Territories than did the generation of electric power. It may be concluded, therefore, that the end of World War II marked the beginning of a rather sudden conversion of the territorial economy from one whose growth depended upon the harvesting of furs to one dependent upon the development of mineral resources.

This transition from fur to minerals was accompanied by little improvement in the relative importance of the territorial economy within the total non-agricultural primary industry of Canada. From the 1920s to the 1960s the Territories produced only about one per cent of the output of the trapping, mining, fishing, forestry, and electric power industries of Canada.[3]

THE LEVEL OF INCOME

Data relating to the level of income received by persons residing in the Yukon and in the Northwest Territories have been published by the Dominion Bureau of Statistics only since 1951.[4] The national accounting concept of "personal income" measures the income actually received by persons and includes factor incomes (such as wages, salaries, rents, interests, and profits) along with "transfer payments" (such as family allowances, old age pensions, and out-payments of social insurance funds). It does not include income "earned" but not received by persons, such as contributions made to social insurance funds by employees and employers.

The absolute level of personal income in the territorial north showed a

[3]See Table 11.13.
[4]Personal income data for the Yukon and Northwest Territories were included with that for British Columbia before 1951.

marked increase over the decade 1951–61 rising from 21 million dollars in 1951 to 49 million dollars in 1961. As shown in Table 11.14, most of this increase occurred during the first half of the decade when rapid development of mining activity was taking place in the north. Total personal income in the Territories rose rapidly to 47 million dollars in 1956 and then showed only relatively slight growth thereafter. It is likely that this rapid rise in personal income from 1951 until 1956 was a continuation of a longer trend going back to the post-war conversion of the territorial economy from one based on furs to one chiefly dependent upon mining. The development of new employment opportunities for labour not only in the mining industry but also in the transportation and other service industries (including government) related to it must have led to a great increase in recorded salaries and wages in the area. This was probably further augmented by the employment created, again both directly and indirectly, by the construction of the DEW line system. Most of the employment opportunities created by such development during the period from the end of World War II to the middle 1950s were probably filled by migrants coming into the Territories from outside for, as we saw earlier in this chapter, this was the period when net migration was the factor accounting for the rapid expansion of the territorial population. If we assume that such migration was economically motivated, we would expect that during this period an attractive income differential would have existed between the Territories and the alternative places where such employment could be found.

When we examine personal income in the Territories on a *per capita* basis and attempt to compare it with *per capita* income in the provinces it is apparent that the peculiar composition of the territorial population (and society) will make such comparisons extremely hazardous. Especially in the Northwest Territories, as we have seen, a very large part of the total population even in 1951 was composed of natives still living the life imposed upon them by the economics of the fur trade—or floundering in the unemployment created by the structural changes being experienced in the territorial economy as a result of the collapse of that industry and of the way of life associated with it.

With approximately 50 per cent of the total population officially designated as "native" in 1951 it is perhaps surprising to find in Table 11.15 that in that year the *per capita* personal income in the Yukon and the Northwest Territories exceeded that reported for Newfoundland, Prince Edward Island, Nova Scotia, and New Brunswick, and that it compared not unfavourably with the level in income in Quebec. In view of the growth in government welfare programmes in the Territories during the post-war period it might be suspected that this relatively good showing was attributable to a rapid influx of government transfer payments. This does not, however, appear to have been the case for, as shown in Table 11.15, government transfers accounted for a very much smaller part of personal income in the Territories than in any of the provinces named (or, for that matter, in any of the provinces in Canada).

It will be seen from the table just referred to that by 1956 the level of personal income *per capita* had risen dramatically in the Territories despite the large increase in population which occurred simultaneously. This growth of income was much more rapid than in any of the provinces, with the result that in 1956 the level of personal income *per capita* had risen to $1,516 in the Yukon and Northwest Territories combined, a level exceeded only by that recorded in Ontario and British Columbia which had $1,610 and $1,618 respectively. At the same time, the importance of government transfers as a source of personal income for residents of the Territories declined from 5 per cent in 1951 to 4.3 per cent in 1956. This compared to percentages ranging from 10 to 15 per cent in the Maritime provinces, 8 to 10 per cent in the western provinces, 6 per cent in Ontario, and 9 per cent in the province of Quebec in the latter year.

In the later 1950s the rapid growth of personal income in the Territories ceased. The total in 1961 was only two million dollars above that recorded in 1956. But, as we saw earlier, the population of the Territories continued to expand rapidly with the result that its income *per capita* declined to $1,324 in 1961. Because income *per capita* continued to rise in the provinces, however, the substantial differential in income which had favoured the Territories in the middle of the decade narrowed sharply. This was not, however, inconsistent with the continued rapid growth of population for, by the later 1950s, as we have seen, population growth there had for the first time in the area's history become primarily a function of the rate of natural increase instead of the rate of net migration. It would, however, be easy to underestimate the population drawing power of the level of income throughout this period by taking the *per capita* income statistics at their face value. If labour is attracted to an area by an income differential, the individuals concerned will not be influenced by the large aggregate factors we have been discussing here, but rather by individual wage, salary, and other income rates in particular employments. Because a very much larger proportion of the territorial population must receive virtually no money income than is the case in even the poorest provinces, the incomes of those who are in commercial or industrial employment in the Territories must be much higher than the *per capita* averages cited here would suggest and they must consequently compare even more favourably with those prevailing in the provinces. If we assume, for example, that in 1961 40 per cent of the territorial population had no regular money income at all, except for government transfers, the *per capita* personal income of the remaining 60 per cent of the territorial population would have exceeded $2,000, or more than the *per capita* annual personal income even in Ontario or British Columbia. And because of the large number of Métis who, while not officially classed as "native" people in the Territories, are by and large often worse off economically than those who are classed as "natives" because they lack access to specialized welfare services available to the latter, our estimate of 40 per cent with no "earned" income may in fact be much too low for a year when trapping provided such a meagre part of the total income earned.

With regard to the "earned" portion of personal income it should be noted that in the early 1960s it consisted almost entirely of wages, salaries, and "supplementary labour income."[5] In 1961, 42 million dollars or 86 per cent of the 49 million dollars of personal income earned in the Territories was so derived. The bulk of this income was attributable to employment in four major types of activity—mining, construction, transportation, and government activities of various kinds.

It will be apparent from the foregoing that so far as that largely "white" part of the territorial population in modern industrial employment was concerned, income levels in the post-World War II period were apparently most attractive in comparison with those prevailing elsewhere in Canada. For the rest of the population in the territorial north incomes were probably at or even below the classic subsistance level, no matter how harshly one might conceive of that measure. But, in fact, even the apparently high *per capita* income levels which may be arrived at by removing the latter part of the population from the *per capita* calculations were largely illusory. This does not necessarily deny their effectiveness as a device for pulling population into the north from outside. But it does have important implications for the ability of the Territories to avoid the economic costs of rapid labour turnover and, in the broader context of territorial development, to acquire and hold a

[5]Supplementary labour income consists of other expenditures by employers on labour account that can be regarded as payment for employee's services, as, for example, contributions by employers to pension funds.

permanent population capable of filling the type of modern employment opportunities being created in the territories as they develop.

The illusory quality of the high levels of personal income in the territorial north was the result of a larger differential existing between the level of money income and the level of real income in the Territories than was the case elsewhere in Canada. Because of the notorious difficulties associated with making inter-regional comparisons of the "cost of living" (which are aggravated for our purposes here by an acute shortage of comparable data for the Territories and outside points), it is not feasible to attempt here any precise estimation of how much the cost of living in the Territories generally exceeded the cost of living in places to the south. The size of this differential must also have varied enormously from one place in the north to another depending upon the adequacy of the transportation facilities involved. And alterations in the adequacy of such facilities over the years surely caused large changes in the cost of commodities in any one centre as well. Not all of this cost of living differential was attributable to costs of transportation, although there is no doubt that this was the largest factor involved. Some of the higher cost of living was attributable to the cost of offsetting physical disadvantages of northern living. The heating of houses, for example, must obviously be more costly in the north than in many parts of Canada lying further south—although again, there is probably little disadvantage in this respect when the northwest is compared to the mining areas of northern Ontario and Quebec. In the mid-1950s the cost of heating a six-room house in a western Canadian city was approximately $80 per year, whereas in Yellowknife the cost was closer to $500. Even in such instances as this, however, the higher cost of northern living was partly attributable to the cost of transportation. As we have seen, the cost of fuel in the north was much higher than in western Canada, for example, because of the heavy transportation costs involved in making it available to northern consumers. Table 11.16 compares fuel costs in three northern centres with fuel costs in a typical prairie city (Regina, Saskatchewan) in the late 1950s.

It is difficult to locate other elements of the high cost of northern living which were not also largely the consequence of high transportation costs. Utilities are one such exception, however. The reasons for the high costs of these commodities have already been discussed. Table 11.17 compares electricity rates in three major territorial centres with those prevailing in Regina, Saskatchewan, during one year in the late 1950s.

Other than the costs of fuel and utilities the chief factors contributing to the high cost of living in the Territories were the prices of food and shelter.

Because of violent seasonal fluctuations in food prices and the extent to which they vary from place to place in the north it is virtually impossible to generalize about them. Official sources are reluctant to attempt even rough estimates, and there are many technical difficulties associated with comparing them with prices elsewhere. Some impression of the differential which existed in the late 1950s may be gained, however, from a spot-check made by the writer on forty-five standard grocery items in Yellowknife, Dawson, and Whitehorse in the summer of 1958. This indicated that food costs in these centres were from 55 to 100 per cent higher than those then prevailing even in the relatively expensive prairie cities of Regina and Saskatoon.

An extreme illustration of the effects high transportation costs could have on certain commodities in the north is the price of fresh produce, meat, and frozen foods in Yellowknife during the 1950s before the Mackenzie Highway was completed to the settlement. Such products were shipped north from Edmonton along the Mackenzie Highway to Hay River on the south shore of Great Slave Lake. They were then flown into Yellowknife, a one-hour flight across Great Slave Lake. Freight charges amounted to 15.5 cents per pound per shipment. Hence, as shown in Table 11.18, on some low-value goods the freight charges exceeded the Edmonton wholesale price for the commodity. Such high prices did not reflect only the costs of transportation, of course. Retailing in small northern centres was itself a more costly process than in the south, partly because of the high cost of labour in the north, but also because of the large inventories which merchants had to hold, and the higher costs of heating, lighting, and shelter. There is some evidence to suggest that during the 1950s the cost of retailing was reduced in a number of northern communities once they had reached such a size as would permit the introduction of modern retailing techniques. In Whitehorse, for example, a large self-service food store opened in 1957 had a perceptible effect upon the level of retail food prices in that area. The high profits which some retailers in territorial centres appeared to be earning obviously drew capital into these lines of activity. In Yellowknife during the 1950s it was apparent that the retailing system there was undergoing a marked transformation as stores initially devised to operate on the low volume high-mark-up basis associated with the fur trade converted to a volume trade with a competitive pricing policy.

Another large factor contributing to high living costs in the Territories has been the cost of housing. Because of certain procedures of the Dominion Bureau of Statistics, data relating to the construction industry in the Yukon and Northwest Territories are not available. It has been estimated, however, that building costs may have been about 40 per cent higher in many northern centres than outside. In the Yukon Territory during the early 1950s building costs were estimated at approximately $16 per square foot as compared to $11 in Vancouver.[6] This was again partly a result of the need for more expensive construction to overcome climatic disadvantages such as severe winter cold and the presence in many areas of permafrost conditions on the building site. In Dawson City, for example, it was necessary to sink heavy piling through many feet of frozen ground to solid bedrock to obtain a solid foundation for buildings. Labour costs also contributed to higher building costs. And, once again, transportation costs greatly increased the cost of building materials. Table 11.19 compares costs of certain standard building materials in Whitehorse and in Vancouver in the mid-1950s. The prices of heavy items such as cement, it will be noticed, were four times the Vancouver price in Whitehorse.

In Whitehorse, Dawson, and Yellowknife in particular, there was considerable construction during the post-war years and in the late 1950s much new construction was in evidence in these as well as many smaller centres. In Whitehorse, for example, a large subdivision was developed by the federal government in the late 1950s to house some of its employees. It is of interest, however, that housing failed to grow at the same rate as population and that, as in many other parts of Canada, the Territories experienced an acute housing shortage throughout much of the post-World War II period. This shortage was aggravated by the fact that the Territories did not benefit equally with the rest of Canada from the provisions of the National Housing Act, which attempted to encourage residential construction by making credit available to would-be home builders at reasonable interest rates. The amount of the loan available in specific circumstances was proportionate to the cost of the building and had a maximum limit which depended in part upon the size of the building. Consequently, because of the high cost of construction in the Territories, a four-room house there cost as much as a comparable standard five-room house built elsewhere in Canada, yet the amount of credit made available would be the same or less. Because

[6]Whitehorse Board of Trade, *Submission to the Royal Commission on Canada's Economic Prospects*, p. 4.

of this, there were many complaints urging higher basic property evaluations for homes built north of the 60th parallel. In so far as the housing shortage was unusually severe in the Territories, it may have constituted an additional reason for the high cost of living there. It should also be noted, however, that the largest part of the native population in the area and indeed a great part of the population officially considered to be of "white status" continued to live throughout this period in the most primitive and unsanitary of hovels.

In addition to the high cost of living in the Territories there is at least one other factor which has contributed to the unusually large differential between money and real incomes there—the federal income tax. This tax was applied against incomes in the Territories at the same rates as elsewhere in Canada. But because these rates were progressive with respect to money incomes, and because the latter were generally much higher in the Territories than elsewhere in Canada, the rate of tax on real income there was higher than in the provinces.

One factor which could work in the other direction in this analysis of real and money incomes is the probability that many wage and salary recipients in the Territories received significant non-monetary benefits from their employers which would not be made available "outside." Many benefits, such as subsidized housing, free transportation outside for vacations, and other devices calculated to make northern life less rigorous, may in effect represent a significant wage payment. Nevertheless, such offsetting considerations could not be important enough to bring into doubt the existence of a larger differential between money and real incomes in the territorial north than existed on the average in the various provinces during the period being considered here. The existence of such a differential was officially recognized by the federal government, which granted special northern living bonuses to employees stationed in the north. Even in the case of a major centre of northern population such as Whitehorse, it was contended in a brief submitted to a royal commission in 1955 that "if each individual who came into the Yukon Territory because of the high wages assessed his circumstances from a purely financial point of view he would come to the conclusion . . . that he is worse off in the Yukon territory than he would be in similar employments on the outside."[7]

In this chapter we have attempted to indicate, necessarily in a rather impressionistic way because of the lack of reliable data, the general level of development attained in the territorial north up to the early

[7]*Ibid.*, p. 6.

1960s in so far as this can be inferred from the growth of population, output, and income both in terms of absolute levels and also in relation to the rest of the country. It may now be appropriate to ask whether or not this level of development has been satisfactory. If so, there is no "problem of northern development" in Canada—at least so far as the remaining areas under federal jurisdiction are concerned. If the level of development attained is judged to have been unsatisfactory, then there is a problem and it would be appropriate to consider both the reasons for its existence and the approaches which were, or could have been, taken to its solution.

12 Public Policy and Territorial Development

DURING THE DECADES of the 1940s and the 1950s Canadians became increasingly interested in the question of the rate of development in the northern territories. Just what the term "development" refers to in such a context is difficult to define precisely, but today the most general meaning of the term, in its North American context at least, has to do with the establishment of economic activities capable of sustaining a population residing in a given area and the subsequent creation of the political and other social institutions which we have come to regard as being the normal attributes of a civilized community. It is this process of establishing an economic base and the related political organization in the territorial north that has been our concern in this study. Little attention has been given here to the admittedly important social and cultural aspects of the development process or to the institutions associated with them. Our reason for focusing attention upon the political institutions involved in the process is that they, probably more than the other factors mentioned, have not only been determined but *determining* factors influencing strongly the development of the basic economic processes upon which the system of development in the broader sense must always depend. The latter emphasis, which makes the economic base the primary element in the development process for a once "empty" area, is not meant to imply, of course, that the entire process of development is economically determined. Indeed, the history of development in the Territories has amply demonstrated that many kinds of non-economic activities in such an area may serve to support a kind of development, as we have been using the term here. We have seen, for example, how military operations have been a factor in the development of the area. But we have been chiefly concerned with the process whereby conventional civilian goods and services came to be produced there and with how the "living" thereby generated provided the basis for population growth and the subsequent development of political institutions. Consequently, in this concluding chapter we return to a consideration of the relationship between resources and population, especially as this has been influenced by public policy relating to the development of resources and to the "living" gained by the territorial population.

The development of any part of the territorial north was first recognized as a problem, in the sense that it was not proceeding satisfactorily, in the Yukon near the beginning of this century. Significantly, this was apparent chiefly at the territorial level of government. But, as we have seen, the recognition of this problem had little practical significance, for the territorial government lacked the constitutional authority and, more important perhaps, the financial resources to do much more than slow down the retreat of labour and capital following the collapse of the Klondike boom. The federal government, judging from its policies with respect to the Yukon administration, and probably most members of Parliament (judging from debates in the House of Commons), apparently failed to share the concern of the territorial council over the disintegration of the territorial economy and of the political and other institutions which had been so rapidly established there during the placer gold-mining boom. This difference in attitudes is hardly surprising, but it is no less important to the whole question of northern development for that.

While probably most Canadians have held a traditional romantic enthusiasm for "the north," those residing in the area have had definite pragmatic reasons for feeling that development there should be promoted even if this necessitated the sacrifice by the country as a whole of alternative national objectives. The Canadians living outside the north could be expected to be less enthusiastic about the romance of the north when it was translated into such practical terms as federal taxation for the purpose of financing subsidies to northern development. Consequently, it is not surprising to find that policy-makers at the federal level have generally found it easier to view territorial development in apparently "rational" terms than have those operating at the territorial level. This was a consideration only in the Yukon Territory and not in the Northwest Territories for, throughout most of the period examined here, it was only in the Yukon that the formulation of public policy at the territorial level reflected in any significant way the opinion of the territorial population. The policies adopted by the federal government toward events in the Yukon early in this century continued with little fundamental or conceptual alteration as the basic elements of public policies toward territorial development as a whole until the 1940s.

This first stage in the evolution of public policy in regard to the Territories has already been identified as the stage of "developmental *laissez-faire*." The role of government in territorial life was limited to that authorized by Adam Smith—the maintenance of justice and civil order, defence against external enemies, and the undertaking of certain activities which private enterprise could not, or should not, be expected to undertake. The latter category was very narrowly defined in the case of federal policy in the territorial north but, as we have seen, in addition to providing routine administration in the Territories, the government did provide some transportation facilities, it sponsored scientific work and services such as geological mapping, and it provided some communications facilities during this period.

This is not to suggest that the policies adopted were the consequence of Ministers of the Crown having read Adam Smith—but the policies adopted could have been defended intellectually had it been necessary to do so by invoking the authority of the classical economist. The more likely immediate cause of the policies was simple expediency—to foster a more rapid rate of development in the Territories would have necessitated devoting public funds to an undertaking which was relatively low in the electorate's scale of priorities. It can hardly have been a matter of the federal government being generally reluctant or unable to contemplate subsidizing development for this was, if anything, recognized as being the federal government's *raison d'être* during this period in Canadian history. But in the case of the territorial north, federal policy during this period bore all the marks of the narrowest interpretation of the ditcates of reason as embodied in "the dismal science."

Public policy left to the functioning of free markets the process of determining the extent to which northern resources would be developed. In so far as this involved the exploitation of mineral resources, such an approach promised that those who were attracted to the area from outside would have an appropriate living because the income that attracted them would maintain them or, if the development proved to be only a temporary one, they would go back to where they had come from. So far as the aboriginal population of the area was concerned, it seemed that the development of the area's fur resources had already provided a basis for their maintenance. And, while the long term prospects for the fur industry were never promising, the native population was not increasing in size either, with the result that the level of living achieved by this native population could be expected, if not to improve, at least to remain near its customary level.

Given this approach to the matter of resource development, the only appropriate government policy was to leave to private enterprise the initiative for resource development. It was appreciated, as we have seen, that this did not necessarily mean embracing the principle of unrestricted competition among private *entrepreneurs*, for there was evidence, as we have seen, that the public authorities recognized that in mining as well as in fur trapping there could be great advantages of scale realized by large firms undertaking resource development in a new area. Furthermore, if public policy was slanted to encourage large firms to undertake resource development projects, this made it possible for the public authority to leave the initiative even in this field of economic activity to private *entrepreneurs*.

Thus, those responsible for the management of the national public revenues could satisfy the most parsimonius taxpayer that, at least so far as the federal territorial hinterland was concerned, only the minimum outlays required for the maintenance of law and order and national sovereignty were being made—and that these, in large measure, would be recovered by fees and taxes levied upon those who were being permitted to utilize the natural resources of the area.

Even those slight (by today's standards) outlays on social welfare items considered a normal function of government in Canada could be said to have been minimized in the Territories under the policy pursued before World War II for, especially in the Northwest Territories, these responsibilities were also entrusted to a form of private, but non-profit enterprise—that is, to religious organizations and to private charity. The chief exceptions to this were the territorial schools and hospitals in the Yukon and, in the Northwest Territories, the federal government's interesting experiment with a form of welfare scheme combining resource development elements—the reindeer experiment described in Chapter 9.

In the Northwest Territories even the formally recognized federal responsibility for the native population was largely shifted to the agents of the Hudson's Bay Company, the churches, and to nature, with the Hudson's Bay Company providing the native population with a cash income (and extensive credit facilities), the churches providing education and some elements of public welfare, and nature providing what food and shelter the native could not otherwise obtain. In the latter respect it is significant that no Indian reservations were ever established in the

Yukon or in the Northwest Territories, but the native population was guaranteed rather general hunting, fishing and other privileges which would enable it to supplement its earnings from trapping by an even more direct process of living off the land.

This policy, in general, has much to recommend it—especially when it is viewed as an abstraction. It also has a number of conspicuous weaknesses both in its theoretical basis and in the particular application made of it in the Territories. Aside from the already mentioned advantage of permitting a minimization of public expenditure in the Territories, this policy seemed to leave the determination of the appropriate rate of economic development there to an automatic, self-regulating mechanism. Like the broader policies associated with the term *"laissez-faire,"* this one relied on the functioning of the impersonal "natural" forces of supply and demand to allocate resources among alternative uses, and specifically in this case, to direct labour and capital resources into the Territories for use in conjunction with the natural or land resources located there. As we saw earlier, under this system it would be expected that when it appeared more profitable to the private organizers of production to use labour and capital to develop a mine in the far north rather than to develop a new one (or to expand an existing one) in the south, these economic resources would be diverted from applications in the south to applications in the north. Whether or not the private *entrepreneurs* arrived at such an estimate of a relative profitability of alternative locations for their productive activities would depend upon their estimates of the relative costs involved (the supply considerations) relative to the revenues expected (the demand considerations). When these estimates were correct and the productive activity located in the new area proved this by yielding a relatively satisfactory rate of profit, the level of development (as measured by output, population, and income) in the new area would be advanced. If the venture failed to yield a satisfactory rate of return, it was shown to have been uneconomical and the resources with alternative uses elsewhere would be removed to the now most promising (profitable) use. In this way the community would automatically be protected from the loss of potential satisfactions which could result from labour and capital being misused— that is, used in employments which did not yield as large an output as would be possible in some alternative employment.

The general theoretical deficiencies of this approach are catalogued in all elementary text-books in economics and it would not be appropriate here to devote space to elaborating the theory of the market economy in the detail necessary to permit exploration of its internal logical consistency. In any event, given an able statement of this theory, such criticism often appears to be trivial. A more rewarding approach to criticism which may be made in connection with this elaborate (and for many people, intellectually appealing) theoretical system is that levelled at its usefulness in particular applications. Like all theories, the theory of the self-regulating welfare-optimizing market economy embodies assumptions which underlie the various assertions the theory makes about particular relationships. If these assumptions provide an unrealistic basis for any conclusions the theory might lead one to, these conclusions lose their force at best, or at worst lead one into false understanding of what was being studied in the first place. Once again we cannot attempt here a general discussion of all the assumptions underlying the theory of resource allocation in the market economy, but we must draw attention to those assumptions which seem particularly unrealistic in the context of this study and which consequently make the policy implications of the theory questionable so far as the matter of territorial development has been concerned. Those which are suggested by our earlier survey of territorial development during this period are the assumptions embodied in the theory concerning *entrepreneurial* knowledge, the comparability of the various alternative uses for resources, and the mobility of resources.

If the market system is to allocate resources appropriately ("optimally") the individual decision-making units must have a perfect knowledge of the various opportunities available. It is generally conceded that this condition is unlikely to be satisfied in the real world. It would appear, however, that in the case of the territorial north knowledge of opportunities for profitable undertakings there, especially during the period before World War II, was unusually scant. We have seen that despite the extensive work done by the Geological Survey of Canada in the area, prior to World War II remarkably little was known about the land itself—its minerals, water resources, forests, soils, and even its native people. Even more significant, perhaps, was the distorted popular impression of the physical characteristics of the Territories which was (and indeed still is) prevalent throughout the rest of the country. The amount of scientific or organized knowledge of the area was slight and what there was, was often overwhelmed by a public impression of the area as one of perpetual ice and snow. How complete this ignorance of the area's resources and characteristics must have been, especially before the awakening of new public and expert interest in the area during

World War II, is suggested by the fact that even today most Canadians asked to name the most common northern bird would unhesitatingly nominate the penguin. A less dramatic, but perhaps more significant manifestation of this low level of knowledge concerning the area in the "outside," is the myth that the north generally possesses unique physical characteristics which are unknown in more southern climates. This myth, propagated by some residents of the north themselves, is reflected in the notion that whatever "problems" the area has, call out for physical solutions such as plastic domes to put over cities and special motor cars capable of operating at low temperatures.[1]

While the north does possess some unique phenomena, such as permafrost, that have important economic implications, much of the real difference between the north and the outside has been, with no pun intended, a difference of degree rather than of kind. Given such a general lack of knowledge, compounded by a general misunderstanding of the area's environment, it seems unlikely that the north could compete with other better known areas on the basis of its real economic merits in the way presupposed by the theory of the market economy.

The plausibility of the assumption that such a simple mechanism could perform the task of allocating resources appropriately in such circumstances is weakened by yet another factor. It is likely that the private *entrepreneur* who does undertake such an evaluation will tend to exaggerate the costs relative to the returns associated with the activity situated in the remote area. The suggestion here is that the private *entrepreneur* tends to "see" more of the total costs of his activity in the new area than in the other simply because he must face directly the costs of establishing in a previously undeveloped area the elaborate complex of individual and community facilities described in Chapter IX. In a less remote location, while similar costs may be present, they are more likely to be spread over a number of individual firms and, because the institutions of local government are more likely to be well established in such an area, the total burden of such costs is apt to be more broadly distributed over a range of enterprises and even of individuals. If this is the case, the individual firm, unless it is so large and well financed that it can disregard such factors, is likely to eschew the new area because of apparently high costs relative to expected earnings. But from an over-all social point of view the new total costs in the new area may

[1]A remarkable example of this popular approach is to be found in an article "The North Just Won't Go Away," by W. E. Senior in *Maclean's Magazine* (October 17, 1964), LXXVII, 18.

be no greater than in the old where they are more likely to be less conspicuous because of being widely dispersed. Thus, when the development decisions are left to individual private firms there may be a tendency for the system to allocate too few of the community's resources to development of the new area.

The third assumption of the market theory which may be challenged is that labour resources are "mobile." In the context of resource allocation among alternative employments, or in a given employment in alternative locations, it is seldom true that labour can or will move freely in response to fluctuations in the labour markets involved. The experience of the territorial north is particularly instructive in this regard, for it provided a classic demonstration of the fact that such physical factors as distance may be less significant obstacles to labour mobility than more fundamental, social, psychological and broadly cultural considerations.

The market theory assumes that labour markets will function so as to draw labour into its most productive employment, for the rewards available to it there will exceed those in other employments. And, as we have seen in this study, despite all the imperfections characteristic of any real situation, the market did function in this way to direct much of the total labour force (and much of the general population of which it was a part) from other employments and from other places into the Territories. But it failed to shift labour out of the declining fur-trapping industry into the growing mining and related industries within the Territories. Perhaps one of the most striking examples of this anomaly noted in this study was the way the market functioned to draw off-season farmers from the distant northern prairies into the Great Slave Lake winter fishery—but failed to shift the virtually unemployed natives living in the vicinity of the lake into this employment.

The inability of the market system to cope with this kind of structural change in the northern economy left a large part of the population of the Territories destitute. In the long run it is true that, left alone, the market system would have solved this problem in its own natural and impersonal way—the excess labour resource would have either responded to the pressure of low incomes by adapting to the new kind of labour demand in the area or by leaving the area or, failing such an adaptation, would have been eliminated by famine and disease. But the native population found it difficult to adapt to the changing demand for labour because the lack of education made learning new skills and new ways of life virtually impossible. The same factor, combined with the lack of funds, made moving out of the area equally difficult. And the third possibility should have been unthinkable.

As shown in the last chapter, however, the public policy of *laissez-faire* towards the Territories was adhered to closely enough before World War II to suggest that the public authorities were unlikely to take strong action to ameliorate the condition of the stranded native population. This is not to suggest that the policy was to allow the native population to adapt or perish, for some public money and some public energy was devoted to relieving its distress, especially in the Yukon where the territorial school and hospital system at least formally did not discriminate among ethnic groups in the community. But we have seen that at the federal level the policy was to leave the problem of the indigent native population to the religious missions, institutions which were ill-suited to the task of enabling the native to adapt himself to the new kind of economy which was inexorably replacing the economy of the northern fur trade. The curriculum of the mission schools, for example, was not designed to train Indian and Eskimo children for modern economic life inside or outside the north and the level of school attendance was such that few received even what education the mission schools could provide. There was little chance that such an educational system, even when it received financial help from the state, could effect a significant improvement in the mobility of native labour even on a long-term basis.

Nor did the *laissez-faire* policy do much to treat the short-run symptoms of this basic failure of the system in the north, the Malthusian "season of distress" visited upon the native population in the specific forms of malnutrition, famine, and disease. The basic approach to this problem was again to leave the provision of a kind of emergency health service to the religious missions and to try, through game regulations and conservation measures, to protect the remaining traditional sources of food for the native population from the incursions of white commercial trappers and hunters. The adequacy of these measures may be judged by the vital statistics which we looked at in the last chapter. Had the overall policy of *laissez-faire* been continued it is likely that the decline of the native population would have continued and the general process of economic development in the area would have proceeded much as it had in the past. But the policy of virtually unqualified *laissez-faire* in the Territories was greatly modified after 1940.

The new public policy with regard to the Territories was distinguished by the following elements: first, the federal government showed an increasing readiness to support private directly productive activities in the Territories; second, it began to assume direct responsibility for welfare, and especially for native welfare, in the area. This more direct participation by the principal public authority in the over-all economic life of the Territories might be regarded as merely a particular (and not particularly important from a national point of view) manifestation of the new and more active role being assumed by the federal government in Canadian economic and social life generally as a result of the special circumstances which had been created by the Depression and the war. Other, more specific reasons for the change in policy, so far as the Territories were concerned, have been suggested earlier in this study. These included the re-awakening of public interest in the northern part of the continent as a result of its sudden strategic military significance, the demonstration of the technical feasibility of major construction undertakings in the area, the discovery and evaluation of its natural resource potential, and a belated public recognition of the deplorable condition of the native and Métis populations of the north.

Although it is hazardous to generalize on the basis of the rather sketchy information about the extent and the purpose of public policy in the Territories during the war and early post-war period, the impression one is left with is that the new policy distinguished between the matter of public welfare in the Territories, and the matter of the rate of economic development there. Different criteria appear to have been applied to what we might call the new public *development* activities and the new public *welfare* activities which were undertaken by government in the Territories during this period. That some such criteria were necessary at all was the consequence of the abandonment of the strict, automatic, market system for regulating the economic aspects of territorial life (and thereby those other parts, such as welfare, which were dependent upon it). Once it had been decided to carry public intervention beyond the established functions of routine administration, scientific exploration, and policing, it was necessary to devise some system for regulating the *extent* of the new activities. With the growing appreciation during this period of the possibilities of deficit financing, it became less plausible to think of public intervention being limited by a certain amount of "money" in the federal treasury. But what criteria could be devised to permit determination of the "appropriate" level of public intervention in the rate of territorial economic development? The new appreciation of the territorial north was enough to call for more public spending in the area—but how much more?

It appears that the temporary solution "found" to this question lay, at the very least, in treating the native welfare problem as an emergency situation calling for rapid alleviation of the immediate difficulties of the distressed population by providing it with income and social services of the most urgently needed kind. This task was simplified by the appearance of massive new national welfare programmes which could be extended throughout the territorial north as well as throughout the provincial part of Canada. In addition to this immediate "relief" programme, funds were to be devoted to revolutionizing the educational system and to raising the level of public health in order to upgrade and to improve the mobility of the native labour force both industrially and geographically. Under the circumstances a good case could be made for allocating whatever amounts were necessary to produce the desired results of improving the immediate living conditions of the distressed population and its ability, in the long run, to adapt to the changing economic environment—but at the same time it must have been apparent that such measures could contribute little to the general economic development of the north.

We have also seen that there was some feeling a more rapid rate of development was desirable not only to create employment opportunities more rapidly but also for reasons of assuring future supplies of mineral resources and for reasons of defence. It was obvious that public enterprise could be used to accelerate such development in so far as publicly financed organizations could undertake development projects, even directly productive activities such as mining, when privately financed, profit-oriented organizations could not. But none of the reasons for such an innovation in resource development policy in the Territories were as compelling as the humanitarian reasons for replacing the system of "private" welfare with a system of heavily subsidized state welfare there. Consequently, the resource development policy applied in the Territories by the federal government during this period was designed to leave the initiative for this kind of undertaking in private hands, but to support such activity if it was seen to be commercially feasible to do so. In other words, the market mechanism of supply and demand was to be relied upon to regulate resource development as in the past, but the possibility of getting an appropriate response to such market inducements to develop resources in the area was to be enhanced by adding public enterprises, carefully organized along commercial lines, to the private enterprises already available.

The best example of the kind of public enterprise envisioned in the foregoing was the Northern Canada Power Commission, designed as it was to operate in precisely the type of activity most likely to be "inadequately" developed by private firms for the reasons suggested earlier.

To express the character of the new approach to policy more succinctly, it could be described as a policy of using private investment in directly productive activity to lead publicly supported investment in social overhead capital so far as the latter was designed to promote natural resource development. But public investment in social overhead capital for welfare, and public spending on current account for welfare purposes were paced by a subjectively determined conception of "need." Of course the distinction between the two areas was blurred when the interactions between the two types of public intervention are considered.

The increased public spending upon welfare under such a policy would have important implications for resource development in the long run as, for example, in creating the possibility of a native labour force capable of industrial employment, and in the short run by expanding local markets, creating volume for retailers, improving the load factor on transportation systems and providing advantages of larger scale operation to a variety of local businesses. Furthermore, public expenditures in support of resource development could, by expanding employment opportunities, contribute to the solution of the unemployment and low income conditions which created the need for much of the welfare programme expenditure in the first place. Indeed, some programmes of the "reindeer herding" and Eskimo handicraft type referred to earlier were conceived of as combined welfare and resource development undertakings, although in practice they had had a negligible effect in the context of total production in the territorial economy. In so far as they were usually intended to achieve a commercially self-sustaining status these programmes provide an interesting example of how public initiative and financial support could be used to manufacture, as it were, a "natural" market to supplement those available by creating a new resource, a new product, and new demand, as well as an economic organization required to bring all three together. The arctic char fishery, the Eskimo "art" promotion, and the reindeer "industry" which preceded them, all sought to create employment and income opportunities for natives in such a way. But, while such income- and employment-creating programmes were obviously preferable to the simple income-creating "relief" programmes, they could scarcely be expected to provide a general solution to the problem of low income and unemployment in the territorial north as a whole. Despite the efforts made during the 1940s to improve conditions there for the native population through public undertakings in the field of welfare and, despite the rapid acceleration of privately and publicly organized mining and related activities throughout the area, by the end of the decade it appeared that the over-all situation was worse than ever.

Given the basic economic conditions prevailing in the Territories, it is hardly surprising, in retrospect, that the justifiably enormous expansion of public welfare programmes in the area should have been accompanied by the rapid increase in the rate of natural population growth which was described and analyzed in the preceding chapter. Given the length of time required for the reform of education in the area to show results in the form of increased mobility in the territorial labour force, it would seem that the problem of unemployability in the area would become more rather than less serious. At the same time, with the white and white-status population becoming large enough to contribute to the labour force through natural increase as well, the need to correlate the level of general resource development with the rate of population growth in the area became increasingly conspicuous. Thus, even before the brief but stimulating flirtation of the Conservative Party with the idea of promoting northern development as a means of exercising the national will and reviving the spirit of expansion lost after the settlement of the prairies, we find evidence of a further departure from the principles of *laissez-faire* in the public policy relating to the Territories.

It is difficult to justify applying one criterion for public spending on resource development in an area and another for the provision of welfare assistance to the population of the same area—if for no other reason than that the need for the latter will be a function of the amount spent on the former. But the logic of such a policy is further strained when it is appreciated how the application of the commercial feasibility criterion to public investment in social overhead capital is vitiated by the maintenance of a large public social welfare "industry" in such an area.

As shown in Chapter 9 only the *appearance* of commercial feasibility ("sound economics") is maintained when public investments in power plants, for example, are made on the basis of a total demand largely created by a public institution which owes its own existence not to its commercial feasibility, but to a humanitarian judgment of need. While the latter is no less correct, valuable, or real a demand for a service, it is not one which would be created by a natural market system left to itself. The point here is simply that in a community where the state plays a major role in creating demands for services, productive facilities built to satisfy these demands are unlikely to be successfully represented as the natural products of a freely functioning market system even if, for accounting purposes, they are operated as if they were. Once such inter-relationships between particular acts of investment are recognized it is a relatively easy intellectual step to abandon the effort to apply "sound economics" in the one area and not in the other. And so indeed during the 1950s there were indications that the policy of relying upon commercial feasibility as a guide to publicly sponsored resource-developing activity in the Territories was being modified, if not completely abandoned.

If the evidence of the new northern roads programme, the Great Slave Lake railway decision, and the extension of Northern Canada Power Commission activity is enough to suggest a change in policy it might be taken as marking the beginning of a third stage in the evolution of public policy with respect to the territorial north.

If the first stage was one of rigorously applied *laissez-faire*, the second brought the intervention of the state in the fields of welfare, where the extent of public activity was politically determined, and also in resource development in so far as public investments were made to support private activities if this could be justified in market terms.

The third stage, and at this point it must remain hypothetical that such a new policy had in fact emerged by the early 1960s, would have been one in which the government had decided to abandon commercial feasibility as a guide to public resource-developing activities. If this were done, public investment in infra-structure capital could be used to "lead" private investment in directly productive activity and thereby promote a more rapid rate of resource development than private firms responding to market forces could achieve on their own. But in view of the difficulties associated with such a "radical" innovation, why might such a policy be implemented? In considering this question it might be helpful to distinguish between the emotional or subjective arguments and the economic arguments involved. In Canada, decisions to allocate resources in particular ways have often been based upon subjective considerations which can derive little support from economic or other forms of rational analysis. Obvious examples could be found in Canadian policy with respect to foreign trade and income distribution. Despite popular impressions to the contrary, our analysis of development in the territorial north up to the 1950s would suggest that until that time emotional enthusiasms had played a negligible part in determining the allocation of resources to northern development at least when resources under public control were concerned. The level of economic development attained in the Territories before the 1950s could be justified in terms of the most conservative and business-like criteria. But during the 1950s an apparently emotional basis for the allocation of national resources to this purpose made its appearance.

It has already been argued that northern development had probably acquired a higher national priority by the later 1950s than it had ever had before. Public interest in the area was stimulated, as we have seen, during the years following the war by a variety of factors. One of these was the publicity associated with the DEW line, and a recurring alarm over the extent to which United States military forces were making themselves at home in Canada's far north. The feeling that the area's potential was also being wasted was stimulated by the appearance of a number of articles comparing unfavourably the level of economic development in the Canadian north with the level which had been achieved in Alaska, Siberia, and in northern regions of the Scandinavian countries. Added to this was the fact that the problem of the native population's welfare in the north was becoming increasingly difficult to ignore especially during a period when the rights of depressed minority groups were being more and more urgently asserted. It may even have been that the cessation of economic growth in the Canadian economy as a whole which occurred in the later years of the decade engendered a greater willingness among Canadians to look once again to the possibility of developing new regions as a means of revitalizing the national economy.

Whether or not any of these factors were responsible for motivating the espousal of northern development as an instrument of party politics by the Conservative Party under the leadership of John Diefenbaker is a question beyond the scope of this study, but they, perhaps among others, may help to account for the receptiveness of many Canadians to Mr. Diefenbaker's enthusiasm as manifested, for example, in his speech of February 12, 1958, in Winnipeg, when he said that "we are fulfilling the vision and the dream of Canada's first prime minister—Sir John A. Macdonald. But Macdonald saw Canada from East to West. I see a new Canada. A Canada of the north!"

This was not the first time a Canadian politician had found occasion to invoke the Canadian dream of a northern frontier—Meighen for example, had been almost as eloquent on the subject in the 1920s. But the Diefenbaker vision included an apparently new element—the idea of increasing the rate of northern development by using publicly sponsored investments in infra-structure capital to *lead* private resource exploiting operations. It is not clear why this policy should have appeared to be particularly novel in view of the historical role of the federal government in stimulating resource development by one form or another of public subsidization. Perhaps it was the very low level of development achieved in the past that made the new policy appear hopelessly visionary and consequently risky as a gamble of public resources. But, for whatever reason the wisdom of such policy was questioned, the criticism had to be answered if the policy was to be considered as an alternative to those earlier policies which we have examined. Even if all public policies of this type are ultimately based on assessments of political rather than economic considerations, if they are to survive for any length of time they must be capable of some form of rational justification. The justification obviously does not have to be an economic one and we have seen that historically most of what publicly sponsored activity did take place in the territorial north was justified on other than "economic" grounds.

In so far as Canada shared in the great military undertakings throughout the north, the justification for this diversion of resources from alternative uses was simply that it was "in the national interest." No one asked whether such projects would yield a profit. Similarly, in the field of welfare, despite the qualms of neo-Malthusians, the provision of relief to a population facing famine could be for political purposes adequately justified on humanitarian or moral grounds without recourse to more elaborate argumentation. But it is helpful, if not necessary, to find economic benefit in such undertakings in order to make the tax burden associated with them more palatable politically. Even so, in the late 1950s, it still appears to have been necessary to find more "rational" grounds for justifying the use of public funds to accelerate the rate of resource development in the northern Territories. And the great weakness of the policy of using publicly sponsored investments to lead private resource-developing operations in this way *as a policy* (quite apart from its appropriateness in a particular situation) has been the difficulty of finding readily understandable economic justifications for it. As we have seen, the original policy of virtually complete *laissez-faire* could have been justified by reference to the conventional wisdom of the classical economic analysis. And the modified version of it, in which public activity supported private activity, was defensible in terms of the theory of a modified market economy. On the surface at least, these justifications seemed "natural" and "business-like." Even those suspicious of public intervention in economic life could take comfort from the fact that the *level* of public involvement in these activities was *limited* by "natural" economic forces and also from the fact that the public undertakings involved could be organized in the same way as private business was organized.

The great difficulty with the "third" approach was that there appeared to be no "automatic" or "natural" limiting of the extent to which the public authority diverted resources from alternative uses to the promotion of northern development. How could one be at all sure that serious waste through misuse of national resources might not occur under such a policy especially if the kind of enthusiasm epitomized in Mr. Diefenbaker's Winnipeg speech referred to earlier got out of hand? In some ways the question suggests the same sort of fears as were once expressed by those who opposed abandoning the gold standard. Could a government or government agency be wise enough to create just the right amount of money in the absence of some natural force, such as the quantity of gold in its possession, which could limit the supply of money? Might the Territories not become a kind of sink down which public funds might be poured by wild-eyed visionaries bent upon creating a new Canada out of what an eminent Canadian journalist, commenting on the policy, referred to as "that inhospitable barren land," in the absence of market or other "natural" restraints upon such efforts?[2] As it turns out there are increasingly respectable techniques of economic analysis which can be applied to the determination of the economic feasibility of public investment undertakings of the kind we are concerned with here. It is perhaps significant that one of the best short expositions of the elements of this type of rational approach to public expenditure policy should be found in a publication sponsored by the Canadian "Resources for Tomorrow Conference," a conference of federal and provincial groups involved in resource management which was conceived by the Diefenbaker government's most enthusiastic advocate of northern development, the Minister of Northern Affairs and National Resources, Alvin Hamilton.[3] The interested reader is referred to the

[2]See P. C. Neuman, *Renegade in Power: The Diefenbaker Years* (Toronto: McLelland and Stewart, 1963), p. 223.

[3]W. R. D. Sewell, John Davis, A. D. Scott, and D. W. Ross, *Guide to Benefit-Cost Analysis* (Ottawa: Queen's Printer, 1962).

Guide to Benefit-Cost Analysis, for it is possible here only to consider certain elements of the approach which are of special interest to us in our consideration of territorial development.

POSSIBILITIES OF BENEFIT-COST ANALYSIS FOR THE APPRAISAL OF TERRITORIAL DEVELOPMENT PROJECTS

The application of benefit-cost analysis presupposes the recognition of some kind of "need." In the "ideal" or "natural" market economy such a "need" would be signaled by the creation of a possibly profitable market situation conspicuous enough to attract the interest of private *entrepreneurs.*

In anything less than such an ideal economy of the kind imagined by the liberal economists responsible for creating the intellectual justification for the public policy of *laissez-faire,* the possibility exists that some needs, while real enough, may not be communicated by the market mechanism or, for some reason, not responded to by private enterprise. We suggested earlier, for example, that under the conditions prevailing in the northern Territories, private firms might fail to carry certain kinds of resource-developing activity to the socially desirable level because of lack of information or because of their unwillingness to make certain necessary investments from which the total returns to society (including, perhaps, competitors in the area) exceeded the returns recoverable by the firm making the investment. Or, of course, public policy might deliberately exclude private firms from certain types of activity because of some judgment that they are inherently monopolistic, for example, and that a public monopoly in such instances is preferable to a private one. But for whatever reason public enterprise replaces private, it cannot be assumed that public enterprise necessarily can or should respond to the same mechanisms whereby "needs" are identified in the private sector of the economy.

Probably, in practice, most needs which are thought to require the efforts of public enterprise are revealed through some political channel. Pressure groups of various kinds and the system of regional representation in the legislature itself provide some of the obvious channels for the communication to the public authorities of information concerning such needs. The process is complicated in a federal state where responsibility for different types of public activities may be allocated to different levels of government. The slow, but perceptible, development of such channels of communication between the territorial north and the central government in Ottawa described in Chapter 2 and the strengthening of the territorial governments themselves after World War II helped to make both developmental and welfare needs of the north known.[4] The growing national interest in the area also made it increasingly likely that some sort of public action aimed at meeting these needs might be forthcoming. It is at this point that a rather broadly conceived type of benefit-cost analysis becomes relevant as a device for at least helping those responsible for organizing such public activities to make "wise," that is, rational, decisions regarding the use of publicly controlled resources. It is appreciated, of course, that such rational techniques of analysis may find their chief use only in justifying decisions which have already been arrived at on political or other grounds.

To illustrate briefly the general approach of the benefit-cost analysis let us consider how it might have been applied to the Great Slave Lake project referred to earlier. The need for such a railway was created by the alleged inadequacy of the existing river and highway transportation facilities for the successful commercial development of the Pine Point lead-zinc deposits. Private firms were apparently unwilling to undertake the railway project, at least in the foreseeable future. Consequently, it was contended by those anxious to stimulate development in the area to be served by the railroad that the railway should be undertaken as a public project by the federal government. There appeared no doubt about the technical feasibility of the project. And there was no doubt that such a railway would be of benefit to Mackenzie District, not only because of its implications for the Pine Point development, but because it would improve the transportation situation in the district generally. But two questions did exist: first, was a railway the most economical means of achieving these ends, and, second, would the economic resources required for such a project be best used this way rather than for any other purpose in the country, such as for an irrigation dam on the prairies, or a causeway in the Maritimes?

The benefit-cost approach may be used to arrive at reasoned answers to such questions. First, a detailed study would be made to quantify the benefits (the money value of the addition to the country's total output

---

[4]This new interest in the north is reflected in the appearance of an unprecedented volume of writing on the subject both in popular journals such as the *Canadian Geographical Journal* and in more scholarly publications as well.

of goods and services) which could be expected to arise from the construction of the railroad. Secondly, an attempt would be made to calculate the "costs" of the project to the national economy, that is, the money value of the economic resources diverted from other uses to this one—or, to put this more directly, the money value of those benefits which would have been realized from the best alternative use of these economic resources, but which would be sacrificed in order to build the railroad. Once the total benefits and total costs of the railroad project are estimated they may be related in the form of a ratio of benefits to costs. If the total benefits exceed the total costs, the project would appear to be economically justifiable in the limited sense that, considered in isolation, the project would yield a net benefit to the community. If the total benefits were less than the total costs, assuming that the benefits and costs had been estimated as accurately as possible, the project would be uneconomical and, unless this economic criterion was to be over-ridden by others (such as political ones) the project would be abandoned.

Assuming that the benefit-cost ratio of the railway was found to exceed "one," the next step in the analysis would be to evaluate the railway project's relative worth by comparing it with all other approaches which might be used to satisfy the need. This is necessary, for even if the railway was itself economical in the sense that its benefits exceeded its costs, there could be more economical ways of satisfying the same need as, for example, by developing highways, water transportation systems or air transport facilities. Any of these alternatives which appear to be technically possible should then be subjected to the same kind of benefit-cost analysis as the railway was and their benefit-cost ratios determined. The economically optimum use of resources to satisfy this particular need would then be determined by comparing the benefit-cost ratios of all the alternatives for which the ratio exceeded one. (The others would be rejected, of course, on the grounds that they did not meet even the limited test of economic feasibility described earlier.) Now, by choosing the undertaking with the highest ratio of benefits to costs we could be reasonably sure that we had discovered the most economical way of satisfying the need as originally specified. But it would still not have been established that the resources used to satisfy this need were being put to their "best" use, for they might yield greater benefits if put to use satisfying an entirely *different* need. Thus, while the railroad might have a benefit-cost ratio higher than that of a highway, or of an improved waterway, or of any other device designed to satisfy the need for large-scale transportation facilities for southern Mackenzie District, an irrigation and power dam in Saskatchewan, or a new harbour facility in the Maritimes might yield an even higher benefit-cost ratio as an alternative use of the public resources (resources under public control) required for the Great Slave Lake railway. Ideally, then, appropriately calculated benefit-cost ratios would have to be obtained for all the technically feasible and economically plausible uses to which available public resources might conceivably be put during a given period of time. The available resources would then be allocated to those projects with the highest benefit-cost ratios. In this way the community would presumably be assured of having made the best possible use of the available resources in so far as this could be judged in economic terms.

Let us now consider some of the more detailed implications arising out of the possibility of applying this type of analysis to projects, some of which might be located in the territorial north.

Reference has already been made to the relevance of political institutions for the determination of "needs," or for having proposed programmes placed upon the agenda of the appropriate public authority. Just what this authority in a federal state would be would depend upon the constitutional distribution of powers. It is conceivable that it might be a federal, provincial, or even local government department or agency which would be doing the planning of public activities—depending upon the classification of the function involved. The ease or difficulty with which proponents of a particular project may have it brought up for consideration could be strongly influenced by the accessibility of whatever agency of the state is responsible.

Confining our discussion for the moment to resource development programmes it might be thought that one of the advantages of having a regional government charged with this area of responsibility would be that such a government (or its agency) could be more accessible to those proposing programmes involving public participation in such undertakings and would be better able to consider them by virtue of being more closely associated with the problems of the area concerned. Thus, in Canada the administration of natural resources has been, in general, a function assigned to provincial governments with the notable exceptions of the Prairie Provinces before 1930, and the northern Territories to this day.

In the case of the northern Territories, and of the Yukon in particular, one of the functions of the territorial government was to provide a channel of communication between those operating in the area and the federal government. Throughout much of its history, for example, one of the chief activities of the Yukon Council was "memorializing" the federal government in support of some proposal or other to encourage resource development. As we saw in Part I a similar function was served by establishing federal constituencies in the Territories and by giving them direct representation in the legislature. Federal agencies, and employees stationed in the north, also provided such lines of communication. But even so, the contact between the authority constitutionally and financially competent to act in this regard was indirect and this, in combination with the physical remoteness of the area, made the process slow and uncertain. It might appear then that if the techniques of benefit-cost analysis were to be applied in an important way to the determination of significant public and other programmes in the north it might be desirable to entrust such measures to one or more regional governments. One of the obstacles to such a move would naturally be the obvious financial one, for the ability of the territorial government (or any government administering an economically undeveloped area) to command the resources required for such programmes is certain to be very limited indeed. Thus, there appears to be a dilemma confronting us in that, for planning purposes, it would appear advantageous to do the planning at the regional level close to the scene of the proposed activity, but when much of the land under the jurisdiction of such a regional government is undeveloped, the government will have little ability to draw upon the other kinds of resources needed for serious public development programmes. In other words, those regional governments most likely to be faced with resource-developing needs will be least able to do anything about satisfying them. Thus, many projects which they might otherwise find to be economically feasible in terms of benefits and costs would have to be rejected at the outset because they were not *financially* feasible given the taxing, borrowing, and subsidy-attracting powers of the regional public authority involved.

The difficulty is compounded by the existence of conflicting alternative uses for public funds at the regional level. Many responsibilities of government will in practice be carried out without the kind of rational processes of economic justification being applied here to resource-developing programmes. Especially where critical public welfare needs exist, if responsibility for such matters has been assigned to the regional level of government, as has been the general practice in Canada, expenditures designed to alleviate distress in the short run will tend to receive priority over resource development programmes evaluated in terms of costs and benefits, many of the latter being realizable only over a relatively long period of time.

It would appear, then, that it is extremely important when applying the techniques of benefit-cost planning in connection with the public programmes for regional development to consider the nature of the public institutions involved and especially the level of government at which such planning should be undertaken. There would seem to be a number of practical advantages and disadvantages associated with both decentralization and centralization of these processes.

In addition to such practical questions as the accessibility of the planning authority and its financial competence, there are a number of theoretical or conceptual questions involved in the benefit-cost approach to the regulation of public enterprise which have significance for the way such enterprise should be organized—especially when undeveloped regions are involved in the process. To discover them we must go to the heart of the benefit-cost analysis and consider the techniques for determining benefits and costs more closely.

The initial appearance of simplicity which characterizes the benefit-cost approach to the determination of public expenditures policy is rapidly dispelled when it is appreciated that this analysis seeks to take into account more than the immediate and direct effects of the projects being evaluated. That is, in the case of the Great Slave Lake railway project, for example, the effect of the railroad on the delivered costs of the Pine Point mines output would not be the only effect considered. To this would be added the effects of the railroad on the costs of imported goods at centres all along the Mackenzie, its implications for the Great Slave Lake fishery, its effects upon local forest industries, upon labour markets in the area, the level of income in the area served by it and so on. As the *Guide* referred to earlier states, "one of the principal objectives of benefit-cost analysis is to take these related secondary and indirect effects into account."[5] It is this inclusiveness of effects which makes the benefit-cost approach so promising a technique for assessing the real economic merits of public undertakings of the type we are concerned with here. But this inclusiveness also accounts for many of the important difficulties associated with making good use of the analysis and, in some applications at least, it would appear that the more thorough and inclusive the analysis is made, the less reliable its results become as a guide to policy.

[5]Sewell *et al.*, *Guide to Benefit-Cost Analysis*, p. 5.

By the "inclusiveness" of effects here we are referring to the extent to which the analysis takes into account the economic effects of the project not only geographically but also over time as well. In other words, how broad and how distant is the "planning horizon"? This will depend upon the kind of agency doing the planning. A single individual, a small privately owned firm, a large privately owned firm, a publicly owned firm, a municipal government, a regional government, a central government, will all have different fields of vision for planning purposes. As suggested in earlier chapters, a private mining company, for example, will be unlikely to take into account in its planning any benefits or costs which will not show up in its own balance sheet. It would be unlikely to include in its estimates of returns from clearing a new road through the bush the income and employment benefits accruing to the local community as a result of the work created for unemployed native labour in the area. But this might be an important factor in the benefit-cost assessment the regional government might make of such a project if it was faced with the possibility of undertaking it. This regional government would not, however, likely treat as a cost of the project machinery used up in its construction if this machinery was provided in the form of a capital grant from the central government, which stipulated that the funds be used for no other purpose than this one. But the central government, were it evaluating the project, would certainly treat such machinery as a cost because it would see an alternative benefit to the national economy sacrificed in order to make these capital resources available for the project it was actually used for.

Obviously then, the extent to which costs and benefits associated with a particular project are "tracked down" for planning purposes will depend upon what kind of organization is doing the planning simply because of differences in the kinds of effects recognizable by different kinds of agencies. Similarly, these different kinds of organization may be more or less disposed to look far into the future in assessing the effects of a programme. Small private firms with uncertain financial backing may wisely take into account only those returns from an investment which are realizable over a period of a few years. A government agency on the other hand may conceivably take into account returns from a project which will be realized only decades hence.

The extent, then, to which "secondary" (or "indirect") effects of a project and even the "primary" (or "direct") effects are taken into account will depend in practice upon the kind of agency doing the planning. If we assume that the object of such planning is to permit society to make the optimum use of its scarce resources, it should follow that the planning would best be done by the agency most likely to have the broadest and longest possible field of vision. In a country with a unitary system of government this would unquestionably be the government itself—but in a federal state, especially when resources and welfare have been made the responsibility of regional governments, the answer is not so clear. We will return to consider some political aspects of this question shortly. But first, it should be noted that there is another reason inherent in the benefit-cost analysis for favouring centralized, broadly based agencies as the planning units. Because of the breadth of view of such organizations, some of the difficulties associated with the most troublesome part of the analysis, the evaluation of indirect or secondary effects, may be avoided. This would be particularly important in the case of the Territories for, on the basis of what we have seen of the characteristics of the territorial economy, there may be unusually large and important secondary effects (especially benefits) of particular acts of investment there simply because of the importance of marginal increases in the *scale* of operations in so undeveloped an area.

The reason it is difficult to handle the secondary effects of the project, and consequently the reason it is important to cast the analysis in such a way as to minimize their influence on its conclusions, is simply that, being only indirectly attributable to the project, their existence and their magnitude tend to remain more conjectural than is the case for the direct effects of the project. In considering the secondary effects of the Great Slave Lake railway, for example, some of the more obvious secondary benefits would include a reduction in grain-shipping costs for agricultural producers in northern Alberta, the possibility of expanding lumbering operations in the southern part of Mackenzie District and lower retail food costs throughout the entire Mackenzie valley north to the arctic ocean. In the case of the timber operations mentioned, the net income of the firms involved would be a typical secondary benefit of the railway so far as the regional economy was concerned. Any other kind of productive activity created in the area would be similarly treated. It should be noted, however, that such production might merely represent a transfer of productive activity from somewhere else to the area affected by the railroad. Lumber produced locally for local consumption in the area might merely replace that amount of production somewhere outside the area, so that from a national point of view the effect might be of much less significance than it would seem to be from a regional point of view. In general, the broader the field of vision of the planning authority the more likely it is that secondary effects of alternative programmes may simply be cancelled out of the problem. And the more of this that can be done the better, for it reduces the chance of making errors in the course of adjusting the relatively precise estimates of primary costs and benefits. This is especially important when it happens that a series of inter-related secondary effects appears or when these effects are "intangible" in the sense that they are not readily measurable in pecuniary terms. The usual examples of such hard-to-measure indirect effects of a project given in the literature have to do with such things as aesthetic effects of the project—as, for example, the destruction of a view by a line of power pylons or the recreational values of a reservoir created by a dam. Given our concern here with the possible applications of these techniques to a little-developed area like the territorial north, however, certain other forms of such indirect effects inevitably come to mind as a result of our earlier examination of this area's past economic development. We might refer to these as "developmental" secondary effects.

These developmental secondary effects would be in the form of economies realized in the exploitation of natural resources as an indirect consequence of a particular project being undertaken in a previously undeveloped area. Because of this, they might better be thought of as reductions in the costs of such projects than as positive additions to the benefits associated with them. In a sense, they might be thought of as "economies of scale" for, from our earlier study of particular industries in the territorial north, it would seem that most of the activities under-taken there have suffered heavily from the high unit operating costs imposed, not so much by the smallness of the particular resource-exploiting operations themselves, but by the relative smallness of the demand they created in any particular area for such productive inputs as labour, fuel, electrical power, and transportation. Under such circum-stances, any undertaking which expands such markets in an area may make possible real economies in the provision of such services. Further-more, these may not be offset by comparable losses elsewhere, for if the alternative locations for such undertakings are in more developed areas, the marginal benefits from scale would probably be lower both abso-lutely and in relation to the sum of the total primary and secondary effects being assessed in such locations.

Examples of developmental secondary benefits arising from a particu-lar public undertaking such as the Great Slave Lake railroad might serve to illustrate the point. By making possible a large mining development at

Pine Point, the railroad (or possibly some such alternative as a highway) would indirectly greatly expand the demand for electrical energy in the area south and southwest of Great Slave Lake. So large a demand for power would conceivably justify the development of a new hydroelectric site in the area. If such a plant could supply power more efficiently (cheaply) than alternative sources for many of the existing and future users of power in the area, real benefits would accrue to the regional economy. But even more indirect effects of the railroad might also be significant. The lower power costs arising in the way just described might in turn encourage the establishment of what previously were commercially unattractive mining or milling or perhaps even smelting operations in the area. Development of the latter could also create further real benefits in the form of improved utilization rates for the railroad facility itself, it could reduce costs of hiring labour by creating a larger labour pool in the area; and by creating other economies associated with the concentration of economic activity it could reduce the high unit costs of labour and capital inputs associated with the remoteness of the area. Because of the possible importance of such developmental effects of programmes in the remote areas of the country it may be necessary to give more attention to the evaluation of secondary effects when projects located in such areas are included in the range of projects being evaluated at the national level despite the difficulties this type of estimation involves. Or, in other words, when there are gross regional differences, especially differences in existing levels of development, it may be more difficult to rely upon a general cancelling-out technique to reduce the influence of secondary effects upon the comparisons.

Two other elements in the benefit-cost approach that seem particularly relevant here are the treatment of risks and the treatment of welfare effects of projects. Evaluation of the riskiness of a project, that is, of the possibility that it might fail, is important to the benefit-cost analysis because it will influence the benefit-cost ratios either by causing the planning agency to be more or less conservative in its estimates of the future flow of benefits from the project, or by causing it to add a risk factor to its cost calculations. Thus, if there is a general reason for risks being thought to be greater in one kind of project, or for projects located in a particular part of the country, broad application of the benefit-cost technique for evaluating these projects will necessitate the development of procedures for making such estimates of risk as objective as possible. That such regional variations in risk may exist is likely if for no other reason than the variations in regional development levels just referred to. We have seen that, in the case of the Territories, a low level of economic development there has been reflected in the economies being dependent upon at most two industries—fur-trapping and mining. The latter, especially when the activities involved are small and widely dispersed geographically, is a notoriously unstable base for any kind of generalized regional economic activity. Consequently, projects devised for such a region would seem inevitably to be riskier than projects intended for a more mature industrially diversified area. Again, then, if we could assume that riskiness was about the same for all projects under consideration it would be possible to avoid detailed assessment—but when this assumption is not possible, risk factors must be assessed for each project. The degree of risk would consequently influence the comparisons of the benefit-cost ratios arrived at.

Finally, it must be recognized that resource development projects of the kind we are chiefly concerned with here may have important effects upon income and employment levels and that these too may vary greatly from one location to another. Again, the situation in the Territories seems to give this matter special relevance. The fact is that both the Yukon and the Northwest Territories, especially the latter, have become areas of labour surplus because of the decline of the trapping industry and the difficulty experienced by the native and Métis population in adapting to employment in mining and related modern industries. The growth of the "white" population base and the high rate of natural increase in it make it increasingly likely that indigenous white labour may also add significantly to this surplus.

Because most of this labour is unable or unwilling to seek employment outside the Territories (even if suitable employment opportunities could be assumed to exist there) it has no economic cost to society when employed in any projects which might be undertaken in the Territories. That is, in so far as projects created employment for such labour, the labour costs of the project to society would be zero. It is unlikely, of course, that much of this labour could be utilized without some training (and perhaps general education) being provided first. The costs of such training would consequently constitute indirect labour costs chargeable to the project for which the labour was being prepared. If similarly "free" labour exists in other locations where projects are being proposed, this factor will not be significant with respect to the relative benefit-cost ratios arrived at. The possibility of using economically "cheap" labour in particular projects depends not only upon the existence of such labour but upon the nature of the project itself and the possibilities for varying the productive inputs it calls for. If the real costs of a project are to be minimized it must be technically possible to use such labour and it must also be culturally possible to substitute labour for capital when it would be economical to do so. In building the railway, for example, where labour is a free good in the sense that it has no alternative use, it may be technically possible and economically desirable to use labour instead of machinery to clear brush from the right-of-way, to build up the roadbed, to lay the ties, and to set the rails. But there may be emotional obstacles in the way of putting men to "unnecessary" manual labour and impatience with the time lost using such methods. These subjective social "costs" of such a substitution of labour for capital might be offset by subjective benefits such as are often claimed to arise out of earning a living as an alternative to living on "relief." If the wages paid on the project exceeded the welfare outlays in amount, this utilization of free labour would have a desirable multiplier effect upon the general level of income and perhaps even employment in the area. Whether this would be an added benefit or an added cost for the national economy as a whole when the effect spilled over into other parts of it would depend upon whether or not the national economy was operating near a full employment level or not.

These, then, are some of the considerations that are involved in the application of benefit-cost techniques of analysis to resource development projects generally and they seem particularly relevant when some of these projects might be located in a virtually undeveloped region like the Canadian territorial north. We have attempted to show that, ideally, in order to realize the potential of this approach as a guide to the optimum economic use of resources under public control for development purposes, the planning should be done by the authority capable of taking the broadest possible account of the effects of specific programmes upon the national economy as a whole. The objective in the allocation of resources under such programmes should be to maximize the level of production and income for the entire country. But, especially in a country characterized by marked regional disparities both in the kind and in the level of economic development, even if there were no political, administrative, or legal obstacles to organizing public development programmes of the kind we have been concerned with in recent chapters, there would be particular difficulties in applying rational planning techniques such as the extended type of benefit-cost analysis looked at in this chapter.

This is not to suggest that these technical problems would be any less difficult at a regional level of planning, for as we have seen, the need to include many secondary or indirect effects at that level might be even greater than at the national level. But when, because of the locational disparities created for national planning purposes by inclusion of a virtually undeveloped area like the territorial north in the national field of planning vision, these effects must be treated as cardinal elements in the analysis, the technical advantages of centralized planning are greatly reduced. In view of this and the various political factors relevant to the application of the kind of public development policies we have been concerned with, how should public policy with respect to the development of the territorial north of Canada be determined and implemented in the future?

So far in this chapter we have attempted to trace the evolution of public policy from a remarkably pure *laissez-faire* with respect to both the long-run resource-developing and short-run welfare problems in the area up through the policy of federal support for private resource development, the extension of the new national welfare services of government into the area, and the appearance of public activities apparently intended to lead private resource development. Along with this evolution of economic policy, the political organization of the area developed as described in Part I, and by the 1950s it appeared to be assumed that eventually the territorial political organization would evolve into the familiar provincial form of government known elsewhere in Canada. In the light of our earlier discussion of the economic development of the Territories to date and of the various public policies applied in the area, does the past record of economic and political development in the Territories as set out in Parts I and II of this study provide any guide to the appropriate course of public policy in the area in the future?

To begin with, it should be noted that the special type of political organization which has been used in the territorial north to date has apparently not been intended to serve as a means for accelerating the rate of development in that area. Within the context of the Canadian constitution it is conceivable that the territorial system of government could have been used to bring the full weight of the federal government to bear upon whatever special development problems these northern areas might have experienced. While it is true that, especially after World War II, federal funds were used to encourage resource development in the Territories, ways had by then been found to give this type of aid to the provinces as well (for example, through cost-sharing programmes). But despite the limited use made of the territorial form of government as a device to speed northern development by direct federal planning and financing of public projects there in the past, it does not follow that this could not become a reason for continuing this system of government for the northern areas in the future.

We have seen that the chief reason why extensive use was not made of the territorial form of government for such purposes in the past was simply the federal government's lack of interest in programmes which would accelerate the rate of development in that area. This brings us back to the fundamental question: Why *should* the federal government have singled out this particular area for special encouragement? Those Canadians with a financial or emotional involvement in any particular region of the country have always been able, of course, to find arguments to support their claims for preferential treatment of that area—as the debates in Parliament attest. Those concerned with less-developed or less prosperous areas have been particularly well equipped in this regard, for they could advance the "equity" and "equality of opportunity" arguments in support of their claims. Certainly many such arguments could be found to support the contention that the territorial north is worthy of special treatment. These arguments may be politically important, as are the channels for communicating them to the public and to the federal government itself. But we are unable here to consider such arguments in detail, nor is it necessary to do so—for our present purpose is merely to establish the issue of northern development in some kind of national perspective.

As we have seen, once the development of the north was made an issue, it became necessary to consider rational approaches to assessing the economic validity of the claims, even if this was only to be a first approximation to an ultimately political judgment. At this point it becomes obvious that the claims of various parts of the country for development assistance must be evaluated in accordance with national objectives, despite the constitutional and administrative difficulties which the federal distribution of powers creates. If policies of regional development are to have a rational basis it would appear that the ultimate responsibility for establishing the allocation of resources to such purposes must be made at the national level. It is apparent from our study of past policies in the north that these general policies will be political in nature and that they will reflect more than a concern with maximizing the return to the national economy measured in terms of goods and services. Military and humanitarian considerations as well as more narrowly political considerations may be involved. The political "fairness" of this step in the determination of policy presupposes, of course, appropriate representation of all the areas concerned, but since the principle of territorial representation at the federal level was recognized at the end of World War II, no special problem appears to exist here—in principle, at least.

Once this political decision as to the extent of the development programme for the particular region has been taken, the next step is to consider how it should be implemented. The most important conclusion to which our study of past development in the territorial north leads us is that in future it must be viewed in terms of a co-ordinated development programme.

The basic reason for advocating a co-ordinated programme of development for the territorial areas is fundamentally an economic rather than a political or administrative one, although considerations relating to both these other factors are also relevant. In the earlier parts of our study attention was drawn again and again to evidence which would suggest the extent to which economic activities in the territories have been affected by the diseconomies of small-scale operations. The "natural" response to such conditions was for many individual operations to combine in an attempt to concentrate demands for productive inputs of various kinds and to undergo various degrees of both horizontal and vertical integration as described in Chapter 7. We also saw how critical certain types of interaction between different kinds of undertakings have often been and why private firms may have been unable to invest to the socially optimum extent because of the discrepancy between the private and social effects of their investments under these conditions. These are, of course, the same kind of phenomena as were considered earlier in this chapter where they appeared as "secondary" or "indirect" effects of publicly sponsored activities. The point is that if the resources made available for promoting regional development are to be used to the best advantage it must be possible to evaluate the alternative uses to which they might be put within the region. This involves being able to at least identify all the relevant effects of each project being considered. If the resources available are distributed among various private and public agencies operating in an area on some other basis, many important costs and benefits attached to their use will be lost sight of. If a number of independent public agencies (such as transportation companies, power commissions, educational institutions, and the wide range of government departments operating in the north) are allocated resources independently on the basis of subjective estimates of need, past budgets, and other subjective grounds, there is little possibility that the total effect of the resources used will be as large as it could be.

In addition to this economic argument for centralized control over regional programmes there are also the political and administrative considerations mentioned above. It would appear that there are obvious administrative efficiencies to be derived from centralized planning in the various public undertakings in the Territories. While it is true that in the past the federal department or branch entrusted with general administration of the Territories has provided a measure of such centralization in overall administration, most of the public undertakings in the area have been planned and supervised by the often bewildering variety of federal departments, territorial departments and crown corporations which have been referred to throughout Parts I and III of this study. The chief political disadvantage of this administrative tangle is an important one, for it involves the serious question of the allocations of political responsibility for the use to which public resources are put. In the case of the territorial north this is a particularly important issue because, if an economically significant development programme should be undertaken there (for any of the reasons referred to earlier) most of the public resources required for it must come from outside the area. In financial terms this means that the programme would be financed largely by taxpayers and by lenders residing outside the territorial area and only partly by those residing in it. Political accountability will consequently be particularly important, for the past experience with public spending (especially for "development" purposes) in the northern areas, as we have seen, has often been a source of controversy. Although the cynic might suggest that this is all the more reason for obscuring the uses to which such funds are being put, it would surely be more satisfactory to make the total financial cost of such a programme as a whole visible to those who are financing it and at the same time to establish without ambiguity where the political responsibility for it should rest.

If such considerations seemed important enough to warrant establishing a centralized agency to plan and to administer a co-ordinated development programme for northern Canada, the next consideration would be the form which it should take. Let us continue our assumption that this agency's budget would be determined at the federal level in accordance with the appropriate criteria for allocating public funds to alternative national purposes. Let us also continue to assume that this process yields a large enough allocation for northern development to justify making provision to use it wisely.

Given these assumptions, what further indications are there, judging from this study of the area's development to date, as to the appropriate form such a regional development agency might take? Specifically, what would its appropriate geographical area of concern be and how would the agency itself be constituted? It is appreciated that we can look to the past experience of the Canadian Territories for only part of the answer to these questions. There is, for example, an increasing amount of information of a comparative nature becoming available on the subject of such regional development organizations in other countries.

As noted at the outset of this study the chief reason for focusing attention upon the area delimited politically by the boundaries of the Yukon and Northwest Territories was neither physical nor economic, but simply a consequence of the special political status of this area within the Canadian federation. Indeed, it was emphasized in Chapter I that if these political boundaries had been based on any geographical or economic considerations at all they would have been located very differently than they were. Consequently, in considering the possibility of establishing a co-ordinated programme for the development of the arctic and sub-arctic regions of Canada it would be appropriate *in terms of economic geography* to create as its area of jurisdiction not only the Yukon and Northwest Territories, but also the large arctic and sub-arctic northern parts of British Columbia, of the Prairie Provinces, and of Ontario, Quebec, and Newfoundland.

The disadvantage of this would be the practical difficulty of co-ordinating undertakings in so many different jurisdictions and of reconciling the various sectional differences of opinion which would inevitably arise. It is difficult to imagine so broadly based an agency having much more than an advisory function. It could have little to do with the actual undertaking of particular projects and the administration of a programme of development in any detail. The equally obvious *advantage* of such a broadly based agency would be that it would not only create a more natural area for planning but, ideally, it would make possible a much more economical allocation of national resources to the purpose of northern development.

In our study we have seen many examples of the powerful economic inter-relationships between development in the territorial north and in the northern parts of the provinces, not only in the field of transportation, where the connection is obvious, but also in such matters as the supply of labour and other productive inputs. Especially when modern techniques of communication are taken into account, it would appear to be both economically desirable and physically feasible to plan future development of all the arctic and sub-arctic regions as a whole. Such an approach would, however, encounter the practical political difficulties arising out of provincial jealousies of their respective northern areas and would create the problem of obtaining provincial co-operation on such a large-scale project. If it is imagined for the moment that the Yukon and Northwest Territories were to be given provincial status, implementing a national programme of northern development would in principle seem to be little different than implementing such familiar programmes as the national Pension Scheme or the proposed Medical Care Scheme. Even with the existing status of the Yukon and the Northwest Territories, such an approach is readily conceivable. Indeed, if the existing Yukon and Northwest Territories structure was dismantled and these lands assigned to geographically appropriate provinces (as has from time to time been suggested) implementation of such schemes would be simplified by reducing the number of provincial units involved.

But let us suppose that for practical political reasons it proved necessary to restrict the type of development programme we have in mind here to the present area of direct federal jurisdiction over natural resources in Canada. Given this, how should the agency entrusted with the detailed planning and administration of the programme itself be constituted?

The most obvious recommendation which our study of past development in the area would suggest is that the agency be so organized as to give representation to all the important specialized agencies, private and public, involved in the economic life of the area. Again the reason for this is the evidence of how important interaction between superficially quite different acts of investment (or other spending) in such an undeveloped area can be. Private and public investments in mining, private investments in the fur industry, private and public spending on health, education, and welfare, and private and public investments in transportation and power facilities are, as we have seen, inextricably inter-related. It is difficult to imagine, for example, how resources could be allocated to road construction without having as much information as possible about the planned undertakings of mining firms in the area to be served. Similarly, decisions to devote resources to vocational training must be taken with some idea of prospective employment opportunities both inside and outside the territorial north. It may be, too, that resources would be better used to subsidize mining development directly in order to create local employment than to use the resources either for "relief" or for promoting a native crafts industry.

Because the fundamental purpose of establishing a regional development agency would be to realize the economies to be gained from co-ordinating all such activities, the structure of the agency would necessarily have to incorporate those involved in its activities. Existing public agencies such as the Northern Transportation Company and the Northern Canada Power Commission might be brought together to form a nucleus for a central planning and administrative agency. We have seen that in the history of the northern Territories even private enterprise has behaved in such a way as to create precedents for this kind of integration. Indeed, one of the small ironies of this history has been that the effect of public policy over most of the period appears to have been to force a greater degree of integration and concentration of *private* activities in the area than of public activities. One possible advantage of this historical fact, however, is that only a relatively few large private undertakings have been established in the area, so the task of organizing a central development agency there would be simpler than it might otherwise have been. Beause of this, and the special and rather fluid political situation in the area, it could prove a useful testing ground for experimentation with some form of the development agency technique for promoting regional growth.

V. TABLES

TABLE 1.1

<small>COMPARATIVE CLIMATIC DATA</small>

Average Daily Mean Temperatures in Selected Months

Location	Years of observation	January	July	November-March	June-August
		(Degrees Fahrenheit)			
NWT					
Yellowknife	10	−18	60	− 8	57
Fort Smith	30	−13	61	− 3	58
Port Radium	11	−15	54	− 7	51
Aklavik	22	−18	56	−12	52
Chesterfield	29	−26	48	−17	44
Frobisher	10	−18	46	− 6	43
YUKON					
Whitehorse	10	5	56	10	55
Mayo Landing	26	−11	58	− 2	56
QUEBEC					
Chibougamau	14	− 3	61	8	58
Knob Lake	5	−13	55	1	52
ONTARIO					
Porquis Junction	12	1	64	11	61
Sudbury	16	10	66	18	64
MANITOBA					
Winnipeg	66	− 3	67	9	64
Flin Flon	23	− 7	66	4	62
SASKATCHEWAN					
Saskatoon	38	− 1	65	10	62
ALBERTA					
Edmonton	56	6	62	16	60

<small>SOURCE:</small> R. G. Robertson, *The Northwest Territories: Its Economic Prospects*, A Brief Presented to the Royal Commission on Canada's Economic Prospects, November, 1955 (Ottawa: Queen's Printer, 1955), Appendix F.

TABLE 2.1

PERCENTAGE DISTRIBUTION OF TERRITORIAL AND PROVINCIAL EXPENDITURES FOR THE FISCAL YEAR ENDING MARCH 31, 1960

Function	YT	NWT	Nfld	PEI	NS	NB	Que	Ont	Man	Sask	Alta	BC	Total
General government	12.2	4.0	5.9	3.3	4.4	4.8	4.6	3.7	5.6	5.3	2.6	5.5	4.3
Protection of persons and property	0.5	1.4	5.0	1.9	3.4	2.6	5.4	5.0	4.4	4.5	5.5	5.0	4.9
Transportation and communications	33.0	4.2	22.2	46.5	30.6	36.0	25.8	28.2	30.2	22.1	25.7	21.4	26.7
Health	12.4	21.6	16.4	13.1	16.0	13.5	12.8	19.3	19.7	25.0	15.5	18.0	17.2
Social welfare	5.4	8.5	14.9	4.4	6.6	5.9	12.9	4.9	5.6	7.5	7.9	9.2	8.1
Education	27.8	45.2	23.7	11.8	22.2	14.6	22.8	23.5	23.7	24.6	31.0	23.0	23.7
Natural resources and primary industries	1.0	2.6	4.1	4.2	4.3	5.5	10.1	4.1	6.6	8.6	9.5	7.6	6.8
Debt charges (exclusive of debt retirement)	1.0	—	3.7	9.5	9.0	8.4	2.0	4.4	-0.3	-0.5	-6.6	1.1	2.3
Contributions to other governments	3.5	5.0	1.5	1.8	1.1	6.9	0.1	3.3	2.1	—	6.5	3.9	2.6
All other expenditure	3.2	7.5	2.6	3.5	2.4	1.8	3.5	3.6	2.4	2.9	2.4	5.3	3.4
Net general expenditure (exclusive of debt retirement)	100	100	100	100	100	100	100	100	100	100	100	100	100

SOURCE: DBS, *Financial Statistics of Provincial Governments: Revenue and Expenditure (Actual) 1959*, p. 8.

TABLE 2.2

TERRITORIAL EXPENDITURES 1959

(thousands of dollars)

Function	YT	NWT
GENERAL GOVERNMENT		
Executive and administrative	262	34
Legislative	18	20
PROTECTION OF PERSONS AND PROPERTY		
Law enforcement	1	—
Police protection	—	—
Other	10	19
TRANSPORTATION AND COMMUNICATIONS		
Airways	5	—
Highways, roads and bridges	663	57
Railways	—	—
Telephone, telegraph and wireless	—	—
Waterways	89	—
HEALTH		
General health	20	36
Public health	133	142
Medical, dental and allied services	3	9
Hospital care	165	201
SOCIAL WELFARE		
Aid to aged persons	32	81
Aid to blind persons	3	20
Aid to unemployed and unemployable	68	60
Mothers' allowances	—	—
Child welfare	38	25
Other social welfare	—	22
RECREATIONAL AND CULTURAL SERVICES		
Archives, art galleries, libraries and museums	2	2
Parks, beaches, and other recreational areas	53	10
Physical culture	—	4
Other	—	2
EDUCATION		
Schools operated by local authorities	903*	616†

*Consists of expenditures on public schools operated by territorial government and grants to denominational schools.

†Includes 423 paid to federal government day schools for pupils other than Indians and Eskimos; 74 as grants to local school districts; and 79 paid to denominational and private schools.

SOURCE: DBS, *Financial Statistics of Provincial Governments: Revenue and Expenditure (Actual) 1959*, pp. 18–21.

TABLE 2.3

PERCENTAGE DISTRIBUTION OF TERRITORIAL AND PROVINCIAL REVENUES BY SOURCE FOR THE FISCAL YEAR ENDING MARCH 31, 1960

Source of revenue	Territory or Province												
	YT	NWT	Nfld	PEI	NS	NB	Que	Ont	Man	Sask	Alta	BC	Total
TAXES													
Corporation	—	—	0.5	0.7	1.0	0.9	4.4	1.9	1.2	0.5	0.7	0.9	2.0
Income—Corporations	—	—	—	—	—	—	14.6	20.7	—	—	—	—	10.1
Individuals	—	—	—	—	—	—	9.0	—	—	—	—	—	2.2
Sales—Motor fuel and fuel oil	11.8	7.3	8.3	17.6	17.0	15.8	15.6	20.6	15.3	14.4	9.2	9.8	15.5
General	—	—	15.2	—	11.3	11.2	11.3	—	—	15.4	—	28.7	8.5
All other sales taxes	4.3	—	0.1	5.2	0.8	2.6	6.1	1.3	0.7	0.1	0.2	1.0	2.2
Succession duties	—	—	—	3.6	—	—	3.7	4.3	12.9	6.1	—	—	2.3
Hospital insurance premiums	—	—	—	—	—	—	—	9.2	—	—	—	1.9	3.8
All other taxes	9.3	0.2	0.6	—	0.2	0.4	0.3	1.2	0.2	0.1	0.1	—	0.7
TOTAL TAXES	25.4	7.5	24.5	27.1	30.3	30.9	65.0	59.2	30.3	36.6	10.2	42.3	47.3
FED.-PROV. TAX-SHARING ARRANGEMENTS	20.1	33.2	33.2	31.8	35.3	34.0	11.3	13.6	39.5	27.6	19.9	21.6	18.7
PRIVILEGES, LICENSES AND PERMITS													
Liquor control and regulation	0.3	3.3	3.1	0.3	0.3	—	2.3	3.2	2.7	—	0.3	0.1	1.8
Motor vehicles	6.3	2.4	3.0	5.3	6.1	5.9	6.3	8.8	7.8	5.2	4.4	5.7	6.7
Natural resources	1.3	3.7	1.2	0.1	1.6	4.7	5.1	4.8	3.9	13.5	53.9	17.6	12.3
Other	2.7	1.9	0.8	0.9	0.6	0.6	1.4	1.2	1.2	1.1	0.6	0.9	1.1
TOTAL LICENSES AND PERMITS	10.6	11.3	8.1	6.6	8.6	11.2	15.1	18.0	15.6	19.8	59.2	24.3	21.9
GOVERNMENT OF CANADA													
SUBSIDIES	1.9	2.8	28.3	22.8	10.6	11.9	0.5	0.5	2.1	1.4	0.9	0.4	2.2
LIQUOR PROFITS	38.8	36.9	4.1	8.6	12.7	10.2	5.5	6.8	10.1	9.0	6.8	8.6	7.3
ALL OTHER REVENUE	3.2	8.3	1.6	3.1	2.5	1.8	2.6	1.9	2.4	5.6	3.0	2.8	2.6
TOTAL NET GENERAL REVENUE	100	100	100	100	100	100	100	100	100	100	100	100	100

SOURCE: DBS, *Financial Statistics of Provincial Governments: Revenue and Expenditure (Actual) 1959*, p. 7.

TABLE 2.4

TERRITORIAL REVENUE 1959

(thousands of dollars)

Source	YT	NWT
Taxes	528	119
Federal tax exemption grant	419	530
Privileges, licences and permits		
Liquor control and regulation	6	53
Motor vehicles	131	38
Natural resources	27	59
Other	57	31
Sales and services	226	46
Fines and penalties	12	11
Interest, discount, premium and exchange	19	—
Other governments	172	248
Government enterprises		
Liquor profits	808	589
Other	—	—
Other revenue	2	1
Non-revenue and surplus receipts	21	75
Total Gross General Revenue	2,428	1,800
Population (000s) estimated as of		
June 1, 1959	13	21
Gross General Revenue Per Capita	187	86

SOURCE: DBS, *Financial Statistics of Provincial Governments: Revenue and Expenditure (Actual) 1959*, p. 16.

TABLE 3.1
TOTAL FUR PRODUCTION OF THE NORTH BY TERRITORIES*

Season	Number of pelts			Value of pelts (current dollars)			Average value per pelt
	YT	NWT	Total	YT	NWT	Total	
1910*				159,672	500,217	659,889	
1919–20	55,354	154,882	210,236	323,467	1,121,026	1,444,493	6.87
1920–21	16,125	208,068	224,193	78,189	1,153,840	1,232,029	5.44
1921–22	69,796	273,288	343,084	203,402	1,834,015	2,037,417	5.94
1922–23	46,198	287,698	333,896	199,522	2,171,424	2,370,946	7.11
1923–24	50,070	164,903	214,973	347,079	1,529,376	1,876,455	8.73
1924–25	36,616	148,885	185,501	309,549	1,780,666	2,090,215	11.27
1925–26	35,767	174,337	210,104	320,803	1,625,875	1,946,678	9.26
1926–27	25,991	203,765	229,756	382,261	2,981,829	3,364,090	14.64
1927–28	64,375	227,136	291,511	610,348	2,000,968	2,611,316	8.96
1928–29	35,736	312,093	347,829	484,919	2,111,543	2,596,462	7.46
1929–30	108,632	219,604	328,236	295,492	1,632,446	1,927,938	5.88
1930–31	61,832	371,281	433,113	145,224	1,945,737	2,090,961	4.83
1931–32	57,679	341,922	399,601	132,268	999,203	1,131,471	2.83
1932–33	52,282	269,319	321,601	146,055	1,095,226	1,241,281	3.86
1933–34	43,803	229,665	273,468	122,999	1,515,077	1,638,076	5.99
1934–35	41,309	212,414	253,723	230,074	1,678,544	1,908,618	7.52
1935–36	42,768	211,551	254,319	276,946	1,188,285	1,465,231	5.76
1936–37	50,308	285,962	336,270	347,558	1,178,129	1,525,687	4.54
1937–38	67,655	523,279	591,034	295,857	1,311,627	1,607,484	2.72
1938–39	77,475	514,894	592,369	267,721	1,274,817	1,542,538	2.50
1939–40	80,617	530,409	611,026	288,292	1,234,529	1,522,821	2.49
1940–41	70,953	447,547	518,500	373,399	2,301,054	2,674,453	5.10
1941–42	66,700	445,336	512,036	398,132	2,840,701	3,238,833	6.33

TABLE 3.1 (concluded)

Season	Number of pelts			Value of pelts (current dollars)			Average value per pelt
	YT	NWT	Total	YT	NWT	Total	
1942-43	52,897	385,440	438,337	338,035	3,165,107	3,503,142	7.99
1943-44	78,005	297,633	375,638	467,188	2,199,132	2,666,320	7.09
1944-45	87,292	258,931	346,223	669,217	1,743,710	2,412,927	6.97
1945-46	107,252	565,065	672,317	677,495	2,750,183	3,427,678	5.10
1946-47	58,777	488,039	546,816	373,176	1,658,754	2,031,930	3.72
1947-48	131,227	482,420	613,647	230,117	1,872,302	2,102,419	3.43
1948-49	151,969	922,136	1,074,105	143,810	1,535,461	1,679,271	1.58
1949-50	153,574	561,400	714,974	199,086	909,504	1,108,590	1.55
1950-51	228,616	643,579	872,195	361,969	2,038,339	2,400,308	2.75
1951-52	171,274	696,245	867,519	173,252	1,448,173	1,621,425	1.87
1952-53	246,379	388,653	635,032	247,001	877,345	1,124,346	1.77
1953-54	176,338	418,871	595,209	182,238	757,079	939,317	1.58
1954-55	213,515	477,611	691,126	242,944	1,166,919	1,409,863	2.04
1955-56	109,576	366,089	475,665	155,777	805,558	961,335	2.02
1956-57	108,102	256,887	364,989	108,873	732,789	841,662	2.31
1957-58	110,512	257,183	367,695	118,607	735,491	854,098	2.32
1958-59	103,604	236,123	339,727	67,571	808,154	875,725	2.58
1959-60	182,982	238,539	421,521	158,232	821,975	980,207	2.33
1960-61	116,787	316,340	433,127	105,031	1,319,748	1,424,779	3.29
1961-62	98,902	337,145	436,047	125,348	888,964	1,014,312	2.33

*Early records of fur production were limited to the decennial census with $262,951 being reported for the Yukon and Northwest Territories in 1901 and $500,217 in 1911. In 1920 the Dominion Bureau of Statistics began reporting raw fur production annually using data supplied by licensed fur traders. Since 1945 provincial game department statements have been used as the basis for these statistics.

SOURCE: Seasons 1919 to 1951 from DBS, *Canada Year Book*, annually; seasons 1951 to 1961 from DBS, *Fur Production*, annually.

TABLE 3.2

TERRITORIAL AND NATIONAL FUR PRODUCTION

	(1) Canada $'000	(2) Y + NWT $'000	(3) (2) as % of (1)
1910	1,928	660	34
1919–20	21,387	1,444	7
1920–21	10,152	1,232	12
1921–22	17,439	2,037	12
1922–23	16,762	2,371	14
1923–24	15,644	1,876	12
1924–25	15,442	2,090	14
1925–26	15,072	1,947	13
1926–27	18,864	3,364	18
1927–28	18,758	2,611	14
1928–29	18,745	2,596	14
1929–30	12,158	1,928	16
1930–31	11,681	2,091	18
1931–32	10,156	1,131	11
1932–33	10,305	1,241	12
1933–34	12,349	1,638	13
1934–35	12,843	1,909	15
1935–36	15,465	1,465	9
1936–37	17,526	1,526	9
1937–38	13,196	1,607	12
1938–39	14,287	1,543	11
1939–40	16,668	1,523	9
1940–41	21,123	2,674	13
1941–42	24,860	3,239	13
1942–43	28,505	3,503	12
1943–44	33,147	2,666	8
1944–45	31,001	2,413	8
1945–46	43,871	3,428	8
1946–47	26,350	2,032	8
1947–48	32,233	2,102	7
1948–49	22,900	1,679	7
1949–50	23,184	1,109	4
1950–51	31,134	2,400	7
1951–52	24,215	1,621	7
1952–53	23,350	1,124	5
1953–54	19,288	939	5
1954–55	30,510	1,410	5
1955–56	28,052	961	3
1956–57	25,592	842	3
1957–58	26,335	854	3
1958–59	25,801	876	3
1959–60	31,186	980	3
1960–61	28,737	1,425	5
1961–62	28,938	1,014	4

SOURCE: As for Table 3.1.

TABLE 3.3

FUR FARMS—YUKON TERRITORY 1920-1944

Year	Number	Year	Number
1920	14	1933	7
1921	16	1934	7
1922	16	1935	8
1923	21	1936	7
1924	20	1937	10
1925	20	1938	10
1926	14	1939	8
1927	14	1940	9
1928	17	1941	10
1929	17	1942	6
1930	15	1943	5
1931	11	1944	nil
1932	7		

SOURCE: *Canada Year Book*, "Fur Farms," annually, 1920-45.

TABLE 3.4

QUANTITY OF FISH LANDED IN THE NORTHWEST TERRITORIES AND IN INLAND CANADA 1945-61

(thousands of pounds)

	NWT	Canada	NWT as % of Total Canada
1945	3291	90,892	3.6
1946	6640	91,275	7.3
1947	3479	79,579	4.4
1948	7805	87,528	8.9
1949	9101	90,208	10.1
1950	7867	91,960	8.6
1951	7477	98,359	7.6
1952	7042	102,929	6.8
1953	6719	106,216	6.3
1954	7021	116,187	6.0
1955	7827	118,959	6.6
1956	6939	124,596	5.6
1957	6584	119,589	5.5
1958	5894	114,613	5.1
1959	5747	117,212	4.9
1960	5543	123,024	4.5
1961	5676	123,073	4.6

SOURCE: DBS, *Canada Year Book*, "Fisheries," annually.

TABLE 4.1

GOLD PRODUCTION

(thousands of fine ounces)

	(I) YT	(II) NWT	(III) Y + NWT	(IV) Canada	(III) as % of (IV)
1900	1078		1078	1350	79.8
1901	871		871	1167	74.7
1902	702		702	1032	68.0
1903	593		593	912	65.0
1904	508		508	796	63.8
1905	423		423	685	61.8
1906	271		271	556	48.7
1907	152		152	406	37.4
1908	174		174	476	36.6
1909	192		192	454	42.3
1910	211		211	494	42.7
1911	224		224	473	47.4
1912	268		268	612	43.8
1913	283		283	803	35.2
1914	248		248	773	32.1
1915	230		230	918	25.1
1916	213		213	930	22.9
1917	178		178	739	24.1
1918	102		102	700	14.6
1919	91		91	767	11.9
1920	73		73	765	9.5
1921	66		66	926	7.1
1922	54		54	1263	4.3
1923	60		60	1233	4.9
1924	35		35	1525	2.3
1925	48		48	1736	2.8
1926	26		26	1754	1.5
1927	31		31	1853	1.7
1928	34		34	1891	1.8
1929	36		36	1928	1.8
1930	36		36	2102	1.7
1931	44		44	2694	1.6
1932	41		41	3044	1.3
1933	39		39	2949	1.4
1934	39		39	2972	1.3
1935	36		36	3285	1.1
1936	50		50	3748	1.3
1937	48		48	4096	1.2
1938	72	6	78	4725	1.6
1939	88	52	140	5094	2.7
1940	80	55	135	5311	2.5
1941	71	74	145	5345	2.7
1942	83	99	182	4841	3.7
1943	41	59	100	3651	2.7
1944	24	21	45	2923	1.5
1945	32	9	41	2697	1.5
1946	45	23	68	2833	2.4
1947	48	63	111	3070	2.2
1948	61	102	163	3530	4.6

TABLE 4.1 (*concluded*)

	(I) YT	(II) NWT	(III) Y + NWT	(IV) Canada	(III) as % of (IV)
1949	82	177	259	4124	6.3
1950	93	201	294	4441	6.6
1951	78	212	290	4393	6.6
1952	79	248	327	4472	7.1
1953	66	290	356	4056	8.8
1954	82	309	391	4366	8.9
1955	72	321	393	4542	8.7
1956	72	353	425	4384	9.7
1957	74	340	414	4434	9.3
1958	68	344	412	4571	9.0
1959	67	406	473	4483	10.5
1960	78	418	496	4629	10.7
1961	67	407	474	4474	10.6

SOURCES: Figures for 1900 to 1956 from DBS, *Canadian Mineral Statistics 1886–1956*, Reference Paper Number 68, pp. 118–20; 1956 to 1961 from DBS, *General Review of the Mining Industry*, annually (26–201).

TABLE 4.2

SILVER PRODUCTION

(thousands of fine ounces)

	(I) YT	(II) NWT	(III) (I + II)	(IV) Canada	(V) (III) as % of (IV)
1899	230		230	3412	6.7
1900	290		290	4468	6.5
1901	195		195	5539	3.5
1902	186		186	4291	4.3
1903	156		156	3199	4.8
1904	133		133	3578	3.7
1905	90		90	6000	1.5
1906	64		64	8473	0.7
1907	36		36	12780	0.3
1908	63		63	22106	0.3
1909	45		45	27529	0.2
1910	87		87	32869	0.3
1911	113		113	32559	0.4
1912	81		81	31956	0.3
1913	88		88	31846	0.3
1914	93		93	28450	0.3
1915	248		248	26626	0.9
1916	360		360	25460	1.4
1917	120		120	22221	0.5
1918	72		72	21384	0.3
1919	28		28	16021	0.2
1920	19		19	13330	0.1

TABLE 4.2 (*concluded*)

	(I) YT	(II) NWT	(III) (I + II)	(IV) Canada	(V) (III) as % of (IV)
1921	393		393	13543	2.9
1922	663		663	18626	3.5
1923	1914		1914	18602	10.3
1924	227		227	19736	1.1
1925	905		905	20229	4.4
1926	2095		2095	22372	9.4
1927	1647		1647	22737	7.2
1928	2840		2840	21936	12.9
1929	3280		3280	23143	14.1
1930	3746		3746	26444	14.2
1931	3695	*	3695	20562	17.9
1932	3015	38	3053	18348	16.6
1933	2204	23	2227	15188	14.7
1934	516	38	554	16415	3.4
1935	55	147	202	16619	1.2
1936	783	317	1100	18334	5.9
1937	3957	135	4092	22978	17.9
1938	2845	582	3427	22219	15.4
1939	3831	484	4315	23164	18.6
1940	2259	60	2319	23834	9.7
1941	857	15	872	21754	4.0
1942	482	23	505	20695	2.4
1943	52	13	65	17345	0.4
1944	32	14	46	13627	0.3
1945	25	2	27	12943	0.3
1946	31	6	37	12544	0.3
1947	372	45	417	12504	3.3
1948	1719	25	1744	16110	10.9
1949	1563	71	1634	17641	9.3
1950	3203	62	3265	23221	14.1
1951	3443	64	3507	23125	15.2
1952	4029	59	4088	25222	16.2
1953	6639	64	6703	28299	23.7
1954	6992	59	7051	31118	22.6
1955	5712	58	5770	27984	20.6
1956	6193	70	6263	28432	22.0
1957	6484	69	6553	28823	22.7
1958	6416	73	6489	31163	20.8
1959	7055	71	7126	31924	22.3
1960	7217	79	7296	34017	21.4
1961	6937	78	7015	31382	22.3

*Small quantity included in Yukon.

SOURCES: DBS, *Canadian Mineral Statistics 1886–1956*; DBS, *General Review of the Mining Industry*, 1956–61, annually.

TABLE 4.3

COPPER PRODUCTION

(thousands of pounds)

*1906 includes some copper mined in earlier years.
†less than 0.1 per cent.

SOURCE: As for Table 4.2.

	YT	NWT	Total	Canada	%
1906*	156		156	55,610	0.3
1907	512		512	56,979	0.9
1908	112		112	63,703	0.2
1909				52,493	†
1910	286		286	55,692	0.5
1911				55,648	†
1912	1,773		1,773	77,832	0.3
1913	1,844		1,844	76,977	2.4
1914	1,367		1,367	75,736	1.8
1915	533		533	100,785	0.5
1916	2,807		2,807	117,150	2.4
1917	2,460		2,460	109,227	2.3
1918	620		620	118,769	0.5
1919	165		165	75,054	0.2
1920	278		278	81,601	0.3
1921					
1922					
1923					
1924					
1925					
1926					
1927					
1928	107		107		†
1929					
1930	43		43		†
1931					
1932					
1933					
1934					
1935					
1936					
1937					
1938		76	76		†
1939		42	42		†
1940					
1941		33	33		†
1942		75	75		†
1943					
1944		12	12		†
1945					
1946					
1947					
1948					
1949					
1950					
1951		2	2		†
1952		7	7		†
1953					
1954					
1955					
1956					
1957		330	330	718,218	†
1958		868	868	690,228	0.1
1959		987	987	790,538	0.1
1960		1,040	1,040	878,524	0.1
1961	882	926	1,808	878,164	0.2

TABLE 4.4

CURRENT DOLLAR VALUE OF METALLIC MINERAL PRODUCTION YT, 1900–61

(thousands of dollars)

	Gold			Silver			Lead			Zinc			Copper			Total value of metallic minerals produced		
Year	$	% Yukon total	% Y and NWT total	$	% Yukon total	% Y and NWT total	$	% Yukon total	% Y and NWT total	$	% Yukon total	% Y and NWT total	$	% Yukon total	% Y and NWT total	Yukon	Y and NWT	Y total as % of Y and NWT
1900	22,275	99.2	99.2	178	0.8	0.8										22,453	22,453	100
1901	18,000	99.4	99.4	115	0.6	0.6										18,115	18,115	100
1902	14,500	99.3	99.3	97	0.7	0.7										14,597	14,597	100
1903	12,250	99.3	99.3	83	0.7	0.7										12,333	12,333	100
1904	10,500	99.3	99.3	76	0.7	0.7										10,576	10,576	100
1905	7,876	99.3	99.3	54	0.7	0.7										7,930	7,930	100
1906	5,600	98.8	98.8	43	0.8	0.8							23	0.4	0.4	5,666	5,666	100
1907	3,150	96.2	96.2	24	0.7	0.7							102	3.1	3.1	3,276	3,276	100
1908	3,600	98.7	98.7	33	0.9	0.9							15	0.4	0.4	3,648	3,648	100
1909	3,960	99.4	99.4	23	0.6	0.6										3,983	3,983	100
1910	4,570	98.2	98.2	47	1.0	1.0							36	0.8	0.8	4,653	4,653	100
1911	4,635	98.7	98.7	60	1.3	1.3										4,695	4,695	100
1912	5,549	94.2	94.2	49	0.8	0.8							290	4.9	4.9	5,888	5,888	100
1913	5,847	94.6	94.6	52	0.8	0.8							281	4.6	4.6	6,180	6,180	100
1914	5,125	95.5	95.5	51	1.0	1.0	2	††	††				186	3.5	3.5	5,364	5,364	100
1915	4,758	94.8	94.8	123	2.5	2.5	45	0.9	0.9				92	1.8	1.8	5,018	5,018	100
1916	4,397	80.3	80.3	236	4.3	4.3	81	1.5	1.5				764	14.0	14.0	5,478	5,478	100
1917	3,673	82.5	82.5	98	2.2	2.2	14	0.3	0.3				669	15.0	15.0	4,453	4,453	100
1918	2,118	90.4	90.4	70	3.0	3.0	1	†	†				153	6.5	6.5	2,342	2,342	100
1919	1,875	96.8	96.8	31	1.6	1.6							31	1.6	1.6	1,937	1,937	100
1920	1,504	95.7	95.7	19	1.2	1.2							48	3.1	3.0	1,571	1,571	100
1921	1,364	77.9	77.9	246	14.0	14.0	142	8.1	8.1							1,752	1,752	100
1922	1,126	63.2	63.2	448	25.2	25.2	207	11.6	11.6							1,781	1,781	100
1923	1,243	41.8	41.8	1,242	41.8	41.8	486	16.4	16.4							2,971	2,971	100
1924	720	76.3	76.3	151	16.0	16.0	73	7.7	7.7							944	944	100
1925	988	55.4	55.4	625	35.0	35.0	171	9.6	9.6							1,784	1,784	100
1926	529	23.8	23.8	1,301	58.4	58.4	396	17.8	17.8							2,226	2,226	100
1927	639	25.5	25.5	1,652	65.8	65.8	219	8.7	8.7							2,510	2,510	100
1928	710	26.2	26.2	1,652	61.0	61.0	329	12.2	12.2				16	0.6	0.6	2,707	2,707	100
1929	742	25.6	25.6	1,738	59.8	59.8	424	14.6	14.6							2,904	2,904	100

Year	Gold $	Gold % Yukon total	Gold % Y and NWT total	Silver $	Silver % Yukon total	Silver % Y and NWT total	Lead $	Lead % Yukon totbl	Lead % Y and NWT total	Zinc $	Zinc % Yukon total	Zinc % Y and NWT total	Copper $	Copper % Yukon total	Copper % Y and NWT total	Total value of metallic minerals produced Yukon	Y and NWT	Y total as % of Y and NWT
1930	734	29.2	29.2	1,429	56.8	56.8	349	13.9	13.9				6	0.2		2,518	2,518	100
1931	956	43.8	43.8	1,102	50.6	50.6	121	5.5	5.5							2,181	2,181	100
1932	953	47.9	47.6	955	48.0	47.7	81	4.1	4.0							1,989	2,001	99.4
1933	1,130	55.5	55.2	834	40.9	40.7	74	3.6	3.6							2,038	2,047	99.6
1934	1,339	82.3	81.4	245	15.1	14.9	43	2.6	2.6							1,627	1,645	98.9
1935	1,257	96.8	89.7	35	2.7	2.5	7	0.5	0.5							1,299	1,401	92.7
1936	1,764	79.5	74.7	354	15.0	15.0	101	4.6	4.3							2,219	2,362	94.0
1937	1,679	44.4	43.7	1,776	46.9	46.2	329	8.7	8.6							3,784	3,845	98.4
1938	2,546	64.3	57.1	1,237	31.3	27.8	174	4.4	3.9							3,957	4,457	88.8
1939	3,171	63.9	45.1	1,551	31.3	22.0	239	4.8	3.4							4,961	7,037	70.5
1940	3,098	75.2	49.4	864	21.0	13.8	157	3.8	2.5							4,119	6,266	65.7
1941	2,732	87.7	45.6	328	10.5	5.5	57	1.8	1.0							3,117	5,991	52.0
1942	3,205	92.8	43.9	203	5.9	2.8	44	1.3	0.6							3,452	7,297	47.3
1943	1,585	91.8	40.7	24	1.5	0.6	7	0.4	0.2							1,616	3,895	41.5
1944	917	98.0	52.6	14	1.5	0.8	5	0.5	0.3							936	1,743	53.7
1945	1,221	98.6	77.6	12	1.0	0.8	6	0.5	0.4							1,239	1,573	78.8
1946	1,664	98.2	65.0	26	1.5	1.0	4	0.2	0.2							1,694	2,560	66.2
1947	1,671	79.7	38.7	268	12.8	6.2	157	7.5	3.6							2,096	4,317	48.6
1948	2,121	50.0	27.1	1,289	30.4	16.5	830	19.6	10.6							4,240	7,816	54.3
1949	2,951	58.2	25.6	1,160	22.9	10.1	846	16.7	7.4	112	2.2	1.0				5,069	11,511	44.0
1950	3,552	40.1	25.6	2,588	29.2	15.6	1,862	21.0	11.3	862	9.7	5.2				8,864	16,549	53.6
1951	2,856	29.9	16.4	3,255	34.1	18.7	2,306	24.2	13.2	1,130	11.8	6.5				9,547	17,429	54.8
1952	2,691	24.6	13.8	3,365	30.7	17.3	2,974	27.1	15.3	1,933	17.6	9.9				10,963	19,499	56.2
1953	2,274	16.1	9.4	5,578	39.6	23.1	4,083	29.0	16.9	2,156	15.3	8.9				14,091	24,123	58.4
1954	2,801	17.6	10.6	5,822	36.5	22.0	4,501	28.2	17.0	2,833	17.8	10.7				15,957	26,519	60.2
1955	2,492	17.5	9.8	5,037	35.3	19.8	3,775	26.4	14.8	2,979	20.9	11.7				14,283	25,427	56.2
1956	2,480	16.4	9.1	5,554	36.7	20.3	3,971	26.3	14.5	3,124	20.7	11.4				15,129	27,341	55.3
1957	2,481	18.1	9.8	5,665	41.3	22.4	3,488	25.5	13.8	2,070	15.1	8.2				13,704	25,268	54.2
1958	2,302	19.2	9.6	5,569	46.4	23.2	2,450	20.4	10.2	1,689	14.1	7.0				12,010	23,978	50.1
1959	2,248	18.2	8.5	6,193	49.7	23.5	2,291	18.6	8.7	1,621	13.1	6.2				12,353	26,334	46.9
1960	2,652	20.4	9.6	6,417	49.3	23.2	2,167	16.6	7.8	1,789	13.7	6.5				13,025	27,606	47.2
1961	2,371	19.1	19.1	6,539	52.7	24.0	1,712	13.8	6.3	1,528	12.3	5.6	257	2.1	0.9	12,407	27,201	45.6

†Less than 0.1%.

SOURCE: As for Table 4.1.

TABLE 4.5

CURRENT DOLLAR VALUE OF METALLIC MINERAL PRODUCTION NWT 1932–61

Year	Gold $	Gold % NWT	Gold % Y + NWT	Silver $	Silver % NWT	Silver % Y + NWT	Copper $	Copper % NWT	Copper % Y + NWT	Total NWT $	Total Y + NWT $	NWT as % of total	Uranium $	Nickel $
1932				12	100	0.6				12	2,001	0.6		
1933				9	100	0.4				9	2,047	0.4		
1934				18	100	1.1				18	1,645	1.1		
1935	7	6.9	0.5	95	93.1	6.8				102	1,401	7.3	248	
1936				143	100	6.1				143	2,362	6.1	159	
1937				61	100	1.6				61	3,845	1.6	414	
1938	239	47.8	5.4	253	50.6	5.7	8	1.6	0.2	500	4,457	11.2	606	
1939	1,876	90.4	26.7	196	9.4	2.8	4	0.2	0.1	2,076	7,037	29.5	877	
1940	2,124	98.9	33.9	23	1.1	0.4				*2,147	6,266	34.3	1,045	
1941	2,865	99.7	47.8	6	0.2	0.1				*2,874	5,991	48.0	1,122	
1942	3,827	99.5	52.5	10	0.3	0.1	3	0.1	0.1	*3,845	7,297	52.7	410	
1943	2,273	99.7	58.4	6	0.3	0.2	8	0.2	0.1	2,279	3,895	58.5	925	
1944	800	99.1	45.9	6	0.7	0.3	1	0.1	0.1	807	1,743	46.3		
1945	333	99.7	21.2	1	0.3	0.1				334	1,573	21.2		
1946	861	99.4	33.6	5	0.6	0.2				866	2,560	33.8		
1947	2,188	98.5	50.7	33	1.5	0.8				2,221	4,317	51.4		
1948	3,557	99.5	45.5	19	0.5	0.2				3,576	7,816	45.8		
1949	6,390	99.2	55.5	52	0.8	0.5				6,442	11,511	56.0		
1950	7,635	99.4	46.1	50	0.7	0.3				7,685	16,549	46.4		
1951	7,820	99.2	44.8	61	0.8	0.3	1	‡‡‡	‡‡‡	7,882	17,429	45.2		
1952	8,485	99.4	43.5	49	0.6	0.3	2	‡‡‡	‡‡‡	*8,536	19,499	58.5		
1953	9,979	99.5	41.4	53	0.5	0.2				10,032	24,123	41.6		
1954	10,513	99.5	39.6	49	0.5	0.2				†10,562	26,519	39.8	15,486	
1955	11,092	99.5	43.6	52	0.5	0.2				†11,144	25,427	43.8	13,232	
1956	12,149	99.5	44.4	63	0.5	0.2				12,212	27,341	44.7	9,176	
1957	11,408	98.7	45.1	60	0.5	0.2	96	0.8	0.4	11,564	25,268	45.8	8,802	734
1958	11,684	97.6	48.7	63	0.5	0.3	221	1.9	0.9	11,968	23,978	49.9	9,573	2,649
1959	13,627	97.5	51.8	62	0.4	0.2	292	2.1	1.1	13,981	26,334	53.1	8,156	2,689
1960	14,195	97.4	51.4	71	0.5	0.3	315	2.2	1.1	14,581	27,606	52.8	9,232	2,670
1961	14,449	97.6	53.1	74	0.5	0.3	271	1.9	1.0	14,794	27,201	54.4	—	2,605

*Excludes some tungsten produced.

TABLE 4.6

SOURCE: As for Table 4.2.

CURRENT DOLLAR VALUE OF MINERALS EXPORTED FROM THE YUKON AND NORTHWEST TERRITORIES ANNUALLY COMPARED TO TOTAL CANADIAN PRODUCTION OF THESE MINERALS ANNUALLY*

(thousands of dollars)

Year	YT	NWT	Total YT and NWT	Total Canada	% of total Canada produced in YT and NWT
1900	22453		22453	30648	73.26
1901	18115		18115	27394	66.13
1902	14597		14597	23575	61.92
1903	12333		12333	20554	60.00
1904	10576		10576	18510	57.14
1905	7930		7930	17780	44.60
1906	5666		5666	27881	20.32
1907	3276		3276	28130	11.65
1908	3648		3846	29942	12.18
1909	3983		3983	23561	16.91
1910	4653		4653	34880	13.34
1911	4694		4694	27136	17.30
1912	5888		5888	44808	13.14
1913	6180		6180	49149	12.57
1914	5364		5364	43507	12.33
1915	5018		5018	52212	9.61
1916	5478		5478	71352	7.68
1917	4453		4453	66681	6.68
1918	2342		2342	69162	3.39
1919	1937		1937	50733	3.82
1920	1571		1571	46722	3.36
1921	1752		1752	31463	5.57
1922	1781		1781	44511	4.00
1923	2971		2971	45549	6.52
1924	944		944	58933	1.60
1925	1784		1784	72979	2.44
1926	2226		2226	69399	3.21
1927	1787		1787	67594	2.64
1928	2691		2691	67397	3.99
1929	2904		2904	68670	4.23
1930	2512		2512	66646	3.77
1931	2181		2181	71495	3.05
1932	1989	12	2001	82700	2.42
1933	2038	9	2047	96469	2.12
1934	1627	18	1645	118765	1.39
1935	1299	102	1401	136987	1.02
1936	2219	143	2362	154561	1.53
1937	3784	61	3845	174692	2.20
1938	3957	500	4457	246429	1.81
1939	4961	2076	7037	266743	2.64
1940	4119	2147	6266	229459	2.73
1941	3117	2874	5991	293990	2.04
1942	3452	3845	7297	272753	2.68
1943	1616	2279	3895	165094	2.36
1944	936	807	1743	132098	1.32
1945	1239	334	1573	127257	1.24
1946	1694	866	2560	138482	1.85
1947	2096	2221	4317	160659	2.69
1948	4240	3576	7816	195962	3.99

TABLE 4.6 (*concluded*)

Year	YT	NWT	Total YT and NWT	Total Canada	% of total Canada produced in YT and NWT
1949	5069	6442	11511	288407	3.99
1950	8995	7685	16680	333683	5.00
1951	9725	7882	17607	526755	3.34
1952	11248	8540	19788	505495	3.91
1953	14568	10032	24600	309550	7.95
1954	16387	10562	26949	323131	8.34
1955	14643	11144	25787	358085	7.20
1956	15545	12212	27757	653500	4.25
1957	14020	12298	26318	531551	4.95
1958	12254	14617	26871	491733	5.46
1959	12534	16670	29204	548194	5.33
1960	13234	17251	30485	604805	5.04
1961	12407	14794	27201	595181	4.56

*Includes gold, silver, copper, lead, zinc. Excludes uranium.

SOURCE: Calculated from data in DBS, *Canadian Mineral Statistics 1886-1956* for the years 1900 to 1956 and from DBS, *General Review of the Mining Industry*, annually 1956 to 1961.

TABLE 4.7

TERRITORIAL GOLD PRODUCTION 1900-61 AND CANADIAN DOLLAR AVERAGE ANNUAL PRICE OF GOLD 1942-61

	'000 fine ounces			'000 Canadian $			Average annual Canadian dollar price
Year	YT	NWT	Total Y and NWT	YT	NWT	Total Y and NWT	
1900	1,078		1,078	22,275		22,275	
1901	871		871	18,000		18,000	
1902	702		702	14,500		14,500	
1903	593		593	12,250		12,250	
1904	508		508	10,500		10,500	
1905	423		423	7,876		7,876	
1906	271		271	5,600		5,600	
1907	152		152	3,150		3,150	
1908	174		174	3,600		3,600	
1909	192		192	3,960		3,960	
1910	211		211	4,570		4,570	
1911	224		224	4,635		4,635	
1912	268		268	5,549		5,549	
1913	283		283	5,847		5,847	
1914	248		248	5,125		5,125	
1915	230		230	4,758		4,758	
1916	213		213	4,397		4,397	

TABLE 4.7 (*concluded*)

	'000 fine ounces			'000 Canadian $			Average annual Canadian dollar price
Year	YT	NWT	Total Y and NWT	YT	NWT	Total Y and NWT	
1917	178		178	3,673		3,673	
1918	102		102	2,118		2,118	
1919	91		91	1,875		1,875	
1920	73		73	1,504		1,504	
1921	66		66	1,364		1,364	
1922	54		54	1,126		1,126	
1923	60		60	1,243		1,243	
1924	35		35	720		720	
1925	48		48	988		988	
1926	26		26	529		529	
1927	31		31	639		639	
1928	34		34	710		710	
1929	36		36	742		742	
1930	36		36	734		734	
1931	44		44	956		956	
1932	41		41	953		953	
1933	39		39	1,130		1,130	
1934	39		39	1,339		1,339	
1935	36		36	1,257		1,257	
1936	50		50	1,764		1,764	
1937	48		48	1,679		1,679	
1938	72	7	79	2,546	239	2,785	
1939	88	52	140	3,171	1,876	5,047	
1940	80	55	135	3,098	2,124	5,222	
1941	71	74	145	2,732	2,865	5,597	
1942	83	99	182	3,205	3,827	7,032	38.50
1943	41	59	100	1,585	2,273	3,858	38.50
1944	24	21	45	917	800	1,717	38.50
1945	32	9	41	1,221	333	1,554	38.50
1946	45	23	68	1,664	861	2,525	36.75
1947	48	63	111	1,671	2,188	2,859	35.00
1948	61	102	163	2,121	3,557	5,678	35.00
1949	82	177	259	2,951	6,390	9,341	36.00
1950	93	201	294	3,552	7,635	11,187	38.05
1951	78	212	290	2,856	7,820	10,676	36.85
1952	79	248	327	2,691	8,485	11,176	34.27
1953	66	290	356	2,274	9,979	12,253	34.42
1954	82	309	391	2,801	10,513	13,314	34.07
1955	72	321	393	2,492	11,092	13,584	34.52
1956	72	353	425	2,480	12,149	14,629	34.45
1957	74	340	414	2,481	11,408	13,889	33.55
1958	68	344	412	2,302	11,684	13,986	33.98
1959	67	406	473	2,248	13,627	15,875	33.57
1960	78	418	496	2,652	14,195	16,847	33.95
1961	67	407	474	2,371	14,449	16,820	35.46

SOURCES: Physical and value data as for Tables 4.1, 4.4, and 4.5. Canadian dollar gold prices from DBS, *General Review of the Mining Industry 1961*, Table 21, p.A-19.

TABLE 4.8

ANNUAL AVERAGE PRICES OF SILVER 1900–61 AND OF LEAD 1942–61

(current Canadian dollars)

	Silver ($ per troy oz.)	Lead ($ per lb.)		Silver ($ per troy oz.)	Lead ($ per lb.)
1900	0.6133		1931	0.2987	
1901	0.5895		1932	0.3167	
1902	0.5216		1933	0.3783	
1903	0.5345		1934	0.4746	
1904	0.5722		1935	0.6479	
1905	0.6035		1936	0.4513	
1906	0.6679		1937	0.4488	
1907	0.6533		1938	0.4348	
1908	0.5286		1939	0.4049	
1909	0.5150		1940	0.3825	
1910	0.5349		1941	0.3826	
1911	0.5330		1942	0.4217	0.034
1912	0.6083		1943	0.4525	0.0375
1913	0.5979		1944	0.4300	0.045
1914	0.5481		1945	0.4700	0.050
1915	0.4968		1946	0.8365	0.0675
1916	0.6566		1947	0.7200	0.1367
1917	0.8142		1948	0.7500	0.1804
1918	0.9684		1949	0.7432	0.158
1919	1.1112		1950	0.8098	0.1445
1920	1.0090		1951	0.9440	0.184
1921	0.6265		1952	0.8355	0.1619
1922	0.6753		1953	0.8403	0.1293
1923	0.6487		1954	0.8329	0.1333
1924	0.6678		1955	0.8814	0.1438
1925	0.6907		1956	0.8970	0.1551
1926	0.6211		1957	0.8743	0.1396
1927	0.5637		1958	0.8678	0.1136
1928	0.5818		1959	0.8779	0.1061
1929	0.5299		1960	0.8892	0.1068
1930	0.3815		1961	0.9439	0.1021

SOURCES: Silver data after J. W. Patterson, *Silver in Canada*, Mineral Survey 3, Mineral Resources Division, Department of Mines and Technical Surveys (Ottawa: 1963), p. 74. Lead prices from DBS, *General Review of the Mining Industry 1961*, Table 21, p. A-19. (1942–47 prices set by Canadian Government; 1947–50 prices based on New York; 1951–61 prices based on Montreal).

TABLE 4.9

NICKEL PRODUCTION (tons)			
Year	NWT	Canada	Territorial as percentage of total Canada
1957	528	187958	0.3
1958	1933	139559	1.4
1959	1921	186555	1.0
1960	1907	214506	0.9
1961	1705	232991	0.7

URANIUM PRODUCTION ('000lbs.)			
Year	NWT	Canada	%
1954	N/A	N/A	
1955	N/A	N/A	
1956	874	4561	19.2
1957	838	13271	6.4
1958	911	26805	3.0
1959	919	31784	2.9
1960	1077	25495	4.2
1961	—	19281	0

CADMIUM PRODUCTION ('000lbs.)			
Year	YT	Canada	%
1950	56	848	6.6
1951	66	1327	5.0
1952	129	949	13.6
1953	238	1118	21.3
1954	253	1087	23.3
1955	212	1919	11.0
1956	245	2339	10.5
1957	186	2368	7.9
1958	161	1756	9.2
1959	142	2160	6.6
1960	145	2357	6.2
1961	143	2399	5.9

SOURCE: DBS, *General Review of the Mining Industry*, annually.

TABLE 4.10

COMPOSITION OF TOTAL METALLIC MINERAL PRODUCTION OF NWT 1932–61

Year	Total gold, silver, copper	Total gold, silver, copper, nickel	Total gold, silver, copper, nickel, and uranium	Uranium as % of NWT total	Nickel as % of NWT total including uranium
	('000 $)	('000 $)	('000 $)	(%)	(%)
1932	12	12	12		
1933	9	9	9		
1934	18	18	266	93.2	
1935	102	102	261	60.9	
1936	143	143	557	74.3	
1937	61	61	667	90.9	
1938	500	500	1,377	63.7	
1939	2,076	2,076	3,121	33.5	
1940	2,147	2,147	3,269	34.3	
1941	2,874	2,874	3,284	12.5	
1942	3,845	3,845	4,770	19.4	
1943	2,279	2,279	NA		
1944	807	807	"		
1945	334	334	"		
1946	866	866	"		
1947	2,221	2,221	"		
1948	3,576	3,576	"		
1949	6,442	6,442	"		
1950	7,685	7,685	"		
1951	7,882	7,882	"		
1952	8,536	8,536	"		
1953	10,032	10,032	26,048	40.6	
1954	10,562	10,562	26,048	40.6	
1955	11,144	11,144	24,376	54.3	
1956	12,212	12,212	21,388	42.9	
1957	11,564	12,298	21,096	41.7	3.5
1958	11,968	14,617	24,190	39.6	11.0
1959	13,981	16,670	24,826	32.9	10.8
1960	14,581	17,251	26,483	34.9	10.1
1961	14,794	17,464	20,246	13.7	13.2

SOURCE: As for Table 4.1.

TABLE 4.11

ALLUVIAL GOLD RECOVERED AND QUANTITY OF MATERIAL HANDLED
IN YUKON 1944–61

	Material handled* (cubic yards)	Gold recovered† (fine ounces)	Ounces recovered per cubic yard	Value per cubic yard $
1944	4,687,174	23,816	0.0050	0.1956
1945	2,981,599	31,721	0.0106	0.4081
1946	5,917,740	45,283	0.0076	0.2793
1947	7,054,753	47,679	0.0067	0.2365
1948	7,813,449	60,606	0.0078	0.2715
1949	9,263,700	81,970	0.0088	0.3185
1950	7,860,497	93,339	0.0118	0.4490
1951	7,266,422	77,504	0.0107	0.3942
1952	6,727,353	92,789	0.0138	0.4729
1953	5,155,826	66,080	0.0140	0.4832
1954	6,889,820	82,208	0.0119	0.4065
1955	6,379,755	72,201	0.0113	0.3907
1956	5,716,389	71,736	0.0125	0.4306
1957	7,559,882	73,709	0.0097	0.3271
1958	6,808,991	67,745	0.0099	0.3380
1959	6,824,062	66,960	0.0098	0.3294
1960	5,519,729	78,115	0.0141	0.4787
1961	4,672,554	66,107	0.0141	0.5018

*Data partly conjectural and includes some over-burben and barren material.
†Fine gold received at Royal Canadian Mint.
SOURCE: DBS, *The Gold Mining Industry*, 1944–62, annually.

TABLE 4.12

CANADIAN* PLACER GOLD-MINING STATISTICS FOR SIGNIFICANT YEARS 1921–59

Year	Number of establish- ments	Number of employees	Total salaries and wages	Cost of fuel and electricity	Cost of process supplies and containers	Gross dollar value of products	Net value of production†
			$	$	$	$	$
1921	197	428	671,783	—	—	1,516,222	—
1929	68	488	586,193	2,969	—	836,006	—
1931	109	337	682,935	41,745	—	1,226,541	—
1933	74	454	704,151	35,165	—	1,218,250	—
1937	109	1,069	1,689,911	99,072	77,488	3,243,196	3,066,636
1939	104	830	1,439,765	119,692	90,610	4,523,587	4,204,974
1941	110	797	1,954,278	155,518	68,489	4,132,503	3,800,142
1944	47	211	598,556	43,591	13,703	1,281,125	1,197,021
1946	39	340	1,112,984	84,206	46,870	1,849,511	1,693,568
1949	56	398	1,509,423	86,614	455,371	3,499,823	2,920,290
1951	47	362	1,553 103	44,678	507,830	3,572,516	2,951,342
1954	62	351	1,619,460	146,300	253,128	3,051,665	2,515,038
1956	64	250	1,378,166	81,639	451,933	2,594,312	2,026,790
1957	57	243	1,180,225	55,472	353,186	2,573,853	2,116,716
1958	112	236	1,253,362	63,007	461,375	3,049,743	2,484,524
1959	112	239	1,194,713	74,536	355,837	2,462,727	1,989,431

*Includes some operations in Quebec, British Columbia, and some other provinces, but about 90 per cent
of the production has been in the Yukon.
†Gross value less fuel, electricity, process supplies, freight and treatment charges.
SOURCE: DBS, *The Gold Mining Industry*, 1960, Table 13, p. B-4.

TABLE 4.13

LEAD PRODUCTION

Year	YT ('000 lbs)	YT Short tons	Total Canadian Short tons	YT as % of total Canadian
1913	3	1	18,831	†
1914	48	24	18,169	0.1
1915	810	405	23,158	1.7
1916	955	478	20,749	2.3
1917	128	64	16,288	0.4
1918	9	5	25,699	†
1919			21,914	†
1920			17,977	
1921	2,473	1,237	33,340	3.7
1922	3,324	1,662	46,654	3.5
1923	6,771	3,385	55,617	6.1
1924	904	452	87,743	0.5
1925	1,875	938	126,795	0.7
1926	5,860	2,930	141,901	2.1
1927	4,165	2,083	155,712	1.3
1928	7,191	3,596	168,973	2.1
1929	8,396	4,198	163,261	2.6
1930	8,897	4,448	166,447	2.7
1931	4,455	2,227	133,671	1.7
1932	3,853	1,927	127,974	1.5
1933	3,100	1,550	133,238	1.2
1934	1,786*	894	173,138	0.5
1935	231	115	169,553	0.1
1936	2,569	1,284	191,590	0.7
1937	6,441	3,220	206,000	1.5
1938	5,199	2,600	209,464	1.2
1939	7,545	3,772	194,285	1.9
1940	4,656	2,328	235,925	0.9
1941	1,704	852	230,084	0.4
1942	1,322	661	256,071	0.3
1943	196	98	222,030	†
1944	106	53	152,291	†
1945	120	60	173,497	†
1946	52	26	176,987	†
1947	1,145	573	161,668	0.4
1948	4,599	2,299	167,251	1.4
1949	5,356	2,678	159,775	1.8
1950	12,886	6,443	165,697	3.9
1951	12,533	6,267	158,231	3.9
1952	18,396*	9,184	168,842	5.4
1953	31,591	15,796	193,706	8.2
1954	33,765	16,882	218,495	7.7
1955	26,249	13,124	202,763	6.5
1956	25,604	12,802	188,854	6.6
1957	24,986	12,493	181,484	6.8
1958	21,566	10,783	186,680	5.8
1959	21,592	10,796	186,696	5.9
1960	20,287	10,143	205,650	4.9
1961	16,770	8,742	231,197	3.7

*Includes small quantity produced in NWT.
†Less than 0.1 per cent.
SOURCE: As for Table 4.1.

TABLE 4.14

ZINC PRODUCTION

| | YT | | Total | YT as % of |
	('000 lbs)	(short tons)	Canada (tons)	total Canada
1949	847	424	288262	0.1
1950	5507	2754	313227	0.9
1951	5679	2839	341112	0.8
1952	11070	5535	371802	1.5
1953	18027	9014	401762	2.2
1954	23646	11823	376491	3.1
1955	21823	10912	433357	2.5
1956	21053	10526	422633	2.5
1957	17119	8560	413741	2.1
1958	15522	7761	425099	1.8
1959	13247	6623	396008	1.6
1960	13403	6701	406873	1.6
1961	12138	6099	412363	1.5

SOURCE: As for Table 4.1.

TABLE 4.15

OPERATIONS OF UNITED KENO MINES LTD.

Year	Daily production	Value per ton	Total revenue	Net profit	No. of employees	Ore reserves
1952	373.2	50.47	5,161,290	711,673	468	437,028
1953	429.3	53.41	8,368,775	744,953	499	612,937
1954	493.8	52.84	9,524,776	879,686	520	616,868
1955	445.0	53.80	9,549,604	1,602,467	490	587,830
1956	425.0	54.99	9,750,219	2,005,000	450	598,020
1957	438.0	52.59	8,196,261	1,001,748	450	601,165
1958	479.6	42.79	7,665,013	586,840	510	587,940
1959	475.0	52.22	9,958,292	1,423,836	575	549,565
1960	483.0	49.75	8,793,284	1,123,649	575	549,565
1961	509.0	45.88	8,540,143	978,035	575	514,369
1962	504.0	52.33	9,635,252	1,218,131	575	445,630

SOURCE: Compiled from *Annual Reports of the Alberta and Northwest Chamber of Mines*, 1958 and 1962.

TABLE 4.16

YUKON SILVER PRODUCTION BY SOURCE

('000 troy ounces)

Year	Alluvial	Lode	Total
1926	6	2,089	2,095
1927	7	1,640	1,647
1928	8	2,832	2,840
1929	8	3,272	3,280
1930	8	3,738	3,746
1931	10	3,685	3,695
1932	9	3,006	3,015
1933	9	2,195	2,204
1934	9	507	516
1935	8	47	55
1936	11	772	783
1937	11	3,946	3,957
1938	16	2,829	2,845
1939	19	3,812	3,831
1940	18	2,241	2,259
1941	16	841	857
1942	17	465	482
1943	9	44	53
1944	5	27	32
1945	6	19	25
1946	9	22	31
1947	10	362	372
1948	12	1,706	1,718
1949	18	1,545	1,563
1950	20	3,182	3,202
1951	17	3,426	3,443
1952	16	4,012	4,028
1953	13	6,626	6,639
1954	17	6,976	6,993
1955	15	5,697	5,712
1956	14	6,178	6,192
1957	16	6,469	6,485
1958	15	6,400	6,415
1959	14	7,041	7,055
1960	16	7,201	7,217

SOURCE: J. W. Patterson, *Silver in Canada*, Mineral Survey No. 3, Mineral Resources Division, Dept. of Mines and Technical Surveys, Ottawa, 1963, Table 9, pp. 62–5. (NWT production removed from 1932 figure and 1933–35 breakdown estimated.)

TABLE 5.1

COAL PRODUCTION YUKON TERRITORY 1901–61

Year	Output Tons	$	Year	Output Tons	$
1901[1]	5,864	86,230	1932	808	3,491
1902	4,910	37,280	1933	862	3,670
1903	1,849	29,584	1934	638	2,217
1904	—	—	1935	835	3,483
1905	7,000	21,000	1936	510	2,286
1906	7,000	28,000	1937	84	812
1907	15,000	60,000	1938	361	3,400
1908	3,847	21,158	1939	—	—
1909	7,364	49,502	1940	—	—
1910	16,185	110,925	1941	—	—
1911	2,840	12,780	1942	—	—
1912	9,245	44,958	1943	—	—
1913	19,722	95,945	1944	—	—
1914	13,443	53,760	1945	—	—
1915	9,724	38,896	1946	—	—
1916	3,300	13,200	1947	—	—
1917	4,872	29,232	1948	3,801	25,857
1918	2,900	11,600	1949	3,156	29,382
1919	—	—	1950	3,703	40,960
1920	—	—	1951	3,696	60,597
1921	233	2,472	1952	8,442	139,345
1922	465	4,650	1953	10,611	169,736
1923	313	1,485	1954	14,113	202,772
1924	1,121	8,265	1955	7,040	81,806
1925	730	7,147	1956	9,372	111,104
1926	316	800	1957	7,731	91,595
1927	414	2,052	1958	4,344	56,379
1928	414	2,915	1959	3,879	58,200
1929	458	1,848	1960	6,470	97,156
1930	653	3,110	1961	7,703	114,221
1931	904	5,039			

[1]Partly mined in 1900.

SOURCE: 1901–56, DBS, *Canadian Mineral Statistics 1886–1956*, Reference Paper No. 68. 1956–1961, DBS, *General Review of the Mining Industry*, annually.

TABLE 5.2

PETROLEUM PRODUCTION OF THE
NORTHWEST TERRITORIES 1932–61

Year	Barrels	Year	Barrels
1932	910	1947	227,474
1933	4,608	1948	350,541
1934	4,438	1949	155,528
1935	5,115	1950	186,729
1936	5,399	1951	227,449
1937	11,371	1952	314,217
1938	22,855	1953	316,689
1939	20,191	1954	369,887
1940	18,633	1955	404,219
1941	23,664	1956	449,409
1942	75,789	1957	420,844
1943	293,750	1958	457,086
1944	1,233,675	1959	430,319
1945	345,171	1960	468,545
1946	177,282	1961	516,979

SOURCE: DBS, *General Review of the Mining Industry*, annually.

TABLE 5.3

PETROLEUM EXPLORATION AND DEVELOPMENT YT AND NWT 1920–60

	NWT		Exploration permits YT		Arctic		Total expenditures on development $
	No.	Acres	No.	Acres	No.	Acres	
Prior to 1951							4,812,165
1951	28	1,705,450					32,040
1952	384	23,300,284					156,879
1953	482	35,244,751	24	1,331,885			1,717,317
1954	281	13,868,465	52	3,446,852	·		1,309,957
1955	186	9,894,641	13	683,969			2,048,951
1956	188	10,148,197	42	2,216,600			2,629,789
1957	414	22,008,200	225	10,006,955			3,609,573
1958	1,163	55,413,971	324	14,639,168			5,752,539
1959	1,534	73,060,852	431	19,928,722			8,219,478
1960	1,129	53,390,824	277	13,037,238	864	46,631,455	11,430,057

SOURCE: Adapted from Department of Northern Affairs and National Resources, *Statistical Report on Oil and Gas Activities 1920–1960*, Ottawa, 1962, Tables 1 and 2.

TABLE 5.4

ANNUAL AMOUNT OF TIMBER CUT FOR SAWING, FUEL, AND ROUND TIMBERS
YT AND NWT* 1934–62

Fiscal year ending March 31	Board feet of lumber		Linear feet round timber		Cords of fuel wood	
	NWT	Y	NWT	Y	NWT	Y
1934	201,884	NA	41,052		85	
1935	341,644	67,000	23,923		5,589	9,739
1936	289,320	185,000	50,732		5,788	11,946
1937	364,253	483,760	66,940		5,683	16,401
1938	599,804	400,000	57,372		13,277	19,677
1939	946,743	671,576	38,108		12,167	17,888
1940	763,756	351,157	45,762		11,025	15,387
1941	1,012,826	306,000	82,079		9,760	19,531
1942	1,748,649	300,000	29,660		17,656	12,847
1943	1,760,863	1,305,000	26,230		18,594	13,658
1944	NA	1,408,657	NA		NA	20,403
1945	1,370,668	6,607,284	15,964		NA	23,567
1946	1,090,549	953,657	NA		NA	11,008
1947	2,393,744	2,539,500	110,437		8,620	14,379
1948	3,708,513	2,446,470	48,859	2,000	10,246	20,838
1949	2,423,835	NA	179,721	48,818	8,237	26,071
1950	2,381,687	1,692,689	63,534	117,627	9,370	27,827
1951	2,173,454	3,788,648	68,947	985,714	5,852	16,003
1952	4,353,647	6,182,751	304,796	1,074,691	6,643	12,629
1953	5,821,328	4,997,918	331,765	2,027,076	4,628	13,135
1954	7,815,740	4,116,910	458,547	2,391,709	6,777	8,401
1955	NA	NA	NA	NA	NA	NA
1956	6,216,604	2,803,579	305,485	948,588	3,627	6,171
1957	21,127,364	4,897,743	968,586	2,159,691	5,708	7,748
1958	12,575,925	3,174,405	449,435	1,413,978	5,272	5,544
1959	12,449,323	2,678,260	328,535	1,175,403	7,814	5,527
1960	15,293,174	4,804,592	303,879	1,167,355	4,800	5,418
1961	19,503,547	7,019,189	613,064	1,183,889	2,475	7,189
1962	16,426,681	3,821,508	140,913	196,724	2,551	4,935

*NWT includes Wood Buffalo National Park from 1953.

SOURCE: 1934–49, *Annual Reports of The Department of Mines and Resources*; 1950–53, *Annual Reports of The Department of Resources and Development*; 1954–62, *Annual Reports of The Department of Northern Affairs and National Resources*.

TABLE 5.5

<small>FOREST PRODUCTION YUKON AND NORTHWEST TERRITORIES 1940–1961:
TOTAL EQUIVALENT VOLUME IN MERCHANTABLE TIMBER</small> ('000 cubic feet)

Year	Logs and bolts for sawing	Fuelwood	Poles and piling	Round wood*	Total	Total value in current dollars
1940	61	1,871		18	1950	170,861
1941	100	2,142		7	2249	222,601
1942	436	2,344		6	2786	312,190
1943	4,194	6,462	244	139	11039	1,561,858
1944	1,596	2,235		3	3834	631,058
1945	401	1,175		2	1578	255,576
1946	987	1,840		17	2844	487,599
1947	1,231	2,487		8	3726	600,288
1948	563	2,745		34	3342	574,294
1949	815	2,976		27	3818	646,152
1950	1,192	1,748		287	3227	511,601
1951	2,107	1,542		375	4024	759,063
1952	2,164	1,421		642	4227	837,762
1953	2,387	1,214		827	4428	693,411
1954	2,066	1,117		717	3900	668,333
1955	1,804	784	5	311	2904	514,135
1956	5,204	1,076	2	564	6846	1,269,207
1957	3,150	865	4	336	4355	826,945
1958	3,067	2,067	98	698	5930	1,104,340
1959	1,276	1,153		375	2804	552,339
1960	4,203	663	830	0	5697	1,086,737
1961	1,146	564	105	0	1815	220,000

*Includes fence-posts, mining timber, and miscellaneous round wood.

<small>SOURCE:</small> Based on DBS, *Operations in the Woods, Revised Estimates of Forest Production 1940–1953 with Final Estimates for 1954–1955*, Table 17, pp. 60–1. Brought to 1961 from the annual publication No. 25-201.

TABLE 5.6

MANUFACTURING: YT AND NWT, 1939–61

Year	Establishments No.	Employees No.	Selling value of factory shipments $
1939	5	55	242,968
1940	9	78	266,745
1941	9	59	341,377
1942	9	68	417,773
1943	8	62	395,943
1944	12	67	489,256
1945	12	64	704,663
1946	13	92	646,295
1947	14	145	1,344,109
1948	17	137	1,330,110
1949	18	148	1,377,453
1950	19	123	1,741,531
1951	18	152	2,018,909
1952	23	164	2,288,039
1953	30	177	2,215,683
1954	31	191	3,536,300
1955	26	170	4,751,000
1956	24	175	5,130,497
1957	22	166	3,221,268
1958	16	145	3,979,489
1959	12	115	2,832,386
1960	14	124	3,071,218
1961	13	138	3,434,135

SOURCE: DBS, *The Manufacturing Industries of Canada,* Section F, 1959 (and annually thereafter).

TABLE 5.7

NUMBER OF MANUFACTURING ESTABLISHMENTS IN THE Y AND NWT

	1952	1953	1954	1955	1956	1957	1958	1959	1960	1961
Bread and other bakery products	3	3	3	3	2	2	1	1	2	2
Carbonated beverages	2	2	3	3	3	3	3	3	3	3
Furniture and sawmills	11	17	18	14	13	11	8	4	4	4
Printing and publishing	3	3	3	2	2	2	2	1	3	
Statuary, art goods and novelties	1	1	1	—	—	—	—	—		
Acids, alkalies, and salts	1	1	1	1	1	1	1	2		4
Jewellery and silverware	1	1	1	1	1	1	—	—		
Petroleum products	1	1	1	1	1	1	1	1	1	
Sheet metal products	—	—	—	1	1	1	—	—		
Total	23	30	31	26	24	22	16	12	14	13

SELLING VALUE OF FACTORY SHIPMENTS ($'000)

Foods and beverages	132	151	204	211	230	269	313	230	241	219
Wood	654	689	645	513	657	482	455	260	396	476
All other groups	1501	1676	2687	4027	4244	2470	3312	2343	2434	2740
Total	2283	2516	3536	4751	5131	3221	3980	2833	3071	3435

EMPLOYMENT

Foods and beverages	14	20	22	22	18	23	12	13	20	16
Wood	56	74	76	63	60	54	48	21	31	42
All other groups	94	83	93	85	97	89	85	81	73	80
Total	164	177	191	170	175	166	145	115	124	138

SOURCE: DBS, *The Manufacturing Industries of Canada*, Section F, 1959 (and annually thereafter).

TABLE 6.1

AVERAGE HOURLY WAGE RATES FOR SELECTED OCCUPATIONS IN AURIFEROUS
QUARTZ GOLD-MINING IN NWT, QUEBEC, ONTARIO AND BRITISH COLUMBIA

OCTOBER 1, 1961

Occupation	Average wage rate* per hour (time work)				
UNDERGROUND WORKERS	$ Industry	$ NWT	$ Quebec	$ Ontario	$ BC
Cage and skiptenders	1.52	1.90	1.45	1.52	—
Hoistman	1.63	2.08	1.52	1.63	—
Labourer	1.40	1.69	1.35	1.40	—
Miner	1.50	1.86	1.40	1.50	1.86
Motorman	1.46	1.84	1.38	1.46	
Mucking machine operator	1.42	1.90	1.38	1.45	
Timberman (shaft timberman)	1.51	1.94	1.42	1.52	1.87
SURFACE AND MILL WORKERS					
Carpenter, maintenance	1.62	2.03	1.45	1.62	
Electrician, maintenance	1.67	2.14	1.55	1.67	
Labourer	1.32	1.71	1.24	1.33	
Machinist, maintenance	1.67	2.14	1.56	1.67	
Mechanic, maintenance	1.61	2.01	1.52	1.62	1.97
Millman	1.51	1.87	1.44	1.51	
Pipefitter, maintenance	1.56	2.04	1.44	1.59	
Steel sharpener	1.52	1.80	1.41	1.51	
Tradesman's helper	1.45	1.73	—	1.46	
STANDARD HOURS PER WEEK	44.1	46.9	44.3	44.2	41.1
STRAIGHT-TIME EARNINGS (Basic rates plus bonus earnings) Miner	2.07	3.45	1.91	2.09	2.68

*Wage rates for underground workers include basic rates of workers under incentive
bonus plans as well as the rates paid to those on time work.

SOURCE: Industry, Quebec, Ontario, and British Columbia data from Canada, Department
of Labour, Economics and Research Branch *Wage Rates, Salaries and Hours of
Labour, 1961*, Report Number 44, Ottawa, 1962, Table 3 p. 36. Northwest Territories
data from special sample compilation provided by Economics and Research Branch,
Department of Labour, August 29, 1962.

TABLE 6.2

AVERAGE HOURLY WAGE RATES FOR SELECTED OCCUPATIONS IN METAL MINING
(EXCEPT GOLD AND IRON)* IN Y AND NWT, NEWFOUNDLAND, QUEBEC,
ONTARIO, AND BRITISH COLUMBIA OCTOBER 1, 1961

Occupation	Time work basic rate per hour†					
	Y and NWT $	Nfl'd $	Quebec $	Ontario $	BC $	Industry $
UNDERGROUND WORKERS						
Miner	2.04	1.67	1.97	2.26	2.27	2.18
Miner's helper	1.76	1.50	1.75	1.79	—	1.77
Standard hours per week	44.9	48	41.5	40.4	40.2	41.0

*Copper-gold-silver, nickel-copper; silver-cobalt; silver-lead-zinc and miscellaneous
metal-mining.
†Rates include basic rates of workers on incentive bonus plans as well as rates per hour
for those on time work.

SOURCE: As in 6.1 except read Table 5, p. 40 in Wage Rates, Salaries, and Hours of Labour.

TABLE 6.3

PREVAILING HOURLY WAGE RATES FOR SELECTED OCCUPATIONS IN CONSTRUCTION
(BUILDINGS AND STRUCTURES ONLY)*

Occupation	Y and NWT	Edmonton	Saskatoon	Winnipeg	Fort William and Port Arthur	Sudbury	Chicoutimi
	$	$	$	$	$	$	$
Bricklayer and mason	2.90	2.90	2.58	2.70	3.00	2.55	2.05
Carpenter	2.65[1]	2.65	2.25	2.50	2.85	2.57	1.95
Electrician	2.95	2.95	2.48	2.80	3.00	2.55	1.95
Painter	2.20	2.20	2.14	2.20	2.35	1.88	1.75
Plasterer	2.70	2.70	2.45	2.70	2.90	2.45	2.05
Plumber	2.80[2]	2.80	2.55	2.80	2.85	2.75	1.90
Sheet metal worker	2.85[3]	2.85	2.35	2.50	2.83	2.50	1.85
Truck driver	1.65	1.90	1.64	1.75	1.85	1.63	1.60
Labourer	1.65	1.90	1.63	1.65	1.80	1.59	1.55

*Yukon and Northwest Territories data is for all centres on the mainland lying west of
110° longitude and was collected as of November 1, 1961. Data for other centres was
collected as of October 1, 1961.

Notes:
[1]Yukon $2.98
[2]Yukon $2.90
[3]Yukon $2.90

SOURCE: As Table 6.1 except read Table 70, pp. 184–5 in Wage Rates, Salaries and Hours of
Labour.

TABLE 6.4

DIRECT LABOUR COSTS IN THE AURIFEROUS QUARTZ-MINING INDUSTRY AT YELLOWKNIFE COMPARED WITH OTHER CENTRES IN CANADA*

	Producing mines	Ore milled	Employees	Salaries and wages	Average salaries and wages	Average labour cost per ton of ore milled
	(no.)	(tons)	(no.)	($)	($)	($)
1960						
NWT	9	604,450	709	3,952,100	5,574.18	6.53
British Columbia	12	256,364	771	3,284,383	4,259.90	12.81
Manitoba and Saskatchewan	3	136,642	218	781,900	3586.70	5.72
Ontario	48	9,328,120	11,732	44,783,710	3817.20	4.80
Quebec and Nova Scotia	74	3,841,667	3,347	12,717,019	3799.50	3.31
1961						
NWT	7	613,109	734	4,326,308	5894.15	7.05
British Columbia	9	194,216	490	2,448,551	4997.04	12.60
Manitoba and Saskatchewan	5	149,942	238	902,832	3793.41	6.02
Ontario	56	9,004,518	11,403	46,170,029	4048.90	5.13
Quebec and Nova Scotia	63	3,873,579	3,011	11,617,795	3858.40	2.99

*Salaries and wages are at per ton of ore milled and are based on Standard Industrial Classification Revised 1960.

SOURCE: DBS, *The Gold Mining Industry* (26-209).

TABLE 6.5

STATISTICS OF PLACER GOLD- AND SILVER-LEAD-ZINC-MINING IN YT, 1950 AND 1960*

	Tons of ore milled	Employees	Salaries and wages	Cost of fuel and electricity	Cost of process supplies and containers
1960					
Total mineral industry of YT	—	743	4,369,445	746,227	1,942,695
Placer gold-mining†	—	207	1,188,160	75,173	334,048
Silver-lead–zinc-mining	174,482	536	3,181,285	671,054	1,608,647
1961					
Total mineral industry of YT	—	719	4,256,748	725,724	408,105
Placer gold-mining‡	—	234	1,278,406	104,548	46,100
Silver-lead–zinc-mining	187,167	485	2,978,342	621,176	362,005
1953					
Total mineral industry of YT	—	843	4,389,189	702,359	904,569
Placer gold-mining	—	218	1,030,978	40,010	147,822
Silver-lead–zinc-mining	193,861	625	3,358,211	662,349	856,747
1951					
Total mineral industry of YT	—	695	3,219,555	341,397	630,208
Placer gold-mining	—	290	1,242,482	35,742	406,264
Silver-lead–zinc-mining	—	405	1,977,073	305,655	223,944

*It is likely that since 1956 the published data for the placer gold-mining industry is in fact that reported from the Yukon. Since that date figures for material handled, etc., in British Columbia do not appear.

†Estimated from Placer Gold Mining Statistics. In 1960, for example, three per cent of total placer gold output was produced in British Columbia and virtually all the other 97 per cent in the Yukon. Data for the combined output was broken down by attributing three per cent of total outlays to British Columbia. Because the only other major mining operation in the Yukon in 1960 was silver–zinc-mining, deducting the estimated placer gold outlays from the totals for all mining provides an estimate of the silver-lead–zinc-mining industry's outlays.

‡N.B. In placer gold-mining, fuel and electricity fluctuate greatly from year to year. Process supplies in 1961 were unusually low compared with 1949–60. Employment is relatively stable.

TABLE 6.6

PRODUCTION COSTS IN THE SILVER–LEAD–ZINC-MINING INDUSTRY

	Ore milled (tons)	Employees (no.)	Salaries and wages ($)	Cost of fuel and electricity ($)	Cost of process supplies ($)
1961					
Canada	5,859,086	4,352	22,098,610	2,446,827	6,628,804
Yukon	187,167	485	2,978,342	621,176	362,005
Canada-YT	5,671,919	3,867	19,120,268	1,825,651	6,266,799
1960					
Canada	5,802,525	4,215	21,304,035	2,245,901	8,517,725
Yukon	174,482	536	3,181,285	671,054	1,608,647
Canada-YT	5,628,043	3,679	18,122,750	1,574,847	6,909,078
1951					
Canada		9,324	30,380,859	3,090,958	10,382,057
Yukon		405	1,977,073	305,655	223,944
Canada-YT		8,919	28,403,786	2,785,303	10,158,113
1953					
Canada	7,508,241	7,144	28,695,473	3,836,581	10,074,160
Yukon	193,861	625	3,358,211	662,349	856,747
Canada-YT	7,314,380	6,519	25,337,262	3,174,232	9,217,413

SOURCE: See notes at bottom of Table 6.5.

TABLE 6.7

DIRECT LABOUR COSTS IN THE SILVER-LEAD–ZINC-MINING INDUSTRY OF THE YT
COMPARED TO THOSE OF PRODUCERS ELSEWHERE IN CANADA*

	Ore milled (tons)	Salaries and wages	Average salaries and wages	Average salaries and wages per ton of ore milled
1961		($)	($)	($)
Yukon	187,167	2,978,342	6,141	15.912
Other	5,671,919	19,120,268	4,945	3.371
1960				
Yukon	174,482	3,181,285	5,935	18.232
Other	5,628,043	18,122,750	4,926	3.22
1953				
Yukon	193,861	3,358,211	5,373	17.322
Other	7,314,380	25,337,262	3,887	3.464

*The salaries and wages are as per ton of ore milled.

SOURCE: DBS, *The Silver-Lead-Zinc Mining Industry*, and as for Table 6.5.

TABLE 6.8

COST OF PROCESS SUPPLIES* USED PER TON OF AURIFEROUS
QUARTZ MILLED AT YELLOWKNIFE AND IN THE PROVINCES

	Ore milled (tons)	Cost of process supplies used	Cost of process supplies per ton of ore milled
1960		$	$
NWT	604,450	1,333,158	2.20
British Columbia	256,364	777,182	3.03
Manitoba and Saskatchewan	136,642	187,291	1.37
Ontario	9,328,120	16,449,845	1.76
Quebec and Nova Scotia	3,841,667	3,938,850	1.03
1961			
NWT	613,109	1,028,104	1.68
British Columbia	194,216	211,746	1.09
Manitoba and Saskatchewan	149,942	112,081	0.75
Ontario	9,004,518	4,643,114	0.52
Quebec and Nova Scotia	3,873,579	1,365,040	0.35

*Explosives, chemicals, etc.

SOURCE: DBS, *The Gold Mining Industry*, 1960 and 1961.

TABLE 6.9

COST OF PROCESS SUPPLIES USED PER TON OF SILVER-LEAD-ZINC ORE
MILLED IN THE YT AND ELSEWHERE IN CANADA

	Ore milled (tons)	Cost of process supplies used ($)	Cost of process supplies per ton of ore milled ($)
1960			
Yukon	174,482	1,608,647	9.219
Other	5,628,043	6,909,078	1.227
1953			
Yukon	193,861	856,747	4.419
Other	7,314,380	9,217,413	1.260

SOURCE: As for Table 6.7.

TABLE 6.10

FUEL AND ELECTRICITY COSTS PER TON OF AURIFEROUS QUARTZ
ORE MILLED AT YELLOWKNIFE AND IN THE PROVINCES

	Ore milled (tons)	Fuel and purchased electricity ($)	Cost of fuel and purchased electricity per ton of ore milled ($)
1960			
NWT	604,450	897,886	1.49
British Columbia	256,364	301,199	1.17
Manitoba and Saskatchewan	136,642	126,920	0.93
Ontario	9,328,120	4,307,333	0.46
Quebec and Nova Scotia	3,841,667	1,527,716	0.40
1961			
NWT	613,109	913,470	1.49
British Columbia	194,216	259,833	1.34
Manitoba and Saskatchewan	149,942	111,453	0.74
Ontario	9,004,518	4,438,198	0.49
Quebec and Nova Scotia	3,873,579	1,493,073	0.39

SOURCE: DBS, *The Gold Mining Industry*, 1960, 1961.

TABLE 6.11
COST OF FUEL AND ELECTRICITY INPUTS USED IN MINING OPERATIONS IN THE TERRITORIES AND PROVINCES 1960

	Coal*			Gasoline			Kerosene			Fuel oil		
	Tons	$	$/Ton	Imp. Gals.	$	$/Gal.	Imp. Gals.	$	$/Gal.	Imp. Gals.	$	$/Gal.
YT	6,162	155,028	25.16	89,491	40,922	0.46	693	626	0.91	214,594	73,144	0.34
NWT	—	—	—	123,611	60,868	0.49	97	82	0.85	3,778,407	853,713	0.23
BC	27,896	235,193	8.43	1,234,269	418,853	0.34	30,579	7,720	0.25	6,160,808	1,329,021	0.22
Alta	8,917	71,206	7.99	5,440,599	2,009,901	0.37	26,223	5,547	0.21	2,556,423	521,252	0.20
Sask	3,512	16,970	4.83	1,347,248	489,358	0.36	11,956	3,404	0.28	8,939,261	1,621,883	0.18
Man	112	2,162	19.30	773,480	290,046	0.37	1,215	395	0.33	6,783,099	880,184	0.13
Ont	14,339	218,813	15.26	5,652,065	1,961,998	0.35	17,668	5,393	0.31	22,685,283	3,470,485	0.15
Que	7,860	115,308	14.67	3,237,092	1,232,408	0.38	34,303	10,327	0.30	38,525,722	6,075,829	0.16
NB	2,822	23,277	8.25	368,401	127,671	0.35	32,311	6,855	0.21	872,195	173,403	0.20
NS	48,819	514,352	10.54	334,450	124,317	0.37	1,951	892	0.46	1,302,527	226,496	0.17
PEI	—	—	—	18,316	6,690	0.37	—	—	—	29,991	9,593	0.32
Nfld	1,307	20,921	16.01	410,079	175,526	0.43	1,920	446	0.23	5,297,242	1,179,465	0.22

	Wood			Gas (liquified petroleum)			Electricity purchased†		
	Cords	$	$/Cord	Imp. Gals.	$	$/Gal.	KWH	$	$/KWH
YT	427	11,570	27.10	1,570	1,981	1.26	30,699,000	462,956	.0151
NWT	981	17,769	18.11	10,637	2,309	.22	37,074,920	545,459	.0147
BC	5,853	81,347	13.90	93,731	31,277	.33	121,934,622	1,348,366	.0111
Alta	250	2,645	10.58	873,768	62,182	.07	156,566,352	3,260,933	.0208
Sask	—	—	—	190,239	34,756	.18	149,949,281	1,567,355	.0105
Man	562	5,547	9.87	92,371	26,065	.28	146,422,570	2,277,632	.0156
Ont	5,731	69,163	12.07	270,405	76,532	.28	2,293,894,237	14,328,530	.0062
Que	350	3,475	9.93	98,659	31,792	.32	1,136,071,757	8,961,998	.0079
NB	55	275	5.00	—	—	—	20,888,049	459,577	.0220
NS	330	4,025	12.20	150	92	.61	153,281,877	2,277,888	.0149
PEI	—	—	—	1,200	480	.40	460	23	.0500
Nfld	—	—	—	4,456	2,117	.48	85,983,344	1,057,807	.0123

*Bituminous.
†For light and power.
SOURCE: Calculated from DBS, *General Review of the Mining Industry 1960*, Table 38, p. A40.

TABLE 6.12

LABOUR COSTS FOR CONTRACT DRILLING IN THE MINING INDUSTRY

	Footage drilled	Av. no. of employees	Total salaries and wages paid	Av. salaries and wages	Labour cost per drilled foot
1960					
NWT	156,176	47	202,660	4311.91	1.30
YT	14,362	10	50,173	5017.30	3.49
Can.	5,521,211	1,912	7,977,782	4172.48	1.44
1959					
NWT	122,173	42	174,830	4162.62	1.43
YT	14,828	8	39,917	4989.63	2.69
Can.	5,435,971	1,902	7,967,756	4189.14	1.47
1958					
NWT	137,156	47	183,481	3903.85	1.34
YT	12,361	6	33,894	5649.00	2.74
Can.	4,426,594	1,717	6,921,761	4031.31	1.56
1957					
NWT	177,270	99	230,699	2330.29	1.30
YT	16,571	9	57,769	6418.78	3.49
Can.	6,296,128	2,951	10,831,483	3670.40	1.72
1956					
NWT	248,792	108	285,438	2642.94	1.15
YT	31,472	30	99,835	3327.83	3.17
Can.	7,840,670	3,415	12,644,217	3702.50	1.61
1955					
NWT	251,959	91	324,748	3568.66	1.29
YT	39,046	18	82,945	4608.06	2.12
Can.	6,443,641	2,840	9,852,432	3469.16	1.53
1954					
NWT	185,432	82	276,877	3376.55	1.49
YT	60,188	30	168,769	5625.63	2.80
Can.	5,639,574	2,352	7,833,645	3330.63	1.39
1953					
NWT	327,222	98	359,519	3668.56	1.10
YT	21,263	36	121,033	3362.03	5.69
Can.	5,258,870	2,238	7,110,188	3177.02	1.35
1952					
NWT	125,289	43	169,274	3936.60	1.35
YT	3,306	24	85,521	3563.38	2.59
Can.	5,180,783	2,345	7,119,714	3036.12	1.37

SOURCE: DBS, *Contract Drilling in the Mining Industry*, annually.

TABLE 6.13

AVERAGE MILLING CAPACITY OF OPERATING GOLD MINES
BY PROVINCE AND TERRITORY 1960

Area	Number of producing mines	Milling capacity of operating mines	Av. capacity
Quebec	17	9,650	568
Ontario	34	28,035	825
Manitoba	3	550	183
British Columbia	10	1,229	123
Northwest Territories	5	1,661	352
Canada	69	41,125	674

SOURCE: Calculated from DBS, *The Gold Mining Industry*, 1960, Tables 18 and 26.

TABLE 7.1

TERRITORIAL AIR TRANSPORT PASSENGER TRAFFIC, 1957–62

		Northbound	Southbound	Within area
1957				
CPA	NWT	9,696	7,407	4,701
	YT	9,825	7,549	1,667
PWA	NWT	NA	NA	20,628
	YT			5,200,000
Mining Co.'s	NWT	669	676	NA
	YT	NA	NA	NA
1958				
CPA	NWT	9,066	7,327	4,884
	YT	7,508	7,464	3,512
PWA	NWT		15,713	15,553
	YT			
Mining Co.'s	NWT	907	809	NA
	YT	NA	NA	NA
1959				
CPA	NWT	5,398	3,996	3,047
	YT	7,667	7,555	4,108
PWA*	NWT	7,230	NA	NA
	YT	—	—	—
Mining Co.'s	NWT	633	648	NA
	YT	NA	NA	NA
1960				
CPA	NWT	—	—	—
	YT	22,350	22,450	5,819
PWA*	NWT	20,160	NA	NA
	YT	—	—	—
Mining Co.'s	NWT	1,241	1,461	
	YT	NA	NA	NA
1961				
CPA	NWT	—	—	—
	YT	9,088	9,511	2,554
PWA	NWT	12,644	NA	NA
	YT	—	—	—
Mining Co.'s	NWT	377	385	NA
	YT	NA	NA	NA
1962				
CPA	NWT	—	—	—
	YT	9,357	9,625	2,863
PWA	NWT	13,490	NA	NA
	YT	—	—	—
Mining Co.'s	NWT	247	298	NA
	YT	NA	NA	NA

*North from Edmonton.

SOURCE: Annual Reports of the Alberta and Northwest Chamber of Mines, 1957–62.

TABLE 7.2

TERRITORIAL AIR TRANSPORT FREIGHT TRAFFIC 1957–62*

		Northbound	Southbound	Within area
1957				
CPA	NWT	2,754,189	423,940	1,568,589
	YT	516,775	100,340	190,270
PWA	NWT	—	—	—
	YT	—	—	—
Mining Co.'s	NWT	1,470,980	1,382,966	N/A
1958				
CPA	NWT	2,091,851	390,094	2,005,072
	YT	557,419	81,507	162,723
PWA	NWT ⎫	7,387,716		2,271,199
	YT ⎭			
Mining Co.'s	NWT	1,160,202	1,185,989	N/A
1959				
CPA	NWT	1,218,086	185,987	824,511
	YT	494,447	88,795	111,922
PWA	NWT†	1,630,700	NA	N/A
	YT	—	—	—
Mining Co.'s	NWT	777,144	758,300	N/A
1960				
CPA	NWT	—	—	—
	YT	513,721	98,176	43,170
PWA	NWT	3,105,600	NA	N/A
	YT	—	—	—
Mining Co.'s	NWT	1,157,000	1,183,000	N/A
1961				
CPA	NWT	—	—	—
	YT	437,878	92,125	28,347
PWA	NWT	2,612,100	NA	N/A
	YT	—	—	—
Mining Co.'s	NWT	229,032	278,083	N/A
1962				
CPA	NWT	—	—	—
	YT	471,133	90,899	15,658
PWA	NWT	2,732,801	NA	N/A
	YT	—	—	—
Mining Co.'s	NWT	222,774	95,834	N/A

*Pounds of freight.
†North from Edmonton.

SOURCE: As for Table 7.1.

TABLE 8.1

EXPENDITURES ON RURAL ROADS AND TOTAL MILEAGE
IN THE TERRITORIES 1946–61

	Expenditures ($)			Mileage		
Year	YT	NWT	Total Y and NWT	YT	NWT	Total Y and NWT
1946			4,438,774			1,461
1947			4,563,991			1,652
1948			4,236,289			1,652
1949			3,567,593			1,445
1950			3,984,643			1,627
1951			3,676,962			2,027
1952			2,582,068			2,092
1953			4,825,132			2,128
1954			5,624,299			2,128
1955			5,794,207			2,263
1956			6,605,806			3,067
1957			7,013,901			* 2,313
1958	6,082,057	3,941,808	10,023,865	1,631	364	* 1,995
1959	8,147,812	4,478,339	12,626,151	1,660	455	2,115
1960	7,657,035	3,807,482	11,464,517	1,785	513	2,298
1961	7,618,060	2,481,521	10,099,581	1,751	500	2,251

*Decrease in total due to elimination of duplication in reporting.

SOURCE: 1946–57 DBS, *Highway Statistics 1945–1957*, memorandum; 1958–61 DBS, *Roads & Street Mileage and Expenditure* (53–201).

TABLE 8.2

Station	Owner*	Installed 1st unit	Last unit	No. of units	Unit capacity of generators	Total capacity of generators	Capital cost of NCPC plants
HYDRO STATIONS					(kw)	(kw)	($)
North Fork	YCGC	1911	1935	1	3,600	10,520	
				1	2,700		
				1	4,220		
Bluefish Lake	CMSC	1941		1	3,360	3,360	
Snare Rapids	NCPC	1948		1	7,000	7,000	4,558,812 (1961)
Mayo River	NCPC	1952	1957	1	2,550	4,950	4,306,218 (1953)
				1	2,400		457,652 (1958)
Whitehorse Rapids	NCPC	1958		2	5,695	11,390	7,200,000 (1959)
Snare Falls	NCPC	1960		1	7,000	7,000	4,558,812 (1961)
Porter Creek No. 1	YHC	1949		2		1,000	
No. 2	YHC	1954		1	800	800	
THERMAL STATIONS (OVER 1500 KW CAPACITY)							
Port Radium	EMR	1936	1953	2	150	3,639	
				1	864		
				2	650		
				2	400		
				1	175		
				1	200		
Fort Smith	NCPC	1950	1960	1	280	1,880	415,805 (1961)
				1	600		
				1	1,000		
Inuvik	NCPC	1958	1960	2	375	2,500	1,023,174 (1961)†
				1	150		
				1	1,000		
				1	600		
Frobisher Bay	NCPC	1960		2	1,000	3,000	569,062 (1961)
				4	250		
Tungsten	CTMC	1962		4		1,600	

*YCGC: Yukon Consolidated Gold Mining Corporation
 CMSC: Consolidated Mining and Smelting Company
 NCPC: Northern Canada Power Commission
 YHC: Yukon Hydro Company
 EMR: Eldorado Mining and Refining Company
 CTMC: Canada Tungsten Mining Corporation
†Power plant only.

SOURCES: Department of Northern Affairs and National Resources, Water Resources Branch, Bulletin 2722-61 March 1962; NCPC Annual Reports; Alberta and Northwest Chamber of Mines Annual Reports.

TABLE 9.1

YUKON SCHOOLS, TEACHERS AND ENROLMENT
SELECTED YEARS, 1938–62

Year	Schools	Teachers	Enrolment
1938	4	—	188
1940	5	10	215
1945	5	12	356
1950	10	23	652
1955	16	65	1,501
1960	—	—	2,755
1962	23	142	3,123

SOURCE: Compiled from data in *Annual Reports
of the Commissioner of the Yukon Territory.*

TABLE 9.2

SCHOOLS OF THE NORTHWEST TERRITORIES 1938

Schools	Average yearly attendance
RESIDENTIAL SCHOOLS	
Aklavik (RC)	36.0
Aklavik (CE)	51.0
Providence (RC)	8.0
Resolution (RC)	11.5
Hay River (RC)	5.0
DAY SCHOOLS	
Aklavik (RC)	33.16
Aklavik (CE)	33.69
Baker Lake (CE)	5.8
Eskimo Point (CE)	22.0
Fort Smith (RC)	13.03
Fort Smith (CE)	9.42
Hay River (CE)	7.99
McPherson (CE)	5.5
Pangnirtung (CE)	9.5
Providence (RC)	18.25
Simpson (RC)	9.28
Simpson (CE)	5.78
Resolution (RC)	35.9

SOURCE: Memorandum dated January 10, 1939,
in *Minutes of the Council of the Northwest
Territories,* Vol. 7, pp. 1651–1652.

TABLE 9.3

CONSTRUCTION OF AND IMPROVEMENTS TO
PUBLIC BUILDINGS IN YT AND NWT

Fiscal year ending March 31	Expenditure	Fiscal year ending March 31	Expenditure
	($)		($)
1962	808,223	1950	669,952
1961	2,179,071	1949	1,072,025
1960	2,898,666	1948	762,135
1959	2,229,861	1947	535,535
1958	982,298	1946	113,606
1957	36,379	*1945	No constr.
1956	278,571	1944	None
1955	362,290	1943	None
1954	1,347,043	1942	None
1953	642,991	1941	None
1952	292,664	1940	None
1951	575,404	1939	None

*Construction only 1945 and before. Small amounts were spent on improvements.

SOURCE: Compiled from *Annual Reports* of the Department of Public Works for the years indicated.

TABLE 9.4

PERCENTAGE OF SCHOOL-AGE POPULATION ENROLLED
IN SCHOOL IN NWT 1950–51 AND 1961–62

Population	1950–51			1961–62		
	School-age	Enrolled	% Enrolled	School-age	Enrolled	% Enrolled
Eskimo	2,464	194	8	3,171	1,870	59
Indian	1,027	368	36	1,375	1,101	80
Other	1,627	621	38	2,123	2,019	95
Total	5,118	1,183	23	6,669	4,900	75

SOURCE: Department of Northern Affairs and National Resources, *Annual Report 1961–2,* p. 87.

TABLE 9.5

FEDERAL HEALTH AND HOSPITAL CONSTRUCTION GRANTS TO THE
YT AND NWT

Fiscal year ending March 31	General health		Hospital construction	
	YT ($)	NWT ($)	YT ($)	NWT ($)
1962	44,342	69,684	112,649	199,299
1961	41,714	67,384	72,127	132,336
1960	35,556	57,047	20,214	33,567
1959	34,556	56,047	50,897	107,191
1958	33,556	55,047	51,492	73,736
1957	32,056	54,147	42,910	59,299
1956	31,556	52,347	34,328	44,862
1955	27,936	46,611	25,746	43,311
1954	26,052	43,262	8,582	14,437
1953	20,018	33,663	8,585	14,437

SOURCE: Canada, *Estimates.*

TABLE 9.6

HOSPITALS AND INDUSTRIAL HOMES IN THE NWT, 1940

Location	Year opened	Number of beds	Federal construction grant ($)
Fort Smith (RC)	1913	30	Nil
Resolution (RC)	1939	20	5,000
Hay River (CE)	1925	6	Nil
Rae (RC)	1939	25	10,000
Simpson (RC)	1931	25	20,000
Norman (CE)	1940	18	10,000
Aklavik (RC)	1933–34	48	Nil
Aklavik (CE)	1936	25	10,000
Chesterfield (RC)	1931	30	Nil
Pangnirtung (CE)	1930	8	Nil

SOURCE: *Minutes of the Council of the Northwest Territories*, Vol. 9, p. 2117.

TABLE 9.7

FAMILY ALLOWANCE AND OLD AGE SECURITY PAYMENTS
PER CAPITA IN 1961

Location	'000	Per capita
FAMILY ALLOWANCE		
Newfoundland	15,960	34.84
Prince Edward Island	3,124	29.75
Nova Scotia	21,242	28.82
New Brunswick	18,878	31.57
Quebec	154,185	29.32
Ontario	162,611	26.08
Manitoba	24,385	26.45
Saskatchewan	25,849	27.95
Alberta	37,365	28.05
British Columbia	41,433	25.44
Yukon and Northwest Territories	1,160	31.35
OLD AGE SECURITY		
Newfoundland	11,355	24.79
Prince Edward Island	4,944	47.09
Nova Scotia	27,610	37.46
New Brunswick	20,350	34.03
Quebec	124,322	23.64
Ontario	214,626	34.42
Manitoba	36,089	39.14
Saskatchewan	37,573	40.62
Alberta	39,688	29.80
British Columbia	75,451	46.32
Yukon and Northwest Territories	405	10.95

SOURCE: DBS, *Canada Year Book 1962*, Table 1, pp. 252–3, and
Table 3, p. 254.

TABLE 11.1

TERRITORIAL POPULATION AS A PERCENTAGE OF TOTAL
CANADIAN POPULATION: CENSUS DATES 1921–61

Year	(1) Total population of territories		(2) Total population of Canada ('000)	(1) as % of (2)
	YT	NWT		
1921	4,157 +	8,143 = 12,300	8,788	0.14
1931	4,230 +	9,316 = 13,546	10,376	0.14
1941	4,914 +	12,028 = 16,942	11,507	0.15
1951	9,096 +	16,004 = 25,100	14,009	0.18
1956	12,190 +	19,313 = 32,503	16,081	0.21
1961	14,628 +	22,998 = 37,626	18,238	0.21

SOURCE: Decennial Census of Canada.

TABLE 11.2

	(A) Growth of the total population		
	1931–41	1941–51	1951–61
Yukon and Northwest Territories	25.1%	48.2%	49.9%
Canada (excluding Newfoundland)	10.9%	18.6%	30.3%

	(B) Growth of the population by broad age groups			
	Age group	1931–41	1941–51	1951–61
Yukon and Northwest Territories	0–14	20.2%	52.8%	71.1%
	15–64	25.5%	49.9%	40.2%
	65+	57.6%	−0.7%	19.2%
Canada (excluding Newfoundland)	0–14	−2.5%	28.5%	46.0%
	15–64	15.7%	12.4%	22.9%
	65+	33.3%	38.4%	28.4%

SOURCE: Census of Canada, *Census Bulletin 7.1–4*, Table VIII, p. 4–21.

	(C) Percentage change in the size of the population by decades for the YT from 1901 to 1961 and for the NWT from 1921–61						
	YT		NWT		Y and NWT		Canada
Year	Population	Change[1]	Population	Change[1]	Population	Change[1]	Change[1]
1901	27,219	—	—	—	—	—	—
1911	8,512	−68.7	—	—	—	—	34.2
1921	4,157	−51.2	8,143	—	12,300	—	21.9
1931	4,230	+ 1.8	9,316	+14.4	13,546	10.1	18.1
1941	4,914	+16.2	12,028	+29.1	16,942	25.1	10.9
1951	9,096	+85.1	16,004	+33.1	25,100	48.2	21.8
1961	14,628	+60.8	22,998	+43.7	37,626	49.9	30.2

[1]Percentage change from preceding Census.

SOURCE: *Census of Canada 1961.*

432

TABLE 11.3

Year	NWT	YT	Total
1914	4,928	1,528	6,456
1915	4,003	1,528	5,531
1916	3,764	1,528	5,292
1924	4,543	1,456	5,999
1929	4,150	1,264	5,414
1934	3,854	1,359	5,213
1939	3,724	1,550	5,274
1949	3,772	1,443	5,215
1954	4,023	1,568	5,591
1959	4,598	1,868	6,466
1960	4,758	1,913	6,681
1961	4,915	2,006	6,921
1962	5,108	2,096	7,204

SOURCE: Quinquennial Census of Indians for 1916, 1924, 1929, 1934, 1939, 1949, 1954, 1959. Since 1959, Canada, Department of Citizenship and Immigration (Indian Affairs Branch), *Annual Report*, Ottawa, for fiscal years ending March 31, 1960, 1961, 1962, and 1963.

TABLE 11.4

RATE OF NATURAL INCREASE* IN THE YUKON AND NORTHWEST TERRITORIES AND CANADA QUINQUENNIAL AVERAGES 1926–60

Year	YT	NWT	Canada
1926–30	−5.2	−3.1	12.9
1931–35	−2.9	5.3	11.7
1936–40	−0.8	4.5	10.7
1941–45	1.7	4.2	13.7
1946–50	20.3	15.9	18.1
1951–55	33.6	23.0	19.5
1956–60	32.3	31.4	19.6

*Rate per 1000 of population.

SOURCE: Calculated from DBS, *Vital Statistics 1962*, Table 55, p. 75.

TABLE 11.5

NATIVE POPULATION AS A PERCENTAGE OF TOTAL TERRITORIAL
POPULATION: CENSUS DATES 1941–61

Population and Year	YT	NWT	Y and NWT
1941			
Total population	4,914	12,028	16,942
Native Indian		4,052	
Native Eskimo		5,404	
Total native	1,509	9,456	10,965
Total native as % of total population	30.7%	78.6%	64.7%
1951			
Total population	9,096	16,004	25,100
Native Indian	1,533	3,838	5,371
Native Eskimo	30	6,822	6,852
Total native	1,566	10,660	12,226
Total native as % of total population	17.2%	66.6%	48.7%
1961			
Total population	14,628	22,998	37,626
Native Indian	2,167	5,256	7,423
Native Eskimo	40	7,977	8,017
Total native	2,207	13,233	15,440
Total native as % of total population	15.1%	57.5%	41.0%

SOURCE: Census of Canada 1941, 1951, 1961.

NOTE: 1931 Census did not distinguish between full-blood Indians and those of mixed blood.

TABLE 11.6

RATE OF DEATHS PER 1000 OF POPULATION:
YUKON AND NORTHWEST TERRITORIES AND CANADA

Year	YT	NWT	Can.
1926–30 (Av.)	13.5	21.0	11.2
1931–35 (Av.)	14.5	13.7	9.9
1936	16.4	16.1	9.9
1937	16.2	13.4	10.4
1938	12.6	16.5	9.7
1939	16.4	16.2	9.7
1940	11.2	15.6	9.8
1941	13.4	25.6	10.1
1942	21.6	18.5	9.8
1943	24.0	25.3	10.1
1944	20.0	29.1	9.8
1945	17.4	39.8	9.5
1946	10.0	21.7	9.4
1947	9.6	23.5	9.4
1948	14.0	23.1	9.3
1949	10.8	27.1	9.3
1950	12.4	20.8	9.1
1951	9.4	17.8	9.0
1952	10.4	21.3	8.7
1953	12.9	18.4	8.6
1954	8.5	14.7	8.2
1955	6.5	13.9	8.2
1956	7.1	15.3	8.2
1957	7.8	17.1	8.2
1958	7.1	16.7	7.9
1959	6.8	13.8	8.0
1960	6.9	14.2	7.8
1961	6.4	11.4	7.7

SOURCE: DBS, *Vital Statistics 1963*, Table D 1, p. 94.

TABLE 11.7

FACTORS IN THE GROWTH OF THE TERRITORIAL
POPULATION 1941–61 BY DECADES

Decade	Population
1941–51	
Population of the Y and NWT 1941	16,942
Natural increase	2,638
Actual increase	8,158
Net migration	5,520
Population 1951	25,100
1951–61	
Population of the Y and NWT 1951	25,100
Natural increase	9,034
Actual increase	12,526
Net migration	3,492
Population 1961	37,626

SOURCE: Census Data 1951 and 1961.

TABLE 11.8

RATE OF LIVE BIRTHS PER 1000 OF POPULATION:
YT AND NWT AND CANADA

Year	YT	NWT	Can.
1926–30 (Av.)	8.3	17.9	24.1
1931–35 (Av.)	11.6	19.0	21.6
1936	7.6	20.8	20.3
1937	16.6	19.2	20.1
1938	15.2	20.5	20.7
1939	12.6	19.5	20.6
1940	16.8	20.0	21.6
1941	14.4	26.3	22.4
1942	19.2	30.8	23.5
1943	19.8	33.6	24.2
1944	27.2	26.3	24.0
1945	24.6	42.6	24.3
1946	18.3	37.1	27.2
1947	28.0	39.1	28.9
1948	34.3	40.3	27.3
1949	38.6	40.3	27.3
1950	39.5	38.9	27.1
1951	38.0	40.6	27.2
1952	43.3	40.1	27.9
1953	42.6	42.3	28.1
1954	42.5	37.1	28.5
1955	47.6	40.7	28.2
1956	40.1	41.3	28.0
1957	41.2	47.4	28.2
1958	36.4	47.3	27.5
1959	41.3	47.1	27.4
1960	38.4	49.7	26.8
1961	38.1	48.6	26.1

SOURCE: DBS, *Vital Statistics 1963*, Table B-1, p. 69.

436

TABLE 11.9

INFANT DEATH RATE:* Y AND NWT AND CANADA

Year	YT	NWT	Can.
1926–30	131	136	94
1931–35	86	110	76
1936	79	170	68
1937	145	100	77
1938	66	133	64
1939	79	111	61
1940	119	113	58
1941	83	209	61
1942	229	160	55
1943	111	154	55
1944	44	187	56
1945	65	225	52
1946	48	133	48
1947	36	152	46
1948	102	136	44
1949	61	113	43
1950	57.0	159.2	41.5
1951	55.6	107.9	38.5
1952	48.7	134.0	38.2
1953	49.6	112.4	35.6
1954	58.8	107.8	31.9
1955	51.5	123.0	31.3
1956	47.8	149.0	31.9
1957	54.7	143.3	30.9
1958	42.3	151.3	30.2
1959	26.1	129.3	28.4
1960	48.3	144.4	27.3
1961	41.2	111.0	27.2

*Per thousand live births.

SOURCE: DBS, *Vital Statistics 1963*, Table D 12, p. 163.

TABLE 11.10

CRUDE FERTILITY RATES OF THE TERRITORIES
AND PROVINCES 1957–61*

Year	YT	NWT	Provinces
1961	187.2	253.6	127.6
1960	199.3	266.8	130.2
1959	214.8	260.5	132.3
1958	181.9	255.4	131.6
1957	190.0	243.2	134.0

*Per thousand of total women aged 15 to 44.

SOURCE: Adapted from DBS, *Canada Year Book 1963–4,* Table 7, p. 232.

TABLE 11.11

AGE COMPOSITION OF THE POPULATION
PERCENTAGE DISTRIBUTION OF POPULATION BY BROAD AGE GROUPS

Age	Area	1951	1956	1961
0–14	Y and NWT	33.8	34.9	38.6
	Can.	30.3	32.5	34.0
15–64	Y and NWT	62.6	62.0	58.6
	Can.	61.9	59.8	58.4
65+	Y and NWT	3.6	3.1	2.8
	Can.	7.8	7.7	7.6

SOURCE: *1961 Census Bulletin 7.1-4,* Table VII, p. 4–17.

TABLE 11.12

POPULATION OF THE TERRITORIES BY CENSUS SUBDIVISIONS

Area	1901	1911	1921	1931	1941	1951	1956	1961
YUKON TERRITORY	27,219	8,512	4,157	4,230	4,914	9,096	12,190	14,628
Unorganized	18,077	4,772[1]	2,851	2,870	3,117	5,478[2]	8,520	8,374[3]
Cities								
Dawson	9,142	3,013	975	819	1,043	783	851	881
Whitehorse		727	331	541	754	2,594	2,570	5,031
Towns								
Mayo						241	249	342
NORTHWEST TERRITORIES			8,143	9,316	12,028	16,004	19,313	22,998
Franklin District			205	2,626	2,968	3,424	4,408	5,758
Keewatin District			992	1,404	1,766	2,301	2,413	2,345
Mackenzie District			6,946[4]	5,286	7,294	10,279	12,492	14,895
Fort Simpson L.I.D.							495[6]	563
Fort Smith L.I.D.							1,164[6]	1,681
Hay River M.D.						792[5]	942	1,338
Inuvik L.I.D.								1,248[7]
Yellowknife M.D.						2,724[5]	3,100	3,245
Unorganized			6,946	5,286	7,294	6,763	6,791	6,820

[1] Moose Hide Village included in Unorganized. [2] Mayo Town detached from Unorganized. [3] Part of Unorganized annexed to White-horse City. [4] Includes part of Franklin District. [5] Hay River and Yellowknife created as Local Administrative Districts 1949–51 and re-organized as Municipal Districts in 1953. [6] Fort Simpson and Fort Smith Local Improvement Districts created in 1954 and removed from Unorganized. [7] Inuvik Local Improvement District removed from Unorganized.

SOURCE: Adapted from *1961 Census of Canada*, Bulletin 1.1-10, Table 6, p. 89.

TABLE 11.13

A. NET VALUE OF PRODUCTION YT AND NWT, 1920–61

Year	Trapping $ '000	%	Mining $ '000	%	Fishing $ '000	%	Forestry $ '000	%	Manu-facturing $ '000	%	Electric power $ '000	%	Total $ '000
1920	1,445	44	1,577	49	33	1.0						3	3,058
1921	1,232	38	1,750	—	NA	—					NA	—	2,982
1922	2,037	50	1,779	44	12	*						3	3,831
1923	2,371	43	2,974	54	11	*						2	5,358
1924	1,876	66	952	33	20	*						*	2,848
1925	2,075	53	1,792	46	15	*					74	2	3,956
1926	1,947	51	1,751	46	13	*					80	2	3,791
1927	3,344	66	1,599	32	9	*					76	2	5,028
1928	2,594	51	2,335	46	41	*					105	2	5,075
1929	2,579	45	2,980	52	19	*					123	2	5,701
1930	1,928	41	2,583	55	23	*					125	3	4,659
1931	2,091	47	2,253	51	23	*					61	1	4,428
1932	1,158	37	1,845	60	20	*					69	2	3,092
1933	1,236	43	1,516	54	17	*					55	2	2,824
1934	1,633	58	1,091	39	15	*					49	2	2,788
1935	1,909	60	1,187	37	21	*					54	2	3,171
1936	1,461	42	1,927	56	13	*					66	2	3,467
1937	1,518	36	2,629	62	9	*					90	2	4,246
1938	1,599	37	2,568	60	5	*					94	2	4,266
1939	1,543	22	5,397	76	5	*			92	1	105	2	7,142
1940	1,516	23	4,631	71	5	*	142	2.1	153	2	104	2	6,551
1941	2,672	32	5,302	60	7	*	205	2.4	200	2	66	1	8,452
1942	2,912	29	6,327	64	3	*	276	2.7	263	3	125	1	9,906
1943	3,496	38	3,958	43	2	*	1,398	15.1	238	3	125	1	9,217
1944	2,665	47	2,087	37	3	*	563	9.8	281	5	99	2	5,698
1945	2,413	49	1,429	29	115	2	228	4.6	518	11	181	4	4,884
1946	3,428	51	1,951	29	293	4	440	7	409	6	248	4	6,769
1947	2,032	28	3,450	49	150	2	531	8	525	7	366	5	7,054
1948	2,102	21	6,272	62	387	4	510	5	380	4	451	5	10,102
1949	1,679	13	9,155	69	549	4	564	4	605	5	651	5	13,203
1950	1,109	6	13,975	80	612	3	453	3	569	3	777	4	17,495
1951	2,400	13	13,530	72	535	3	682	4	759	4	890	5	18,796
1952	1,621	8	15,053	75	735	4	739	4	1,023	5	977	5	20,148
1953	1,124	5	16,955	79	471	2	612	3	1,012	5	1,415	7	21,589
1954	939	2	32,515	86	636	2	595	2	1,856	5	1,364	4	37,905
1955	1,410	4	31,098	84	742	2	449	1	1,733	5	1,462	4	36,894
1956	961	3	26,543	83	787	2	1,152	4	1,076	3	1,641	5	32,160
1957	842	3	25,014	82	720	2	625	2	1,410	5	1,768	6	30,379
1958	854	3	26,163	83	682	2	952	3	859	3	1,946	6	31,456
1959	876	3	27,980	84	703	2	497	1	650	2	2,707	8	33,413
1960	980	3	29,125	80	702	2	1,026	3	1,326	4	3,172	9	36,331
1961	1,425	5	23,954	79	675	2	201	1	738	2	3,487	11	30,480

*Less than 1%.

440

TABLE 11.13 (*concluded*)

B. NET VALUE OF PRODUCTION IN TRAPPING,
MINING, FISHING, FORESTRY*,
AND ELECTRIC POWER INDUSTRIES YT AND NWT
AND CANADA SELECTED YEARS 1926–61

Year	Canada	YT and NWT	YT and NWT as percentage of total Canada
1926	315,305	3,791	1.2
1931	307,113	4,428	1.4
1936	456,675	3,467	0.8
1941	752,691	8,252	1.1
1946	979,228	6,360	0.7
1951	1,916,570	18,037	0.9
1956	2,717,031	31,084	1.1
1961	3,190,736	29,742	0.9

*Forestry excluded from Canadian and territorial totals in 1926 and 1931.

SOURCES: Figures for 1926 to 1951 from DBS, *Survey of Production 1925–56*, Table 7, pp. 16–22; 1951 to 1961 from DBS, *Survey of Production*, annually.

TABLE 11.14

PERSONAL INCOME YT AND NWT 1951–61

Year	Total	Per person
	'000,000	$
1951	21	840
1952	23	920
1953	24	960
1954	27	1,000
1955	34	1,172
1956	47	1,516
1957	42	1,355
1958	43	1,303
1959	41	1,206
1960	50	1,389
1961	49	1,324

SOURCE: 1951–56, DBS, *National Accounts, Income & Expenditure 1926–1956*; 1957–60, DBS, *National Accounts, Income & Expenditure 1960*; 1961, DBS, *National Accounts, Income & Expenditure 1963*.

TABLE 11.15

PERSONAL INCOME AND GOVERNMENT TRANSFER PAYMENTS FOR THE
PROVINCES AND TERRITORIES 1951, 1956, 1961

Province or territory	Personal income		Govt. transfers		Transfers as a percentage of personal income*	Population
	Total	Per person	Total	Per person		
	$'000,000	$	$'000,000	$	%	'000
1951						
Nfld	205	568	27	75	13.7	361
PEI	60	612	7	71	12.1	98
NS	499	776	48	75	10.0	643
NB	383	742	40	78	10.9	516
Que	3,763	928	274	68	7.8	4,056
Ont	6,093	1,325	306	67	5.4	4,598
Man	881	1,135	54	70	6.5	777
Sask	1,106	1,329	70	84	6.6	832
Alta	1,228	1,308	71	76	6.1	940
BC	1,568	1,346	132	113	9.2	1,165
YT and NWT	21	840	1	40	5.0	25
1956						
Nfld	305	735	46	111	15.1	415
PEI	76	768	11	111	14.5	99
NS	694	999	72	104	10.4	695
NB	509	917	61	110	12.0	555
Que	5,423	1,172	490	106	9.0	4,628
Ont	8,702	1,610	543	101	6.2	5,405
Man	1,109	1,305	88	104	7.9	850
Sask	1,212	1,376	107	122	8.8	881
Alta	1,592	1,418	122	109	7.7	1,123
BC	2,264	1,618	222	159	9.8	1,398
YT and NWT	47	1,516	2	63	4.3	32
1961						
Nfld	429	937	78	170	18.2	458
PEI	102	971	20	191	19.6	105
NS	881	1,195	135	183	15.3	737
NB	637	1,065	119	199	18.7	598
Que	7,248	1,378	949	181	13.1	5,259
Ont	11,484	1,842	1,130	181	9.8	6,236
Man	1,392	1,510	177	192	12.7	922
Sask	1,131	1,223	187	202	16.5	925
Alta	2,122	1,593	243	181	11.5	1,332
BC	2,957	1,815	383	235	13.0	1,629
YT and NWT	49	1,324	4	105	8.2	37

*Percentages calculated before rounding of Personal Income and Government Transfers data.

SOURCES: 1951 data from DBS, *National Accounts, Income and Expenditure 1926–56*; 1956 and 1961 data from DBS, *National Accounts, Income and Expenditure 1961*.

TABLE 11.16

FUEL COSTS IN THREE PRINCIPAL NORTHERN CENTRES
AND IN REGINA, SASKATCHEWAN, 1956

Fuel	Whitehorse	Dawson	Yellowknife	Regina
	($)	($)	($)	($)
Coal (anthracite) per ton	—	55.00	—	17.50
Fuel oil per gallon	0.30	0.45	0.29	0.16
Kerosene per gallon	1.00	1.00	0.54	0.25
Wood per cord	21.44	24.00	24.00	15.00

SOURCE: Dominion Bureau of Statistics, *Special Compilation*, Prices Division, 1958.

TABLE 11.17

ELECTRICITY RATES IN PRINCIPAL NORTHERN CENTRES AND REGINA 1956

Whitehorse	Dawson	Yellowknife	Regina
($)	($)	($)	($)
First 10 kwh. at .20	Flat rate at .25 per kwh.	First 20 kwh. at 3.15	First 15 kwh. at 1.00
Next 20 kwh. at .15		Next 25 kwh. at .12	Next 85 kwh. at 0.04
Next 70 kwh. at .10		Next 55 kwh. at .06	Next 900 kwh. at 0.035
		OR	
Over 70 kwh. at .05		First 100 kwh. at 9.45	Over 1000 kwh. at 0.03
		Over 100 kwh. at .03	

SOURCE: As for Table 11.16.

TABLE 11.18

WHOLESALE PRICE AND TRANSPORT CHARGES ON FRESH
VEGETABLES IN EDMONTON AND YELLOWKNIFE 1958

Produce	Edmonton cost price	Freight charges	Yellowknife cost price
	($)	($)	($)
Cabbage (per bag)	3.75	3.81	7.56
Onions (per bag)	4.75	3.81	8.56
Turnips (per bag)	2.25	4.72	6.97
Corn (per six dozen)	4.95	6.65	11.60

SOURCE: Courtesy Hudson's Bay Company store, Yellowknife,
NWT, 1958.

TABLE 11.19

VANCOUVER AND WHITEHORSE PRICES OF CERTAIN
BUILDING MATERIALS

Material	Vancouver	Whitehorse
	($)	($)
Cement (bag)	1.00	4.00
Wallboard (sheet)	2.40	3.70
Gyproc (sheet)	2.40	4.75
Shingles (210 wt.)	10.00	21.25

SOURCE: Whitehorse Board of Trade, *Submission
to the Royal Commission on Canada's
Economic Prospects*, Vancouver, 1955, p. 4.

Index